NAZISM, THE JEWS, AND AMERICAN ZIONISM

NAZISM
THE JEWS AND
AMERICAN
ZIONISM

1933~1948

AARON BERMAN

WAYNE STATE UNIVERSITY PRESS DETROIT

Copyright © 1990 by Wayne State University Press,
Detroit, Michigan 48202. All rights are reserved.
No part of this book may be
reproduced without formal permission.
94 93 92 91 90   5 4 3 2 1

Library of Congress Cataloging-in-Publication Data

Berman, Aaron, 1952–
  Nazism, the Jews, and American Zionism, 1933–1948 / Aaron Berman.
    p.   cm.
  Includes bibliographical references.
  ISBN 0-8143-2231-X (alk. paper)
  1. Jews – United States – Politics and government. 2. Zionism –
United States. 3. Holocaust, Jewish (1939–1945) – Public opinion.
4. Public opinion – United States 5. United States – Ethnic
relations. 6. Public opinion – Jews. I. Title.
E184.J5B492   1990
320.5′4′0956940973 – dc20   *90–11942*
                                                        CIP

CONTENTS

ACKNOWLEDGMENTS

I owe my thanks to the many people who have contributed to this book. I am particularly grateful to the librarians and archivists who patiently responded to my numerous requests. Sylvia Landress and her staff at the Zionist Archives and Library were especially helpful as was Miriam Leikind of the Abba Hillel Silver Memorial Archives. I also appreciate the efforts of the staffs of the American Jewish Historical Society, the Herbert H. Lehman Papers, the National Office of Hadassah, and the Jabotinsky Institute. Daniel Schnurr, the social science reference librarian of Hampshire College, generously provided me with references and support.

I owe a special debt to Professor Walter P. Metzger of Columbia University and Professor David S. Wyman, of the University of Massachusetts at Amherst. Professor Metzger was an excellent dissertation sponsor. His insightful comments and probing questions were numerous and his editorial suggestions invaluable. Professor Wyman, as a friend and mentor, was generous with his time and support. I can honestly say that this book would not have been completed without their help.

Professors James P. Shenton, Paula Hyman, and Rosalind N. Rosenberg read most of this manuscript and offered important suggestions. I would like to especially thank Professor Shenton and Professor Peter Onuf for their support and encouragement during my years as a graduate student at Columbia University. Professors Henry Feingold and Monty Penkower helped me understand the complex history of American Jewry during the 1930s and 1940s. Many colleagues at Hampshire College offered their encouragement and posed difficult and probing questions. Leonard Glick was an important source of inspiration. I relied upon Penina Glazer, the Dean of the Faculty, for friendship, advice, and

9

Acknowledgments

release time. I am also grateful for the support of Egbal Ahmad, Nancy Fitch, Allen Hunter, Bob Rakoff, and Miriam and Paul Slater.

I have been lucky enough to be assocated with a group of scholars who have been true comrades for many years. A special thanks to Elizabeth Capelle, Dan Richter, Diana Shaikh, and Herbert Sloan. Thanks also to Harriet Goldstein, Howard Berman, my late grandmother Sarah Feller, the late Leo Mittelman, Bea Mittelman, Midge Wyman, and Kirsten and Lia Meisinger who provided support and love for many years.

Both Ms. Anne Adamus and Dr. Robert R. Mandel of Wayne State University Press have been very helpful and unusually patient. I hope that this book will meet their expectations. As should be obvious, while many individuals have contributed to the appearance of this book, I am solely responsible for any errors of fact and judgment.

I cannot adequately express my gratitude to my parents, Rose and Harry Berman. All I can do is dedicate this book to them and to my wife, Amy Mittelman. To Amy I owe much. As a talented historian she set an example I tried to emulate and as a friend and companion she successfully got me through more crises than I care to remember. Finally, I thank my son, Louis, for the hearty laughs and big hugs which helped me keep the task of writing this book in perspective.

INTRODUCTION

In 1943, the American Zionist leader Hayim Greenberg accused American Jewish organizations of "moral bankruptcy" for failing to mobilize to come to the aid of European Jewry. Greenberg, writing in the Yiddish press, marveled at the lack of a frenzied response on the part of a people who had learned that millions of their brethren were being brutally eliminated.[1] His claim that the great number of competing organizations that made up the American Jewish community divided rather than united American Jewry, anticipated the judgment of historians. Greenberg and subsequent scholars, however, tended to ignore an intriguing fact: during the Holocaust era, American Zionist organizations experienced tremendous growth and Zionists became the leaders of the American Jewish community.[2]

In 1933, the year Adolf Hitler came to power in Germany, Zionism was a weak movement struggling to survive within the American Jewish community. The major American Zionist organizations in 1933 claimed a combined membership of slightly over sixty-five thousand.[3] In the midst of a major depression, Zionists vainly fought to convince American Jews to join a movement that seemed to be doing little to uplift the Jewish condition either at home or abroad. To make matters worse, within the United States powerful American Jewish organizations, such as the American Jewish Committee and the entire Reform Judaism establishment, refused even to accept the very concept of Jewish nationhood.

On the eve of the Nazi nightmare, Zionist leaders in the United States, like their counterparts in Palestine, did not expect to see the establishment of a Jewish state in their lifetimes. Instead, they looked forward to a slow but steady Jewish settlement of Palestine under the supervision of Great Britain, which held a League of Nations Mandate to prepare

11

the Holy Land for eventual independence. While this strategy did not promise to immediately alleviate the "Jewish problem" in Europe, it would allow for social experimentation and, through the kibbutz movement, the establishment of a class-less Jewish society in Palestine. Slow-paced development would also provide Zionists with time to forge a peaceful relationship with the Arab residents of Palestine. While Palestine's Arab majority might be uncomfortable with Jewish settlement in 1933, most American Zionist leaders optimistically looked forward to the time when the Arabs would realize that the Zionist experiment in the Holy Land was serving their own best interests, as well as those of the Jews.

Following the Nazi's rise to power in 1933, many German Jews sought to flee from their oppressors. The Jewish refugee crisis dramatically transformed American Zionist organizations. The plight of assimilated German Jewry seemed to validate the Zionist claim that Jewish nationalism was the only suitable survival tactic for Diaspora Jewry. American Zionists energetically set out to provide the Jewish refugees with a home in Palestine. Their ability to provide a practical solution to the refugee crisis won the movement new prestige and members.

The thousands of Jewish refugees who found a home in the Holy Land frightened Palestine's Arab majority. Dreading the possibility of becoming "second class citizens" in their own land, the Arabs began a long and bitter armed insurrection in 1936. Arab opposition to Jewish immigration led Great Britain in 1939 to renounce its support of Zionism and eventual Jewish statehood. The necessity to defend Palestine against Arab attacks and to fend off American and British critics of Jewish nationalism slowly changed the priorities of American Zionists. Whereas they had previously been able to focus their attention on presenting Palestine as the most practical and feasible refugee haven, they were now forced to use the refugee crisis as a means to defend the Jewish settlement of the Holy Land.

World War II seemed to offer American Zionists one last opportunity to create a Jewish state. Believing that the Second World War would follow the pattern of the First, American Zionists looked forward to a "second" Versailles conference, which would redraw boundaries and settle territorial and national disputes. To make this dream a reality, Zionists would have to gather massive political and popular support during the war. Knowledge of Hitler's ongoing extermination of European Jewry did not force American Zionists to alter their thinking or strategy; rather it confirmed their conviction that Jewish statehood was the best response to genocide. As American Jews learned about the fate of their European co-religionists, they seemed to flock to the Zionist banner.

Historians have generally conceived of the American Jewish response to the Holocaust and the triumph of American Zionism as two separate events. In fact, they are inseparably linked. Hitler's persecution of European Jewry (which began long before the implementation of an extermination policy) fundamentally determined the development of American Zionism.

American Jews completely transformed their political world between 1933 and 1948. By the end of 1947, Zionist organizations, with nearly one million members,[4] hegemonically controlled the American Jewish community. Zionists had spearheaded a long, bitter political struggle resulting in the November 1947 United Nations vote to establish a Jewish state in Palestine. Much of this campaign was waged against a British Empire that, in the minds of American Zionists, had been transformed from a benign benefactor into an accomplice in the extermination of six million European Jews. The struggle for Jewish statehood also fundamentally altered Jewish perceptions of the Arabs. American Zionist leaders no longer looked upon Palestinian Arabs as a people merely needing to recognize the benefits of Jewish development of the Holy Land. Instead, American Zionists viewed their Arab opponents as reactionary neo-Nazis who were attempting to complete the work that Adolf Hitler had begun.

This book is neither a diplomatic history of American Zionism nor an analysis of organizational developments. Other historians have undertaken these tasks.[5] Rather, this is a study of how the worldview, or *weltanschauung*, of American Zionists evolved during the critical decades of the thirties and forties. Particular attention will be given to the dynamic and complex relationship between the Zionist worldview and the policies they pursued during their confrontation with nazism.

Studying how the worldview of American Zionists developed and changed during the critical years between 1933 and 1948 requires a sensitive analysis of sometimes neglected sources. Abba Hillel Silver, Stephen Wise, and their fellow Zionist leaders delivered numerous speeches and published many articles aimed at both Jewish and Christian audiences. The verbatim transcripts of American Zionist conventions total thousands of pages, recording the words of both movement leaders and rank-and-file members. Of course, many of these speeches and comments were repetitious and unoriginal, but some Zionists like Silver and Wise could express themselves eloquently and powerfully. Regardless of the quality of construction or delivery, the speeches and comments of American Zionists provide us with a wonderful means of understanding how Jewish nationalists in the United States attempted to make sense of their world.

American Jews in the 1930s and 1940s lived through times of confusion and tragedy. In the midst of a major economic depression, which at times seemed to threaten the social and political stability of the United States, they confronted the rise of Nazi anti-Semitism. However, these acts of hatred were usually associated with "unenlightened" Eastern Europe. Hitler's success at enacting anti-Semitic policies reminiscent of the Middle Ages in "civilized" Germany seemed incredible and without precedent. The dilemma of American Jews deepened after the outbreak of the Second World War when they learned about the ongoing mass murder of European Jewry. The systematic, "scientific" extermination of millions of souls was horrifying, all the more so because the victims were not strangers. The overwhelming majority of Jews in the United States had roots that stretched across the Atlantic to Nazi-occupied Europe. It was their kinfolk riding the railcars to German gas chambers. During World War II, American Jews desperately struggled both to understand and respond to the European Jewish tragedy.

American Zionists shared in the despair and anguish of the entire American Jewish community. However, they discovered that the ideology of Jewish nationalism allowed them to understand events almost defying comprehension and provided them with a means of responding to Hitler's death camps. For Zionists, the Holocaust proved that national homelessness caused anti-Semitism and that only through the creation of a nation of their own could Jewry achieve salvation. Convinced that the Second World War offered Zionists their last best chance to create a Jewish state, they were determined not only to rescue European Jewry, but, through the revolutionary step of Jewish statehood, to rescue the entire Jewish people, born and unborn, from the threat of continued persecution. Failure to create a Jewish state would be criminal, as they were sure that it would condemn future generations to death and suffering.

Once Zionists intellectually "understood" the extermination of their European kin, they offered their explanation and solution to the wider Jewish and Christian publics. The powerful Zionist message appealed to the American Jewish masses and to the many Christians desperately searching for an answer to Auschwitz. They flocked around the blue and white flag of Zionism and joined in a crusade that ended with the establishment of the State of Israel.

The pages that follow tell the story of how American Zionists struggled to comprehend and respond to Nazi anti-Semitism and the consequences of their actions.

I | AMERICAN ZIONISM AND THE EXTERNAL THREAT, 1933–1936

The Zionist quest began in 1896, when Theodor Herzl published his classic political manifesto, *The Jewish State*. Herzl, born in Budapest in 1860, grew up in an assimilated Jewish home and received his education in Vienna, where he became a prominent journalist and aspiring playwright. A devout believer in the liberal credo, the young Herzl optimistically expected that the advance of progress in Europe would completely emancipate Jewry from discrimination and persecution.

Herzl's optimism did not survive several personal encounters with anti-Semitism, including the Dreyfus affair, which he covered as a correspondent for the Viennese *Neue Freie Presse*. By 1896, as *The Jewish State* demonstrates, Herzl had undergone a conversion experience. He no longer believed that Christians could be "educated" to tolerate Jews, no matter how assimilated they became. Rather, he maintained that Christians would always perceive of Jews as strangers and that anti-Semitism would increase as the concentration of Jews in a given territory grew. That being the case, it made no sense for Jews to respond to anti-Semitism by emigrating to a more "tolerant" land, since Jew hatred in their new homes would surely increase as a result of their arrival.

Having determined that anti-Semitism could not be escaped through either assimilation or emigration, Herzl proposed a radical solution: Jewish statehood. In their own country, he wrote, Jews would escape their minority status and would be free to develop and progress like the great nations of Europe. He thought that most of the world's Jews would eventually settle in the Jewish state, and predicted that anti-Semitism would decline as the number of Jews in the Diaspora decreased.[1]

Herzl was not the first writer to suggest a national solution to the Jewish problem. In 1882, Leo Pinsker, a Russian Jewish intellectual, had published his pamphlet *Autoemancipation*, which in many respects foreshadowed Herzl's later work.[2] However, if Herzl was not an entirely original or critical thinker, he was a magnificent politician. Shortly after completing *The Jewish State*, he began to plan the formation of a political movement that would seek to establish an independent Jewish nation. Herzl's work culminated in the First Zionist Congress, which held its opening session in Basel, Switzerland, on August 29, 1897. The 197 delegates who attended the Congress came to hail Herzl and to form the World Zionist Organization.[3]

Even before the close of the Basel Congress it became apparent that Zionists were divided on a number of significant issues. Herzl's conversion to Jewish nationalism had not been accompaneid by a corresponding growth in his interest in and commitment to Jewish culture and tradition. The Jewish state he intended to build would be liberal, secular, and bourgeois, and would be located in whatever territory Jews might acquire through negotiations with European imperial powers. The East European Jews who quickly became the backbone of the Zionist movement held a very different vision. They wanted to *recreate* a Jewish state in Palestine, the ancient and unforgotten homeland of the Jews. Many of the East Europeans were attracted to the ideas of Ahad Ha-Am, a Russian Jewish scholar and Zionist, who believed that a Jewish homeland would not only answer the problem of anti-Semitism, but would also provide the environment in which a new vibrant Jewish culture could evolve. Other East European Jews attempted to fuse Jewish orthodoxy and Zionism. They organized the Mizrachi Zionist Organization in 1902, which was dedicated to the establishment of a religious Jewish state in a Palestine whose legal system and culture would be built on the foundation of Torah and Talmud.[4]

While the Mizrachi looked to the Jewish holy books for guidance, other East European Zionists read Karl Marx. Like Herzl, the socialists planned to build a secular Jewish state, but based on socialist principles. Greatly influenced by Russian populism, the socialist Zionist organizations of Europe, including the Poale Zion (1907), specialized in dispatching small groups of Jewish "pioneer" youth to Palestine to "return" to the soil and live as laborers and farmers. These young people established the kibbutzim (communal agricultural settlements) and became the dominant force in the Palestinian Jewish community (the Yishuv) until the creation of Israel in 1948.[5]

Zionist organizations in the United States reflected the ideological splits of the world movement. Orthodox religious Zionists formed the Mizrachi Organization of America in 1912, whose principal goal was the "Rehabilitation of Palestine in the spirit of Jewish Torah and Tradition" and which was affiliated with the international Mizrachi Movement. The American Mizrachi, which claimed to have twenty thousand members on the eve of the depression, had a limited constituency in the United States. The Mizrachi tended to find its best audiences in the immigrant communities of New York, but its recruitment efforts suffered as a result of restrictive American immigration quotas, which almost totally eliminated the influx of East European Jews into the United States after 1921.[6]

Socialist Zionism in the United States shared many of the problems of the Mizrachi. It too found it difficult to sink roots deep into the American Jewish community; in 1929 the Poale Zion, the most important socialist Zionist group in America, claimed to have only five thousand members. Generally hostile to the Soviet Union and the American Communist Party, which branded Zionism a form of bourgeois nationalism, the Poale Zion supported the organizing efforts of Jewish workers in Palestine and the United States. Perhaps one of the most important contributions of the American socialist Zionists was the publication of their journal, *Jewish Frontier*, which first appeared in 1933. Edited by Hayim Greenberg, a talented writer and humanitarian, *Jewish Frontier*'s substantive and thoughtful articles attracted the attention of many American Jews who never joined a socialist Zionist organization.[7]

Both the Mirachi and Poale Zion were loyal participants in the World Zionist Organization. On the eve of Hitler's rise to power in 1933, members of both organizations, like most Zionists, believed that they would probably never live to see the establishment of a Jewish state in Palestine. This, the final stage of Zionism, would have to wait until the Jews of Palestine, who in 1931 made up only 17 percent of the country's population, achieved majority status. In the meantime, the first priority of Zionists was to carefully nurture the social and economic development of the Yishuv, preparing it for eventual independence. The patience of the Mizrachi and the Poale Zion generally reflected their essential trust of Great Britain, the Mandatory Power in Palestine. While both organizations criticized specific British policies in Palestine, neither doubted that London remained committed to the spirit of Foreign Minister Arthur Balfour's 1917 declaration that "His Majesty's Government view with favour the establishment in Palestine of a national home for the Jewish people."[8]

Revisionist Zionists did not share these views. Vladimir Jabotinsky, who established the Revisionist party in 1925, was a powerful orator (his opponents called him a demagogue) and a charismatic leader. The movement he established seemed to many to be uncomfortably similar to Mussolini's fascist organization. Revisionists were passionately anti-socialist and seemed to be fascinated with military-like discipline and rituals. By 1930, Jabotinsky was angrily attacking other Zionist leaders for their failure to recognize that Great Britain was deserting them. He was particularly upset by the Zionist movement's failure to prevent Great Britain's establishment of the Arab kingdom of Transjordan in the territory west of the Jordan River, which had originally been included within the Palestine Mandate. Jabotinsky's anti-British stance finally forced him and the Revisionist movement to break from the World Zionist Organization in 1931.[9]

Revisionism did not win many adherents in the United States and existed only on the fringes of the American Zionist community. The Zionist Revisionist Organization of America (which later changed its name to the New Zionist Organization), whose goal was to establish a Jewish state on both sides of the Jordan River, did not even come close to approaching the numerical strength of Poale Zion.[10]

The Zionist Organization of American (ZOA) and Hadassah were the most important American Zionist organizations between the end of World War I and the establishment of Israel in 1948. Hadassah, the largest organization of Zionist women in the world, theoretically was affiliated with the Zionist Organization of America, but actually exercised total autonomy. The organization concentrated its efforts on practical programs and its financial backing was vital in the construction of Palestine's impressive health care system. Both Hadassah and the ZOA prided themselves on being the only American Zionist bodies solely committed to reestablishing the Jewish nation in Palestine. Like the Poale Zion and Mizrachi, the ZOA and Hadassah were part of the World Zionist Organization, but they criticized their Zionist competitors for diluting their Jewish nationalism with other ideologies and philosophies. Generally, Hadassah and ZOA members saw their mission as providing the pioneers in Palestine with financial and, when necessary, political support. Few actually intended to settle in Palestine themselves. Most supported the kibbutzim and the powerful Jewish labor organization in Palestine, although they were not socialists, and a great many were also concerned with furthering and ecouraging the growth of Jewish culture in the United States, although few were Orthodox.[11]

During World War I, under the leadership of Louis Brandeis, the ZOA was able to boast of a membership of two hundred thousand, which included prominent young Jews like Felix Frankfurter who joined the Zionist ranks at Brandeis's request. After the war, however, American Zionism went into a period of steady decline, largely because Zionists lacked an issue with which to capture the attention and loyalty of American Jews. During the world conflict, the starvation, dislocation, and persecution of East European Jewry stimulated American Jewish concern and propelled large numbers into the Zionist ranks. With the return of peace, the condition of Jews on the continent significantly improved and American interest in Zionism dwindled. Many American Jews also seemed to believe that the Zionist movement had already achieved its goal when the British government in 1917 expressed support for a Palestinian Jewish homeland in the famous Balfour Declaration. This commitment was reaffirmed by the League of Nations when it awarded the Palestine Mandate to Great Britain. Finally, a bitter struggle for the leadership of the world Zionist movement between Louis Brandeis and Chaim Weizmann, the Russian-born Zionist who had been principally responsible for winning Britain's support for Zionism, further sapped Jewish nationalist strength in the immediate postwar years. Weizmann's supporters within the ZOA, who resented the assimilated Brandeis's lack of concern with Jewish culture, defeated the forces of the Supreme Court justice, but only at the expense of membership and prestige. On the eve of the stock market crash, the

ZOA and Hadassah claimed a combined membership of sixty-five thousand. In 1929, Zionists did not and could not claim to speak for the more than four million Jews of the United States.[12]

The stock market crash of 1929 and the depression that followed struck a severe blow at the already weak Zionist body politic, as the fear and actuality of unemployment turned the attention of American Jewry inward. The reestablishment of a Jewish state in the distant future seemed a trivial matter when compared to the urgency of unpaid rent and grocery bills. In a time of economic emergency even many Zionist veterans concluded that membership dues were a luxury that had to be sacrificed.[13]

At many National Board meetings in the early 1930s, Hadassah's leaders heard reports describing the organization's declining membership.[14] Hadassah leaders tried to slow the rate of desertion by allowing members to forgo paying their four dollar annual dues for two years before striking their names from the movement's mailing list.[15] In August 1932, officials declared that the continued loss of membership threatened the whole Hadassah framework, and in November, when they learned that over one thousand members had left the organization during the preceding year, they immediately decided to hire a professional publicity worker to oversee a coordinated recruitment drive.[16]

The aggressive campaign to attract women to Hadassah seemed to achieve quick success. At the end of December 1932, board members learned that "for the first time in three years reports indicated a temporary increase in membership." By February 1933, 2,096 new members had joined the Zionist ranks, making Hadassah leaders believe that their own personal depression was over. Reports in March indicated, however, that while over two thousand women had entered the movement, a greater number of veterans had failed to renew their Hadassah membership. By July it was clear that the success of the campaign had been an illusion. Almost five thousand women had left Hadassah since the drive began, and the extraordinary efforts of the organization's leaders couldn't attract even half that many new women into the movement.[17]

JEWISH REFUGEES AND AMERICAN IMMIGRATION RESTRICTION

As American Zionist organizations struggled to survive, Adolf Hitler began the long process that would result in European Jewry's near-extinction. While no plans existed for the physical annihilation of German Jewry in 1933, Hitler certainly intended to segregate and impoverish the Jewish population to the point where they would be forced to flee. The Nazis quickly organized large-scale, anti-Jewish demonstrations, dismissed Jews from government positions, urged "good" Germans to boycott Jewish professionals and businessmen, and used all the resources of the German state to spread the anti-Semitic virus throughout the German populace.[18]

Hitler's persecution of German Jewry horrifed American Jewish leaders, but it also had an unintended benefit. At its 1933 annual convention, ZOA president Morris Rothenberg declared that "the calamity that had overtaken the 600,000 Jews in Germany has cast a shadow over everything else in Jewish life."[19] Rabbi Stephen S. Wise, one of American Jewry's most respected Zionist leaders, agreed but also pointed out that a "tragic vindication has come to Zionism in these unhappy days." The assimilated German-Jewish community had rejected Theodor Herzl and had denied the existence of a Jewish people. Wise even speculated that the German obsession with Aryanism might have been "evoked" by the "repudiation" of Jewishness by German Jews and their espousal of "pseudo-Aryansim," but he called on Zionists to forgive German Jewry its errors, confessing that "our hearts are full of compassion for them that have sinned against Jewish history."[20]

All segments of the organized American Jewish community concerned themselves with the German Jewish crisis, and all American Jews supported efforts to pressure the Nazi government into recognizing the civil rights of its Jewish citizens. American Zionists did too, but because they feared that Hitler's anti-Semitic policies would not be easily overturned, they also believed that salvation for many Jews would only come with emigration from the Nazi Reich.[21]

Between January 1933 and September 1, 1939, 226,000 German Jews, approximately one-third of Germany's Jewish population, left the Third Reich. During the spring and summer of 1933, between four hundred and five hundred Jews a day visited the Berlin offices of the *Hilfsverein Der Deutschen Juden* (Relief Organization of German Jews) to gather information about emigration from Germany. Their prospects for settlement were not particularly bright. Very few countries were willing to allow large numbers of refugees to enter their borders.[22]

The League of Nations responded to the German refugee crisis by appointing a High Commissioner for Refugees. James G. McDonald, an American lawyer and foreign policy specialist, assumed the office and for two years attempted to rationalize and streamline the refugee emigration process. In June 1935, McDonald resigned his position, frustrated by the failure of League members to support his efforts to provide new homes for German refugees.[23]

France, which shared a common border with Germany and was therefore a likely candidate to become a major refugee haven, did allow many German Jews to enter its borders, but encouraged them to leave again as soon as possible. A large number of Jews used France as a major way station; in late 1933, over thirty thousand German Jews found temporary salvation in France. By early 1938, the number had dwindled to ten thousand. Great Britain was also willing to do its "fair share" to solve the refugee crisis, but like France was unwilling to open its doors to all or even a majority of those in need, and London also encouraged arriving Jewish refugees to look for a permanent home elsewhere.[24]

The United States was less generous than the European powers. America's traditional policy of open immigration came to an end when Congress enacted restrictive quota systems in 1921 and 1924. Legislation stipulated that no more than 153,774 immigrants could enter the United States annually. The quota system allowed 25,957 Germans to immigrate to the country every year.[25]

After the stock market crash of 1929, restrictionist sentiment in the United States grew as the average American believed that every immigrant allowed into the country would add to the already intense competition for a limited number of jobs. Representatives in Congress began to demand an additional reduction of immigration. Existing legislation allowed American consular officials to deny immigration visas to those individuals judged "likely to become a public charge." In September 1930, President Herbert Hoover ordered American officials vigorously to enforce the "Likely to Become a Public Charge" clause and to award visas only to those individuals who could either prove that they had enough savings to care for themselves after they came to the United States or who possessed affidavits from Americans who pledged to provide them with financial support. As Hoover had hoped, the new American policy significantly reduced immigration to the
United States; during the last year of his administration, State Department officials distributed only 35,576 immigration visas.[26]

State Department officials continued to use the "Likely to Become a Public Charge" clause as a restrictive measure after Franklin Roosevelt's inauguration in March 1933. The government's failure to liberalize its immigration policy as the refugee crisis worsened reflected the nativism of many State Department bureaucrats, Roosevelt's concentration on drawing up legislation to combat the depression, and the new president's wariness about advocating unpopular positions. Roosevelt, however, soon had to confront the German Jewish dilemma, as American Jews, including leading Zionists, took advantage of their official positions and prominence to intercede with the administration on the refugees' behalf. Louis Brandeis, Stephen Wise, the directors of Hadassah, and other American Zionists believed that the United States had a moral responsibility to provide a haven for at least some of the German Jewish refugees.

Several months after President Paul von Hindenburg named Hitler chancellor of Germany, Stephen Wise pressed Secretary of State Cordell Hull to support an executive order that would allow refugees from Nazi persecution to enter the United States. Wise was shocked to find Hull "weirdly uninformed" about the Jewish crisis in Germany.[27] In April 1933, Felix Frankfurter, a professor at Harvard Law School and one of America's most respected Zionists, suggested to President Roosevelt that a larger number of German refugees be allowed to enter the United States. Hull, responding for Roosevelt, assured Frankfurter that Germans applying for entry into the United States were experiencing no delay in receiving visas as a result of immigration quotas.[28] Unsatisfied with this response, Frankfurter arranged a meeting between Hull and Louis Brandeis. Brandeis told Hull that he was "more ashamed of my country than pained by Jewish suffering." He did not want the United States to do away with quotas altogether, but he did argue that Washington could reasonably be expected to relax its policy of restricting immigration.[29]

Hull agreed to discuss the matter with Roosevelt, and eventually some executive action was taken to streamline the torturous visa application process. In 1933, only 5 percent of the German quota was filled. Over the next two years the number of Germans entering the United States increased fourfold, and by 1937, 42 percent of the available visas for German nationals were used. After Hitler's annexation of Austria in March 1938, the refugee crisis intensified as Austrian Jewry joined the visa line, and finally, in 1939, State Department officials issued all of the visas available under the combined German-Austrian quota.[30]

Brandeis's actions were not solely responsible for the very slow but steady liberalization of American immigration policy. Many American Jewish organizations and leaders made their requests and feelings known to the Roosevelt administration. Stephen Wise, an early and ardent supporter of the New Deal, played a critical role in informing Roosevelt about the refugee tragedy and in 1938 became a member of the newly created President's Advisory Committee on Political Refugees. In spite of their concern and good intentions, however, neither Wise nor any other Zionist or Jewish leader in the United States mounted an aggressive campaign aimed at breaching the American quota system, which insured that most Jewish refugees would never be able to reach America.[31]

During the depression decade, the American public's opposition to a large influx of immigrants was even more intense than it had been in 1921 and 1924, when the immigration quota laws were enacted. Nazi anti-Semitism and the frantic search of German Jewish refugees for a new home did not force many Americans to change their attitudes about immigration. Throughout the thirties, public opinion polls revealed, a majority of Americans opposed opening the country's doors to Jewish refugees. In 1938, five years into Hitler's "war against the Jews," 83 percent of those polled responded "no" to the question: "If you were a member of Congress, would you vote yes or no on a bill to open the doors of the U.S. to a larger number of European refugees than are now admitted under our immigration quotas?" This overwhelming response was partly due to the sincere belief of many that there were simply not enough jobs or resources in the country to accommodate a large number of newcomers. Sadly, however, the opposition of many others to a more liberal refugee policy reflected the growing problem of anti-Semitism in the United States.[32]

During the thirties, American anti-Semitism never came close to approaching the intensity of Jew-hatred in Nazi Germany. The government of the United States did not pursue anti-Semitic policies, and Jews in the United States continued to hold prominent positions in the public and private spheres. Nevertheless, American Jews throughout the decade knew that some of their neighbors thought ill of them.

Pollsters found that significant numbers of Americans believed that Jews had both admirable and objectionable qualities. During the spring of 1938, over 60 percent of those quizzed admitted that they admired Jews, primarily because of their business and intellectual achievements.[33] During the same period, another survey found that 65 percent of Americans objected to certain "Jewish qualities," including their supposed greed, dishonesty, aggressiveness, and clannishness.[34] Only 13 percent of those polled in May 1938 would support a hypothetical anti-Semitic campaign, but an amazing 58 percent claimed that European Jewry was at least partly responsible for its persecution.[35] A much more threatening sign was the growth of rabidly anti-Semitic movements on the fringes of American politics. Father Charles E. Coughlin, the charismatic radio priest, often inserted anti-Semitic statements into his broadcasts without suffering censure from his church superiors. William Dudley Pelley's Silver Shirts and the German-American Bund had the support of only a very small number of Americans, but they loudly and repeatedly denounced "traitorous" American Jews and accused Roosevelt of being under their control.[36]

The intensity of restrictionist sentiment in the United States and the latent anti-Semitism of many Americans made Franklin Roosevelt's feeble efforts to liberalize immigration policy seem impressive. American Jewish leaders feared a restrictionist victory in Congress; these fears were not unwarranted. In early 1939, American Jewry and its supporters made their one serious attempt to breach the United States quota walls. In February, Senator Robert Wagner (D., N.Y.) and Representative Edith Rogers (R., Mass.) introduced bills in both houses of Congress that would have allowed 20,000 refugee children to enter the United States above the quota limit. In spite of impressive support from Eleanor Roosevelt, Hollywood personalities, and Jewish and humanitarian organizations, the bill was amended out of existence. Restrictionist representatives, responding to the opposition of various American "patriotic" organizations (including the American Legion), would allow the bill only to give the children first priority in the existing and already oversubscribed quota. Wagner was disgusted by his mutated bill and withdrew it.[37]

Their inability to change significantly American immigration policy concerned American Zionists, but did not depress them. They were convinced that many German Jewish refugees would be able to find a permanent and prosperous home in Palestine.

A PALESTINIAN SOLUTION TO THE REFUGEE CRISIS

American Zionists and their European and Palestinian counterparts enthusiastically accepted the challenge of providing German Jews with a much-needed refuge.

Chaim Weizmann wrote to an American supporter in the spring of 1933: "The German tragedy is absorbing—and seems likely to absorb for some time to come—every ounce of my time and energy. . . ."[38] Max Shulman of the ZOA defined the settlement of German refugees in Palestine as one of the major tasks of the American Zionist movement.[39]

At the 1933 ZOA convention, Rabbi Stephen Wise expressed the opinion of all American Zionists that "Jews cannot permanently remain in Germany." Zionists, Wise noted, had long ago prepared a solution to this tragic situation: "The emergency conference through which to meet the German situation was called by Theodor Herzl in 1896. . . . The answer to the Hitler program is a Jewish program, and the Jewish program is Zionism or Jewish nationalism."[40]

Speaker after speaker at the convention echoed Wise's message and stressed Palestine's role in the solution of the German Jewish crisis. Abraham Goldberg, a delegate from New York City, enthusiastically supported Zionist plans to settle one hundred thousand German Jews a year in Palestine. Jewish nationalists, he said, "will not be satisfied merely with protests, although we took an important part in the protest demonstrations. We must have a constructive plan which will help German Jewry and vindicate Jewish honor."[41]

American Zionists believed that Palestine could accommodate large numbers of refugees, but during the first years of Hitler's reign they carefully admitted that Zionism was not the only solution to the problem of German anti-Semitism. This not only reflected a commitment to the ideal of Jewish political and social equality in Europe, but a genuine uncertainty about the absorptive capacity of Palestine and an uneasiness about the suitability of many of the prospective immigrants. *The Jewish Frontier*, the prestigious socialist Zionist journal, suspected that some of the Jews fleeing to Palestine were not truly committed to the Zionist program. Many of the former professionals and businessmen among the refugees seemed to be unwilling to adapt themselves physically and culturally to their new homes, and many of them were not willing to become farmers or laborers. In order to preserve the Zionist experiment in Palestine, the journal advocated a more careful screening of prospective immigrants, noting that, "Palestine has a right to expect of the new immigrant not merely the devotion of his energies to the struggle for economic survival, but also a readiness to participate, socially and culturally, in the reconstruction of the Jewish homeland."[42]

Chaim Weizmann, the president of the World Zionist Organization from 1920 to 1931 (he would be reelected to the post in 1935), also recognized that massive Jewish immigration to Palestine could be troublesome. In 1933, he warned members of the Zionist Organization of America at their annual convention not to expect too much from the Jewish homeland. He feared that too rapid an influx of refugees would overwhelm the resources of the Jewish agricultural settlements and would cause overcrowding in Palestine's towns and cities. Such a situation would imperil the entire Zionist project, since the collective agricultural village was the source of the morals, culture, and civilization that Zionists were creating in Palestine. Weizmann hoped that Zionists would realize that

> if we are going to repeat the mistakes which Jews have made in all countries that we settled in towns and the country was somebody else's we shall not have a normal national home. A normal national home is based on the right balance between town and country; on the right proportion between town dwellers and peasants. And, therefore, colonization on the land may be more difficult; it may be slower; it may be costly, but it is the essential prerequisite if our national home is going to be stable at all.[43]

Weizmann also confessed some skepticism about the ability of German Jewry to adapt to the new Jewish society of Palestine. Many refugees were crippled by a tradition of 150 years of assimilation, which "hollowed out the spirit and the heart of a great many Jews." Like Stephen Wise, he believed that German Jews bore some responsibility for their plight. Had they and other Western Jews "not sneered so much at Palestine, had they believed in it as we did, . . . why they could walk in today in Palestine in the hundreds of thousands."[44]

Weizmann's concern for Palestine and his ambivalence about the moral character of German Jewry was matched by a strong commitment to fight German anti-Semitism. He believed that Palestine could play a role in the fight against Hitler by accepting 40,000 refugees during the next year, and he hoped that a total of 250,000 could be accommodated within the next five or six years.[45]

Emanuel Neumann, one of American Zionism's young and promising leaders, disagreed with Weismann's assessment. Neumann and his followers within the ZOA believed that too much attention had been given to the building of small, socialist agricultural communities by the Zionist movement. They favored increased private investment in the country, industrialization, and the recruitment of middle-class immigrants. Jews with money to invest in industry would create many jobs in Palestine and would increase the country's capacity to absorb masses of German Jews. Neumann urged Zionists to be honest with the Jewish world and admit that the German refugee problem could not be solved by taking a number of Jews and "physically" and "literally" settling them in Palestine. Instead, he argued, "we can do it chiefly by opening the whole of Palestine to Jewish development on such a scale that there will be room and possibilities for tens of thousands and hundreds of thousands to come into Palestine."[46]

Many Zionists at the 1933 Convention seemed to favor large-scale settlement of Jewish refugees in Palestine without sharing Weizmann's fears about destabilizing the Jewish community already there. Solomon Goldman, a future president of the ZOA, argued that Zionists had to engage in "a scheme of colonization that will make all our previous efforts look insignificant." Palestine, he continued, must be made ready to act as a haven for all needy Jews.[47] However, in spite of significant support for Neumann's position, ZOA leaders were unwilling to endorse a plan that might undermine the agricultural and communal settlement of Palestine because such a step would have alienated those ZOA members who sympathized with the idealistic founders of the Jewish kibbutzim in Palestine. ZOA convention delegates instead unanimously voted for a compromise resolution requesting the world Zionist leadership to settle at least a quarter of a million Jews in Palestine during the next four years.[48]

Although Zionists worried about Hitler's anti-Semitic policies and their impact on Palestine's development, they were also optimistic about the future. The experiences of German Jewry seemed to prove the Zionist dictum that Jewish nationalism, not assimilation, was the correct Jewish strategy for survival. Costly Zionist efforts to develop Palestine had prepared that land to serve as one of the few havens available to Germany's Jews. Zionists were proud to contribute to the refugee problem's solution, and they also realized that the refugees could benefit their beloved Palestine. ZOA president Rothenberg observed: "We are profoundly convinced that tragic as the present situation is, it at the same time points to a historic duty and historic opportunity to enlarge the possibilities of the Jewish National Home for greater immigration."[49]

Some Zionists even hoped that the influx of refugees into Palestine would allow Jewish colonization to expand out of the confines of the Palestine Mandate. Emanuel Neumann, who had been actively involved in negotiations to open Transjordan to Zionist colonization, argued that a solution to the refugee problem required Jewish settlement on both sides of the Jordan River.[50] Stephen Wise's vision was even grander than Neumann's. He hoped that England, the United States, and the League of Nations would respond to the refugee crisis by coupling Syria and Iraq with Palestine so that they could "claim their share in the enriching processes which Jews have brought to Palestine in our generation."[51]

Following the 1933 ZOA convention, American Zionists and their European and Palestinian partners devoted considerable energy to implementing plans for the settlement of German Jews in Palestine.[52] The Jewish Agency (which represented Jewish interests in Palestine) and the Zionist Executive, however, were not legally responsible for regulating Palestine's immigration policy. Great Britain, internationally recognized as Palestine's legitimate protector and governor, held that power.

Hitler's rise to power and the refugee exodus that followed strained Zionist-British relations. In April 1933, Stephen Wise optimistically predicted that Great Britain would increase the number of Jews it allowed into Palestine each year in order to capitalize on world Jewry's resentment of Hitler. Shortly afterwards, however, Britain began to refuse Zionist requests for increased Jewish immigration to Palestine. A massive influx of Jewish workers, British administrators hypothesized, could stimulate the Jewish economic sector and threaten the jobs of those

Arabs employed by Jewish businessmen, farmers, and industrialists. Accordingly, for the six months form October 1, 1932, to March 31, 1933, the British, following a policy enacted before Hitler's assumption of power, issued 4,100 labor certificates allowing Jews without capital and their families to enter Palestine. During the next six-month period (April–September 1933) the British increased the number of certificates they issued only by 550.[53]

Robert Szold believed that the British were responding to Arab pressure, and he called on Zionists to begin a program of counterpressure.[54] Louis Lipsky, a close associate of Chaim Weizmann, who had led the struggle against Brandeis's leadership after World War I, asked James McDonald of the League of Nations Commission on Refugees to join the campaign against British immigration restrictions. Justice Brandeis personally made his objections known to Sir Herbert Samuel, who had served as Britain's first high commissioner in Palestine.[55]

In spite of his concerns about British immigration restrictions, Brandeis did not expect British hostility to continue. David Ben-Gurion, the leader of the Zionist establishment in Palestine, also minimized the Mandatory Power's opposition to the Jewish settlement of Palestine. Ben-Gurion advised Felix Frankfurter against adopting too aggressive an anti-British policy, writing: "I have a feeling that the Government is not unfriendly disposed towards us, but that it is beset with doubts and misgivings."[56]

The optimism of Ben-Gurion and Brandeis was quite realistic. In 1932, 9,553 Jews emigrated to Palestine. In spite of the restrictive British policy, that number increased to 30,327 in 1933. More importantly, the British in 1934 finally began to open the doors of Palestine wider, issuing 6,275 labor certificates for the period from April 1 to September 30, 1934, and 7,200 certificates for the six months following. The more liberal policy allowed 42,359 to reach Palestine in 1934, a number that climed to 61,854 in 1935.[57]

THE REFUGEE CRISIS AND THE REBIRTH OF AMERICAN ZIONISM

As they championed the refugees' cause, American Zionists quickly learned that a mutually beneficial relationship existed between their efforts to rescue German Jewry and the advancement of the Zionist movement in America. As early as April 1933, Stephen Wise had written Louis Brandeis: "We feel that time has come which almost parallels the 1914 situation, and that we may now be able to reawaken the interest of American Jews in Palestine and Zionism."[58] Robert Szold concurred with Wise's judgment and wrote: "There is no doubt that the German persecution of Jews has aroused Jewry, as nothing has done for a long time. It is impossible to over-estimate the extent of the feelings around; — and the possible effect on

Palestine. Many discussions have taken place in this country looking toward large schemes of Palestine development."[59] Many American Jews were realizing that Zionism seemed to offer a simple and practical solution to the refugees' plight. While other Jewish organizations futilely attempted to convince Adolf Hitler to alter his anti-Semitic policies, Zionist settlements in Palestine offered German Jews security and a future. By the summer of 1934, Hadassah and the ZOA reported that thirteen thousand American Jews had joined their organizations during the previous twelve months and that their total membership had risen to seventy-eight thousand.[60]

By February 1934, Hadassah leaders recognized that the German situation might allow the organization to reverse the downward plunge of its membership rolls. The board resolved that Hadassah must capitalize on the growing public interest in Palestine as the one available refuge for German Jewry.[61] By the end of March, Hadassah leaders were able to celebrate the continued influx of members into the organization, and they enthusiastically looked forward to continuing good times for the movement.[62]

Hadassah's leaders understood the extent to which their good fortune resulted from American Jewish concern for their brethren caught in Hitler's grasp. In the spring of 1934, Dr. Mordechai Kaplan, the founder of Reconstructionism and a widely respected theologian, urged Hadassah to concentrate its resources on solving the problem of "white slavery," which "blighted" the lives of many Jewish girls in Europe. Zip Szold (wife of Robert Szold) and the other leaders of Hadassah politely listened to Kaplan and promised to study the problem,[63] but continued to center their activites around Palestine and German Jewry. They had little other choice, as the local chapters of the organization would have tolerated no deviation from the German problem. National leaders were even beginning to feel pressure to abandon the organization's traditional emphasis on Palestinian health care. As they explained:

> There is a growing feeling in many Hadassah groups, . . . that Hadassah cannot always confine itself to a medical program in Palestine. The German situation had intensified this feeling, and Hadassah has found it difficult to convince its Chapters that they are serving the German immigrants in Palestine more effectively by providing them with good medical service than by undertaking other projects for their welfare.[64]

Jewish nationalists at the July 1934 convention of the ZOA were clearly aware of the refugee problem's centrality to Palestine's development and the success of American Zionism. President Morris Rothenberg observed that "the world Jewish situation, with the resultant emphasis upon the Zionist position, has brought the Zionist Organization closer to the appreciation and understanding of the Jewish public." While the rest of the world closed their doors to the Jewish refugees, the Zionist community of Palestine held out their hands to their beleaguered German kin. American Jewry's acknowledgment of Palestine's central role in the solution of the refugee problem had stimulated Zionist growth and fund-raising activities throughout the country. He reported that the ZOA had reduced its deficit from $133,161 to $53,321 and predicted that Jewish public interest in Palestine would continue to grow because many expected that Nazi anti-Semitism would spill over Germany's borders. He pointed to a general rise in European anti-Semitic activities and said that the only bright spot for world Jewry was Palestine.[65]

Louis Lipsky, the leader of the anti-Brandeis ZOA faction in the twenties struggle, and Robert Szold, a devoted disciple of the Supreme Court justice, agreed with Rothenberg's analysis. Lipsky feared that anti-Semitism would permeate Europe, turning the continent into a large concentration camp. Palestine, of all the world's lands, was willing to open its doors to the refugees. He confidently predicted that the refugee situation would make it difficult for any group or individual to maintain an anti-Zionist position.[66] Szold declared that the most important problem facing Zionists was "how to open the gates of Palestine to Jewish immigration." Echoing Rothenberg, he called upon Zionists to get the maximum number of European Jews into Palestine in the shortest possible time.[67]

While concern about Hitler's anti-Semitic policies significantly contributed to the growing prestige and strength of American Zionism, some Jewish nationalists feared that too strong an emphasis on the refugee crisis would dilute their movement. American Jews who had joined the Zionist ranks before the rise of Hitler could not help but question the ideological commitment of their new comrades who seemed only to be concerned about solving an immediate refugee problem. Did they understand that Hitler was not a unique phenomenon and that Theodor Herzl had established a revolutionary movement designed to end Jewish homelessness, the principal cause of anti-Semitism? Were they aware of the movement's past accomplishments as well as the history and culture of the Jewish people? Would they continue to be Zionists after the refugee crisis was solved? In the summer of 1934, ZOA president Rothenberg called upon American Jews to enlist in the Zionist crusade to bring the maximum number of refugees into Palestine, but he added that

> Zionism aims not merely to secure a place of refuge for those of our race seeking to escape persecution, but also to provide for the Jewish people the opportunity of a free, creative life, and to reproduce its national culture. . . . Hence it has always been considered sound Zionist philosophy and practice to participate in the cultural and spiritual development of Jewish life everywhere.[68]

Zionists had to become actively involved in every facet of the American Jewish community, particularly in the field of education. Rothenberg favored strong efforts to combat the progress of assimilation among American Jews.[69]

Jacob de Haas opposed Rothenberg's plan for expending Zionist resources on a wide range of projects. De Haas, a native of Great Britain, had come to the United States as an emissary for Theodor Herzl to oversee the development of American Zionism. He urged ZOA members to focus all their efforts on supporting the settlement of Jewish refugees in Palestine. It would be a great mistake, he said, for the organization to involve itself with questions not directly linked to the task of Jewish settlement.[70] Jewish youth, de Haas explained, were attracted to the Communist party because they preferred action and concrete programs to education courses. The same young people would flock to the ZOA if the Zionists followed the Communist lead and instituted an activist program.[71]

Several Zionists attacked de Haas and condemned him for not being sufficiently concerned with the fostering and encouragement of Jewish culture in the Diaspora. Louis Lipsky supported the Rothenberg plan that de Haas had attacked. He explained:

> You do not win a Zionist only when you get him to go to Palestine. You win a Zionist also when he becomes a Zionist in the Golus [exile] and acquires all those attributes, with the exception of the political rights and political status, of every Jew who lives in Palestine. The business of the Zionist movement is to create in the Golus such nationally constructed human beings that they become fit candidates to enter into the National Home even before they touch it. The Zionist organization therefore has an eye on all things that happen in the Jewish world.[72]

The strongest opposition to de Haas came from a small group of Jewish and Yiddish intellectuals and journalists who argued that Zionists must concern themselves with combating the advance of assimilation among American Jewry. Several expressed concern with the central role the German refugee movement was playing in the Zionists' progress. Ludwig Lewisohn, a Jewish author, confessed that almost every Jew he met claimed to be a Zionist because of the refugee situation. Lewisohn condemned this position explaining that persecution was not the greatest danger confronting the Jews. "True" Zionists understood that a larger problem was posed by the emancipation of Jewry under a misguided liberalism that denies that "mankind is forever divided into peoples."[73] A. H. Friedland agreed with Lewisohn and reminded de Haas that Zionism was more than a movement of settlement and a political machine.[74] They and their followers heartily backed Rothenberg and hoped that the Jewish nationalist movement would not become solely obsessed with the settlement of refugees in Palestine.

In spite of the contrary views of several leading American Zionists, the refugee crisis in Europe would increasingly define the tactics, strategy, scope, and success of Jewish nationalism for the next fifteen years. It could not have been otherwise. Zionist leaders knew that many of the new members flocking to their organizations lacked a proper appreciation of Jewish culture, did not understand the danger of assimilation, and were primarily interested in doing anything that might relieve the suffering of European Jewry. However, there could be no arguing with the fact that the new members increased the strength, prestige, and resources of the Zionist Organization of America. Judge Bernard A. Rosenblatt, a respected veteran member of the ZOA, showed that he understood the situation well in the summer of 1934, when he told a ZOA convention: "Before that epoch-making year [1933], anyone might have questioned the experiment of a Jewish Palestine. Today no serious critic of our efforts in Eretz Israel can deny the ultimate success of our program." Hitler's policies ensured that Jews would someday make up a majority of Palestine's population. Rosenblatt explained that just as the Russian czar's anti-Semitism had led to the rise of the American Jewish community almost half a century earlier, so would Hitler's persecution lead to the development of a Jewish Palestine, which would become the "Little America of the East."[75]

THE WIDENING APPEAL OF AMERICAN ZIONISM

Events and developments during the last half of 1934 and 1935 continued to force Zionists to focus their attention on Palestine's role in the solution of the refugee crisis. On Rosh HaShanah (the Jewish New Year) in the fall of 1934, Rabbi Abba Hillel Silver, a Reform rabbi form Cleveland and one of the most talented Zionist orators, described the past Jewish year in very bleak terms. Not only had Hitler strengthened his grip on Germany, but Austrian Jews now feared that their government would mimic Hitler's programs. Pointing to anti-Semitic activities in Greece, Algeria, and Canada, and the development of fascist organizations in England and the United States, Silver lamented, "What a year of bitterness, stress and heart-ache this has been for our people."[76] The death of Poland's Marshall Joseph Pilsudski in early 1935 threatened the existence of three million more Jews. Poland's new leaders were much more willing to adopt anti-Semitism as an official government policy than the old general was. Only the continuing development of Palestine seemed to brighten the gloomy Zionist perception of world Jewry's condition.[77]

In response to the refugee crisis, ZOA president Morris Rothenberg spearheaded the organization of the National Conference for Palestine. Rothenberg hoped that the conference, which would be attended by non-Zionists as well as Zionists, would mobilize support for the Jewish homeland. He wrote to Justice Brandeis:

> The rapid disintegration of the Jewish position in many lands, particularly in Germany and Eastern Europe, and the unparalleled development of Palestine as a permanent haven of refuge for the victims of oppression . . . makes it

imperative that the full strength of the Jewish people be mobilized to enlarge the scope and possibilities of Jewish settlement in Palestine, if large segments of our people are not to perish.

Palestine, Rothenberg maintained, was the "greatest center for the salvaging of Jewish life."[78]

Representatives of every segment of the organized American Jewish community attended the National Conference for Palestine, which opened on January 20, 1935. Fifty-two national Jewish organizations and 141 cities sent two thousand delegates to the conclave. Franklin Roosevelt dispatched a message, and Secretary of the Interior Harold Ickes and Charles Edward Russell addressed the assembly. Ickes's strong support of Jewish efforts to develop Palestine thrilled Zionist leaders. The cabinet secretary applauded the imagination and creativity of Jewish pioneers in Palestine and compared the Jewish program to the New Deal. Both, he explained, aimed to provide the people with a more abundant life through hard work and planning.[79]

One observer described the conference as a "big demonstration" supporting the Palestinian solution to the European refugee problem. Joseph Saslaw, a Zionist veteran, was heartened to see the leaders of the American Jewish Committee and B'nai B'rith supporting the rebuilding of Palestine. Many delegates at the conference felt like they were living in "miracle days" when Rabbi Abraham Simon expressed the approval of the traditionally anti-Zionist Reform Rabbinate for the Jewish development of Palestine. Rabbi Simon, representing the Central Conference of American Rabbis (the national association of Reform Judaism), stated that "the tragedy of our people today is greater than the ideology of the Rabbinate," Saslaw reported.[80]

Actually, the "miracle" was not as great as some believed. German Jewish immigrants had formed the B'nai B'rith in 1843, and it quickly became the largest Jewish fraternal organization in America with a membership exceeding 75,000 in 1935. Wealthy Jews of German descent had organized the American Jewish Committee in 1906 to protect Jewish interests in the United States and to combat anti-Semitism at home and abroad. Both organizations were hostile to Zionism before World War I, reflecting the view common to American Jews of German heritage that Jews had found their "Zion" in the United States and that a Jewish state was unnecessary. Following World War I, however, the American Jewish Committee found itself challenged by the American Jewish Congress founded by Stephen Wise, whose membership was dominated by Jews of East European descent. The members of the Congress resented the elitism and conservatism of the Committee and subjected it to bitter attack. Partially in response to the American Jewish Congress's criticism, the Committee began to rethink its position on Zionism, as did the B'nai B'rith, whose membership now included significant numbers of East Europeans. Both organizations adopted a so-called non-Zionist position. They continued to oppose the establishment of a Jewish state; the American Jewish Committee, in particular, fearing that the creation of a Jewish nation might raise doubts among Christians about the "dual loyalty" of American Jews. However, the B'nai B'rith and the Committee both supported Jewish immigration to and settlement of Palestine. Their support of a Palestinian solution to the refugee crisis at the 1935 national conference did not therefore represent a significant change of policy.[81]

The 1935 endorsement of Jewish immigration to Palestine by the Central Conference of American Rabbis was a more important development. German Jewish immigrants brought Reform Judaism to America in the middle of the nineteenth century. The Reform movement, dedicated to the "modernization" of Judaism, borrowed much from Protestant religious practices, including Sunday instead of Saturday Sabbath services and the use of choirs and organs. Most importantly, Reform Jews defined their Jewishness purely in terms of religion, denying all claims of separate nationality. Reform, unlike Orthodox or Conservative Judaism, rejected the belief that a messiah would one day come to rescue Jews from their exile and return them to Palestine. Reform doctorine led most Reform rabbis, with the notable exceptions of Abba Hillel Silver, Stephen Wise, and a few of their compatriots, to oppose Zionism.

By 1935, the problems of German Jewry, the Zionist success in colonizing Palestine, and the maneuverings of Silver and other pro-Zionist Reform rabbis combined to force the Reform establishment to modify its views on Jewish nationalism. The Central Conference of American Rabbis gave their approval to the settlement of Jewish refugees in Palestine at the 1935 national conference and during their own 1935 convention passed a "Neutrality Resolution" stating in part that: "In the rehabilitation of Palestine, the land hallowed by memories and hopes, we behold the promise of renewed life for many of our brethren. We affirm the obligation of all Jewry to aid in its upbuilding as a Jewish homeland by endeavoring to make it not only a haven of refuge for the oppressed but also a center of Jewish culture and spiritual life." The Reform movement, however, continued to oppose Jewish statehood.[82]

The refusal of important elements of the American Jewish community to recognize the need for a Jewish state did not particularly trouble American Zionists in 1935. Most continued to believe that the establishment of a Jewish nation was the long-term goal of the Zionist movement. The determination of the exact political nature of that nation, whether it would be a totally independent state, a member of the British Commonwealth, or a part of a larger Middle East federation, would wait until Jews achieved majority status in Palestine. For the immediate future, all that was necessary was for Zionists to build support for large-scale Jewish immigration to Palestine.[83]

Of course, some Americans insisted on searching for other havens for European Jewry. In August 1935, Oswald Garrison Villard noted with some sarcasm that "no nation had done more to aid the Jews in this crisis of the race's history than the wicked and godless Soviets." Villard, a respected journalist and the one-time owner of the liberal periodical *The Nation*, believed that Birobidzhan, the Jewish autonomous region of the Union of Soviet Socialist Republics, would absorb large numbers of Jewish refugees.[84]

The *Jewish Frontier* was particularly upset by Villard's article. The socialist Zionist editors of the journal were profoundly anti-Soviet and had devoted considerable space in their magazine to proving that Palestine was a far more suitable haven for refugees than Birobidzhan. They warned Villard to "guard against unwittingly aiding those who seek to disperse the energy which the Jewish people must concentrate on Palestine."[85]

Rabbi Abba Hillel Silver shared the *Jewish Frontier*'s concern. The young rabbi argued that there could be no "ersatz" for Palestine because "Palestine is not a colonization project or a relief measure. It is nation building. It is not an emergency place or refuge, a night's lodging. It is Home!"[86]

Many American Jews in 1935 probably did not share Silver's concern for the revival of Jewish culture and language, but they did consider Palestine to offer the best possible haven for European Jewry. Motivated by deep concern and sympathy for those suffering under Nazi rule, interested Americans felt that they owed a debt of gratitude to the Zionists. Palestine had proven its ability to absorb large numbers of Jews while Birobidzhan and other suggested havens had not. The Yishuv's generosity and willingness to accept refugees contrasted vividly with the selfish, restrictionist sentiment of most of the American population. Finally, Palestine's availability as a refugee haven probably made it easier for American Jews to live with the fact that there seemed to be little they could do to change American immigration policy. By the middle of 1935, the ZOA and Hadassah claimed a joint membership of 80,500, leading several Zionist leaders to question whether "the Zionist organization can in its growth keep pace . . . with Jewry's interest in Palestine."[87] It was a unique situation, which American Zionists could not afford to miss, for as one ZOA member noted: "Up till now, even when there was danger, there was no opportunity; and when there was opportunity there was no danger. I say it is providential – danger on one side opportunity on the other; and they come together in a fatefully most fruitful hour in our life. We must make use of that fact.[88]

Of all the American Zionist organizations, Hadassah probably was most successful in latching onto and exploiting American Jewry's growing concern for their European co-religionists. The organization's sponsorship of the Youth Aliyah program, designed to settle refugee children in Palestine and to provide them with an education and trade, won it many new adherents, huge resources, and an enviable reputation for success within the American Jewish community.

Zionists developed the Youth Aliyah program because they realized that Hitler's early anti-Semitic policies had a particularly cruel effect on Jewish children. The Jewish Agency, the quasi-official government of the Jewish community in Palestine, designed the Youth Aliyah project (*aliyah* is a Hebrew word meaning immigration or to go up), which took children out of Hitler's grasp and settled them on cooperative and communal agricultural settlements in Palestine. On the kibbutzim (communal settlements) and moshavim (collective settlements), the refugee children received a basic education and learned a trade. The Zionist leadership placed Henrietta Szold in charge of Youth Aliyah. Szold had been born in the United States where she founded Hadassah, the women's Zionist organization. She moved to Palestine shortly after World War I and took a particular interest in social and health projects there. Under Szold's brilliant leadership Youth Aliyah settled over fifty thousand children in Palestine between 1934 and 1948. The first large group of children arrived from Europe in February 1934.[89]

In America, Hadassah began the "age of Hitler" in 1933 with protests against German policy, but with little revision of the organization's original strategy of focusing on and improving Palestine's health care system. However, by mid-1935, some change in priority was clearly mandated. The many new members attracted to the organization questioned whether better hospital care in Palestine was the most pressing need of the German refugee. Moreover, thanks to Hadassah's efforts, a modern hospital and public health system existed in Palestine. Hadassah's leaders were left looking for a program to support.[90]

In searching for a solution to this dilemma, Rose Jacobs, president of Hadassah, traveled to Palestine, hoping to discover some new project that could capture the imagination of American Jewish women. As she traveled through the Holy Land with Henrietta Szold, Jacobs was able to observe the efforts of Youth Aliyah workers, and she marveled at their energy and dedication. When Jacobs returned to the United States, she urged America's women Zionists to play a special role in supporting the Youth Aliyah program.

The National Board of Hadassah enthusiastically accepted the idea, discussed it with refugee experts, and began to plan a large publicity campaign.[91] American Zionist men did not fully approve of the project. Morris Rothenberg and Louis Lipsky feared that Hadassah's efforts to raise money for Youth Aliyah would jeopardize other Zionist fund drives, particularly the American Palestine Campaign, which they ran. Lipsky and Rothenberg maintained that Youth Aliyah's potential as an organizing slogan was too significant to entrust solely to Hadassah.[92]

Encouraged by Louis Brandeis, who was probably only too happy to strike a blow against his old enemy Louis Lipsky, the women of Hadassah persisted in their efforts to assume exclusive control over the Youth Aliyah campaign in America.[93] In order to defuse the crisis that threatened to end the cordial relationship between the ZOA and Hadassah, the Jewish Agency dispatched Berl Locker to America to serve as a mediator. Locker, a Palestinian Zionist leader, asked Rose Jacobs and the Hadassah leadership to put Zionist unity ahead of their own organization's interest. Youth Aliyah, he explained, was an "important project," but it also was a "good slogan" and Hadassah would have to share it with Lipsky and Rothenberg. Locker probably expected the women of Hadassah to acquiesce; male Zionist leaders generally considered Hadassah to be a woman's auxiliary. However, Jacobs refused: "Hadassah wants the project as a means of arousing Zionist interest and promoting Zionist education among American Jewish women." After some effort, Locker finally negotiated a settlement under which Hadassah would serve as the exclusive American agent for Youth Aliyah, but its financial campaigns would have to be conducted within the framework of the United Palestine Appeal.[94]

Events quickly demonstrated that Hadassah's leaders had been correct to hitch their organization's fortunes to the Youth Aliyah bandwagon. The plight of refugee Jewish children attracted the attention of many Americans. Entertainer Eddie Cantor threw himself into Hadassah work and in ten months raised over $25,000. During its first year of fund raising, Hadassah collected over $125,000 for Youth Aliyah and gained a reputation for being at the vanguard of American Jewish efforts to aid European Jewry and Palestine.[95]

By the beginning of 1936, American Zionism bore little resemblance to what it had been during the bleak days of 1932. Roosevelt's New Deal had stopped the downward spiral of the economy, and American Jews were more prepared than they had been to invest some of their earnings in Zionist projects to develop Palestine. At the same time, Nazi policies forced many American Jews to turn their attention away from their own problems to the worsening plight of German Jewry. Zionists were pleased to find that they could offer concerned American Jews a practical solution to the refugee problem and that resettlement projects in Palestine were supported by individuals who had never before been interested in Jewish nationalism. Zionist leaders effectively exploited opportunities created by German Jewry's persecution to further the cause of Jewish nationalism in America.

AMERICAN ZIONIST PRIORITIES

American Zionism prospered in the years following Hitler's rise to power, but this is not to imply that its use of the refugee crisis was callous or Machiavellian. Jewish nationalists understood that both Palestine and Zionism would benefit as a result of the refugees' plight, but they knew that their primary mission was to aid their less fortunate brethren. From 1933 to 1936, no contradiction existed between working to rebuild Palestine and aiding Jewish refugees. Hitler's treatment of the Jews under his control was clearly not improving in these years, and emigration was the only solution available to many sufferers. Unfortunately, there were few countries willing to accept large numbers of refugees. Immigration quotas and a Congress unwilling to open the country's doors to newcomers during a time of economic depression kept the United States from assuming its traditional role as an immigration center. England and France were somewhat more willing to accept refugees, but they did so reluctantly. Only the Jewish community of Palestine was willing to accept refugees freely and happily. Palestinian Jewry provided the refugees with the resources and services necessary to rebuild lives in a new location. American Zionists were proving in these years that you could "have your cake and eat it too." They were in the rare and much enviable position of being able to help themselves and save others.

One sign that they were not putting Zionist designs ahead of the safety of their co-religionists was their unrelenting effort to improve the lot of Jews in Germany. Zionists were extremely vocal in their appeals for international condemnation of Hitler's anti-Semitic policies. At the 1933 summer convention of the Zionist Organization of America, the movement's most prestigious leaders argued that immigration to Palestine should not be the only response to Hitler's persecution of Jewry. The entire convention enthusiastically resolved that the civilized world had to save those Jews whom the Nazis were threatening to destroy.[96]

American Zionist organizations often supported the relief and protest campaigns of other American Jewish organizations. For example, Hadassah helped the American Jewish Congress plan a New York City parade to protest the burning of Jewish literature in Germany.[97] The ZOA also supported the American Jewish Congress's efforts to improve the quality of life of those Jews who chose or were forced to remain in Germany.[98]

It should be noted that the line separating Zionist bodies from other Jewish communal organizations was extremely blurry. Many members of the Zionist Organization of America also belonged to the American Jewish Congress, while Hadassah had well-developed organizational ties with the American Jewish Committee. Several Zionist leaders also held important positions in other organizations. Stephen Wise, in particular, transcended the boundaries of American Jewish organizational life. Wise was one of the founding members of the ZOA and was also the "father" of the American Jewish Congress. As the tragedy of German Jewry deepened and the specter of anti-Semitism spread through Europe, Wise was instrumental in the organization of the World Jewish Congress, which attempted to monitor and resist anti-Semitic policies and movements around the world.[99]

American Jews and Zionists were able to develop a dramatic method of striking a blow against Hitler. Among the first anti-Semitic acts of the new Nazi state was to declare a nationwide boycott of Jewish businesses. Jewish communities in Europe and North America reacted to the Nazi attack swiftly and organized a counterboycott of German imports. The American boycott campaign was particularly effective and militant. Several established American Jewish organizations, including the American Jewish Congress and the Jewish War Veterans, spearheaded the anti-Nazi boycott. Unsuccessful attempts were made to unify the disparate boycott organizations, but a lack of cohesion did not seem to handicap the boycott's effectiveness. After concerted pressure, Macy's, Gimbels, Sears and Roebuck, and Woolworth's agreed to comply with the boycotters' demands and pledged not to stock or sell German-produced merchandise.[100]

American Zionists actively supported the anti-German boycott. Abba Hillel Silver served as vice president of the American League for the Defense of Jewish Rights, one of the most important pro-boycott organizations (in December 1933 the organization's name was changed to the Non-Sectarian Anti-Nazi League to Champion Human Rights). Hadassah took part in the anti-Nazi boycott from its inception, and members of the organization served on the American Jewish Congress's boycott committee.[101] The Zionist Organization of America and the Poale Zion, a socialist Zionist group, also supported efforts to use economic coercion in order to force Germany to alter its anti-Semitic policies.[102] Stephen Wise helped to supervise the American Jewish Congress's boycott activities and was especially effective in explaining the boycott to Christian Americans. Louis Brandeis encouraged Wise to compare the Jewish boycott of German products to the boycott of British goods by American patriots during the pre–Revolutionary War crisis, explaining that "the American is an essentially manly being and he admires nothing more than courage. We have got to fight and fight. We must, of course, fight fairly."[103]

Leaders of the boycott organizations hoped that the Nazi desire for prosperity and profit would prove to be more powerful than their hatred of the Jews. Abba Hillel Silver, one of the most articulate architects of the boycott, believed that the anti-German import campaign would ultimately force Hitler to ease his persecution of the Jews. Nazi anti-Semitism, Silver explained, was political and "must be attacked with political weapons and the strongest political weapon, when all others fail, is the economic boycott."[104] Jews were fighting a life and death battle with Nazi Germany. If Hitler succeeded in depriving all German Jews of their rights, other tyrants would attempt to solve their "Jewish problem" in a similar manner. The Jewish leadership, Silver declared, should wage political and economic war against the Nazis in defense of German Jewish rights. Providing a refugee haven was simply not enough.[105]

While Silver and other American Zionists were participating in the boycott campaign, the Jews of Palestine were attempting to provide a home for the German refugees. Nazi expropriation laws ensured that many of the refugees from the Reich would arrive in their new home practically penniless. Jewish social service and charitable organizations struggled to meet the needs of the impoverished refugees. In response to this particular difficulty, the Jewish Agency for Palestine entered into negotiations with the Nazi government of Germany. Within a year of Hitler's rise to power, these talks resulted in the signing of the Haavara (Transfer) Agreement between representatives of the German government and the Zionist movement. Under this accord, a portion of the expropriated wealth of Jewish exiles would be deposited in closed German bank accounts. This money would then be used to pay for German-manufactured goods that would be shipped to the Jewish community of Palestine. When the refugees reached Palestine's shores, the Jewish Agency, the official recipient of the German equipment, would reimburse the refugees.[106]

All groups seemed to benefit under the Haavara Agreement. Germany gained a valuable new export market, Palestine received farm machinery, and the refugees avoided the threat of poverty in their new homeland. However, many American Zionists were not pleased with the German-Zionist contract, which threatened to sabotage Jewish efforts to organize a worldwide boycott of Nazi exports. Stephen Wise accused the Jewish Agency of surrendering to Hitler's blackmail.[107] Abba Hillel Silver angrily attacked the Jewish Agency for betraying its duty to lead world Jewry in the fight against oppression. Silver declared that "Palestine failed the Diaspora. The interest of Palestine clashed – or seemed to clash – with those of the Diaspora and the Diaspora was sacrificed." Diaspora Jewry refused to profit from trade with Germany, while the "whole-wheat Jews of Palestine were exempt from such sacrifices."[108] Silver sadly concluded that the Haavara Agreement was not an example of "the sort of leadership which the Jews of the world have been taught and promised to expect from Palestine."[109]

Zionists debated the Haavara Agreement at the July 1935 convention of the Zionist Organization of America when a few members introduced a resolution condemning the accord. Several speakers argued that trade between Jewish Palestine and Nazi Germany was a source of embarrassment for the American Zionist movement. One delegate from Massachusetts called the trade contract dishonorable and accused the Jewish Agency of behaving like simple merchants. Louis Lipsky and other ZOA members defended Palestinian Jewry's actions. Trade with Hitler was distasteful, but necessary if the orderly resettlement of German Jews was to continue, Lipsky maintained. As the debate grew more acrimonious, Abba Hillel Silver presented his own compromise resolution. Silver's proposal, which the convention subsequently passed, expressed the Zionist Organization of America's continued support of the anti-Nazi boycott and called on the organization's delegation to the next World Zionist Congress to investigate relations between Palestine and Germany.[110]

The entire Zionist movement was given the opportunity to discuss the Haavara Agreement at the World Zionist Congress held at Lucerne, Switzerland, in August 1935. The majority of delegates, representing Zionist organizations of varying ideologies, threw their support behind the agreement.[111] However, in the United

States, American Zionists continued to question the propriety of the Jewish Agency's behavior. When Hadassah learned that it could buy German medical equipment under the Haavara Agreement, the organization's leadership began to question whether they should remain loyal to the boycott campaign. Henrietta Szold, who was then visiting the United States, urged the American women Zionists to take advantage of the Haavara accord, but the National Board decided not to follow her advice. The organization was very reluctant to breech the boycott of German goods that was still being waged in America, fearing that Hadassah acceptance of the Haavara Agreement could jeopardize financial contributions from American Jews who strongly opposed doing any business with the Nazi regime.[112]

The priorities of most American Zionists during the first years of the Third Reich were clear. Hitler's rabid anti-Semitism shocked and grieved almost every Jew. Zionists shared world Jewry's horror at Hitler's excesses, but their pain was accompanied by a growing sense of righteousness that their longstanding views had been vindicated. German Jewry, the loudest advocates to the strategy of assimilation and the most stubborn opponents of Jewish nationalism, now had to rely on the Zionists for survival. Long-time members of the ZOA and Hadassah were gratified to discover that the years and riches spent developing Palestine now made it possible to rescue thousands of Jews. Palestine's significant contribution to the solution of the German Jewish crisis in the early thirties had won new prestige and members for Zionist organizations in the United States. The American leaders of the Jewish nationalist movement were confident that, with time, an ever-developing Palestine would be able to absorb even greater numbers of Jews from the European continent where anti-Semitism seemed to be spreading ominously. If Zionists successfully met this challenge, they assumed, rewards would follow. Palestine would prosper and Jewish nationalism would be recognized by all Jews as the correct strategy for survival. However, all depended on providing refuge and relief for persecuted Jewry. Zionism, after all, had developed as a response to threats to the survival and well-being of Jewry and Judaism. The first priority of American Zionists was to rescue as much of German Jewry as they could. If they accomplished this, the future of the Jewish National Home would be bright.

Unfortunately, events soon began to unfold that seriously altered the priorities of American Zionists and undermined their optimistic perception of the future. By September 1939, when German troops poured over the Polish border, Zionists feared that there might not be any future at all for Jewish Palestine.

II | A REORDERING OF PRIORITIES: THE HOMELAND UNDER SIEGE

AMERICAN ZIONISTS AND THE ARABS

The exodus of Jews from Europe that began in 1933 greatly strengthened the Zionist position in Palestine. An official British census in 1931 found that 175,000 Jews comprised 17 percent of Palestine's total population. By December 31, 1935, the number of Jews in Palestine had more than doubled, and the tremendous growth of the Yishuv showed few signs of slowing. During the first six months of 1936, an additional 19,000 Jews immigrated to the Holy Land, allowing Zionist leaders proudly to claim the loyalty of 28 percent of Palestine's population. The Zionist dream seemed to be well on the way to fruition.[1]

Zionists in Palestine, preoccupied with the monumental task of settling tens of thousands of Jewish refugees, generally did not worry about how the Arabs of Palestine would react to the astonishing growth of the Yishuv. For the most part, Palestinian Jewry clung to the belief that the Jewish development of Palestine would enrich Arabs as well as Jews and that a grateful Arab population would ally themselves with the Zionist campaign. Theodor Herzl was among the first Zionists to articulate this position in his utopian novel, *Altneuland* (1902), and succeeding generations of Zionists religiously adopted the position. Arab. demonstrations against Zionists, including anti-Jewish riots that erupted in several Palestinian towns and cities in 1920 and 1929, did not destroy Zionist faith in peace through economic progress, but did lead Jews to temper their idealism with a heavy dose of pragmatism. By the early thirties, Yishuv leaders believed that the steady growth of Jewish power in Palestine would not only enrich the Arabs, but would also convince them of the futility of resisting Zionist settlement. Shortly after Jewish refugees from nazism

41

began to arrive in Palestine, David Ben-Gurion predicted that the Arabs would be forced to reconcile themselves to the Zionist settlement of the country if Palestine's Jewish population reached one-half million within five years.[2]

American Zionist leaders' understanding of Arab interests and views differed little from that of their counterparts in the Yishuv. Publicly, they expressed their sincere belief that the Zionist colonization of Palestine would benefit Arabs as well as Jews. Two years before Hitler's coming to power, Professor Felix Frankfurter of the Harvard Law School wrote that the Zionists returning to Palestine were willing to share Palestine with the Arabs; he promised that Arab standards of living would rise as a result of Jewish settlement. For the moment, he continued, Zionists demanded only the right to bring Jews to Palestine; the political future of the territory would not be determined for some time, and, when it was, the interests of the Arabs would surely influence Jewish actions. Zionism was a movement of liberation not enslavement, and Frankfurter's credo was simple: "If the Jewish homeland cannot be built without making the fellaheen's [peasant's] lot worse rather than better, it ought not be be built."[3]

In December 1934, as the tremendous growth of the Jewish population of Palestine continued, Hayim Greenberg, a prestigious American socialist Zionist leader and the editor of the *Jewish Frontier*, reported on his recent trip to the Middle East. During his travels in the Holy Land he had repeatedly asked himself, "Was I justified in claiming for years that we have not harmed the Arabs economically; that the Arabs were better off with us than without us?" His answer was an unequivocal yes. He had observed that the closer an Arab community was to a Jewish settlement, the more prosperous and healthy the inhabitants were. The reverse was also true:

> The farther an Arab village was situated from a center of Jewish colonization, the more dirt and mud were visible; the larger the number of blind wrecks — men in rags and women in tatters. The hungry, barefoot children suffered from sick, inflamed eyes; their camels were scrawny, their donkeys undersized — desert creatures without the romance of the desert.

Greenberg's findings did not completely cheer him, for he, unlike Frankfurter, realized that Arab-Jewish relations in Palestine were not solely a matter of economics. An Arab, he noted, could be convinced that "he has lost nothing through Jewish colonization" and that additional Jewish immigration would benefit him. It was much harder though to prove to the Arab that he would not lose his dignity during the process. No people, the Bible taught, wished to be beholden or dependent on another. Esau sold his birthright to Jacob for a pot of lentils, but, after his hunger was satisfied, he wanted his birthright too. Jacob tried to persuade Esau that "he does not need the birthright; that the difference between Jacob and Esau is not the difference between greater and lower, but merely a difference in kind." Tragically, Esau could not be persuaded, and he hated Jacob for robbing him and his children of their birthright and dignity.

Greenberg could propose no simple solution to this dilemma, which seemed to be more psychological than economic or political. The Zionist task, he concluded, was to "discover the therapeutic measures which will heal the sore spots in the relations between Jew and Arab." Unfortunately, he could not provide a more specific remedy.[4]

A number of Greenberg's associates were less optimistic than he about the prospect of "therapeutic measures" insuring Arab acceptance of Zionism. They, like Frankfurter and Greenberg, believed that the Jewish settlement of Palestine benefited the Arabs, but if necessary they were prepared to deal with the Arabs in terms of power and not accommodation. In mid-1933, Abraham Goldberg, a veteran American Zionist, predicted that there would be no security problem if an additional half million Jews emigrated to Palestine.[5] In March 1934, Emanuel Neumann (then an American representative on the Zionist Executive in Palestine) happily reported: "The proportion of Jews to Arabs has increased, and if the government continues to permit the present rate of immigration, we will soon have quite a favorable representation in the country." The Jewish birthrate was growing as was the number of men capable of bearing arms. Neumann concluded that "in time, with all these factors operating, the Jews would be in an 'impregnable position.'"[6]

Some American Zionists even hoped that the mass immigration of Jews to Palestine would allow them to expand the very boundaries of the national home. For years Zionists had resented Britain's 1922 amputation of the eastern part of Palestine, which resulted in the creation of Transjordan. Many had never accepted the legitimacy of the British act and hoped that, in the future, Jewish settlements would straddle both sides of the Jordan River.[7]

When Emanuel Neumann arrived in Palestine in 1932 to assume a position on the Zionist Executive, he immediately asked British authorities about the possibility of Jewish settlement in Transjordan.[8] Neumann's own interest in the matter had been reinforced by Louis Brandeis, who had asked the young Zionist leader to investigate the Transjordan situation.[9] In the fall of 1932, Neumann was intrigued to learn from Heschel Farbstein, a Mizrachi (Orthodox Zionist organization) representative on the Zionist Executive, that the Arab leader of Transjordan, Emir Abdullah, was interested in selling some of his country's land to Zionist settlers. Neumann met secretly with Abdullah and obtained an option to purchase land east of the Jordan River. In spite of an exchange of money, there was no actual transfer of land from the Arab ruler to the Zionist organization. British and radical Arab disapproval convinced Abdullah that the time was not right to conduct business with the Jewish settlers of Palestine. Nevertheless, Abdullah's offer and Neumann's negotiations stimulated the interest of many Zionists, particularly those in America.[10] Neumann himself was committed to the opening of Transjordan to Jewish settlement and confided to Stephen Wise: "I would be willing to lay down my life for the opening up of Transjordan if need be and I know there are tens of thousands who feel as I do."[11] After Abdullah's cancellation of the land sale deal, Supreme Court Justice Brandeis wrote Neumann: "Even if the cancellation should prove definite and final, you have, in my opinion, achieved much for the cause. The crack in the Transjordan wall which you affected will be widened, and opportunity opened for Jew and Arab by the Jewish immigration."[12]

The rise of Hitler and the onset of the refugee exodus naturally fueled Zionist interest in the settling of Jews in Transjordan.[13] Neumann reported that Abdullah's approval for the land sale could be easily obtained if British support could be won for the scheme. Neumann planned to establish a Development Corporation for Transjordan, which would oversee the Zionist purchase and development of land acquired from Abdullah. Among the first subscribers to the corporation was Louis Brandeis who invested $25,000 in the project.[14] Felix Frankfurter also supported the establishment of a charter development company, arguing that Transjordan and Great Britain, as well as the Zionist movement, would benefit from the movement of Jewish settlers east of the Jordan River.[15]

American Zionist leaders attached great importance to the Jewish settlement of Transjordan. The very success of the Jewish nationalist movement seemed to depend on it. Abdullah's decision to do business with the Zionists would be an important step in the normalization of the Arab-Jewish relationship in the Middle East. Additional land would also allow the Zionists to demand more immigration certificates from the British on the grounds that their capacity to absorb Jewish refugees had increased. The Jewish settlement of Transjordan, Zionists also realized, would allow Jews to increase the size and stretch the boundaries of their homeland. As Emanuel Neumann wrote:

> [T]he success of our effort in Palestine, in the larger sense will depend ultimately upon our ability to penetrate T.J. [Transjordan] and colonize it. Without T.J., Palestine is an awfully tiny strip on the seashore—hardly a sufficient basis for any large-scale immigration settlement scheme. Unless the Hinterland is opened up, the strong immigration and development in Western Palestine will receive a check in the not distant future.[16]

Early in the summer of 1934, Felix Frankfurter, then a visiting professor at Oxford, attempted to enter into informal negotiations with British officials on the Transjordan question. Britain at this time still maintained ultimate control of Transjordan, which did not become a totally independent state until 1946. Colonial Secretary Sir Philip Cunliffe-Lister claimed to sympathize with the Zionist desire to move Jews into Transjordan, but refused to endorse any immediate Jewish movement into the territory because he feared that the Arabs of Transjordan would resist Jewish colonization.[17]

In spite of Britain's failure to support Jewish settlement projects in Transjordan, Zionist interest in the land east of the Jordan River continued, fueled by the ever-worsening plight of Jewry in Europe. By the summer of 1935, the virus of anti-Semitism seemed to be spreading beyond Germany's borders and Jewish leaders in the West worried especially about the virulent anti-Jewish policies being adopted by the Polish government. Some Zionists even feared that the persecution of Polish Jewry soon might become more severe than that of their German co-religionists. Palestine, which had proven itself to be one of the most important havens for Jewish refugees from Nazi Germany, now confronted the possibility of receiving millions of Jews from Eastern Europe.

Abba Hillel Silver told the annual ZOA convention in July 1935 that they were not involved in building little settlements in Palestine, but a "great Jewish nation." He prophesied that the influx of millions of refugees would stretch the boundaries of the Jewish homeland, noting that: "The little land now known as Palestine will be too small for the hosts of our people who will go there. And we will become in that land stretching beyond the Jordan, stretching north and stretching south on the shores of the Mediterranean, one of the great imperial, one of the mighty spiritual and not only physical peoples of the coming world."[18]

Abba Hillel Silver could not know in the summer of 1935 that within a year his dream of an expanding, vibrant Jewish homeland would lie in shambles. Even as he spoke, Arabs were becoming increasingly fearful about the consequences of the expanding Jewish population of Palestine.

THE ARAB UPRISING OF 1936: DEFENDING THE JEWISH HOMELAND

Zionists in the United States and Palestine had seriously underestimated Arab opposition to the growth of the Yishuv. Jewish settlement, as Zionists predicted, had provided Palestinian Arabs with one of the highest standards of living in the Middle East, but as Hayim Greenberg had reported, many Arabs, from all class and social backgrounds, feared that they would soon become second-class citizens in a Jewish-dominated land. Even as the influx of Jewish refugees into the Holy Land gave Zionist leaders a false sense of security, Arab notables from Palestine's elite landowning class were using the fear of Jewish domination to recruit peasants and city workers into a Palestinian-Arab national movement. Haj Amin Muhammad al-Husseini, the Mufti (Moslem religious leader) of Jerusalem, was the most prominent of these Arab nationalist leaders. Husseini, an Arab nationalist since 1919, was ardently anti-British and blamed the Mandatory Power for encouraging and fostering the Jewish "take over" of Palestine.[19]

Arab resentment about Zionist advances in Palestine finally resulted in violence on April 15, 1936, when a group of Arabs intercepted a bus and killed two Jewish passengers. The murders set in motion a tragic chain reaction of retaliation and counter-retaliation. On the night of April 16, Jews killed two Arabs and set off a number of Arab riots and protests throughout Palestine. The Mufti and other nationalist leaders in Palestine seized the occasion to declare a general strike aimed at forcing Great Britain to prohibit further Jewish immigration to Palestine. The general strike, which lasted almost seven months, was not the only form of Arab resistance to growing Zionist power. In the hills of Palestine, Arab guerrilla bands, with the covert support and guidance of the Mufti, attacked nearby Jewish settlements. Violence raged until October 1936, when the British were finally able to defeat the Arab rebels. In this first round of fighting, 197 Arabs, 80 Jews, and 28 British soldiers fell.[20]

The Arab revolt created a serious dilemma for the British authorities. Arab violence could not be tolerated, but Arab goodwill was an essential ingredient of British imperial policy. At the same time, Mandatory officials also found themselves under increasing pressure from Jewish community leaders to suppress violence and restore law and order. British leaders tried to follow a balanced policy. They refused to halt Jewish immigration to Palestine, but also would not take drastic measures to repress the Arab strike and revolt. London administrators hoped that the Arab "disturbance" would run its course quickly, and they tried to encourage Arab restraint by pledging to investigate Arab grievances and the causes of Arab unrest as soon as peace was restored. However, ongoing Arab resistance forced the British to take stronger measures. By the end of the summer of 1936, the British had doubled the number of Jewish policemen in Palestine and had recruited the assistance of 2,700 Jewish supernumerary police. The British also rushed military reinforcements to Palestine, including Royal Air Force detachments, which carried out bombing and strafing attacks on Arab guerrilla bands.[21]

In Palestine, Jews responded to the Arab revolt by taking up arms themselves. The Haganah, the quasi-legal underground defense force of the Jewish Agency, expanded in size and strength during the Arab revolt with the encouragement of the British. Following a policy of *Havlagah* (self-restraint), the Haganah organized the defense of threatened Jewish settlements, but refrained from carrying out acts of counterterrorism against Arab civilians. The Jewish community of Palestine imposed taxes on themselves to pay for defense measures, and financial donations from abroad also contributed to the increased military strength of Palestine's Jews. Among the most prominent of these foreign contributors was Louis Brandeis of the United States.[22]

Besides sending money to Palestine,[23] American Zionists during the early stages of the revolt also mounted efforts to encourage the British to take a firmer stand against Arab violence and protest. In May 1946, the Pro-Palestine Federation, a Zionist-sponsored support group of prominent Christians, sent a petition to the

British asking for a stronger pro-Jewish policy in Palestine.[24] Congressman Emanuel Celler of Brooklyn, a supporter of the Zionist cause, attacked the British for failing to adopt "stringent measures" to defend Palestinian Jewry. Celler supported David Ben-Gurion's charge that the Arab revolt was caused by Great Britain's failure to demonstrate its full support of Jewish settlement of Palestine. Had the British fully embraced Zionism, the Arabs would never have felt confident enough to violently resist the return of the Jews to Palestine. Celler urged Britain to "punish the foul wrongdoers, suppress the agitators and do all in its power to prevent a recurrence of the evil."[25]

The intensity and longevity of the Arab revolt physically challenged Zionists in Palestine, but ideologically and intellectually challenged supporters of Jewish nationalism in the United States. Widespread Arab violence made it difficult for Zionist spokesmen to claim that there was no basic conflict between Jews and Arabs and that material progress would create Jewish-Arab friendship in Palestine. Stephen Wise even feared that the Arab attacks would strengthen the position of those Jews who supported the Soviet-sponsored Jewish homeland in Birobidzhan. Suddenly, American Zionists, who had been concentrating their efforts on proudly portraying Palestine as the most effective solution to the refugee crisis, found themselves having to defend the very right of Jews to build a national home in the Holy Land.[26]

Six days after the Arab revolt began, the *New York Times*, whose assimilated Jewish publisher Arthur Hays Sulzberger was one of the most prominent American Jewish opponents of Zionism, editorialized that the clash between Arabs and Jews disclosed the "irreconcilable" conflict between the two peoples. The newspaper explained that: "The inertia and conservatism of an economically backward people intensify their natural resentment against the thrust of expanding, energetic newcomers, some of whom are not responsive to the sensibilities of their Arab neighbors." The *Time*'s editors believed that peace in Palestine could be achieved only if Jewish and Arab leaders stressed the need for practical cooperation. Neither Jews nor Arabs, the paper argued, "no matter what the pretensions of extremist leaders, can reasonably look forward to sole control over Palestine."[27]

Journalist Albert Viton (a pseudonym) concurred with the *Time*'s gloomy analysis of the Palestine situation. Traveling in the Middle East at the height of the riots, Viton wrote back to the *Nation* that nationalism was gripping the whole Middle East as it had gripped Europe in the nineteenth century. The Jews came to Palestine to escape anti-Semitism and paid dearly for every piece of land they bought, but despite some good intentions, there was little Arab-Jewish cooperation in the country. Viton gloomily predicted that bloodshed was inevitable because: "An Arab nationalist sees in a Zionist his mortal enemy who comes to rob him of his fatherland. . . . Every good Zionist sees the Arabs as an unnecessary obstacle to his homeland dream."[28]

47

William Ernest Hocking, a professor of philosophy at Harvard University, advanced a strongly pro-Arab argument in the pages of the *Christian Century*, a prestigious liberal Protestant periodical. Hocking, an anti-imperialist, portrayed the general strike and violence in Palestine as a desperate attempt by the Arabs to resist Jewish domination. He then went on to challenge the very basis of the Jewish claim to Palestine, claiming:

> Palestine does not belong to the Jews. It does not belong to them on historical grounds. They had full possession of it for less than five hundred years. The Arabs have had it for thirteen hundred years. The Jews were not driven out of Palestine by the destruction of Jerusalem under Titus. Their dispersion for several hundred years had been a voluntary diaspora.

If Zionists truly wanted to aid persecuted Jewry, Hocking concluded, "let it above all refrain from forcing them into Palestine under the shelter of British guns."[29]

Arab-Americans tried to assist Hocking and other opponents of Zionism in explaining the Palestine situation to the American public, but their ability to shape public opinion in the United States was limited. While pro-Arab supporters outnumbered Zionist sympathizers in the State Department and American missionary societies, there simply was not a large enough Arab population in America to support a major anti-Zionist propaganda campaign. Shah-Mir, an Arab living in Brooklyn, could only write a letter to the *New York Times* complaining about the anti-Arab bias of most of the New York press, which did not understand that the Arab nation was struggling against an invasion of foreigners. No matter what Zionists maintained, he wrote, no Arab welcomed the penetration of Palestine. He sympathized with the suffering and persecution of European Jewry, but condemned as hypocritical those who wanted to help refugees reach a safe haven as long as it was on somebody else's territory.[30]

Zionist spokesmen responded to the doubts and attacks of their critics. Jacob de Haas, the English-born Jew whom Theodor Herzl selected to spread the Zionist gospel in the United States, argued that Jews were not really the cause of Arab unrest. In a letter to the *New York Times*, he explained that the Jewish pioneers in Palestine had become pawns in the struggle between Arab nationalists and the British authorities. He claimed that the British used the Jews as their "goat" because the legal basis for the British presence in Palestine was their undertaking to develop the Jewish national home, and he argued that "there are fair reasons for assuming that a Zionism minus British overlordship would be compatible with the Pan-Arab and Pan-Islamic movements."[31]

Unlike de Haas, most Zionists in the United States and Palestine were not willing to do without the British. Moshe Shertok, the head of the Political Department of the Jewish Agency in Palestine, a post roughly equivalent to that of a foreign minister in a legitimate state, attempted to convince an American audience that the issue in Palestine was not between the Jews and Arabs of the Holy Land, but between the Jewish and Arab peoples in general. Palestine was the only country in the world where the Jewish people could achieve "national salvation," but "the national existence of the Arab race as a whole, its political self-determination and the prospect of its achieving the full stature of independent nationhood" did not depend on Palestine. Zionists had brought prosperity to all Palestinians, and, Shertok promised, the Jewish nationalist program would make no Arab suffer. The same could not be said of the Arab nationalist movement in Palestine and he warned that: "If the claims of the Palestine Arabs were granted, if Jewish immigration were stopped, not only would Jews in Germany, Poland and other countries for whom Palestine offers the only possible refuge be doomed, but the hope of the Jewish people to become again a nation rooted in a homeland would become extinct."[32]

Albert Viton's *Nation* article published on June 3, 1936, infuriated several Zionists who rushed to refute his contention that "every good Zionist sees the Arab as an unnecessary obstacle to his homeland dream." The *Jewish Frontier* dismissed his claim as distortion and "poppycock," and Marie Syrkin, the daughter of the prominent socialist-Zionist theoretician Nahman Syrkin, condemned him for failing to discuss the great benefits Jewish development had brought to all of Palestine's residents.[33]

The attacks on Zionism by William Hocking and other anti-imperialists troubled those Zionists who were themselves critical of colonialism. Maurice Samuel, a Zionist author and a student of Yiddish literature, spoke for those "radical Zionists" who at "first glance" seemed to be allied with reactionary British interests. Socialist Zionists, he wrote, dealt with Great Britain not by choice, but out of necessity, because the League of Nations had made London responsible for Palestine. Why, he asked, if Zionism furthered imperialism as some claimed, did not British authorities adopt a stronger pro-Jewish position in Palestine? Why hadn't Mandatory officials immediately taken drastic steps to crush the Arab general strike and revolt at its inception? Going on the offensive, Samuels charged that the real reactionaries in Palestine were not the Zionists, but the elite leaders of the Arab national movement.[34]

Samuels was not the only Zionist to attack the legitimacy of the Arab nationalist movement. Hayim Greenberg had pointed perceptively to some of the sources of Arab anti-Zionism sixteen months before the outbreak of violence in Palestine. The Mufti's militant demand for a cessation of Jewish immigration, which, if fulfilled, would have denied many refugees a haven and have doomed the Zionist dream of building a homeland, significantly diminished his ability to empathize with the Arab experience. In June 1936, while Arab workers and peasants continued their general strike and guerrilla attacks, Greenberg wrote that the Arab masses had absolutely no reason to oppose Zionist development, which economically benefited Arabs as well as Jews. Earlier, he had recognized that economic progress would not ease the Arabs' fear of becoming second-class citizens in a Jewish-dominated Palestine, but now he argued that the Arab masses had become the unknowing tools of reactionary leaders like the Mufti. "Peaceful Jewish colonization is the Industrial Revolution of Palestine," he explained, and "the Jewish cooperatives and communes are the cells of a new socialist economy." Arab peasants and workers were prospering as a result of Jewish settlement, and they were learning the virtues of efficiency, democracy, and equality from their Zionist teachers. "The present Arab chauvinist leaders seek to head off and destroy this resolution," Greenberg wrote, and he scolded American critics of Zionism for having "hitched their wagon to the Grand Mufti's counter-revolution."[35]

In December 1936, the debate over Palestine intensified as Albert Viton, in a two-article series for the *Nation*, attacked the Zionists for refusing to recognize the existence of Arab nationalism in Palestine. Although Zionists claimed to be a "movement of liberation" for the native Arab population, they were increasingly playing a "reactionary role." He accused Jews of relying on British protection instead of trying to reconcile themselves with the Arabs and concluded that there could be no peace in Palestine as long as Zionists clung to their dream of a Jewish state. Millions of Jews might have to escape European persecution, he added, but Palestine would not be able to offer them security.[36]

Viton, by this time, had earned the deep ire and hatred of many American Zionist leaders. Philip Bernstein, a Rochester, N.Y., rabbi and a rising young leader of the ZOA, assumed the task of doing battle with Viton in the pages of the *Nation*. Before the Arab revolt, Zionists had conceived of Palestine as the means through which the Jewish refugee problem could be solved. Now, Bernstein altered the equation and used the refugee crisis as a weapon to defend the Jewish position in Palestine. He began his essay by pointing to the horrible condition of Jews living in Germany, and he forecast that their problems would continue even if Hitler's regime was to be overthrown because Nazi authorities had thoroughly indoctrinated German children, so the conditions that produced anti-Semitism would continue to exist. Emigration offered the only immediate salvation for European Jewry, but where, he asked, would Jewish refugees go if denied access to Palestine? No nation in the world was willing to extend the victims of Hitler's persecution the same degree of hospitality and generosity as the Yishuv did. Once in Palestine, he continued, Jews, the victims of countless persecutions, sought to elevate not dominate others. Finally, he accused Arab nationalist leaders of opposing Zionism because it threatened to undermine their feudal status, a view that was becoming increasingly popular among American Zionists.[37]

Sensing a victory, Zionists and their allies rushed letters to the *Nation* to reinforce Bernstein's rebuttal of Viton. John Haynes Holmes, a prominent New York minister and a close friend of Stephen Wise, wrote to say that he had seen genuine cooperation between the Jewish and Arab masses in Palestine. He claimed that the tensions in the Holy Land were caused by British imperialists and "feudal landowners" who saw "a rapidly growing Jewish population refusing to go 'native' or take the status of 'natives.'" With time, Holmes believed, Jews and Arabs would solve Palestine's problems peacefully.[38] Stephen Wise congratulated Bernstein, and the socialist editors of the *Jewish Frontier* celebrated the appearance of a pro-Zionist tract in the *Nation*, a journal that seemed to be hostile to the Jewish nationalist cause.[39]

THE PEEL COMMISSION AND THE PARTITION OF PALESTINE

In November 1936, as American Zionists struggled to present their own interpretation of the Arab revolt, a Royal Commission of Inquiry arrived in Palestine to determine for itself why Arab Palestinians so violently resisted Zionist settlement. The commission, headed by Lord (Earl) Peel, chairman of the British Wheat Commission and a former Secretary of State for India, thoroughly investigated the social, political, and economic conditions of Palestine.[40] American Zionists did not have the opportunity to give testimony to the commission, but the Jewish nationalist position was presented by very able witnesses.[41]

Professor Maurice Hexter, director of the Jewish Agency's Colonization Department, detailed Jewish agricultural and industrial achievements in Palestine, aiming to prove that the territory had enough resources to absorb large numbers of additional Jewish immigrants without economically displacing the native Arab population.[42] David Ben-Gurion told the commission that the Zionists wanted to bring as many Jews as possible to Palestine, but did not seek to dominate the Arabs. He was even willing to share political power with the Arabs provided that they end their opposition to Jewish immigration.[43] Chaim Weizmann's testimony was particularly eloquent. He reviewed the history of the Balfour Declaration for the commission and went into a lengthy description of the deteriorating condition of Polish and German Jewry. For many European Jews, he said, "the world is divided into places where they cannot live and places they may not enter." Only Palestine offered the refugees the possibility of redemption. Weizmann, like Ben-Gurion, asked the commission to support the continuance of mass Jewish immigration to Palestine.[44]

Arab nationalists also appeared before the Royal Commission. Kahil Totah, headmaster of the Quaker school at Ramallah and an associate of the Mufti, blamed British administrators and Zionist leaders for the alienation and despair of many of his students who felt cut off from the rest of the Middle East.[45] The Mufti himself appeared before the Peel Commission, barely concealing his contempt for its members. His prescription for peace in Palestine was simple: he demanded that all Jewish immigration cease and that the British withdraw from the territory and grant its Arab inhabitants independence.[46]

After weeks of private and public hearings, the Peel Commission returned to Great Britain in January 1937 to draft its report. Commission members knew that the task of reconciling Jewish, Arab, and imperial interests in Palestine would be difficult, if not impossible. Ben-Gurion, Weizmann, and the other Jewish witnesses were clearly willing to have Great Britain continue its rule over the Holy Land provided that large-scale Jewish immigration continued. Arab nationalists, on the other hand, seemed to be convinced that a Zionist-British conspiracy existed to displace and "imprison" them. Stephen Wise feared that the commission might resolve this dilemma by denying the Arabs independence, while at the same time drastically limiting, or even suspending, Jewish immigration to Palestine.[47]

There seemed to be good reasons for Wise to expect such a serious British act. On November 5, 1936, the day the Peel Commission left England, London announced a new six-month immigration schedule that gave the Jewish Agency only 17 percent of the labor certificates it had requested. The *New Palestine*, the official journal of the ZOA, correctly analyzed this action as a British attempt to win Arab support.[48] British policymakers, particularly Foreign Office officials, hoped that the reduction in Jewish immigration would convince Palestinian Arabs that Britain was concerned about their interests in spite of its violent response to Arab guerrilla attacks.[49] Most Zionists believed that the British action would just be a temporary setback. Eliezer Kaplan, treasurer of the Jewish Agency in Palestine, confidentially confided to Hadassah leaders that in spite of the British action, "enormous possibilities" for further immigration continued to exist.[50] The editors of *Jewish Frontier*, believing that the British reduction was just a temporary action, praised the British for not giving in to terror tactics and for allowing at least some Jewish immigration to continue.[51]

The editors' good cheer ended in May 1937 when Great Britain announced a new four-month immigration schedule that gave the Jewish Agency so few certificates that the Zionist body refused to accept them as a matter of principle.[52] Zionists knew that British immigration restrictions threatened to limit their ability to respond to the Jewish refugee crisis. Jews caught in Hitler's Germany would be the immediate victims of such a development, but the Zionist movement would also suffer a loss of prestige and power. The American Zionist response to the British reduction was not particularly intense, however, because the attention of Jewish nationalists was occupied by a crisis that seemed even more serious.

In April 1937, three months before the publication of the Peel Commission's report, Zionists learned from friendly British sources that one of the plans the commission was considering called for the division of Palestine into separate Jewish and Arab states. The rumor did not surprise Chaim Weizmann, the London-based president of the World Zionist Organization. During one of its closed meetings, the Peel Commission had asked him how he would respond to the partition of Palestine. At the time, Weizmann's response was negative, but by April 1937 his opposition was wavering. An independent Jewish state, he reasoned, would allow the Zionist movement to determine its own immigration policy in Palestine, freeing both the Jewish nationalists and the refugees from the burden of endless negotiations with British officials who controlled all their futures. The surrender of territory would be a high but not disastrous price to pay for autonomy.[53]

Among American Zionists, the rumored British division of Palestine met with almost universal derision.[54] Hadassah immediately informed British and American officials that it would oppose any attempt to limit the Jewish claim to Palestine.[55] Hayim Greenberg of the socialist *Jewish Frontier* condemned any "Balkanization" of the Holy Land, which would severely reduce the number of refugees who could find a haven in Palestine,[56] while the orthodox Mizrachi Zionist Organization announced that the British division of Palestine would be a crime as heinous as the "Italian rape of Ethiopia."[57] The ZOA vowed to fight any partition plan and warned Great Britain that Zionists would not repeat the error they had made fifteen years earlier when they had failed to mobilize against the 1922 British division of Palestine that established Transjordan.[58] To reinforce their threat, the ZOA decided to switch its summer convention from Baltimore to New York City in order to hold a massive anti-British demonstration at Madison Square Garden.[59]

Several American Zionist leaders doubted whether the anti-partition consensus within the American Zionist community could long endure. Robert Szold and Louis Brandeis both knew that Chaim Weizmann was flirting with accepting the British partition proposal, and they feared that Louis Lipsky would eventually adopt the views of his mentor.[60]

Despite Szold's concern, the Fortieth Convention of the Zionist Organization of America, held ten days before the official release of the Peel Commission plan, reached an unusual consensus on the issue of partition. Stephen Wise, ZOA president, declared that the commission was appointed to investigate the Arab disorders, not to "consider the problem of partition or division or cantonization or amputation." Palestine's partition would bring new disorders, not peace, and Wise, thinking of Weizmann, criticized those Zionists who were sympathetic to the plan. He wondered whether "partition has not made too lurid an appeal to some histrionic hotheads among us who are more avid to the name 'Jewish State' than the reality of a Jewish National Home." He passionately maintained that "a partitioned, divided, truncated Palestine would no more be Palestine than England would be England without Scotland and Wales, without Yorkshire and Northumberland."[61]

Robert Szold seconded Wise's position and reminded the assembled delegates that there had already been one partition of Palestine in 1922. Partition, he explained, was even worse than a temporary halt of immigration because "partition means a permanent cutting off of the land." Partition would be "geographically impossible, economically infeasible and morally suicidal." Drawing the applause of his audience, Szold asserted that the fate of all Jewry, present and future, was jeopardized by the division of the Holy Land and that no Zionist organization had the right to surrender any part of the Jewish birthright.[62]

Louis Lipsky, to Szold's satisfaction, joined in the anti-partition clamor saying: "The Sovereignty we thought we were to have a chance at is now being broken, halved and quartered, to serve the needs of Empire – the Empire of the British and the soon-to-be Empire of the Arab people."[63] Morris Rothenberg, a past president of the ZOA, and Senator Robert Wagner, one of Zionism's most important congressional supporters, also opposed the partition of Palestine. Rothenberg argued that in a time of "unprecedented Jewish homelessness," England should not restrict immigration to or reduce the size of Palestine.[64] Senator Wagner told the ZOA convention that Palestine was an "outpost" of "civilization" and freedom, and concluded: "The colonization of Palestine must be encouraged. The promises made for Palestine must be kept. That is the test of fair treatment toward the Jewish people. That is the test of wisdom and humanity on the part of the civilized world."[65]

The case against partition was presented most eloquently by Abba Hillel Silver. Silver, a Reform rabbi with a prosperous Cleveland congregation, was a brilliant orator with a forceful personality that at times angered his associates. Zionists, Silver told his audience, had transformed a "wilderness" into a "flowering land." He agreed with Szold, Wise, and Brandeis, predicting that a Jewish state in a partitioned Palestine would be a political and economic "absurdity." The Zionists had not "conquered" Palestine with a sword and bloodshed, but with "labor." The Arabs had prospered as a result of Jewish settlement and were no longer "illiterate" and oppressed by a "semi-feudal oligarchy." The partition of Palestine, Silver warned, would do incalculable harm to the Jewish people because a divided Holy Land would not be able to absorb masses of Jewish refugees and the "Jewish problem" would never be solved:

> The aim of Zionism, my friends, is not to shift the diaspora. It is to put an end to it. The aim of Palestine, if we cannot put an end to it, is to transform the diaspora through the establishment of a large scale Jewish National Home which will be enabled to draw in millions of our people. The aim of Zionism is not to take masses of our people from one place where they are an insecure minority and put them in another where they will continue to be an insecure minority. The aim of Palestine is to create somewhere on this God's footstool a place where the Jews will finally be masters of their own political destiny – at home.

Jews were a people with a culture who needed a land "into which our culture can sink its roots and from which it can draw sustenance." Silver pleaded with those Zionists who were willing to accept the principle of partition not to "sacrifice the ultimate ideal for the sake of a few seeming concessions and rewards. Think of the ultimate. We want a Jewish homeland." Silver asked his audience to "rededicate" themselves "to this ancient covenant, to rebuild, if not tomorrow, if not by ourselves, . . . by our own children and our grandchildren, the land in its historic boundaries, the Jewish land."[66]

The ZOA delegates rose, applauded vigorously, and sang the Zionist anthem *Hatikvah* (The Hope). The convention then adopted resolutions strongly opposing partition and requested that the United States intercede with the British on their behalf.[67]

Not everyone was happy with the ZOA's actions. During the proceedings, Chaim Weizmann telephoned from London to tell Stephen Wise, Louis Lipsky, and Felix Frankfurter that the Peel Commission would definitely recommend Palestine's partition. Weizmann felt that the commission's suggestion might be better than a continuance of the status quo, and he unsuccessfully tried to convince the ZOA leadership not to take a stand against the partition issue.[68] He also wrote Frankfurter that if the partitioned Jewish state was big enough to allow growth and included Jerusalem, "we have gone a long way towards realization of a dream, which might compensate us a little for the nightmare of Jewish life at present."[69] Weizmann hoped that all Zionists would remain united and calm. He told Frankfurter that "it is our destiny to get Palestine, and this destiny will be fulfilled someday, somehow." Once a Jewish state existed the problem of its "expansion" could be left to "future generations."[70]

On July 7, 1937, the Peel Commission finally published its long-awaited report. The commission's detailed analysis of the Arab-Jewish conflict reflected the remarkable sensitivity and objectivity of its members. Lord Peel and his associates found that many of the Zionist claims about Palestine were in fact accurate, and they praised the economic and physical accomplishments of the Yishuv. The Arabs, the report acknowledged, "have shared to a considerable degree in the material benefits which Jewish immigration has brought to Palestine," and enjoyed a substantially higher standard of living than they had in 1920.[71] The commission determined, however, that Zionist-inspired economic progress had not succeeded in winning Arab acceptance of Jewish settlement in Palestine. Arab nationalism was a much more powerful movement than Zionists recognized, Peel reported, and Arab opposition to Jewish immigration was intense and widespread.[72]

The Peel Commission sadly concluded that the status quo could not continue in the Holy Land. Both Arabs and Jews had legitimate rights to Palestine, but their programs and goals were irreconcilable.[73] The continued settlement of refugees in Palestine would exacerbate Arab fears of Jewish domination and would surely result in renewed violence. Ending Jewish immigration to Palestine would enrage the Zionists and condemn thousands of Jews to a miserable existence. The commission reported that it could recommend only one solution to this quandary: the partition of Palestine into Jewish and Arab states. The Jewish state, much smaller in size than the Arab, would encompass those regions of Palestine with heavy Jewish settlement: the coastal plain stretching from Tel Aviv to Haifa and part of the Galilee. Great Britain would retain control of several small strategic areas including Jerusalem, a holy place for Christians, Jews, and Moslems, and Bethlehem, the birthplace of Jesus. The rest of Palestine, including Transjordan, would constitute an independent Arab nation.[74]

Peel and his colleagues knew that their partition proposal would be controversial and that neither Jews nor Arabs would be pleased with the sacrifices they would have to make. They hoped, however, that both Zionists and Arab nationalists would ultimately be satisfied with a partial victory. Peel notified his superiors: "Partition seems to offer at least a chance of ultimate peace. We can see none in any other plan."[75] He added that it would be necessary to restrict (but not to end) Jewish immigration to Palestine until partition could be affected, so as not to provoke new Arab attacks. He warned that if the partition proposal was not accepted, England would be forced to allow only twelve thousand Jews to enter Palestine annually for the next five years.[76]

The British government of Prime Minister Neville Chamberlain (Conservative party) accepted the Peel Commission's suggestions, although Foreign Secretary Anthony Eden objected that the establishment of a Jewish state would incite anti-British sentiment throughout the Middle East. In an official policy statement, Colonial Secretary William Ormsby-Gore, a major proponent of the Peel plan, wrote that the "irreconcilable conflict" between Jewish and Arab "aspirations" made it impossible for Britain to continue its present mandate in Palestine and that, "a scheme of partition . . . represents the best and most hopeful solution to the deadlock."[77] During parliamentary debates on the Peel plan, opponents of the Conservative party took the opportunity to attack partition and the Chamberlain government. Liberal party leader Sir Archibald Sinclair condemned the Peel proposal for according the Jews much too small a part of Palestine. Tom Williams, speaking for the Labor party, objected to the partition proposal, calling it "hopelessly inconclusive" and "hazardous." Conservative party maverick Winston Churchill, regarded by many Zionists as one of their closest allies, also objected to the division of Palestine. The opposition of these impressive individuals was not strong enough to defeat the government's plan, although the House of Commons refused to commit itself totally to partition and instead authorized Chamberlain to continue negotiations on the plan before submitting it for final approval.[78]

The Peel Commission's recommendations outraged many leading American Zionists, including Hayim Greenberg, Louis Brandeis, Louis Lipsky, Stephen Wise, and Abba Hillel Silver. Wise confessed, "I never dreamed that we would fare so badly at Britain's hands." Brandeis and several of his disciples, whose distrust of Chaim Weizmann was rooted in the factional disputes of a decade and a half earlier, feared that the president of the World Zionist Organization would accept the British plan. David Ben-Gurion, the leader of the powerful Labor Zionists of Palestine, had initially condemned the British offer, but the Brandeis cohort suspected that he might "be carried away by the lure of an immediate Jewish state."[79]

Following the publication of the Peel Commission's report, American Zionists focused their attention on Zurich, Switzerland, where the Twentieth Zionist Congress would consider the British proposal to partition Palestine. American delegates to the congress included Stephen Wise, Louis Lipsky, Abba Hillel Silver, and many of the Hadassah leaders. Robert Szold decided to attend the congress after his mentor, Louis Brandeis, urged him to aid Wise in the fight against partition.[80]

The delegates who met in Zurich in August 1937 reflected the factionalized world of Jewish nationalism. Chaim Weizmann presented the case for partition, warning that if the Jews rejected the Peel scheme, the British would severely and permanently restrict Jewish immigration to Palestine. Jews would then remain a permanent minority in the Holy Land and the Zionist dream of sovereignty and a national home would die. A Jewish state in a divided Palestine was not an ideal situation, but it would guarantee Jewish autonomy and control of immigration into at least part of Palestine. Weizmann agreed with critics of partition that the size of the Jewish state suggested by the Peel Commission was unacceptably small, but he believed that Britain would agree to increase the size of the proposed Jewish nation.[81]

Several American Zionists who had fought Weizmann immediately after World War I continued to suspect his motives. Julian Mack wrote Brandeis that "C. W. [Chaim Weizmann] I believe, is not at all a well man. To be king or president of a Jewish state would in his judgement, I fear, put him just one notch above Herzl and the temptation is too great." Robert Szold and Stephen Wise were among those who tried to counter Weizmann's pro-partition position at the Zurich congress. They argued that the Palestine Mandate was workable and that difficulties could be overcome. Szold predicted that a Jewish state would be unable to absorb the large number of Jews seeking to escape Poland and Germany, and he warned that this would break the morale of the Jewish pioneers in Palestine whose strength and courage were "based on their hope that they are assisting in the solution of the Jewish problem." If Britain divided Palestine, he continued, "the dreams of a historic Palestine as a Jewish State or Commonwealth will be gone." Szold concluded that "we have no moral right, because concerned with another temporary crisis, permanently and irrevocably to consent to and deal a moral [mortal] wound to Zionism."[82]

As some American Zionists had nervously anticipated, David Ben-Gurion reversed his original opposition to the partition scheme and supported Chaim Weizmann at Zurich. According to Szold, Ben-Gurion was attracted to the idea of Jewish autonomy, believing that even the best British officials would sometimes "sabotage" the mandate's commitment to Zionism.[83]

Weizmann's reelection as president of the World Zionist Organization reflected the anti-partitionists' lack of a majority at Zurich. Several factions made up the forces opposed to Palestine's division, even if a small Jewish state would be created by the process. The Mizrachi, a world-wide organization of ultra-religious Zionists, opposed Weizmann because they believed that God had given the Jewish people all of Palestine, and that no one had the right to surrender even a part of this treasure.[84] Joining the Mizrachi in a strange alliance was the Hashomer Hatzair, an organization of radical socialist Zionists who believed that cooperation with the Arabs was possible and preferable to the partition of Palestine between the two peoples. Most of the Hadassah delegates at Zurich also opposed the partition scheme as did the representatives of the B group of General Zionists.[85]

The delegates of the Zionist Organization of America, chosen by the 1937 convention that had strongly opposed partition, split over the issue at Zurich. Silver, Wise, Szold, and their supporters opposed Weizmann and the division of the Holy Land, while those delegates, including Louis Lipsky, who had supported Weizmann in the past continued to do so. Joining the pro-Weizmann ZOA group were the delegates of General Zionist faction A, which was Weizmann's power base. The Ben-Gurion–led Labor Zionists, who were particulary strong in Eastern Europe and Palestine, lent critical support to the partition plan. The representatives of the small, American labor Zionist groups (excluding the Hashomer Hatzair) cooperated with their European and Palestinian comrades. In an address delivered at the end of the congress, Hayim Greenberg, who had originally opposed partition, confessed that he still had grave doubts about whether the division of Palestine was practical. However, he was convinced that it should at least be attempted.[86]

The Twentieth Zionist Congress passed a resolution that seemed to straddle the partition issue, but which actually handed a victory to Weizmann, Ben-Gurion, and the pro-partitionists. While labeling the Peel proposal unacceptable, the congress authorized the Zionist Executive to negotiate with the British in hopes of winning better boundaries for the proposed Jewish state. The resolution, however, prohibited the Executive from agreeing to any particular British proposal without first getting the approval of another World Zionist Congress.[87]

The Zurich resolution did not prevent the outbreak of an intense conflict over partition, which threatened to divide American Zionists. Shortly after returning from Zurich, Dr. David de Sola Pool, a respected rabbi and scholar, tried to explain his pro-partition vote at Zurich to the National Board of Hadassah. Dr. Pool said his vote was not for partition but to give the Zionist Executive authority to negotiate with Britain. The unwillingness of Great Britain to encourage Jewish immigration in the face of Arab opposition made it imperative for Zionists to enter into negotiations that might lead to the creation of a viable Jewish state in part of Palestine. Pool argued that if Zionists rejected the Peel Commission's recommendations, they would antagonize the British people and government, "the only country and the only people to show any real interest in the Jewish problems." Total rejection would also lead Great Britain to limit severely Jewish immigration into Palestine, thereby guaranteeing that the Jews would never achieve majority status in the Holy Land. Pool hoped that negotiations with Britain would result in "the establishment of a Jewish State which would meet the urgent and immediate needs of the Jewish people."[88]

The continued debate over partition threatened to disrupt the autumn 1937 convention of Hadassah. The leadership of the women's Zionist organization found themselves in a quandary. Hadassah delegates had voted against the Weizmann position at Zurich, but Hadassah leaders felt duty-bound to maintain the group's traditional commitment to acting only in accordance with official policy as decided at Zionist congresses. The National Board resolved to prepare a compromise resolution that would express Hadassah's desire for the full implementation of the Mandate while also supporting ongoing negotiations between the Zionist Executive and Great Britain in accordance with the decision of the Twentieth Zionist Congress. Hadassah leaders hoped that the resolution, which would neither clearly support nor oppose partition, would preserve the internal unity of the organization and also "would attest to Hadassah's position as a disciplined group within the Zionist organization."

Hadassah's compromise strategy broke down at the organization's convention, when some Board members urged that an anti-partition resolution be presented to the delegates. The National Board then reversed its original decision and decided to allow Hadassah members to choose between a resolution that would support partition and one that would oppose the division of Palestine. Unfortunately, when the convention began to decide the issue, a partition supporter on the National Board introduced the original compromise resolution. After Henrietta Szold spoke in favor of the compromise, the chair found it impossible to rule the resolution out of order. Before the pro- and anti-partition resolutions could be introduced, nearly 60 percent of the Hadassah delegates voted to support the compromise resolution.

This unexpected development angered Zip Szold, an anti-partitionist and the wife of ZOA leader Robert Szold. She was determined to discover the true feelings of Hadassah's members. When Szold asked the delegates to indicate their approval or opposition to the Zurich decision, she was pleased to see 95 percent of the delegates express their opposition to Palestine's partition. Szold and the majority of anti-partitionists on the Board viewed the delegates' vote as a "mandate" to undertake anti-partition activity in the United States.[89] They rationalized that "propaganda conducted in a friendly and fair manner could not be construed as an expression of disloyalty to the [World Zionist] Executive."[90] Pro-partitionists were not as "good natured" as the Hadassah leaders and one high-ranking world Zionist leader even appealed to Stephen Wise for help in "taming" the women Zionists.[91]

While Hadassah was wrestling with the partition issue, anti-partition forces within the ZOA were also marshalling their forces. Veterans of the anti-Weizmann/Lipsky fight within the ZOA were at the forefront of the anti-partition effort. Stephen Wise, a confirmed anti-partitionist, was president of the ZOA, but Louis Lipsky, a Weizmann supporter, served as editor of the ZOA's official journal, *New Palestine*, making it difficult for opponents of partition to reach the organization's large and dispersed membership. In order to solve this problem, Bernard Flexner and Robert Szold formed a committee dedicated to the production and dissemination of anti-partition propaganda. Szold, Julian Mack, and the Palestine Economic Corporation, an organization heavily funded by Supreme Court Justice Louis Brandeis, provided the anti-partition committee with the capital necessary to carry out an extensive publicity campaign. Stephen Wise also supported the work of the committee, as did Felix Frankfurter, who condemned the Peel plan as "unworkable" and called all the talk of a Jewish state "romanticism chasing a mirage."[92]

American Zionists working against the partition of Palestine found that they had some unusual allies. Wealthy non-Zionists, usually of German-Jewish descent, had helped finance the settlement of pioneers and refugees in Palestine even though they rejected the Zionist notion of Jewish nationality. The possible partition of Palestine into Jewish and Arab states disrupted the uneasy alliance between non-Zionists and Zionists. Several prominent American Jews, including Felix Warburg, feared that the creation of a Jewish state would destabilize American Jewish life by allowing anti-Semites to question the primary loyalty of Jews in the United States. Stephen Wise and Louis Brandeis did not share Warburg's concern about dual loyalty and looked forward to the eventual establishment of a Jewish state in all of Palestine, but they were willing to cooperate with him in order to maintain the physical unity of the Jewish homeland. Robert Szold counted on the non-Zionists to publicize the anti-partition case and reported to Brandeis that the powerful, non-Zionist American Jewish Committee seemed to have budgeted some money for this purpose. Szold said that anti-partition Zionists had decided to keep in touch with the non-Zionists but not to consolidate their efforts. A formal alliance with opponents of Jewish nationalism, Szold explained, would lose the anti-partitionist leaders support and standing with their American Zionist constituents.[93]

While the anti-partitionists within the ZOA organized, Louis Lipsky and his pro-partition supporters also mustered their strength. The battle within the ZOA was bitter, reflecting the belief of both factions that they were fighting to protect the Zionist experiment in Palestine. Opponents of partition were struggling to preserve the birthright of the Jewish people. They were convinced that partition would not solve the Jewish problem because a divided Palestine would be unable to support a viable Jewish state. Pro-partition advocate Louis Lipsky also claimed to be fighting for the survival of the Jewish people. On the night of December 30, 1937, at a meeting of ZOA leaders, Lipsky warned that Great Britain would respond to a Zionist rejection of partition by repealing the Balfour Declaration and by completely abandoning the Jewish national project.[94]

The anti-partitionists found it difficult to respond to Lipsky's dire prediction. Brandeis, Szold, and Wise had successfully composed powerful arguments against the dismemberment of Palestine, but the task of formulating an alternative policy was significantly more troublesome. Shortly after the Zurich World Zionist Congress, Brandeis confidently proclaimed: "it ought to be possible to work out a modus vivendi-temporary [sic]—with the Arabs. . . . Reason and virtue will sometime again have their way. The British . . . will return from their erring way. It is imperative that nothing be done until then in the way of [the] ultimate disposition of the problems."[95]

Unfortunately, by December, the optimism of some anti-partitionists was beginning to crumble as Britain continued to restrict Jewish immigration to Palestine and Arabs renewed their attacks on Jewish settlements. Stephen Wise wrote Brandeis: "I have felt firm in the faith that partition would not come. Many things that are happening tend to shake my faith."[96] By the end of December, Brandeis and Szold were desperate to develop a peace agreement with the Arabs that would make partition unnecessary. They were even considering a plan under which the Zionists would voluntarily limit immigration to ensure that Jews would remain a minority in Palestine for a limited number of years. Brandeis recommended a five- to ten-year limitation on immigration, at the end of which time Jews would not exceed 40 to 45 percent of Palestine's population. Brandeis stipulated that Transjordan's Arab population was to be considered in these figures. Wise, however, was opposed to this scheme and agreed with the Zionist Executive that any temporary self-restriction on immigration would undermine the Jewish claim to Palestine and would condemn Jews to a permanent minority status in the country.[97]

Making the best of a difficult situation, Brandeis and Szold finally concluded that the opponents of partition did not have to develop alternatives to the British scheme because that would only admit that partition was a proper topic for the Mandatory Power to consider. While the present government seemed to be in favor of partition, Brandeis hoped that it might be replaced by a new cabinet with an opposing point of view. He and Szold reasoned that a strong, large Jewish community in Palestine was vital to British interests, and they hoped that "the common sense of the situation will become more and more apparent to responsible Britishers."[98]

While all Zionists anxiously awaited the conclusion of Weizmann's discussions with the British government, the partition debate continued to dominate the American Zionist community. Zip Szold of Hadassah questioned the validity of pro-partitionist claims that the plight of European Jewry required the immediate creation of a Jewish state, even if that state was smaller than most Zionists would prefer. The Hadassah leader, presenting her own variation of an argument often used by anti-Zionists, claimed that a partitioned Palestine would not have the absorptive capacity to satisfy the demand of European refugees for a new home. She remarked that the Jewish position "will be much sorrier when it is the Jewish state itself which has to deny admittance to persecuted Jews than when such admission is denied by the Mandatory power." According to Szold, the pro-partitionists "complete disregard for future generations of Jews is entirely out of harmony with Jewish tradition and with the realistic emergencies which face Jewish survival at the present moment."[99]

ZOA members, who had extensively discussed Palestine's partition the year before, resumed the debate at the next annual convention in July 1938. Robert Szold expected that Louis Lipsky would attempt to succeed Stephen Wise as president of the organization, thereby increasing the strength of pro-partitionists within the ZOA bureaucracy. He left for the 1938 convention determined "to protect the position of the anti-partitionists."[100]

Despite Szold's belligerent stance, Stephen Wise seemed intent on not letting the partition issue tear his organization apart. In his convention address he singled out Louis Lipsky for praise, thanking him for his help, while acknowledging their differences on the partition question. Wise repeated the anti-partition argument, but was generally much more understanding of the opposition's point of view than he had been a year earlier. He pointedly declared that he would willingly comply with the decision of the World Zionist Congress, although he also wanted world Zionist leaders to give American Zionists more power within the international organization. Wise tried to shift the attention of ZOA delegates away from the partition issue and focus it instead on the refugee crisis, which had been exacerbated by Hitler's annexation of Austria in March 1938.[101]

Louis Lipsky also tried to strike a moderate tone in his address to the convention, but he continued to present a cogent argument in favor of Palestine's partition. He confessed that he and other Jewish nationalists, who had thought that the national home would be built slowly, had not foreseen the rise of Hitler. Lipsky argued that Zionists now had to realize that a change in strategy was necessary: "It was never dreamed that the burdens and problems of the Diaspora would be thrown upon Zion, that they would batter at the gates with claims, with appeal." The Jewish refugee problem, Lipsky continued, could only be solved if a sovereign Jewish state existed that would control its own immigration policies. The partition of Palestine was the price Zionists had to pay for their state.[102]

Most of the ZOA delegates seemed to be exhausted after a year of bitter debate about Palestine's future. Abba Hillel Silver had passionately denounced partition in 1937, but after a year of uncertainty and anguish, he called on Great Britain to make up its mind about Palestine's fate. If partition and a Jewish state were to be London's formula, Silver for one was now willing to accept it, even though he continued to find the prospect of partition extremely distasteful.[103]

ZOA members at the Detroit convention, in an attempt to end the dangerous conflict within their own ranks, chose Solomon Goldman to succeed Stephen Wise as their president. Goldman, a Chicago rabbi, opposed partition, but like Abba Hillel Silver was prepared to accept the division of Palestine if the British forced the issue.[104] The convention also passed a compromise partition resolution that gave both pro- and anti-partition forces within the ZOA the freedom to advocate their positions until a new World Zionist Congress finally decided on the issue.[105]

A REORDERING OF PRIORITIES

Even as American Zionists argued over the wisdom of Ben-Gurion and Weizmann's acceptance of the principle of partition, developments in the Middle East were making it extremely difficult for the British to act on the Peel Commission's proposals. Arab nationalists in Palestine adamantly refused to consider the division of Palestine into Jewish and Arab states, and Arab regimes in the Middle East also condemned the British proposals. Palestinian Arab militants responded to the Peel Commission's report by launching a new campaign of anti-British and anti-Zionist violence. To the dismay of the British, the new Arab revolt was more intense and violent than the upheavals that had led to the creation of the Peel Commission.[106]

The British cabinet characteristically responded to the new crisis by appointing yet another royal commission, this one under the direction of Sir John Woodhead who had served the empire in India. The commission arrived in Palestine in April 1938 and began gathering testimony, a task that was seriously complicated by the stubborn refusal of Palestinian Arab nationalists to cooperate with the investigating committee. The Woodhead Commission finally submitted its findings to the cabinet in November 1938, reporting that the Peel Commission's partition proposal was impractical. The Woodhead group suggested several alternative plans, including one of partition that would have created an even smaller Jewish state than the one proposed by Lord Peel. According to this blueprint, the Arab and Jewish states would be economically united and neither state would have autonomy over economic matters.[107]

Both Arabs and Zionists opposed the Woodhead report, forcing the British to abandon partition as a compromise solution to the Arab-Jewish crisis in Palestine.

At the end of November 1938, the British government announced that it was no longer considering any plan for the division or partition of Palestine. Instead, the British cabinet invited the Zionists, Palestinian Arabs, and the Arab states to send representatives to London to negotiate a mutually agreeable solution to the Palestine problem. The cabinet also warned all parties that if they failed to reach a solution, Great Britain would be forced to impose its own policy, even if both Jews and Arabs objected.[108]

American Zionists who had opposed partition welcomed the British announcement that the creation of a Jewish state in Palestine was no longer an immediate prospect. Louis Brandeis wrote, "It is a source of rejoicing for us (and should be of deep humiliation for the British) that the government has reversed itself on partition and recognized the Mandate as binding it." While happy about the demise of the partition proposal, the Supreme Court Justice condemned the British proposal to negotiate with representatives of Arab countries, calling it "as stupid (and craven) as its past proposal of partition." Brandeis urged other Zionist leaders not to propose alternative solutions to the Arab-Jewish dilemma, but rather to demand that London simply fulfill its duties under the League of Nations Mandate. He wrote to his loyal assistant Robert Szold: "My own conviction is, that if once the terrorists are beaten—soundly beaten—we can arrange to get along with the other Palestinian Arabs, but not until then. And that we must divorce Palestinians from all other Arab populations in the settlement of the Palestinian problem."[109]

Emanuel Neumann, the promising young leader of American Zionism, was also pleased with the abandonment of the partition proposal, but he did not share Brandeis's optimism about the future. The best that could be hoped for from England, he gloomily reported, was another "more or less bad" compromise.[110]

The defeat of partition seemed to return Zionists to the situation that had existed before Lord Peel set foot into the land of Palestine. The Arabs stubbornly refused to accept the Zionist presence in the Middle East, and the British, faced with a growing fascist threat in Europe, were tempted to desert the Zionists in order to stabilize a critical part of the empire. However, while the partition controversy might not have radically altered the external political realities of the Middle East, it did profoundly affect the mind-set of American Zionists.

Before the Arab revolt of 1936 and the Peel Commission that followed, American Zionists had focused their attention on the plight of European Jewry. Wise, Silver, Szold, Brandeis, Rothenberg, and Lipsky all expected Palestine to be the destination of most Jewish refugees, and they understood that the Zionist movement in America would win new respect and support with every refugee that the Yishuv successfully absorbed into Palestine. Satisfied that events had proven Theodor Herzl correct, American Zionists set out to transform Palestine into a haven for refugees. However, the Arab riots of 1936 and the British reaction to them subtly changed the priorities of American Jewish nationalists.

Arab violence and the fear that it would seriously undermine British support for the Zionist program led Jewish nationalists in the United States to turn their main attention away from the European refugees to the survival of the Zionist experiment in Palestine. Upset over the British failure to crush the Arab revolt and suspecting that partition would be recommended by the Peel Commission, Brandeis and other American Zionists concluded that London was determined "to prevent Jewish development from becoming too powerful in the Near East." Accordingly, discussions between Zionist leaders and American officials began to focus more on the Palestine situation than on the plight of German Jewry.[111]

Of course, the threat to Palestine's future was connected to the plight of European Jewry. If the British were to restrict Jewish immigration to the country, one of the few havens available to refugees would be lost. Appeasement of the Arabs would deprive many European refugees of a new life and future generations of a Jewish national home. American Zionists also understood that any decrease in the efficiency of refugee resettlement in Palestine would undermine the advances made by Zionists within the American Jewish community.

Zionist organizations did not ignore the worsening plight of European Jewry in this period. American Jewish nationalists collected and distributed money for relief and resettlement work, and protested against the persecution of European Jewry in the German Reich and Poland.[112] Nonetheless, American Zionists increasingly concentrated on what the Diaspora could do for Palestine rather than what the Jewish homeland could do for the world's Jews. In 1934, Abba Hillel Silver and other Zionists attacked the Haavara Agreement, claiming the the Yishuv had an obligation to the Jews of Germany and should not profit financially from their suffering. After the Arab riots, however, Stephen Wise and Louis Brandeis could sympathize with the fear of the Yishuv that "the Diaspora Jews . . . may fail to do their part" to support Zionist efforts in Palestine. Palestine, in the opinion of American Zionists, offered needy Jews "permanent reconstruction" while other resettlement efforts promised only "temporary relief." If American Jewry was to save its European co-religionists, it would first have to defend Palestine.[113] In Morris Rothenberg's words: "Would it not be morally indefensible for the American Jewish community, living in security and comfort in this great and free land, to keep silent as they see their brothers in their tragic plight, . . . being threatened with the deprivation of their last cherished hope for a better future for themselves and their children?"[114]

As the struggle over Palestine's future continued, Zionists began to use the refugee crisis as a means to defend their stake in the Holy Land. In debates with American critics of Zionism, publicists like Philip Bernstein argued that any attack on the Jewish claim to Palestine was also a blow against thousands of refugees who could find no other home. Both sides of the partition debate argued that the well-being of the refugees depended on their victory. Weizmann, Lipsky, and Ben-

Gurion explained that an autonomous Jewish state, even if it encompassed only part of Palestine, could offer sanctuary to Jews escaping German or Polish anti-Semitism. Robert Szold and other anti-partitionists claimed that a state in a divided Palestine would lack the resources necessary to absorb the massive number of needy Jews.

The Peel Commission's proposal to divide Palestine between the Arabs and Jews, and the restriction of Jewish immigration that began in November 1936 seriously undermined American Zionists' confidence in Great Britain. Opponents of partition feared that the Peel proposal was part of a cruel and brutal British plan to crush the Zionist movement. Those Zionists advocating Palestine's division also questioned Britain's loyalty to the Balfour pledge and advocated partition as a means of escaping the dictates and whims of colonial administrators and the London cabinet.[115]

Unfortunately, the Zionists' suspicions about Great Britain proved to be well founded. The growing likelihood of a new European conflict made it imperative for London to secure England's position in the Middle East. British strategists were afraid that, in the event of a war against Germany, continued Arab unrest in the region would drain army manpower away from the European battlefields. Accordingly, after inviting Arab and Zionist representatives to a London conference to be held in early 1939, Great Britain warned that if the negotiations failed, the British cabinet would impose its own settlement on the region.

For the Zionists, the London conference held in February 1939 proved to be a disaster. Arab delegates from Palestine and neighboring Middle Eastern states refused even to sit at the same table with representatives of the Zionist movement.[116] The inability of Jews and Arabs to develop a compromise agreement gave British authorities the opportunity to impose their own will in Palestine. On May 17, 1939, Great Britain published yet another White Paper on Palestine. To the dismay of all Jewish nationalists, the 1939 MacDonald White Paper seemed to repudiate the Balfour Declaration by declaring that:

> His Majesty's Government believe that the framers of the Mandate in which the Balfour Declaration was embodied could not have intended that Palestine should be converted into a Jewish state against the will of the Arab population of the country. . . . His Majesty's Government therefore now declare unequivocally that it is not part of their policy that Palestine should become a Jewish State. They would indeed regard it as contrary to their obligations to the Arabs under the Mandate, as well as to the assurances which have been given to the Arab people in the past, that the Arab population of Palestine should be made the subjects of a Jewish State against their will.

The British proclaimed their intention to establish an independent state in Palestine in ten years, in which Jews and Arabs would share political power. The White

Paper recognized the fear of Arab Palestinians that indefinite Jewish immigration would endanger their well-being. In order to reassure the Arabs that a Jewish state would never emerge, London announced that it would allow only seventy-five thousand Jews to enter Palestine during the next five years. This would insure that the Jews would remain a minority in the Holy Land, outnumbered three to one by the Arabs. After five years, any further Jewish immigration would depend on the agreement of Palestine's Arab community, which was unlikely to ever give its consent. The 1939 White Paper, labeled a "death sentence" by Zionist leader Chaim Wiezmann, also imposed severe restrictions on Jewish land purchases in the Holy Land.[117]

Three and a half months before the outbreak of the Second World War, Zionists in Europe, Palestine, and America seemed to be faced with a gloomy and tragic future. If the British carried out their new policy, a Jewish majority would never be established in Palestine and the Zionist dream of creating a Jewish homeland would go unfulfilled. The German tanks that crossed Poland's borders on the morning of September 1, 1939, ignited a conflict that would result in the death of forty million people. For Zionists, the German attack seemed to offer one last opportunity to win their homeland.

III | WAR AND STATEHOOD

DESPAIR: RESPONDING TO THE WHITE PAPER

At the 1939 World's Fair in New York City, dozens of nations exhibited artifacts illustrating their economic and cultural achievements. Among the many national pavilions, one represented a people without a country. The Palestine pavilion's opening highlighted the forty-second annual convention of the Zionist Organization of America. Many of the ZOA's leaders had supervised the construction of the exhibit, the cornerstone of which came from Kibbutz Hanita, a young Jewish settlement in Palestine whose founders had withstood a sustained Arab attack in 1938. For American Zionists meeting one month after the publication of the MacDonald White Paper, the stone from Hanita seemed to symbolize their intention to continue the building of a Palestine homeland in the face of official British opposition.[1]

The organizers of the ZOA convention were determined to carry on business as usual.[2] Rabbi Stephen Wise told the audience that Lord Halifax, the British ambassador to the United States, had informed him that there were times when moral claims, such as the Zionists' on Palestine, had to yield to administrative necessities like the White Paper. Wise disagreed with the British official and brought the ZOA delegates to their feet when he asserted that: "Jewish history affirms that every administrative necessity yields before the uncancellable moral claim of the Jewish people to live and rebuild Eretz Israel."[3] Rabbi Solomon Goldman, president of the ZOA, also attacked the White Paper, admitting that it was a setback for Zionists but also proclaiming his refusal "to convert a temporary setback into a rout." Former ZOA president Morris Rothenberg predicted that the White Paper would shortly become just "another

68

exhibit in the dusty archives of inept British statesmanship," and Louis Lipsky bravely commented that "the work of Palestine goes on. No power on earth can completely stop it."[4]

In spite of these heroic words of resistance, the ZOA leadership's hopeful good humor was just a facade to camouflage the despair and confusion caused by the new British pro-Arab policy. On May 10, 1939, Justice Louis Brandeis confided to Robert Szold that Zionist leaders in Palestine were "panic stricken" over the imminent publication of the White Paper. Most of the plans they suggested, he continued, were either "impossible" to fulfill or were "unwise."[5]

American Zionists shared the anxiety and pessimism of their Palestinian counterparts. Solomon Goldman, dismissing the strategic imperatives that dictated British policy in Palestine, believed that the new White Paper was the latest in a long series of atrocities committed against the Jews. Equating anti-Zionism with anti-Semitism, Goldman concluded that Nazi racist doctrines had affected Great Britain.[6] Rose Jacobs, a former leader of Hadassah and an American representative on the Jewish Agency in Palestine, compared the British White Paper to the Munich Pact and the betrayal of the Czechs. Zionists, she worried, might have done a terrible disservice to the Jewish people because they had "led a whole generation of youth to believe that they could be secure in Palestine, and that security had now become a myth."[7]

While Jacobs worried about the future, the practical and businesslike leaders of Hadassah began to discuss the decrease in contributions to the Youth Aliyah program that would probably follow the implementation of the new British immigration restrictions.[8] The Hadassah women could not have found much solace in the opinions of Solomon Goldman and Louis Brandeis, who "optimistically" noted that the MacDonald White Paper "at least" gave Zionists five years to organize against the planned total halting of Jewish immigration to Palestine.[9]

The religiously orthodox Mizrachi organization, like Hadassah, also began the painful task of adapting to the post–White Paper world situation. Realizing that the task of resettling the Jewish homeland could not, at least for the time being, be continued, Mizrachi officials decided to concentrate their efforts on the religious education of American Jewish youth who would have to assume the burden of keeping the Zionist dream alive.[10]

There seemed to be little direct action that the Zionists could take against the British. American Zionists wondered how they could adopt a strong anti-British policy and still work with London against their common enemy, Adolf Hitler. Rose Jacobs wearily commented, "This dilemma demonstrated most clearly how alone the Jews are as a people. They have no place to look to for help in the outside world."[11]

Several Zionist organizations tried to organize and coordinate protests against the British policy; two hundred leading Jewish nationalists agreed to travel to

Washington to lobby among representatives and senators. Zionist leaders hoped to demonstrate that "although Zionist membership in this country might be small, Zionist sentiment was very large." Jewish leaders did not expect these demonstrations to have an immediate effect on the British, but they hoped that the public actions would provide the Zionist rank and file with an "outlet" for their "indignation" and would also help "secure their loyalty and support for the long struggle ahead."[12]

While world Jewish leaders organized popular protests, they also struggled to bring the Palestine situation before the League of Nations. The League had incorporated the Balfour pledge into the Palestine Mandate it awarded to Great Britain, and it could censure London for its restrictive immigration policies. However, there was slight chance that the Chamberlain government would give much credence to the desires of the League, which had already proven its impotence in the face of German, Italian, and Japanese aggression.[13]

In the face of catastrophe, Zionist leaders desperately sought reason for hope. Some Zionists found solace in an almost mystical belief in the indestructibility of the Jewish people who had endured so many persecutions and setbacks. Many also looked to the eventual election of a new government in England, which they hoped would be more supportive of the Zionist program than the Conservative party.[14]

During parliamentary debates in May 1939, both the Liberal and Labour parties had vigorously condemned the White Paper. Herbert Morrison, a Labour party member of the House of Commons, attacked the Chamberlain government for its "cynical breach" of the Balfour Declaration, which implicitly pledged to support mass Jewish immigration to Palestine. Now, he continued, alluding to the plight of German Jewry, "the Jews, already victims of other races as a minority in certain countries, are . . . to be made a permanent minority in the country that had been promised to them."[15] Liberal party leader Sir Archibald Sinclair argued that the world would interpret the White Paper as a surrender to Arab violence and he warned that, if the new policy was instituted in Palestine, "we shall create confusion in that country, [and] we shall incur the scorn of Europe.[16] Winston Churchill, an arch-opponent of Chamberlain's policy of appeasing Hitler, likened the White Paper to the Munich Pact. He reminded Parliament that the Balfour Declaration's "pledge of home of refuge, . . . was not made to the Jews in Palestine but to the . . . vast, unhappy mass of scattered, persecuted, wandering Jews whose intense, unchanging, unconquerable desire has been for a National Home." He predicted that outside events would not allow Great Britain to carry out its five-year plan of immigration restriction in Palestine, saying:

> Europe is more that two-thirds mobilized tonight. . . . That cannot possibly continue for five years, not for four, nor for three years. It may be that it will

not continue beyond the present year. Long before those five years are past, either there will be a Britain which knows how to keep its word on the Balfour Declaration and is not afraid to do so, or, believe me, we shall find ourselves relieved of many overseas responsibilities other than those comprised within the Palestine Mandate.[17]

While American Zionists waited for Churchill or some other opponent of the White Paper to take possession of 10 Downing Street, Palestinian Jewry, more action-oriented than their American cousins, began to wage war against the British Empire. On May 18, 1939, the day after the publication of the White Paper, Jews throughout Palestine demonstrated against Britain's new policy. In Jerusalem the demonstration turned into a riot as Jewish protesters fought British policemen, wounding four and killing one; 135 members of the Yishuv were hurt in the fight.[18] The Irgun (a small group of Jewish radicals loyal to Revisionist leader Vladimir Jabotinsky), which refused to acknowledge the authority of Zionist leaders in Palestine, responded to the White Paper with a terrorist campaign aimed at British and Arab targets. The Irgun set off a bomb at the Palestine Broadcasting Service on May 17 and blew up the main post office on June 12.[19] In August, Irgun assassins murdered Ralph Cairns, commander of the Jewish section of the British Criminal Investigation Department in Palestine. In retaliation for Arab attacks on Jewish civilians, Irgun terrorists killed over seventy Arabs in a series of explosions in Haifa.[20] A tragedy was fortuitously averted on June 9, when British police arrested a young Irgun woman who was about to plant a bomb among a large group of Arab women and children waiting to visit relatives incarcerated in Jerusalem's central prison.[21]

The Irgun's bloody terrorist campaign against civilians appalled Zionist leaders in Palestine, but they were also determined to respond to the White Paper forcefully. On June 5, 1939, the Jewish Agency in Palestine authorized the secret creation of Haganah Special Squads, which would operate under the direct command of David Ben-Gurion. The Special Squads attacked British targets in Palestine, damaging oil pipelines and sinking a British police boat in August. Although their successes might have been spectacular, the Haganah's military offensive constituted only a minor element of the Yishuv's anti–White Paper campaign. The Zionists devoted most of their resources to Aliyah Bet—the illegal smuggling of Jewish refugees into Palestine.[22]

Actually, the first illegal immigration operation occurred in June 1934, when a Polish Zionist youth organization successfully smuggled 350 refugees into Palestine on board the Greek ship *Velos*. The failure of a second Aliyah Bet attempt in late 1934 convinced Zionist leaders to suspend all further actions in order to avoid a confrontation with British authorities. In 1937, after Britain began to decrease the number of Jews it allowed into Palestine, the Irgun and Revisionist

Zionist organizations in Europe adopted the illegal immigration tactic, bringing between five and six thousand Jews to Palestine before the outbreak of war in September 1939. Late in 1938, the Haganah and the Jewish Agency established the *Mossad L'Aliyah Bet* (Institute for Illegal Immigration) to oversee the illegal transportation of refugees into Palestine. After the publication of the 1939 White Paper, the Mossad intensified its efforts, smuggling over six thousand Jews into Palestine in less than two years. A favorite Mossad tactic was to anchor a transport ship off of Palestine's coast. During the night, small boats would shuttle refugees from the ship to one of the many kibbutzim that dotted the Mediterranean shore. Not all these attempts were successful. On June 1, 1939, British naval vessels intercepted a Greek cattle boat carrying 906 Jews to Palestine. Mandatory authorities transported the refugees, including 360 women and children, to Haifa and announced that they would be allowed to remain in Palestine, but that their number would be deducted from the White Paper quota.[23]

American Zionists, far removed from the action in Palestine, could do little to contribute to the Aliyah Bet campaign. Most generally supported the Mossad's efforts and compared Aliyah Bet to the Boston Tea Party and other "illegal" American colonial attempts to resist tyrannical British taxation.[24] A few Zionist leaders in the United States, however, worried about the potentially serious consequences of illegal immigration. Abba Hillel Silver, chairman of the United Palestine Appeal, a major Zionist fund-raising organization, voiced his concerns at the twenty-first World Zionist Congress, which met in Geneva, Switzerland, in late August 1939. In a rare mood of caution, Silver, who during the next decade would acquire a reputation for aggressive risk taking, asked Zionist authorities to refrain from doing anything that might bring the Yishuv into conflict with British forces. In a public address repeatedly interrupted by hecklers and during private sessions, Silver explained that the Jews could not hope to win a war against Britain and instead should avoid confrontation until British public opinion forced a change in the Mandatory Power's policy. Asked about the plight of Jewish refugees searching for a haven, Silver replied that thousands of Jews could be settled in Palestine even under the White Paper's restrictions.

Berl Katznelson, a Palestinian socialist Zionist leader and editor of the Hebrew daily *Davar*, refuted Silver's position, warning that criticism of Aliyah Bet betrayed the refugees and young Yishuv members who were spearheading the battle against Britain. Katznelson's argument proved to be irresistible for most of the Zionists at Geneva, including many in the large delegation from the United States. Even those Americans who shared Silver's doubts could not bring themselves to censure or disown the courageous Aliyah Bet operatives.[25]

While Aliyah Bet caused some controversy within Zionist ranks, neither it nor the Irgun's terror campaign were having the desired effect of forcing Great Britain to alter its Palestine policy. London, preparing for a possible war with Germany, was determined to pacify the Middle East in order to insure that, in the event of war, British resources could be concentrated on the Western Front, not dwindled away in suppressing Arab revolts or threats to the Suez Canal. In a war, the British coldly calculated, the Jews of Palestine would have little choice but to support those forces battling Hitler. In the meantime, British resources in Palestine were sufficient to limit the impact of the "Jewish revolt" against the White Paper. On August 31, British police in Palestine raided a house in Tel Aviv and arrested most of the Irgun command. Other Jewish terrorists were shot down by the Palestinian police. Even Aliyah Bet proved to be no more than a nuisance for the British authorities.[26]

WORLD WAR II: NEW HOPE

Because American Zionists did not fully comprehend British imperial strategy, the German invasion of Poland on September 1, 1939, and the English and French declarations of war that followed boosted their morale. Many tended to compare the 1939 White Paper with the Munich Pact and anticipated that the outbreak of war would discredit all forms of appeasement, whether it be of Nazis or Arabs. Stephen Wise thought that the White Paper would be one of the first casualties of a new European war.[27] Mrs. Moses Epstein of Hadassah analyzed the Zionist position just four days after German tanks rolled across the Polish frontier and found it to be stronger than it had been before the outbreak of hostilities. The democracies, she naively reported, were finally accepting the fact "that Nazi and Fascist persecution of a Jewish minority inevitably leads to persecution of other minorities, and in the last analysis is a threat to the democratic structure itself." Renewed British support of Zionism would surely follow, she predicted.[28]

American Zionist optimism at the start of World War II was based not only on the conviction that all forms of appeasement would soon end. Of even greater importance was the fact that Zionists, like most Americans, believed that the Second World War would follow the course of the first and would end with an international peace conference where the victorious powers would redraw political boundaries and create new states. At Versailles, Jewish delegations had lobbied for the granting of political and cultural rights to Jews and other European minorities, and had won international support for the Balfour Declaration. ZOA President Solomon Goldman expected the Jewish nationalists at a post–World War II peace conference would be able to improve on the concessions they had won from the Allies following World War I.[29]

American Zionists who had been despondent about the British White Paper now had reason to believe that better times were near. Zionist contributions to the British war effort would win renewed British support of Jewish nationalism and lead to the abandonment of the White Paper, a development that would safeguard the Zionist experiment in Palestine and would benefit the Jewish refugees who were struggling to escape Hitler's grasp.

Chaim Weizmann in London and Jewish leaders in Palestine shared the views of their American comrades and quickly took steps to assure that a Zionist delegation would be present at the peace conference that would end the Second World War. Immediately after the German invasion of Poland, David Ben-Gurion announced that, while the Yishuv would never accept the White Paper's immigration restrictions, Jewish Palestine would use all of its resources to help Great Britain defeat Hitler. Weizmann offered the Chamberlain government the total assistance of the world Zionist movement and as a personal contribution to the war effort he cooperated with British scientific efforts to produce artificial rubber and high-octane fuel.[30]

Even the Irgun decided to support the British war effort. On September 9, 1939, the organization's high command announced a suspension of all anti-British actions and offered their services to the imperial forces.[31] Avraham Stern, a leading member of the Irgun, refused to accept the dictates of his superiors and with a small number of followers bolted from the organization in order to carry on the struggle against the British. In no mood to tolerate resistance, Mandatory security forces hunted Stern down, finally apprehending him in a Tel Aviv apartment where he was summarily executed.[32]

Stern's anti-British program found practically no support within Zionist ranks. Ben-Gurion, Weizmann, and their comrades looked forward to London accepting their offers of cooperation and expected the British to mobilize the Yishuv youth into Jewish fighting units, perhaps even a Jewish army. The Jewish soldiers would enter battle with two goals in mind. Their primary mission would be the defeat of the hated Hitler. Their sacrifices in the field would also allow Zionist statesmen to demand recognition as a co-belligerent with Great Britain and would insure that Jewish Palestine's interests would be considered in the reconstruction of the postwar world.

To the dismay of all Zionists, the Chamberlain government was reluctant to accept their help. British officials were convinced that the advantages of Yishuv support would be outweighed by the wave of Arab unrest that an alliance with the Zionists would surely spark. Accordingly, London continued to enforce its White Paper policy and allowed only a small number of Jews to serve in military support units in Palestine. The German conquest of France in the spring of 1940 forced the British to reconsider their position. The new government of Winston Churchill was more prepared than its predecessor to accept Zionist assistance and allowed a larger number of Palestinian Jews to enter military service. In the spring of 1941, with Rommel's Afrika Korps threatening the entire Middle East, the British army cooperated with the Haganah in the creation of the Palmach, a small unit of Jewish youth that would operate as a guerrilla force in the event of a German conquest of Palestine. However, in spite of England's grave military condition, the British General Staff and, in particular, Foreign Secretary Anthony Eden remained convinced that the empire's security depended on the continued appeasement of Arab leaders and nationalist movements. They knew that the Arabs, unlike the members of the Yishuv, were not eager to enlist in the British army, but they also realized that Britain could not afford to divert any military resource to the suppression of a new Arab revolt in Palestine. Churchill, heeding the advice of his cabinet, refused to authorize the total mobilization of the Yishuv and rejected repeated Zionist requests for the revocation of the White Paper.[33]

Britain's behavior forced Ben-Gurion and Weizmann to conclude that a full-scale political campaign would be required to force London to accept the Zionist movement as an ally. The actual task of negotiating with British officials would remain in their hands, but American Zionists would also have an important role to perform. If enough American public support for a Jewish army could be amassed, Britain, desperate for American assistance in the war against Hitler, might be forced to change its policies. Weizmann traveled to the United States in early 1940 in order to rally American Zionist support,[34] and in June 1940 Ben-Gurion sent an urgent message to the ZOA annual convention informing the already concerned organization: "Never has our people, never has our country faced as great danger as today." Nearly five million Jews were now in Hitler's control and Nazi armies were themselves threatening Palestine, whose conquest would wipe out all the great Zionist achievements of the preceding half century. He warned that "history" would never forgive American Jewry, the largest free Jewish population in the world, if they did not do everything possible to give the Yishuv the chance to defend itself.[35]

American Zionists enthusiastically responded to Ben-Gurion's call for action. The Mizrachi, representing Orthodox religious Zionists in the United States, proclaimed: "We must in this grave and critical hour concentrate all efforts for the defense of Eretz Israel."[36] Louis Lipsky called on American Zionists to sacrifice and do everything possible to support Palestinian Jewry in their "great defensive effort."[37] Almost eight hundred ZOA delegates, recognizing that American Jewry represented "the last bulwark of moral and material support for the development of the Jewish Homeland in Palestine,"[38] urged Winston Churchill to allow Palestinian Jewry to form combat units to fight in defense of the Middle East.[39]

American Zionists attempted to demonstrate that the Jewish and British war efforts were inextricably linked. Zionists repeatedly pointed out that the Jews were the first victims of "Nazi aggression." According to ZOA president Solomon Goldman, while German Jewry struggled through years of persecution, the democratic powers attempted to avert war by ignoring Nazi atrocities and militarism. Zionists, he claimed, being among the first to understand that nazism was a threat to all democracies, welcomed the British to the battle against fascism. Jewish nationalists could, more easily than anyone else, understand the terror and despair of those peoples struggling to free their countries from German domination because their nation, Palestine, had been conquered by Roman armies two thousand years before. Members of the Yishuv were already contributing to the British battle to halt Nazi aggression and free Europe; all they asked was to be allowed to enlist in larger numbers. After Hitler was defeated, Goldman concluded, Zionists would expect their allies to complete the crusade for liberation by allowing the Jews to return to Palestine.[40]

The American Emergency Committee for Zionist Affairs (AECZA) attempted to coordinate Zionist efforts in the United States to build public support for the creation of a Jewish army and the revocation of the White Paper. Established in late 1939, the AECZA had twenty-four members representing all the major American Zionist organizations. Although Stephen Wise served as chairman of the AECZA, Emanuel Neumann directed the day-to-day work of the organization.[41] Personal and organizational rivalries crippled the AECZA and frustrated Neumann who resigned his position and complained that AECZA members "were acting not as a unified body, but as ambassadors from sovereign organizations. Some of them insisted that they had to consult their respective organizations – their 'governments'– before any action could be taken." The ZOA, Hadassah, Poale Zion, and Mizrachi refused to supply the AECZA with the $250,000 Neumann felt was necessary to mount an effective political campaign.[42] Louis Brandeis and his supporters, unwilling to let old conflicts die, were suspicious about the activities and loyalty of their old opponent Louis Lipsky, an AECZA member. Robert Szold and Morris Rothenberg of the ZOA opposed Neumann's organizational activities because they worried that a politically powerful and independent AECZA would absorb "Zionist work in this country so as to leave the ZOA with nothing except membership work to do."[43]

In fact, American Zionism desperately needed just the type of organization Rothenberg and Szold dreaded. In the years following Hitler's seizure of power, Zionist groups in the United States experienced tremendous growth. By the summer of 1941, the ZOA and Hadassah claimed a joint membership of two hundred thousand, while the much smaller Mizrachi and Poale Zion had both more than doubled their membership since 1933.[44] However, without some organizational structure that would transcend petty organizational and personal rivalries, Zionists could not hope to develop the resources and skills necessary to build political support outside of the American Jewish community. The impotency of the AECZA was primarily responsible for the failure of Zionists to mount any effective drive in support of a Jewish army or against the White Paper before the Japanese attack on Pearl Harbor.

Political immaturity was not the only difficulty American Zionists confronted during this period. Their strong support of Britain's war effort pitted them against powerful isolationist forces in the United States, including Robert R. McCormick, publisher of the *Chicago Tribune*, the famous aviator Charles Lindbergh, and socialist leader Norman Thomas. Lindbergh attacked American Jews for their strong support of Great Britain and accused them of conspiring to push the United States into war.[45] Even the Reverend John Haynes Holmes, a supporter of Jewish nationalism, spiritual leader of New York's Community Church, and a close friend of Stephen Wise, who had defended Zionist interests during the Arab Revolt of 1936, preached the doctrine of isolationism.[46]

Holmes, a life-long pacifist and admirer of India's Mahatma Gandhi, often spoke out against any American support for Britain's war against Hitler. In December 1940, the *Christian Century*, a liberal Protestant periodical, asked Holmes if he would support the United States if it was "drawn into the war." His response was an unequivocal no. Hitler, the Protestant clergyman wrote, was not the source of the world's troubles, but was only one symptom of mankind's moral decay. The war between Britain and Germany was a "fundamentally immoral clash of competing imperialisms" and, Holmes concluded, "if America goes into the war, it will not be for idealistic reasons but to serve her own imperialistic interests so closely identified with those of Britain."[47]

Holmes's refusal to support the British war effort troubled Stephen Wise, who admired his friend's allegiance to Gandhi and pacifism. More than twenty years before, the rabbi and the minister had both applauded Woodrow Wilson's neutrality policies and worked to insure the President's reelection in 1916. When the United States declared war against Germany in April 1917, the two parted ways as Holmes condemned Wilson's "betrayal" of neutrality, while Wise, believing that German militarism made war unavoidable, offered his services to the administration, even working one summer as a unskilled worker in a military shipyard.[48] After the armistice, Wise slowly drifted back into pacifism and reconciled his differences with Holmes. He even encouraged his congregation to see *If This Be Treason*, an antiwar play coauthored by Holmes and Reginald Laurence, which received little critical acclaim.[49]

The fascist threat again led Wise to revise his views on war. Following the German invasion of Poland, Wise, believing that a German victory "would mean the blackest night for civilization,"[50] led the effort to rally American Jews and Zionists to Great Britain's defense saying:

> The question has ceased to be one of war versus peace, but is rather become a question whether unbridled might and unmoral [sic] power shall again rule over the destinies of men and nation. Insofar as England and France have taken up the gage, insofar as the two great democracies of Western Europe dared to say to Hitler after his threat to Poland, "Thus far shalt thou go and no further," it is for peoples who are, and for men who would remain free,

their most sacred obligation to give moral, political and material aid and furtherance to Britain and France.[51]

Wise urged all ZOA members to cooperate with William Allen White's efforts to awaken the American public to the Nazi threat.[52] In 1941, as president of the American Jewish Congress, he directed financial campaigns within the American Jewish community that netted over $100,000 for Britain's defense.[53] Following the German conquest of France in June 1940, Wise, saying that England was "the Maginot Line of the United States," urged Americans to extend to Britain all support short of war.[54]

Although Wise never called on the United States to actually declare war against Germany, he supported all the president's efforts, which slowly made Washington an ally of London, including Lend Lease and the use of American ships against German U-boats. In May 1940, Wise, referring to Roosevelt's opposition to isolationism, called the president the "one clear voice in the world today" and "the earth's foremost statesman."[55] It was a view most American Jews and Zionists shared. At its annual convention in June 1940, the ZOA unanimously and without debate passed a resolution urging all Americans to support Roosevelt's efforts to supply London with the resources it needed to defeat the totalitarian regimes that threatened to "plunge" America into "catastrophe."[56] As political scientist Lawrence H. Fuchs noted, "there was no stronger interventionist group in the United States than the Jews." Understanding that every Nazi conquest subjected thousands of their co-religionists to terrible persecution, American Jews in overwhelming numbers turned to the anti-isolationist Roosevelt for salvation and security. According to surveys by the American Institute of Public Opinion and by the National Opinion Research Center at the University of Denver, more than 90 percent of Jewish voters cast their ballots for Roosevelt in 1940.[57]

Significantly, most American Jews supported Roosevelt in spite of his failure to take a strong stand on Zionism. The President respectfully sent welcoming messages to Zionist conventions, but his administration did little to further the Zionist quest. For example, Roosevelt and the State Department did not endorse the 1939 British White Paper, but neither did they seriously attempt to convince London to revoke it. Generally, Roosevelt seemed to believe that the future of Palestine was a British concern.[58]

MOVING TOWARD STATEHOOD

Even as Wise and Roosevelt cooperated in the campaign to build public support for American intervention in a second world war, Zionists began to comprehend the profound contradictions that plagued their wartime program. The war against

Hitler, Chaim Weizmann noted, put Jewish nationalists in the paradoxical position of supporting their "British friends," while their would-be ally's policies threatened to destroy the Zionist project in Palestine.[59] The schizophrenic nature of this situation was apparent at the November 1940 convention of the National Labor Committee for Palestine, which drew together delegations representing several American Zionist groups. The convention delegates supported Stephen Wise's demand that the United States do everything "short of war" to strengthen Britain in its defense of civilization. Shortly afterwards, the same audience enthusiastically responded as Wise condemned Britain's decision to deport 1,800 "illegal immigrants" from Palestine.[60] Infuriated by this dilemma, an angry Abba Hillel Silver protested:

> Our desire to help Great Britain in this war is maneuvering us into a policy distinctly harmful to Zionism. We are asked not only to withhold criticism of outrageous acts . . . , but actually . . . [to] become apologists for the Palestine Government. In the meantime England intends to pursue her policy of appeasing the Arabs even more aggressively than she did before the war. . . . This is an intolerable situation into which we are being moved. Every people speaks up for its own rights in this desperate time, . . . The Jews alone, the most hard-pressed of all, must speak up only in behalf of Great Britain.[61]

Britain's cruel and insensitive wartime policies exacerbated the dismay and intensified the fury of Silver and his fellow Zionists. London not only continued to refuse to establish a Jewish army, but also strictly enforced the 1939 White Paper in spite of the desperate plight of Europen Jewry. As German armies raced across Western Europe in the spring of 1940, the "free world" knew that Jews in Nazi-occupied lands were singled out for special abuse. This was particularly true for the three million Jews of Poland who, in 1940, were forcibly moved into small, overcrowded ghettoes. Cut off from their Christian neighbors, Polish Jewry struggled to survive the famine and disease that characterized ghetto life.[62] Small groups of European Jews, sometimes with the aid of Mossad or Revisionist agents, were able to board ships in order to seek refuge in Palestine. These ships were usually small and barely seaworthy; not all of them made it safely to Palestine's shores.

In the fall of 1940, Bulgaria, a German ally, exiled several hundred Jews from Dobrudja, a territory it acquired from Romania in September 1940. From this group, 380 chartered the *Salvador*, a sixty-ton Bulgarian sailing vessel, on which they hoped to reach Palestine. After the ship encountered stormy seas, the Turkish government allowed the vessel to anchor temporarily in the Strait of Bosporus. When the weather improved on December 13, the Turks, unwilling to have their country become a haven for Jewish refugees, ordered the *Salvador* to sail. Sixty miles from Istanbul, heavy winds knocked out the ship's small auxiliary motor. The captain and crew struggled to maintain control of the boat, but, as one refugee remembered: "Suddenly a violent shock aroused us. We had been hurled onto

79

a reef. The ensuing scenes were terrible. Prayers and shrieks mingled with the howling of the gale, and in the pitch darkness the white-crested waves broke over us and water poured through thousands of fissures as the ancient craft began to break up." That night, 231 refugees drowned.[63]

Some refugee boats were lucky enough to reach Palestinian waters, but the Royal Navy usually apprehended the vessels before their Jewish passengers could disembark. At first, British authorities allowed the "illegal immigrants" (who often spent months in internment camps) to remain in Palestine after subtracting their number from the White Paper immigration quotas. The British cabinet in late 1940, intent on discouraging European Jews from seeking refuge in Palestine, decided to deport illegal immigrants to British detention camps on the island of Mauritius. Government leaders explained, with very little evidence, that the Nazis were using the refugee exodus to smuggle spies and saboteurs into Palestine.

In November, nearly two thousand illegal immigrants boarded the British ship *Patria* for transport to Mauritius. After London refused to consider repeated Zionist appeals for clemency, Munia Mardor, a Haganah agent, smuggled explosives onto the *Patria*. His intent was to disable the ship in order to prevent its sailing. Tragically, Mardor's demolition skills were weak, and the bomb that exploded on November 15 was much more powerful than expected, killing more than two hundred of the refugees. The British announced that the *Patria* survivors would be allowed to remain in Palestine, but refused to extend the same hospitality to the 1,581 immigrants who had reached Palestine on board the *Atlantic* the day before the *Patria* catastrophe. On December 9, two British ships began the voyage to Mauritius carrying the despondent refugees.[64]

A year after the *Patria* incident, the *Struma*, a decrepit old steamer, slowly made its way into Istanbul Harbor. The almost eight hundred Jews on the ship had wanted to reach Palestine, but the *Struma* was dangerously unseaworthy, and the refugees decided to request sanctuary from the Turkish government. Turkey refused to grant the Jews' request, and the ship remained in Istanbul for months while Jewish leaders attempted to convince British officials to give the refugees special permission to enter Palestine. The English, unwilling to stray from the 1939 White Paper policy, refused to give the *Struma* passengers any type of visa, and the Turkish government finally gave orders for the removal of the ship. On February 24, 1942, tugboats pulled the *Struma* beyond Turkey's territorial waters. Shortly afterward the ship sank; 767 men, women and children drowned.[65]

Angered and disillusioned by Britain's seemingly unshakeable hostility to the Zionist cause, Yishuv leaders began to reconsider their tactics and philosophy. The Zionists' wartime strategy, developed after the German invasion of Poland, assumed that the White Paper was an aberration, a temporary reversal of London's traditional support of Jewish settlement of Palestine. Jewish nationalists believed that Zionist material and political assistance to Great Britain would convince London to conclude that the empire's interests would be best served by an alliance with the Yishuv, not by appeasement of the Arabs. With the anticipated reversal of Britain's anti-Zionist policies, the situation in Palestine would revert back to that of the pre–Arab-revolt "golden age" of 1933–36. Those refugees who could escape Nazi-occupied Europe would find a home in Palestine, and in the postwar period mass Jewish immigration to the Holy Land would resume. Within a short period of time a Jewish majority would emerge in Palestine and Zionists could then realize their ultimate goal—the creation of a Jewish state.

By late 1940, David Ben-Gurion and some of his Palestinian colleagues had concluded that time was no longer on their side. The White Paper was over one year old, and the British gave no hint of its imminent demise. Continued immigration restriction would insure that the Jews would remain a permanent minority in Palestine; the "Jewish National Home," it seemed, was destined to become an Arab state.

Desperate times demanded radical action. Armed struggle against the British was, as least for the moment, completely out of the question. The Yishuv simply was materially unprepared for revolution, nor could Jews, in good conscience, do anything that might contribute to Hitler's triumph. Instead, Ben-Gurion, in consultation with several of his closest advisers, decided that the Zionist movement must alter its timetable. Sovereignty could no longer remain the distant long-term goal of the movement. Recent experience with the British proved that large numbers of Jews would enter Palestine only when the Zionists themselves were free to establish and administer the territory's immigration policies. Therefore, it was imperative for Zionists to mount, as quickly as possible, a powerful pro-statehood political campaign. Ben-Gurion understood that the success of this venture would depend, in no small measure, on the ability of American Zionists to become a potent political force.[66]

During two long stays in the United States, Ben-Gurion explained his views to American Zionist leaders. On December 5, 1940, shortly after the *Patria* disaster, Ben-Gurion met with eight prominent American Zionists, including Abba Hillel Silver, Stephen Wise, Israel Goldstein, and Louis Lipsky of the ZOA, and Tamar de Sola Pool of Hadassah. Ben-Gurion told his compatriots that the European war would leave four to five million Jews destitute and demoralized. Palestine could easily absorb these pitiful victims of anti-Semitism, but the British White Paper threatened to prevent the Zionist movement from accomplishing its mission of mercy. Statehood, Ben-Gurion argued, was the only "means" through which future Jewish emigration to Palestine could be ensured. Remembering the bitter conflict over the Peel Commission's partition proposal, he quickly pointed out that the question of the future state's boundaries and its relationship to Britain could be left to future discussion. The reconstituted Jewish nation might opt for membership in the British Commonwealth or could even join in a postwar federation of Middle Eastern states.[67]

Ben-Gurion was not naive. He knew that London, intent on keeping Jews out of Palestine, would not simply comply with the Zionist request for statehood. However, Ben-Gurion believed that World War II would substantially reduce Great Britain's influence in the Middle East. The long series of British military disasters since the German invasion of Poland proved that the empire, on its own, could not defeat the Axis. American material support was sustaining Churchill's armies; it would have to increase if Europe was to be liberated. Ben-Gurion, with an eye on a future peace conference, calculated that Washington, not London, would control the destiny of Palestine. Therefore, it was imperative for all American Zionist groups to set aside their differences and join together in a concerted drive to build public and political support for Jewish statehood. As Ben-Gurion told the AECZA in November 1941: "There was no doubt that England will be influenced by what America says, and it was most important to develop political Zionism in America. Public opinion must be convinced that Palestine is the only solution to the Jewish problem. If the Jews here were won over to faith in our cause, then . . . we could win over the government."[68]

At the December 5 meeting, Abba Hillel Silver, who was thoroughly disgusted with British anti-Zionism, agreed with Ben-Gurion's analysis. Silver had opposed Palestine's partition during the Peel Report controversy, but now that the issue of boundaries was no longer being debated, he wholeheartedly adopted the goal of Jewish statehood. Nahum Goldmann also supported Ben-Gurion. A German-born Zionist who served as a representative of the Jewish Agency in Washington, Goldmann predicted that the tactic of using a postwar refugee problem to justify the establishment of a Jewish state would be very effective. American Jews were extremely concerned about the fate of their European co-religionists and doubted, given the American public's strong opposition to mass immigration, whether the refugees would be able to find a home in the United States after the war. Therefore, if Zionists could suggest a large, dramatic solution to the predicted refugee problem, wide public support would follow.[69]

Stephen Wise also supported the goal of statehood at the December meeting, but the elderly rabbi found his colleagues' rhetoric to be excessively militant. He warned that the aggressive political campaign Ben-Gurion was suggesting would add to London's burdens just at a time when British armies were barely holding off the Wehrmacht and Luftwaffe. He reminded his comrades that they too had a stake in Britain's war; the defeat of Hitler was the prime objective of all Jews.[70]

Silver disagreed with Wise's position, arguing that the New York rabbi "was talking himself into a position disastrous to Zionism." Ben-Gurion agreed with Silver and added that Wise's policy would be an injustice to the British cause. He explained that London's failings had to be publicized and corrected so that the moral basis of England's fight could be preserved.[71]

Ben-Gurion's persistent arguing of his case and Britain's uncompromising enforcement of the White Paper steadily convinced most American Zionist leaders to accept the goal of statehood. On December 12, 1940, the American Emergency Committee for Zionist Affairs voted, with Ben-Gurion's encouragement, to adopt a stronger stand against the White Paper.[72] At the end of January 1941, Abba Hillel Silver delivered a stirring address to the annual convention of the United Palestine Appeal, the largest American Zionist fund-raising organization. Responding to Silver's call for American Jewry to go on a "war-footing," the two thousand delegates of the convention resolved that the refugee problem that would arise at the end of the war could only be solved by the creation of a Jewish commonwealth in Palestine.[73]

In September 1941, Stephen Wise, who had voiced reservations at his meeting with Ben-Gurion nine months earlier, asked the annual ZOA convention to approve the policy of making Palestine's postwar autonomy the goal of their movement. The statement of principle unanimously ratified by the convention repeated many of the arguments used by David Ben-Gurion at the December 1940 Winthrop Hotel meeting. It maintained that the millions of uprooted Jews who would survive the war could only find peace and salvation if "afforded the opportunity to re-establish themselves in a land of their own." The rapid resettlement of refugees depended on "the reconstitution of Palestine in its historic boundaries of the Jewish Commonwealth."[74]

At the convention, Henry Montor, an officer of the United Palestine Appeal, called on his fellow Jewish nationalists to "go forward in comradeship and dedication, to the achievement of the unequivocal, the unexpressed and the inexpressible post-war aim of the Zionist movement, the creation of a Jewish state in Palestine."[75] Solomon Goldman told the ZOA audience that the Jews suffering Nazi persecution wanted to live a creative and idealistic life in freedom. He pleaded with Winston Churchill to give a sign so that all would know that "Eretz Israel is the assured, the guaranteed Homeland, the sovereign Homeland, dependent Homeland, self-governing Homeland of the Jewish people."[76]

Ben-Gurion eventually even won the cooperation of his arch rival Chaim Weizmann. Since the outbreak of the war, the two men had been moving in opposite directions. The Palestinian believed that Weizmann's love of Great Britain kept him from realizing that London had become one of Zionism's major adversaries. Ben-Gurion was determined to unseat Weizmann from his position as president of the World Zionist Organization so that the movement could adopt a more aggressive stance against the British. Weizmann, for his part, considered Ben-Gurion to be a dangerous extremist who would deprive Palestine of the great benefits Britain could bestow. Like the Palestinian leader, Weizmann looked forward to the creation of a Jewish state, but was more willing to compromise this long-term goal for immediate political gains. In May 1941, while Ben-Gurion was rallying American Zionists to the statehood goal, Weizmann organized a meeting of thirty-three prominent American Jewish leaders, including representatives of the American Jewish Committee (AJC). Wanting to insure the Committee's support of mass Jewish immigration to Palestine after the war and knowing that the AJC opposed the establishment of a Jewish nation because it would raise questions about the loyalty of Diaspora Jewry, Weizmann deviated from the statehood formula. He explained that the Zionists would be satisfied with the creation of a semi-autonomous Palestine, preferably under Britain's protection, in which Jews would have control over immigration and colonization policies.[77]

Weizmann, by late 1941, seems to have found the momentum toward statehood irresistible. In an article for the prestigious American journal *Foreign Affairs*, he spelled out his plans for Palestine's future. Like Ben-Gurion, he anticipated a major postwar Jewish refugee problem, which would be exacerbated by a major economic crisis as nations made the transition to peacetime economies. Given this situation, "it would probably be unduly optimistic to assume that countries like the United States, Canada, and some of the South American republics, will radically change their immigration policy after the war." The Yishuv, on the other hand, had the desire and the capacity to absorb millions of homeless Jews.[78]

While Weizmann extolled the virtues of Palestinian settlement, he did not follow Ben-Gurion's example and justify the establishment of a Jewish nation on the grounds that the White Paper experience proved that mass Jewish immigration could take place only under a sovereign Jewish government. Instead, he argued that Jewish statehood was not only a political necessity, but also a moral imperative. The Jews, the "most abject of all the abject victims" of Nazi terror, deserved and demanded a radical solution to the problem of anti-Semitism. That, Zionist doctrine taught, could only be statehood, which would allow Jews, who were everywhere a minority, to prosper and mature as a "normal nation." Weizmann concluded:

> A Jewish state in Palestine would be more than merely the necessary means of securing further Jewish immigration and development. It is a moral need and postulate, and it would be a decisive step toward normality and true emancipation. . . . The latest manifestation of Nazi ingenuity is the decree by which every Jew under Nazi rule must bear on his chest a so-called "badge of shame"–the Shield of David. We wear it with pride. The Shield of David is too ancient and too sacred a symbol to be susceptible of degradation under the pagan Swastika. Hallowed by uncounted ages of suffering and martyrdom, patiently and unrevengefully borne, it will yet shine untarnished over Zion's gate, long after the horrors of our present night are forgotten in the light of the new day that is to come.[79]

As the statehood idea gained in acceptance, Emanuel Neumann explained to American Zionists that the political task Ben-Gurion asked them to assume would not be easily accomplished. Neumann knew that Franklin Roosevelt was tremendously popular with American Jews and Zionists who approved of the president's New Deal and interventionist policies. Stephen Wise revered Roosevelt and would tolerate no criticism of him even though the White House had actually done little to support the Zionist cause beyond sending annual greetings to ZOA conventions and issuing a mild rebuke of the White Paper. Recognizing that Roosevelt was "off-limits," Neumann attempted to separate the president from his government. Neumann told a large group of leading Zionists that Roosevelt was genuinely sympathetic to the plight of European Jewry and to the cause of Jewish nationalism. However, he maintained, American diplomats were "not yet in their hearts, prepared to say that the solution [to the Jewish problem] must . . . be the reconstitution of Palestine as the Jewish Commonwealth." The State Department was primarily concerned with providing Great Britain with aid and was inclined to accept London's explanation that military necessity required the denial of Jewish rights to Palestine. Whether Roosevelt would prevail over Zionism's opponents depended on American Jewry, because Neumann explained: "it is obvious that the lengths to which he can go now or later will depend upon the strength of public backing— not only backing but urging—which he will have on the part of the public." The successful establishment of a Jewish commonwealth in Palestine depended on the support of the American government, and Neumann urged Zionists to organize mass support for their cause.[80]

Toward this end, the American Emergency Committee for Zionist Affairs in late 1941 began preparations for a major meeting of American and world Zionist leaders. At the conference, Ben-Gurion hoped, the entire Zionist movement in the United States could formally unite around the goal of immediate statehood. If Zionist groups could pool their resources they would be able to set out to win the support of the entire American Jewish community. With this base secured, Zionists expected that their movement would become a potent political force.[81]

The Japanese attack on Pearl Harbor sped up the statehood drive within the Zionist movement. America's entrance into World War II ended any doubts about whether the United States would occupy an important seat at a future peace conference. The eminent Jewish historian Salo Baron observed in June 1942 that "it is enough for us to recollect the transformations in the American Jewish community which took place as a result of the First World War to get an inkling of what changes might be expected from the Second War which is so much greater in the issues at stake, so much more profound in the depth of its upheaval, and so much more encompassing both area and apparent duration."[82] Time was running out. World War II offered Zionists their last best chance to change the destiny of the Jewish people. If an international peace conference failed to endorse the creation of a Jewish state in Palestine, Diaspora Jewry would be doomed to further persecution when a new anti-Semitic demagogue arose to resume Hitler's work.

With this sobering thought in mind, 586 American Zionists gathered at New York's Biltmore Hotel for the Extraordinary Zionist Conference, which would plan the redemption of the Jewish people. They were joined by 67 guests from abroad including Chaim Weizmann and David Ben-Gurion. The organizations included all of the major and minor American Zionist groups with the exception of the small right-wing Revisionist organization, which still refused to accept the authority of the world Zionist movement and was considered a pariah by most American Jewish nationalists.[83]

The delegates who gathered at the Biltmore Hotel in May 1942 knew that they were meeting at a time of grave danger, yet one that also held the possibility of great promise. It was clear that the goal of Jewish statehood would be the major topic at the Biltmore Conference. Naturally, delegates also devoted much discussion to the Jewish refugee problem, which had rejuvenated and strengthened the Zionist movement during the decade preceding Biltmore and was expected to reach crisis proportions after the war. The six hundred Zionists in the New York hotel could not know that Adolf Hitler had already begun his "final solution" to the refugee problem. When German troops crossed the Soviet Union's borders in June 1941, select units of the SS followed, executing Jews, gypsies, and Communist party leaders in Nazi-occupied Russia. Shortly after the invasion of Russia, the Nazis also began to build huge extermination centers in Poland where they could efficiently and quickly gas Jews to death. By the end of 1942, trains packed with Jews were arriving at Auschwitz, Sobibor, Treblinka, and other extermination camps, where most of the passengers were immediately executed.[84]

Jewish leaders in the United States did not learn about the Nazi plan to systematically murder all of European Jewry until three months after the Biltmore Conference. However, Chaim Weizmann and his compatriots did know that Nazi rule subjected European Jewry to starvation, persecution, and murder. Weizmann was deeply troubled by the suffering of the European Jews and at Biltmore he identified himself with their suffering by declaring: "Like all of you, I am a deeply wounded Jew." Jews were the first targets of Hitler and while many other people were caught in the grip of the German oppressor, Weizmann believed that "our tragedy is both in quality and quantity, different from that of the world around us." The "father" of the Balfour Declaration mournfully predicted that 25 percent of East European Jewry would perish as a result of Nazi brutality and atrocities. Those Jews who survived the war would "float" between heaven and hell and as many as four million would be homeless. Much of the world would experience a period of great economic dislocation after the war, and Weizmann believed that the United States and other nations would be unable to absorb many of the Jewish survivors. Palestine was the only practical solution to this dilemma and he argued that "the very weight of the tragedy and the lack of a rational solution except through Palestine, will . . . focus and force the attention of the world to this solution." The Biltmore audience enthusiastically responded to Weizmann's declaration: "I would like to relieve the non-Jewish world of the trouble of settling our problems. We can do it ourselves. We can do it ourselves, and with God's help, we shall do it ourselves."[85]

David Ben-Gurion, who was still battling Weizmann for control of the Zionist movement, agreed with his competitor's assessment of the Jewish situation. He told the Biltmore delegates that Jewish suffering in World War II was greater than it had been in World War I and that the condition of European Jewry after Hitler's defeat would be much worse than it had been in 1919. Zionists, Ben-Gurion proclaimed, demand that the Allies unequivocally reaffirm the Balfour Declaration and agree to the postwar reestablishment of a Jewish commonwealth in Palestine. Until the commonwealth could be established, Ben-Gurion continued, the Jewish Agency should be given sole responsibility for the colonization and immigration policies of Palestine.[86]

American Zionists, like Ben-Gurion, also emphasized the need to create a Jewish homeland in order to solve an anticipated postwar refugee problem. According to Rabbi Abba Hillel Silver, most Americans understood that large numbers of Jewish refugees would have to go to Palestine after the war, but, he lamented, most of these people were also unsympathetic to the goals of political Zionism. They favored massive Jewish immigration to Palestine, but could not comprehend why it was necessary for the Zionists to create a Jewish state. They failed to understand that political Zionism was the only possible solution to the postwar Jewish refugees' plight. It was impossible to argue for Jewish immigration to Palestine on "philanthropic" grounds. The Holy Land had already absorbed a huge number of refugees, and the British could legitimately claim that Palestine had done its part in the humanitarian solution of European Jewish homelessness. Silver explained: "Unless we have our political claim to Palestine, our historic claim to Palestine, . . . internationally reaffirmed, that Jews have a right to Palestine in the same self sense as Englishmen have a right to England, then we won't have a leg to stand on at the Peace Conference after the war." Only the creation of a Jewish state in Palestine would insure the right of all Jews to emigrate to that land. The American public, Silver concluded, had to be taught that the "distinction between political Zionist and philanthropic, humanitarian action for Jews in Palestine is an unreal, a spurious and a dangerous distinction."[87]

Palestine's importance to the solution of a postwar refugee problem, as outlined by Ben-Gurion and Silver, became the primary basis for pro-Zionist agitation and diplomacy during the years following the Biltmore Conference. While many

American Jews would be drawn to Zionism because of their concern about postwar Jewish refugees, the delegates at the Biltmore Hotel knew that their own support of Jewish statehood rested on other rationales. Most of them had been Zionists long before Hitler came to power in Germany, and their commitment to Jewish nationalism went beyond any desire to solve an immediate Jewish refugee crisis. They were fully convinced that Zionism would solve, once and for all times, the 2,000-year-old problem of anti-Semitism.

David Ben-Gurion addressed this issue when he warned the Biltmore assembly to "beware of the dangerous illusion that the destruction of Hitlerism alone will free the world from all ills and the Jewish people from its misery." There was something fundamentally wrong with a world that consistently singled Jews out for extreme punishment and persecution. The task of Zionism was to remake Jewish history by reestablishing a political entity that would end the long nightmare of Jewish homelessness. In the style of a biblical prophet, Ben-Gurion foresaw that "a Jewish Palestine will arise. It will redeem forever our sufferings and do justice to our national genius. It will be the pride of every Jew in the diaspora and command the respect of every people on earth."[88]

According to Robert Szold, Zionists were trying to do more than create a refugee haven or a "cultural outpost"; they were struggling to change the fate of all the Jewish people. Leon Gellman of Mizrachi supported Szold's position and added that "Palestine is not just a place to send refugees." Louis Segal, a member of Poale Zion, a socialist and secular Zionist organization, essentially agreed with the ultra-religious Gellman and the capitalist Szold, asserting: "If Zionism can only answer the momentary tragedy that happens to a few Jewish people, then it's of no importance. It must give an answer to the national folk beliefs and folk traditions." Nahum Goldmann joined his colleagues in distinguishing between Zionist and non-Zionist supporters of Jewish immigration to Palestine. The Biltmore audience responded loudly and proudly as Goldmann defined a non-Zionist as a Jew who wants to develop Palestine for those who "need" it. However, a Zionist, according to Goldmann, wanted to settle Palestine for the "Jewish people" of which he was a "living part."[89]

Of all the Zionists at the Biltmore, Abba Hillel Silver most clearly articulated the belief that Jewish statehood was not merely a practical solution to the Nazi persecution of European Jewry. For Silver, like many Jews, Jewish history for two thousand years seemed to be one long chain of persecution and tragedy. Silver could see nothing unique about the experience of Jews in Nazi-occupied territories. Their plight was no different than that of their ancestors who had endured forced conversions, expulsions, inquisitions, and pogroms. Anti-Semitism predated Hitler and the defeat of the Nazis would not be the final cure to this affliction. "We Jews," Silver said, "stand to come out of the war, even after an Allied victory, defeated, unrequited and betrayed." An American and British victory would do nothing to solve the cause of all Jewish suffering—national homelessness. As a Zionist, Silver believed that the entire course of Jewish history could be changed by the bold act of reestablishing the Jewish state destroyed two millennia before by the Roman Empire. The American people, he said, had to understand:

> what has been the basic fact in Jewish tragedy right through the ages, the fact of our national homelessness, of our abnormal political status in the world, and that now, after a second World War, in which Jews by the millions are already casualties . . . in a war in which Jews suffer doubly and trebly in relation to every other people, that . . . the ultimate solution of the Jewish problem must finally be sounded, and the ultimate solution is the establishment of a Jewish Nation in Palestine.[90]

Following Silver's address, the conference overwhelmingly voted to ratify a declaration making the creation of a Jewish commonwealth the immediate and major goal of the American Zionist movement. The conference called on Great Britain to give the Jewish Agency full control of Palestine's immigration and colonization policies.

Zionists articulated two sets of ideas to justify and explain this historic act. In the propaganda they prepared for Christian consumption, Zionists generally argued that only a Palestinian Jewish nation could solve the postwar refugee problem. However, the radical Zionist promise to solve the "Jewish problem" and to put an end to Jewish persecution was especially effective in winning the support of the American Jewish masses who were grieving for their suffering European brethren. As American Jews became more aware of the magnitude of Nazi murder and destruction, the Zionist plan to revolutionize Jewish existence became almost irresistibly attractive.

HIDDEN SCHISMS: THE TRUE MEANING OF BILTMORE

The Biltmore platform's endorsement of a radical Zionist solution to the Jewish problem was carefully and soberly worded. The conference deliberately decided to use the term "commonwealth" instead of state, although many Zionists at the hotel used the two words interchangeably in their addresses. This strategy was partially dictated by a desire not to alienate non-Zionist organizations like the American Jewish Committee, which had traditionally supported the settlement of Palestine while opposing the concepts of Jewish nationality and statehood.[91] Zionist leaders also seized on the ambiguous term "commonwealth" as a tool to link together the many organizations that met at the Biltmore. The Biltmore Conference, organized by the AECZA to celebrate Jewish nationalist unity, in fact revealed just how different Zionist dreams could be. The various organizations that made up the Jewish nationalist community in the United States were committed to radically different visions of a reestablished Jewish homeland.

Even the two most prestigious foreign dignitaries at Biltmore found it difficult to reach common ground. Chaim Weizmann and David Ben-Gurion had both been attracted to the Peel Commission partition plan of 1937, but by 1942 issues of both policy and style divided the leaders. Weizmann, by now the elder statesman of the Zionist movement, remembered the successful negotiations of 1917, which had led to Britain's endorsement of Zionism in the famous Balfour Declaration. In May 1942, his faith in Britain's moral superiority and tradition of tolerance, for which his son Michael, an RAF pilot, had died three months earlier, remained strong.[92] Even after three years of harsh British immigration policies, Weizmann could still express optimism about soon-to-be-improved relations with the Colonial Office. Weizmann called the MacDonald White Paper an aberration of traditional British goodwill, which would soon pass.[93] When he uttered the slogan "Jewish commonwealth," he looked forward to some distant date when Jews would have political sovereignty in at least some part of Palestine, which might even be linked constitutionally to the British Commonwealth.

Ben-Gurion's faith in British virtue was much weaker than Weizmann's. The Palestinian leader told his American audience that British colonial administrators had been trained to deal with "primitive peoples," not the progressive Jewish community they encountered in the Holy Land. Naturally, the officials felt more at ease with Palestine's Arabs, "where they could indulge their colonial habits of maining [sic] the status quo." Ben-Gurion found Weizmann's approach to London too passive and understanding, and he advocated a Zionist policy that recognized that Jewish and British interests were not necessarily identical. He instructed the delegates that "reviewing the history of the past twenty years, and taking into account the needs facing us in the future after the war, our first conclusion is that the Mandate must be entrusted to the Jewish people themselves." When Ben-Gurion called for the establishment of a Jewish commonwealth, he visualized an independent Palestinian state that Zionists could create quickly if they launched a powerful political offensive to win support in the free countries of the West.[94]

Several Zionist delegates at Biltmore even found themselves in the position of having to oppose the creation of a Jewish commonwealth in Palestine. B. C. Sherman confessed in Yiddish: "I know I will not get your approbation if I tell you that I disagree with Mr. Ben-Gurion, that I don't think we can make a Jewish world in Palestine, . . . in spite of the unity that Professor Weizmann spoke of last night."[95] Sherman and other members of the left-wing faction of Poale Zion were particularly committed to the socialist ideals of international brotherhood and cooperation, and they feared that the establishment of an autonomous Jewish political entity in Palestine was both impractical and dangerous because it ignored the Arab question. Sherman warned that "even in liberal movements there is less understanding and less sympathy for us than there was years ago." The creation of a Jewish commonwealth would not meet with Arab support, and Zionist campaigns for its creation would win no new friends in the democratic world. He appealed to Zionist leaders to try and work with the Arab working class in Palestine, whose interests coincided with those of the majority of the Yishuv.[96] Moshe Furmansky reinforced Sherman's position and advocated that the Zionists join with Arabs in order to create a binational state in Palestine.[97]

In a binational state political power would be shared by Jews and Arabs. Proponents of this strategy acknowledged that the Jewish claim to Palestine did not supersede that of the country's Moslem and Christian populations. While only a minority of Palestinian Jewry supported binationalism, several outstanding celebrities championed it, among them Martin Buber, the prominent German-Jewish philosopher; Judah Magnes, the American-born rabbi and chancellor of Hebrew University; and Henrietta Szold, the founder of Hadassah and the director of the Youth Aliyah program of the thirties.[98]

Although the concept of binationalism had few supporters at Biltmore, several delegates worried about the consequences of Jewish statehood for Palestine's Arab population. Hayim Greenberg, an influential socialist Zionist journalist and thinker, argued that "no one can say that there isn't an Arab-Jewish problem in the world." He frankly admitted that there had been times when he had believed that "it would be better to enter upon great compromises, and to reserve to ourselves the hope of expansion later." After serious thought, Greenberg continued, he decided that "there is no possibility in our time that we will be able to agree with Arab factions in Palestine." Since in his view no Arab leader was willing to negotiate with moderate Zionists, Greenberg concluded that any Jewish attempt to compromise would be suicidal.[99]

Louis Segal of Poale Zion had even less patience for binationalists than his fellow socialist Greenberg. Asserting that there was too much concentration on the Arab problem, he declared: "Jews want to come to Palestine to establish a Jewish Homeland. If the Arabs understand that, then there will be peace; if they should refuse to understand it then we cannot make peace with them. That is all."[100]

Hadassah delegates, perhaps influenced by the position of their "patron saint" Henrietta Szold, were less willing than Seigal to condemn the binationalists. Rose Jacobs reminded Zionists that there would be grave consequences if no solution to the Arab-Jewish problem could be found. She could offer no formulas for peace except "that of recommending investigation and inquiry that may ultimately lead to action based on judgement."[101]

Bernard Rosenblatt, a retired New York State judge who had been active in Zionist affairs for almost thirty years, worried about the fate of Palestine's Arab majority. He warned the Biltmore audience that demanding the immediate creation of a Jewish state on both sides of the Jordan River would "run counter to all precedents based upon the liberal philosophy of democracy, with its implicit faith in 'the rights' of the majority of a population." While he supported the creation of a Jewish commonwealth, Rosenblatt's blueprint for the future Jewish homeland radically differed from those of either Ben-Gurion or Weizmann. For almost a decade Rosenblatt had been advocating the creation of a federated Palestine, which would consist of a Jewish commonwealth and an Arab sister state. The federated Arab and Jewish entities would each exercise control over immigration to their respective sectors. He believed that his solution to the problem of conflicting Arab and Jewish claims to Palestine was based on the American precedent of federalism, which had brought peace and justice to "peoples" of diverse "race" and "cultures."[102]

While Rosenblatt and some members of Hadassah might be willing to accept a Jewish commonwealth in only part of Palestine, others at the Biltmore Conference were appalled by such a possibility. The representatives of Mizrachi, the organization of Orthodox religious Zionists, adamantly objected to any compromise plan that involved making concessions to Palestinian Arabs. Leon Gellman of Mizrachi warned that his organization would tolerate "no deviation from the original plans for Palestine, even in the name of Peace." He urged the Biltmore delegates publicly to declare that the one and only objective of their movement was the establishment of a "Jewish world" in "all" of Palestine.[103] Another Mizrachi leader angrily reminded the delegates that all of Palestine belonged to the Jewish people by "tradition" and by "right."[104] Rabbi Wolf Gold, a representative of Mizrachi's international leadership, pledged that his organization would never accept the partition of Palestine.[105]

Many members of the Zionist Organization of America also continued to oppose the principle of partition. They all remembered the long conflict over the Peel Commission's partition proposal. Some, including Stephen Wise, now supported the goal of Jewish statehood, but the New York rabbi pointedly remarked that Jews could not be diverted away from the "high purpose of building a national home for themselves and their children within the borders of undivided and unpartitioned Palestine."[106] Robert Szold, another veteran of the anti-partition struggle of the late thirties, expressed his support for the Biltmore resolution, but he argued against any concessions by Zionist leaders that would whittle down Jewish rights in Palestine. Plans for binationalism, federalism, and partition were impractical and would condemn Jews to a permanent minority status in Palestine.[107] Dr. Israel Goldstein, chairman of the American branch of the Jewish National Fund and another old opponent of partition, stated that the Jewish acquisition of the maximum amount of land possible in Palestine was a "non-debatable" issue within the Zionist movement.[108]

By endorsing the establishment of a Palestinian Jewish commonwealth, the Biltmore delegates skillfully avoided the question of exactly how much of Palestine's territory Jews would control. While most American Zionists were willing to work for the creation of some politically autonomous Jewish entity, no consensus existed on the vital issue of boundaries. Any Jewish nationalist attempting to draw the future Jewish state's borders would have to confront two contradictory positions within the American Zionist body politic. One powerful faction, consisting of the Mizrachi and a sizable number of ZOA members, refused to accept any territorial concessions. For them, religion and tradition dictated that all of Palestine by right belonged to the Jews and that any territorial concession to the Arabs would be comparable to Esau's sale of his birthright. On the other side of the spectrum, several moderate and left-wing Zionists saw some legitimacy in the Arab's claim to Palestine. In return for peace with the Arabs, these Zionists were willing to create their Jewish state in only part of Palestine. Any Zionist attempt to establish Jewish sovereignty over the entire Holy Land, they feared, would ignite a long, bloody, and perhaps suicidal conflict with the more numerous non-Jewish population of the area. United Zionist action in 1942 clearly required that nothing be done that would bring these mutually contradictory positions to the surface and into conflict.[109]

ON THE EVE OF TRAGEDY

Fortunately for American Zionists, the radical and idealistic spirit eloquently expressed at the Biltmore Hotel survived the conference's closing. Five months after the Extraordinary Conference, the annual convention of the Zionist Organization of America heard Morris Rothenberg say that "either Zionism will now offer a comprehensive solution for the problem of Jewish misery and Jewish homelessness, or it will disappear as an answer to the Jewish question. It will take its place as a brave, interesting, but abortive attempt to solve the Jewish problem."[110] Robert Szold, who had often disagreed with Rothenberg in the past, now sided with him, saying, "Zionists feel that now there must be a complete, clear, and unequivocal and permanent solution."[111]

During the months that followed American Jewish espousal of Jewish political sovereignty, Zionist spokesmen continued to formulate arguments designed to attract broad public support in the United States. As they had done at Biltmore, Zionists continued to predict that a major Jewish refugee problem would plague the postwar world and that a Jewish state in Palestine was the only practical solution to this anticipated crisis.[112] Jewish nationalist leaders also understood that they had to link Zionist goals to the postwar interests and ideals of the Allied powers.[113] During World War I, Zionists and other ethnic nationalist groups used Woodrow Wilson's support of self-determination to legitimate their national demands.

Robert Szold believed that the Zionist rhetoric of World War I could not be used in the struggle against Hitler. He suggested that "postwar solutions may not be again based primarily in territorial lines with emphasis on self-determination of nationalities." Instead, the Allied powers would be most concerned with the social and economic measures necessary to facilitate the postwar reconstruction of the world. Szold asked Zionist spokesmen to emphasize the vital role Jews could play in the development of Middle Eastern resources so that Jewish nationalism would be in accord with progressive thought.[114]

The practical work necessary to achieve the goal of Jewish autonomy also continued after the closing of the Biltmore Conference. Emanuel Neumann in late 1942 observed that the United States government was becoming more involved in Middle Eastern affairs, and he remembered that many Zionists had expected Washington to automatically assume a pro-Zionist stance because they reasoned that it was "our America." Unfortunately, the American adoption of Zionism could not be accomplished so easily because, as Neumann said, "there are people in official and unofficial life who are constantly watching out, seeking the weakest spots in our armor, looking for signs of disunity, trying to discover Jewish groups who are not Zionists or who may be prepared to fight Zionism." Politics in the United States, according to Neumann, was also a battle between minorities. In wartime America, there were pro-Zionist and anti-Zionist minorities, while the majority of the public was uninformed and without an opinion. If Zionists were to win their struggle for American support they would have to proceed methodically with a powerful, well-organized political and propaganda campaign. Zionists, Neumann was pleased to announce, had already taken the first step in the campaign at the Biltmore, where there had been "substantial progress" in the development of a common Zionist ideology. Consensus among American Zionists was a precondition for the success of Neumann's second objective, the uniting of American Jews around a pro-Zionist platform. Zionist leaders, Neumann reported, had already begun preliminary discussions with non-Zionist American Jewish organizations. A staunchly pro-Zionist American Jewish community, Neumann confidently predicted, would facilitate winning support from American public and political figures and from important government agencies.[115] Neumann's formula for Zionist victory was endorsed by Chaim Weizmann who told American Jewish nationalists: "Your task is to close the ranks of American Zionism, to win the support of American Jewry and to enlighten American public opinion on the justice and high moral significance of our social cause."[116]

By the end of 1942, Zionist organizations were giving special priority to the task of winning broad American support. The Zionist Organization of America convention in October devoted an entire Thursday afternoon session to a symposium on public relations programs that could be carried out by local ZOA branches. Delegates listened closely as the rabbi of a Pottsville, Pennsylvania, congregation explained how his flock had decided to enroll en masse as ZOA members. The new Zionist recruits had also amended the constitution of their congregation and now required every new member of the synagogue to also enlist in the ZOA.[117]

Zionists hoped that the ideological and propaganda weapons they were refining would allow them to "conquer" the American Jewish community. Hitler's persecution of European Jewry facilitated the task of nationalizing American Jewry, who, as Morris Rothenberg observed, believed that they had a responsibility and an opportunity to "serve" their "bruised" and "lacerated" European cousins.[118] Zionism offered a radical solution to the Jewish problem. A Jewish commonwealth in Palestine would provide postwar refugees with a home, and it would also revolutionize Jewish existence. If Zionists were successful, they would be able to guarantee that there would never again be another Jewish problem in Europe. A Jewish state would permanently solve the crisis of anti-Semitism, which Zionists believed was caused by Jewish homelessness. No other Jewish group in the United States could match the scope and promise of the proposed Zionist solution to the Jewish problem. ZOA President Levinthal insightfully remarked: "every Jew in the country must rally to the support of our cause, and I believe the Jews who are not ashamed of their Jewish identity and who have faith in the Jewish future will come to our support because there is no other alternative."[119]

IV

AMERICAN ZIONISM
AND THE HOLOCAUST

THINKING ABOUT THE UNTHINKABLE

Adolf Hitler's plan to exterminate European Jewry remained a secret until the summer of 1942. Even before the devastating news of Nazi mass murder reached the United States, American Jewish and Zionist leaders knew that their brethren in Hitler's lands were being subjected to terrible atrocities. At the Biltmore Conference of May 1942, Chaim Weizmann reported that the suffering of European Jewry was different in "quality" and "quantity" from that of the rest of the world. Hitler had declared war against the Jews in 1933, and since then Nazi pogroms, atrocities, and ghetto conditions were exacting a heavy toll. Weizmann concluded that "a cold, statistical calculation reveals the cruel fact that probably about 25 per cent of the Jews of Eastern and Southeastern Europe, will be, to use the modern word, 'liquidated.'"[1]

Nahum Goldmann, a brilliant political analyst, almost guessed what the Nazis' true intentions were in the spring of 1942. Goldmann urged the delegates at the Biltmore Hotel not to ignore Weizmann's grim prophesy. Nobody could know what European Jewry's final fate would be because

> Who can foretell what the Nazi regime, once brought into the position of the surrounded killer, will do in the last moment before it goes down to shame? Do to Europe or the Jews under its command in the last moment before the downfall? But even as it is today, sometimes news reaches us, a glimpse of the situation is given, and every time it is a new horror and a new shock. One reports 800 killed a day in the Warsaw ghetto. I think it is exaggerated, because, if it

would be true, then in the course of two years the total of a half million Jews in the Warsaw ghettos may be wiped out. Now you don't have to be a great mathematician to figure out what will be the result of such a process, if it goes another year, two years, three years.

In spite of his fears, Goldmann didn't propose any program to come to the immediate aid of those threatened with annihilation. Instead, he called for the establishment of a Jewish commonwealth, and he urged Zionists to prepare "to enlarge the spheres of Jewish life" in postwar Europe. He specifically demanded new efforts to reach the Jews of the Soviet Union, whose removal from the Zionist world he called the most harmful "blow" directed against the Jewish people since the end of the First World War.[2]

By the summer of 1942, numerous unconfirmed reports of large-scale Nazi murder operations were circulating within the American Jewish community. On August 1, 1942, Dr. Gerhart Riegner, a German Jewish emigré and director of the Geneva office of the World Jewish Congress, received some startling information. Riegner, through a German source, learned that the Nazis were carrying out a plan to murder all the Jews under their control. According to Riegner's source, Nazi extermination centers would gas to death Jews from all German-occupied territories. Riegner asked that the American legation in Switzerland inform Stephen Wise about the Nazi murder plan. The legation sent a message off to Washington, but State Department bureaucrats decided not to forward Riegner's information to Wise. The American officials did not believe the seemingly fantastic information coming out of Switzerland.

Fortunately, Riegner had also sent his report, through British diplomatic sources, to World Jewish Congress leaders in London, who then contacted Stephen Wise in New York City. Wise shortly decided to request aid from the Roosevelt administration, and he contacted Undersecretary of State Sumner Welles, a diplomat who was sympathetic to the plight of European Jewish refugees. In view of the unbelievable nature of Riegner's report, Welles asked Wise to wait for State Department confirmation before making news of the extermination public. Wise felt that he had no choice but to comply. Otherwise, he would alienate the State Department, the branch of the government to which he would have to look for help. Unfortunately, more than three months would pass before Wise could inform the American public about the Holocaust.[3]

While Wise honored his promise not to publicize the report, he did not keep the information secret from other Jewish and Zionist leaders. A few prominent Zionists also had their own European sources who reported similarly terrible news.[4] In mid-October 1942, Wise and several other Zionist leaders who were aware of the ongoing extermination of European Jewry met at the forty-fifth Annual Convention of the Zionist Organization of America.

When Wise first addressed the ZOA audience he refrained from any mention of the terrible fate of European Jewry.[5] He did speak of the European situation in a second speech at the end of the Zionist conclave. The Nazis, Wise declared, had decimated European Jewry, but they had not broken their "unconquerable" spirit. Jewry would not be "liquidated" nor "destroyed." Wise promised the Jews in the German-occupied territories: "we will stand with you and by you and for you until you either go back to your homes in Europe, or forward to Eretz Israel."[6]

Some Zionists at the 1942 meeting were more explicit than Wise. In the midst of a lengthy analysis of Zionist political aims, Nahum Goldmann casually remarked that Zionists did not have a realistic sense of what the position of European Jewry would be after the war. It would be a blessing, he said, if just half the Jews of occupied Europe survived the war. Goldmann continued: "You know what is going on with the deportations. Deportations mean deportation to certain death, and the Hitler regime has in the last months definely [sic] from a period of indirect starvation, discrimination and persecution and the extermination of the Jews, to a period of direct extermination by mass murder and mass slaughter." [7] Judge Morris Rothenberg, a former president of the ZOA, referred to districts in Eastern Poland where Jews from all of Poland were brought to be shot. Rothenberg lamented that mankind had not experienced anything like the "systematic butchery" of innocent civilians that was taking place in Nazi-occupied Europe. He announced that the reported Nazi deportations of Jews to unknown places were, in fact, "part of the ruthless policy to exterminate the Jewish people and to reduce other populations to a state of helpless vassalage."[8]

The almost nine hundred ZOA delegates attending the conference did not seem to grasp the significance of Goldmann's and Rothenberg's comments. Their descriptions of the German extermination policy were buried in the dozens of long and often tedious addresses that characterized most ZOA conferences.[9] Because Rothenberg and Goldmann delivered their speeches without any fanfare, the delegates should be forgiven for not recognizing the importance of their messages.

Rothenberg and Goldmann did not urge American Zionists to take any extraordinary steps to save their European brethren. In fact, all of the small group of leaders privy to Wise's information initially responded to news of Hitler's extermination program by assuming that the Jewish people would somehow survive what seemed to be just the latest in a long chain of tragedies that marked the two thousand years of Jewish exile from their national home. Selig Brodetsky's message to the conference was typical: "Hitler has just reaffirmed his resolve [to] exterminate [the] Jewish people, but in spite of mass murders . . . practiced on our helpless brethren throughout occupied Europe, he will fail as many tyrants before him have failed."[10] With an almost mystical belief in Jewry's ability to persevere, Zionist leaders dedicated themselves to insuring that nazism would be the last crisis the Jewish people would have to endure. Accordingly, their commitment to the Biltmore formula of Jewish statehood increased for, as Louis Lipsky proclaimed, "there must be an end of the homelessness of the Jewish people," the root of all their suffering.[11]

Nahum Goldmann concurred with Lipsky's analysis and lamented: "Our generation is in the tragic position that one-half of the generation is being slaughtered before our eyes, and the other half has to sit down and cannot prevent this catastrophe." Goldmann, however, urged his audience not to despair, but instead to direct their energies to the creation of a Jewish state that would make future tragedies impossible.[12]

Goldmann's call to action, like his warning about Nazi mass murders, did not lead to any spontaneous demonstrations of support by the ZOA delegates, probably because they and the entire American Zionist movement were already following the course set at the Biltmore Conference. Even as Stephen Wise waited for the State Department to corroborate Gerhart Riegner's information about Nazi genocide, he and other American Zionists continued to plan for the opening of a grand and extraordinary meeting of all American Jewish leaders who, they hoped, would give the community's blessing to Jewish statehood.

Leon Feuer, a disciple of Rabbi Abba Hillel Silver, clearly enunciated the Zionist position as it stood by early November 1942 in his monograph, *Why a Jewish State*. The survival of a large number of European Jews was fundamental to Feuer's case for Jewish statehood. Repeating an argument that Zionists had developed at the Biltmore Conference of May 1942, Feuer predicted that after the war, millions of Jewish refugees would find it impossible to return to normal lives in their European homes.[13]

German occupation authorities, according to Feuer, were subjecting European Christians to massive doses of anti-Semitic propaganda, and Jew hatred would continue to be a problem for some time after the Nazi defeat. Unless a solution to the Jewish problem was found, European anti-Semitism would again endanger the world. Hitler had used anti-Semitism as a tool to achieve power in Germany. Other demagogues and tyrants could use the same tool after the war to achieve their own ends, thereby jeopardizing world peace and stability.[14]

Palestine, Feuer argued, could solve both the long-term and immediate problems of Jewish homelessness. A Jewish state would give dignity and power to a people who had been subject to persecution and humiliation for centuries. It would also provide a home to the millions of stateless refugees expected to survive the war. No other country outside of Europe, he forecast, would be willing to open its gates to the millions of impoverished and demoralized Jews now caught in Hitler's grasp. After the war, Feuer explained, "these countries will have their own heavy burdens of readjustment." Only the Jews of Palestine were anxious to welcome their downtrodden brethren.[15]

Feuer, like most Jewish nationalists, believed that Zionists would have their last chance to win international support for Jewish statehood at a great postwar peace conference. If they failed to take advantage of this great opportunity, he soberly warned, "it may never again present itself."[16]

Shortly after the publication of Feuer's pamphlet, Stephen Wise received a telegram from Undersecretary of State Welles asking him to come to the State Department. As he later remembered, a deeply troubled Welles told him on November 24, 1942, "'I have in my hands documents which have come to me from our legation in Berne. I regret to tell you, Dr. Wise, that these confirm and justify your deepest fears.'"[17]

Rabbi Wise immediately called a press conference and released the contents of Riegner's message. He also announced that the Nazis had already exterminated two million Jews. The *New York Times* on November 25, 1942, saw fit to carry news of the murders on page ten. The *Times* informed its readers of the existence of special extermination camps and reported that the State Department confirmed the accuracy of Wise's statements.[18]

The Wise announcement was electrifying. The rabbi and other Jewish leaders declared a day of fast and mourning for the dead and dying Jews of Europe.[19] The Jewish Labor Committee, a non-Zionist left-wing labor organization, called for a ten-minute work stoppage on the day of mourning, December 2, 1942. The International Ladies Garment Workers Union and the Amalgamated Clothing Workers of America agreed to participate in the work stoppage, while Yeshiva University in New York agreed to cancel all classes.[20]

A week later, at the initiative of Stephen Wise, a delegation of American Jewish leaders met with President Roosevelt. The President offered his condolences and sympathy, but he suggested no plan for the immediate salvation of European Jewry.[21]

By this time it was apparent to American Jewish leaders that the immediate fate of European Jews could be determined only by the Germans who sought to destroy them or the Allies who might be able to rescue them. Roosevelt and Churchill had the resources and tools necessary to threaten Nazi leaders and the German people with retribution if they continued to slaughter the Jews. Allied pressure could be exerted on Hungary and other satellite states that had not yet agreed to turn their Jewish populations over to the Gestapo. The State Department and Foreign Ministry could negotiate with Turkey, Spain, Switzerland, Sweden, and other neutral states that bordered the Reich and that could offer haven to those Jews who could escape from German-occupied territory. Only the American and British armies and air forces could launch military rescue operations. Thus,

American Jewish leaders could most effectively contribute to the salvation of their European brethren by making use of their contacts with high government officials and by initiating a national publicity campaign to focus public pressure on the Roosevelt administration and Congress to act on the behalf of European Jewry.

Shortly before the Jewish delegation met with Roosevelt, Peter Bergson, the leader of the Committee for a Jewish Army (CJA), wrote to Judge Louis Leninthal, the newly elected president of the Zionist Organization of America. The CJA was a small organization formed by a group of Palestinians sent to the United States by the Irgun, a right-wing Jewish underground group in Palestine. Prior to Wise's press conference, the CJA had been building American support for the creation of a Jewish Army to fight with the Allies against the Axis Powers. After Wise's announcement, the Bergson group began to devote most of its attention to publicizing the plight of European Jewry by attempting to put pressure on the Roosevelt administration to act. Bergson, in his letter to Levinthal, offered to form an alliance with the ZOA to press for rescue action.[22]

Levinthal refused to join hands with Bergson, but representatives of major Jewish organizations, including prominent Zionists, did respond to the situation by forming the Joint Emergency Committee on European Jewish Affairs, a body that excluded the Bergson group. The committee existed for only a few months, but it did engage in activities aimed at influencing the American government to rescue European Jewry. American Zionists were in the forefront of these efforts, which included the lobbying of representatives in Congress in an unsuccessful bid to convince the legislature to take a stand on rescue. The emergency committee also desperately tried to influence the State Department to develop rescue programs. Primarily, the committee concerned itself with sponsoring mass meetings throughout the nation calling for government action on rescue.[23]

The most important of the American Jewish mass meetings was the "Stop Hitler Now" rally organized by the American Jewish Congress with the cooperation of the American Federation of Labor and the Congress of Industrial Organizations. On March 1, 1943, over 21,000 people jammed into New York's Madison Square Garden as an expression of support for the millions of European Jews threatened with extinction. Jewish leaders presented an eleven-point rescue program to the rally requesting the Allied powers to:

1. Negotiate with Germany and her satellites through neutral states in order to win freedom of emigration for Jews under Hitler's control.
2. Open sanctuaries and havens in Allied and neutral countries for any Jews who might be released by the Axis.
3. Liberalize American immigration practices, so that existing American quotas would be completely filled.[24]
4. Open England's door to as many Jewish refugees as would not constitute a danger to her national security.

    5. Urge Latin American nations to modify their restrictive immigration policies.

    6. Open the doors of Palestine to Jewish immigration thereby ending the White Paper limitations.

    7. Guarantee financial assistance to neutral countries that provide sanctuary for refugees, and promise to provide the refugees with a permanent haven as soon as possible.

    8. Devise a system to provide food to starving Jews under Nazi control.

    9. Establish an intergovernmental agency to implement a rescue program.

    10. Provide financial guarantees for the execution of the rescue program outlined.

    11. Establish a war crimes commission that would outline the procedure by which Nazi war criminals would be brought to justice.[25]

The rally's eleven-point plan was a workable and comprehensive strategy for rescue. In December 1942, the editors of the *New York Times* had sadly noted that the most tragic aspect of Hitler's extermination of European Jewry was "the world's helplessness to stop the horror while the war is going on." After the "Stop Hitler Now" rally, the editors were more optimistic about the Allies' ability to resist Hitler's slaughter and warned that "the United Nations governments have no right to spare any efforts that will save lives, even though dealings with the German and German-controlled states may be necessary."[26] Anne O'Hare McCormick, in her widely read *Times* column "Abroad," wrote that the "Christian world's" failure to support the rescue proposal would be "an act of submission to Hitler."[27]

In succeeding years, various private and governmental agencies would refine and compile plans on how these specific suggestions could be put into effect. Point #9, calling for the establishment of a rescue agency, was clearly the most important rescue proposal. The Nazi regime had made the destruction of European Jewry a war aim and had established a sophisticated bureaucracy to coordinate the resources and "skills" necessary to accomplish it. Clearly, only a correspondingly comprehensive effort on the part of the American government held out the hope of halting, or at least impeding, the destruction process. A governmental rescue agency would be able to coordinate the military, diplomatic, and financial resources needed to resist Hitler's "war against the Jews." In fact, it is difficult to justify Franklin Roosevelt's failure to establish such a commission as soon as news of the Holocaust was released.[28]

The other ten proposals also reflected the shrewd perceptivity of American Jewish leaders. Even in March 1943, it was apparent that the major obstacle to rescue was the unwillingness of outside countries to accept Jews. Several of the eleven proposals (numbers 2–7) dealt with that difficult problem. While Germany might not have been willing to negotiate the release of Jews under its control, by 1943 it was clear that some German satellite states, including Bulgaria and Romania, were searching for ways to ingratiate themselves with the Allies who seemed to be on their way to victory over the Third Reich. In order to carry out these delicate negotiations, an Allied rescue agency that could coordinate the activities of the State and Treasury Departments was clearly essential.[29]

American Zionists, particularly Stephen Wise, played important roles in the organization of the "Stop Hitler Now" rally, and they were in the forefront of all of the Joint Emergency Committee's actions. Their attempts to induce the United States government to rescue European Jewry, however, did not divert their attention away from the goal of Jewish statehood. In fact, Zionists generally and understandably responded to confirmed news of the ongoing European tragedy with an increased commitment to their original program. They had, after all, based their demand for Jewish statehood on the belief that the restoration of a Palestinian homeland would once and for all solve the problem of anti-Semitism and Jewish persecution. Only through Zionist work, Chaim Weizmann wrote in December 1942, "can we find consolation – that perhaps a better day will come for those who will survive this holocaust."[30] *Youth and Nation*, the journal of the Hashomer Hatzair, a left-wing Zionist group, similarly asked its readers to devote themselves to the establishment of a "free Jewish nation" that would spare future generations of Jews from the recurrence of such a tragedy,[31] while Rabbi Abba Hillel Silver called for the settlement of one dunam [about a quarter acre] of Palestine's land for every murdered Jew.[32]

This is not to say that Zionist leaders were not also deeply concerned with steps directed at immediate rescue. In early December 1942, Zionist leaders, including Rose Halprin, Tamar de Sola Pool, Meyer Weisgal, and Hayim Greenberg, met to discuss the rescue situation. Most of them agreed that it was of utmost importance to concentrate on steps that might halt the Nazi mass murder of European Jewry. Zionist leaders believed that they should wait until the American public was firmly committed to rescuing European Jewry before they suggested Jewish statehood as the ultimate remedy to Jewish persecution.[33]

Several months after the December meeting, Hayim Greenberg, a leader of the Poale Zion in the United States, published in the Yiddish press a blistering attack on the American Jewish organizations for failing to concentrate their resources on an aggressive campaign to force the U.S. government to attempt rescue actions. Greenberg accused American Jews of behaving in a morally bankrupt fashion, and he marveled at the lack of a frenzied response on the part of a people who had learned that millions of their brethren were being brutally eliminated.[34]

Greenberg's case was overstated. American Jews and Zionists were working for rescue, though not at the pace Greenberg would have preferred. They had met with President Roosevelt and other members of the administration, circulated petitions demanding that the Allies take steps to rescue European Jewry, held news conferences, and released press statements. The March 1 "Stop Hitler Now" rally was a huge success and did produce a valuable list of rescue proposals. The left-wing Zionist journal, *Youth and Nation*, hoped that the rally and other forms of American Jewish pressure would force the United States to abandon its policy of inaction and that the Roosevelt administration would become a leading agent in the rescue of European Jewry.[35]

THE BERMUDA CONFERENCE

American and British Jewish pressure did, in fact, force a response from the Allied governments. In early March 1943, Washington and London announced that they would hold a conference to develop plans to aid European Jewry. British and American officials originally planned to have the rescue conference in Ottawa, Canada, but they later decided to switch the location to Bermuda because reporters and the representatives of Jewish organizations would be less likely to intrude on the privacy of the conferees.[36]

The Bermuda Conference opened on April 19, 1943. On that same day, Jewish resistance fighters in the Warsaw Ghetto rose up against their Nazi oppressors. While the Warsaw Ghetto fighters armed with pistols and Molotov cocktails battled against German SS troops, British and American representatives at Bermuda deliberated about the fate of European Jewry. Harold Willis Dodds, the president of Princeton University, led the American delegation at Bermuda. It also included Senator Scott Lucas (D., Ill.) and Representative Sol Bloom (D., N.Y.). Richard K. Law, the Parliamentary Undersecretary for Foreign Affairs, led the British group. American Jews and Zionists hoped that the Bermuda discussants would develop a plan for the salvation of European Jewry. Jewish organizations submitted memoranda and written rescue plans to British and American authorities, which essentially repeated the proposals made at the "Stop Hitler Now" rally.[37] Unfortunately, even before the opening of the rescue conference, there were signs that the Allied powers were not willing to rise to the challenge of Nazi mass murder.

Any realistic plan to save European Jewry would have to deal with the question of what to do with Jewish refugees once they were freed from Hitler's clutches. Given the experiences of the last decade, there seemed little chance that the American Congress would be willing to liberalize immigration quotas, which severely restricted the entry of East Europeans into the United States. Wartime passions had, if anything, strengthened nativist sentiments in the United States. The British, for their part, were adamant in their determination to abide by the White Paper restricting Jewish immigration to Palestine to 75,000 over the five years from 1939–44. Already hard pressed in the fight against the Axis, British military and political leaders wanted to avoid any unrest or rebellion among the Arabs of the strategically important Middle East. The British were clearly unwilling to ease restrictions on Jewish immigration to Palestine even if it jeopardized attempts to rescue Jews. On February 4, 1943, Lord Halifax, the British ambassador to the United States, sent Stephen Wise the good news that the government of Bulgaria, a German satellite state, had agreed to allow a large number of Jewish children and a smaller group of adults to leave for Palestine. However, the British ambassador was careful to inform Wise that London would continue to abide by the White Paper. He also wrote, "The very considerable difficulties involved in making the necessary arrangements for transport and for the accommodation and sustenance in Palestine of such large parties of refugees may limit the numbers that can be handled under this procedure."[38]

The Bermuda Conference failed to change the fate of the millions of Jews destined for the gas chambers. The American representatives to the conference announced that the most efficient way to rescue European Jewry was to ensure a speedy Allied victory. They implied that the Jewish rescue proposals, if implemented, would hinder the Allied war effort. America's refusal to consider any plan involving a breaching of the nation's immigration quota wall handicapped the Bermuda Conference from the day of its opening, as did the British refusal to deviate from the White Paper restrictions. Despite optimistic statements following the conference by the participants, the only concrete action taken at Bermuda was the revival of the Intergovernmental Committee on Refugees (IGCR) first established by the 1938 Evian Conference. The IGCR, however, proved to be no more capable of effective action in 1943 than it had been in 1938.[39]

Shortly after the Bermuda Conference, Peter Bergson's Committee for a Jewish Army placed a large advertisement in the *New York Times* charging that "to 5,000,000 Jews in the Nazi Death Trap, Bermuda was a Cruel Mockery." The ad demanded that the Allies set up an agency to rescue the Jews of Europe.[40]

The leaders of the established American Jewish organizations responded to the conference's failure to act upon rescue with dismay, incredulity, and disappointment. In a May 2 address to the National Conference for Palestine, Abba Hillel Silver noted that the Allies had been no more supportive of Jewish efforts to save their European brethren from annihilation. They express sympathy, Silver said, and ask us to be patient. That all European Jewry might be dead when victory was finally won, Silver angrily declared, "does not seem to arouse these friends of ours to any extraordinary emergency acts of rescue and deliverance." The Bermuda Conference, ostensibly convened to satisfy popular humanitarian demands, was "never" intended to do anything to adequately respond to the tragedy. Silver sadly concluded that "clearly the friends upon whom we had hoped to lean have turned out to be broken reeds. The enemies of Israel seek us out and single us out, but our friends would like to forget our existence as a people."

Lacking practical expedients, Silver lapsed into the almost mystical rhetoric through which Zionists sustained themselves in adversity: *"The inescapable logic of events! When the doors of the world will be closed to our people, then the hand of destiny will force open the door of Palestine. And that hour is rapidly approaching."* [Italics in original.] Zionists, Silver stressed, had been proven correct in their belief that the lack of a Jewish national home led to persecution and murder. He urged all American Zionists to remain faithful to the cause of Jewish statehood. The Allied powers, according to Silver, would have to provide the Jews with a state in order to achieve a stable postwar world. Reactionary forces had used anti-Semitism, created by Jewish homelessness, time and again in their struggle for power and conquests, and unless the Jewish situation was changed, it would be used again.

Silver concluded his address on a messianic note, which reflected his belief that it was God's will to put an end once and for all to the primary cause of Jewish misery. He told his audience that Jewish sages taught that two arks led the Children of Israel through the desert to the Promised Land. One ark contained the body of the Patriarch Joseph, while the other held the tablets of law, divinely delivered to Moses on Mount Sinai. There were two arks, he repeated, "the Ark of death and the Ark of faith!" Today, Silver continued, another ark of death, this one carrying two million dead Jews was "leading us . . . through the wilderness to Palestine!" Along with the martyred Jews of Europe, an Ark of Faith also moved, "our covenant with the future, our faith in our destiny." If this latest tragedy of persecution was to be the last ever suffered by Jewry, they would have to resolve finally to put an end to Jewish homelessness, the cause of anti-Semitism. He concluded, "we now wish to be noble and free and as a free people in its own land."[41]

The day after Silver's eloquent appeal for continued insistence on a Jewish state, leading American Zionists met to discuss the Bermuda Conference. Moshe Furmansky, a left-wing socialist Zionist and a proponent of a binational Arab-Jewish state in Palestine, argued that Zionists must take immediate action to offset the American and British failure at Bermuda. He suggested that American Zionists immediately organize a mass protest campaign against the White Paper's restriction on Jewish immigration to Palestine. Nahum Goldmann seconded Furmansky's proposal, but added that if Zionists wanted to conduct a massive attack on the White Paper, they would have to cease demonstrating against the massacre of European Jewry. Goldmann explained that the Zionists' limited resources made it impossible to engage in two major campaigns at the same time. He agreed with Abba Hillel Silver that after Biltmore, it was now necessary "to emphasize the preeminence of the Zionist program in relation to the refugee question."

Rabbi Wolf Gold, a leader of Mizrachi, the Orthodox Jewish Zionist organization, disagreed with Goldmann. He believed that action against the White Paper was "long overdue," but he didn't understand why it would preclude mass action against the Nazi extermination program. Gold maintained that the two issues could be linked together, since the only answer to the problem of rescue was to open the gates of Palestine.[42]

While Gold and Goldmann disagreed about the relationship of a drive to press the government to attempt rescue and an anti–White Paper campaign, no one at the meeting questioned whether Nazi extermination policies threatened to undermine the Zionist argument for Jewish statehood. Long after Stephen Wise's terrifying November 1942 announcement, Zionists continued to insist that a large number of homeless Jews would survive the war and that the only practical solution to their plight would be resettlement in a Jewish state in Palestine. Few American Zionists seemed to realize that Nazi gas chambers threatened to solve the whole problem in a most gruesome manner.

In mid-1943, one lone voice within the councils of American Zionism questioned the logic of remaining loyal to the Biltmore resolution's demand for a Jewish commonwealth while the Holocaust continued. Chaim Weizmann, by the middle of 1943, had been engaged in an increasingly bitter personal dispute with David Ben-Gurion for a number of years. Although Weizmann had supported the Biltmore resolution in 1942, he believed that Ben-Gurion and other Zionists were attaching too much importance to its demand for a Jewish commonwealth. The Bitlmore declaration, he maintained, was "just" a resolution, "like the hundred and one resolutions usually passed at great meetings in this country, or in any other country."[43] On June 1, 1943, Weizmann then in the United States for an extended visit, attended a meeting of the American Emergency Committee for Zionist Affairs (AECZA). He told the Jewish nationalist leaders at the meeting that he would soon be leaving the United States with a "heavy heart" and that he wished to make "a few summary remarks." Zionists, he said, had to consider seriously the implications of the Nazi extermination of European Jewry. Where, he asked, will the millions of Jews who were supposed to go to Palestine come from? In Nazi-occupied Europe, only the courageous few who were lucky enough to have the means to endure would survive the war. The Soviet Union would probably not let any Jews left in Russia after the war go to Palestine because of the traditional communist opposition to Zionism. Weizmann also noted that the five million Jews of the United States would not go to Palestine unless "driven." Therefore, given the demographic and internal problems confronting Zionists and the lack of American and British support for Jewish statehood, Weizmann urged Jewish nationalists to abandon "old methods" and "slogans" and to seek out new strategies and positions. These, however, he did not specify. Weizmann explained that when Zionists passed the Bilmore resolution they "were genuinely convinced that the Jewish state would be realized 'tomorrow.'" Unfortunately, that was not to be, and, Weizmann concluded, the Biltmore program was a "symbol" and a "flag" but not practical politics.[44]

Weizmann's stark and depressing analysis of the problems confronting the Zionist movement sparked a lively discussions among the AECZA leaders. Rabbi Meyer Berlin, a Palestinian leader of Mizrachi who was also on a visit to the United States, argued that such a bleak portrayal of the Zionist future would be strongly opposed in Palestine where the Yishuv generally believed that peace would bring the implementation of the Biltmore program. He also pointed out that no one could accurately forecast how many Jews would survive the "massacres" in Europe; millions of Jews might well endure. The rabbi insisted that the establishment of the Jewish right to "Eretz Israel" was still the most important task confronting the Zionist movement.[45]

The furor caused by Weizmann's comments continued after the AECZA meeting. On June 25, Weizmann wrote Stephen Wise that his remarks at the meeting "have been construed as a deviation from the Biltmore program and that as a result a cable has been sent to Palestine in protest against this 'heresy.'" Subjected to censure and criticism, Weizmann retreated from his position. Publicly, he followed the orthodox Zionist line of demanding, on behalf of persecuted European Jewry, the establishment of a Jewish commonwealth in Palestine, while he privately worried about the consequences of European Jewry's demise on the Zionist program.[46]

Writing in 1944 to Meyer Weisgal, his strongest American supporter, Weizmann warned that the successful extermination of European Jewry would undermine the Zionist case for statehood. He wrote:

> The main argument based on pressure due to anti-Semitism loses its force if only a very small number of Jews remain alive in Europe after the war. I am quite sure that our opponents are already reckoning on this in their own minds, though they do not speak about it yet because it would be very ungracious to make political capital out of such a catastrophe. But when everything is over, and the facts become known, they will speak for themselves. And any demand of ours based on the imperative necessity of transferring large numbers of Jews speedily to Palestine will then fall to the ground.

Weizmann counselled Weisgal to begin recruiting large numbers of American youth for settlement in Palestine as a way out of the dilemma caused by the Holocaust.[47]

THE AMERICAN JEWISH CONFERENCE

As Chaim Weizmann despaired about the effects of mass extermination on Jewish nationalism, and while Allied planning for the Bermuda Conference continued, Zionists prepared to continue the work they had began at the Biltmore Hotel in May 1942. Now that American Zionists were united around the statehood goal, they began to organize a national conference representing all American Jews, which would endorse the Zionist program.[48] In early 1943, prominent American Zionists convinced Henry Monsky, the President of B'nai B'rith, to send a letter to the leaders of thirty-four major American Jewish organizations. American Jewry, Monsky wrote, would have to represent the interests of all the Jewish people at the peace conference that would follow the Allied victory over the fascists. Monsky wanted to avoid any conflict between American Jewish groups at the peace conference, and he invited the leaders of the thirty-four organizations to meet with him in Pittsburgh to formulate a united American Jewish plan for the postwar reconstruction of European Jewry.[49] Monsky did not mention the creation of a Jewish commonwealth in Palestine in his letter, but the Zionists who were helping him plan the conference intended to use it to advance their own program.[50]

Jewish leaders met in Pittsburgh three times during the weekend of January 23 and 24, 1943. Many of the seventy-eight delegates were Zionists. Israel Goldstein, Louis Levinthal, and Morris Rothenberg represented the Zionist Organization of America, while Rose Halprin was one of the three Hadassah delegates present. Some of their ablest leaders represented the Orthodox religious Mizrachi organization and the socialist Zionists, including Leon Gellman (Mizrachi), and Hayim Greenberg and David Wertheim (socialist).[51]

Unfortunately for the Zionists, the prestigious American Jewish Committee refused to attend the Pittsburgh conference. The conservative and elitest Committee rejected the concept of Jewish nationhood, but had for sometime supported "nonpolitical" projects to settle Jews in Palestine. However, by early 1943, the American Jewish Committee's leadership was disturbed by the increasing power of American Zionism and by the movement's decision at Biltmore to campaign aggressively for the establishment of a Jewish commonwealth in Palestine.[52]

Participants in the Pittsburgh meetings decided to organize an American Jewish Assembly where representatives of the entire American Jewish community could debate the critical issues of the day. They devised an elaborate election system to ensure that the 500 delegates who attended the assembly would be democratically selected. National Jewish organizations participating in the assembly would select 125 of the delegates. Local Jewish communities would select the remainder. The number of representatives dispatched by each community would depend on the size of its Jewish population.[53]

The original intention of those Zionists planning the American Jewish Conference was to win the support of the entire American Jewish community for the creation of a Jewish commonwealth in Palestine. The failure of the small but influential American Jewish Committee to attend the preliminary Pittsburgh meeting threatened to undermine the success of the conference. It would be difficult for Zionists to argue that they had the support of all American Jews if the American Jewish Committee was absent from the conference. Because the Committee objected to the term *assembly*, arguing that it implied that American Jews were a distinct and separate political group, Monsky and his colleagues agreed to change the name of the assembly to the American Jewish Conference. The American Jewish Committee also convinced the conference's organizers to agree that any decisions made by the delegates would not be binding on any organization that chose to attend.[54]

As they negotiated with the Committee to ensure its participation, Zionist leaders had to confront the fact that even if the Committee chose to attend the American Jewish Conference, there was little likelihood that it would consent to support the Biltmore program. In early 1943, the American Emergency Committee for Zionist Affairs met to discuss what steps to take regarding the American Jewish Committee. Some Zionist leaders stubbornly refused to alter the Biltmore program's support of a Jewish commonwealth even if it meant a complete break with the American Jewish Committee. Others hoped that a way could be found to win the cooperation of the Committee, and they urged that "nothing be done" to alienate those Committee members who might be eventually won over to the Jewish nationalist position. After long deliberation, the AECZA finally decided that Zionists should privately continue negotiating with the American Jewish Committee provided that nothing be done to limit the freedom of the Zionists to present the Biltmore program to the American Jewish Conference.[55]

The leaders of the constituent organizations of the American Emergency Committee for Zionist Affairs organized efficient electoral campaigns to insure that American Jewish communities elected a substantial number of Zionists to the American Jewish Conference. Several leaders of the AECZA understood that Zionists could campaign "too hard," however, and explained that "the impression must be avoided that the Zionists are out to capture all the delegates."[56]

American Zionists, who had been instrumental in the organization of the conference, did remarkably well in the elections held to choose representatives to the assembly. Due to the organizational ability of the Zionist leadership and the hard work of rank and file members, well over half of the 501 delegates at the American Jewish Conference were affiliated with an established Zionist organizations. Conference organizers estimated that "at least 2,225,000 Jews participated directly or indirectly" in the elections, held in all forty-eight states and the District of Columbia, which selected 379 of the delegates. National Jewish organizations, including Zionist groups and the pro-Zionist American Jewish Congress and the B'nai B'rith, appointed the remaining 123 delegates according to a key agreed on at the Pittsburgh meeting. The non-Zionist American Jewish Committee and Jewish Labor Committee were represented.[57]

The original agenda for the American Jewish Conference included only two major items for discussion: the future of Palestine and the postwar reconstruction of the Jewish communities of Europe. Conference organizers added the rescue issue only when Jewish popular pressure demanded it. However, no one doubted that the main task of the conference was to deliberate about the future of Palestine.

According to Joseph Halbert, a delegate from Atlantic City, his community discussed only the commonwealth issue when it voted to select its representatives to the conference.[58]

As the day for the opening of the conference approached, the Zionist political position became even more complex and confused as some Jewish nationalist leaders, continuing their effort to ensure the support of the American Jewish Committee, recognized that they would have to moderate their statehood demand. Officially, the major American Zionist organizations maintained that their delegates at the American Jewish Conference were pledged to support the Biltmore resolution. Louis Lipsky, Emanuel Neumann, Abba Hillel Silver, and others hoped that the conference would give its stamp of approval to the goal of Jewish statehood. However, some Zionist leaders, in particular Nahum Goldmann, pressed for some moderation in the Zionist approach to the conference. They did not oppose the eventual creation of a Jewish state, but they didn't think it was possible to unite the American Jewish community around this goal in 1943. They argued that it would be more profitable for Zionists to win the conference's support for a resolution that would strongly oppose the British White Paper and that would call for unlimited Jewish immigration to Palestine. Through his talks with leaders of the American Jewish Committee, Goldmann knew that they would support the demand for Jewish immigration to Palestine provided it was clearly separated from any call for statehood. While such a position did represent a tactical retreat from the Biltmore resolution, in Goldmann's view it did not undermine the eventual establishment of a Jewish political entity in Palestine. The creation of a Jewish majority, after all, would set the stage for Jewish political control of Palestine.[59]

On August 29, 1943, five hundred delegates and fifteen hundred guests gathered at the Waldorf Astoria for the opening of the American Jewish Conference. To symbolize the seriousness of the occasion, the room was left undecorated except for the American flag and the blue-and-white Star of David flag of the Zionist movement. A memorial service for the European Jewish victims followed the singing of the "Star Spangled Banner" and "Hatikvah" ("The Hope"), the Zionist anthem.[60]

B'nai B'rith president Henry Monsky welcomed the delegates and reminded them that Hitler had declared war against the Jewish people before he attacked the rest of the civilized world. However, he lamented:

> It is with regret that we record the lack of practical measures for the relief of the millions who have been persecuted, pillaged, pilloried and devastated. Many statements of sympathy and compassion have been issued by our Government and its allies. Such statements are reassuring, but distressingly ineffective so far as the plight of the victims is concerned.

American Jews had to act promptly and in unison if they wanted to save European Jewry. Palestine, he continued, had a large role to play in solving the postwar problems that the Jewish people would confront. Monsky demanded that the British White Paper of 1939 be withdrawn, but he avoided calling for the immediate creation of a Jewish commonwealth in Palestine.[61]

Stephen Wise also made no mention of the creation of a Jewish commonwealth in his address to the conference. Jews, Wise said, totally supported the Allied war effort, yet they were singled out by Great Britain and discriminated against. White Paper immigration restriction must end, he proclaimed, and the gates of Palestine must be opened to the Jewish refugees. He was confident that the American Jewish Conference would unanimously and forcefully express its opposition to the White Paper.[62]

Other speakers at the American Jewish Conference followed the trend set by Monsky and Wise and avoided asking the conference to endorse the Biltmore resolution's demand for the immediate creation of a Jewish state. Nahum Goldmann announced that he would be satisfied if Great Britain gave the Yishuv complete control over immigration to Palestine. The creation of a Zionist state, he concluded, could wait until Jews made up a majority of Palestine's population.[63]

The American Jewish Committee, through its president, Judge Joseph Proskauer, responded positively to the Zionists' moderate approach. Proskauer, in his address to the conference, praised the achievements of the Yishuv and said: "We are one in our concern for its [the Yishuv's] preservation and upbuilding, and I do not believe we would ever have a difference in adopting a formula along the lines that Dr. Wise suggested, of keeping the gates of Palestine open."[64]

Not all American Zionists were pleased with the abandonment of the Biltmore program. Emanuel Neumann believed that the very purpose of organizing the American Jewish Conference had been to win the support of American Jewry for the creation of a Jewish commonwealth in Palestine. He approached Abba Hillel Silver, who was also displeased with the course of the conference, and asked him to speak in favor of Jewish statehood. Silver was not scheduled to appear before the conference. Zionist leaders willing to cooperate with the American Jewish Committee apparently feared that Silver, a fiery speaker, might undermine the fragile relationship they had worked out with Proskauer. But Neumann was able to arrange for Silver to address the entire conference on Monday night, August 30, 1943.[65]

ABBA HILLEL SILVER AND THE "RESCUE" OF THE JEWISH PEOPLE

Silver, then fifty years old and at the peak of his capabilities, proved more than able to meet the task that Neumann set for him. In a masterful speech, he championed the ideal of Jewish statehood and defeated all those who had sought compromise. He brilliantly reflected the concerns and hopes of an American Jewry that was living through the hell of a war in which millions of their brethren were being butchered.

Calling on his audience to look beyond the war years, Silver opened his speech by declaring:

> My dear friends, the Jewish people is in danger of coming out of this war the most ravaged of peoples and the least healed and restored. The stark tragedy of our ravage has been abundantly told here and elsewhere – tragic, ghastly, unredeemed. To rehearse it again is only to flagellate oneself and to gash our souls again and again. But what of the healing? What is beyond the rim of blood and tears? Frankly to some of us, nothing.

The rabbi warned that many Jews were falsely hoping that the Second World War would achieve "what an Allied victory failed to give them after the last war, what a whole century of enlightenment, liberalism and Progress failed to give them – peace and security." Putting one's faith in international treaties and guarantees of minority rights was naive. These solutions did not take into account the principal cause of Jewish suffering, "the immemorial problem of our national homelessness." All Jewish history since the exile from Palestine consisted of one long line of tragedies. He explained:

> There is a stout black cord which connects the era of Fichte in Germany with its feral cry of "hep, hep," and the era of Hitler with its cry of "Jude verrecke." The Damascus affair of 1840 links up with the widespread reaction after the Revolution of 1848 – the Mortara affair of Italy; the Christian Socialist Movement in the era of Bismark; the Tisza-Ezlar affair in Hungary; the revival of blood accusations in Bohemia; the pogroms of the 80s in Russia; *La France Juive* and the Dreyfus afffair in France; the pogroms of 1903; the Ukranian blood baths after the last war and the human slaughter houses of Poland in this war.

There was only one solution for the "persistent emergency," the "millennial tragedy" of Jewish life. Resettlement programs, refugee havens, these were not solutions. "There is but one solution for national homelessness. That is a national home!"

Silver declared that there could be no compromise on the commonwealth demand. Jewish statehood was more than ideology. It was the "cry of despair" of a people who had suffered yesterday, were suffering today, and would probably suffer tomorrow if their prayer was not answered. Silver proclaimed that the "crucifixion" of the Jewish people must end, saying:

> From the infested, typhus-ridden ghetto of Warsaw, from the death-block of Nazi occupied lands, where myriads of our people are awaiting execution by

the slow or the quick method, from a hundred concentration camps which befoul the map of Europe, from the pitiful ranks of our wandering hosts over the entire face of the earth, come the cry: "Enough; there must be a final end to all of this, a sure and certain end."

To those who believed that the cause of unity justified compromise on the Biltmore program, Silver explained: "I am for unity in Israel, for the realization of the total program of Jewish life, relief, rescue, reconstruction, and the national restoration in Palestine. I am not for unity on a fragment of the program, for a fragment of the program is betrayal of the rest of the program and a tragic futility besides." As Ben-Gurion had argued several years earlier, Silver maintained that only a Jewish government would allow Jews to enter Palestine in large numbers. Great Britain's betrayal of its Balfour Declaration pledge clearly proved that Zionists could not rely on the goodwill of Christian governments, which would only protect the Jews if it served their own national interests. Silver realized that the survival of his people was a political, not a humanitarian issue, and that it would be insured only if the Jews understood that:

We cannot truly rescue the Jews of Europe unless we have free immigration to Palestine. We cannot have free immigration into Palestine unless our political rights are recognized there. Our political rights cannot be recognized there unless our historic connection with the country is acknowledged and our right to rebuild our national home is reaffirmed. The whole chain breaks if one of the links is missing.

Silver warned the conference delegates that if they failed to pass a resolution that mentioned the need for a Jewish commonwealth, that the Jewish delegation to the Allied peace conference at the war's end would have nothing more than an "immigration aid plea to let Jews go to Palestine, as if Palestine were for us another Santo Domingo?"[66]

As Silver finished speaking, the conference audience spontaneously arose and sang "Hatikvah," the Zionist anthem. The highly emotional ovation that followed sealed Silver's victory over those who had attempted to avoid the commonwealth issue.[67]

The crowd that reacted to Silver's speech and the masses of American Jews who flocked to the Zionist movement in the years that followed were responding to Hitler's extermination of their European brothers and sisters. Like Silver, they saw nothing unique in Hitler's attempt to annihilate the Jewish people. Their sense of Jewish history told them that this had been the ultimate desire of tyrants and demagogues for nearly two thousand years. While some Jewish leaders might come forward with piecemeal plans to save European Jewry, Silver offered American Jews the ultimate rescue plan. Unless they succeeded in creating a Jewish state, there would be little sense in trying to send food to the starving masses in the Jewish ghettos or even in bombing the death camps and the trains that brought Jews to their extinction. Unless the problem of Jewish homelessness, the basic cause of anti-Semitism, was solved, future generations of Jews would have to suffer in other death camps.

The conference's Palestine Committee, charged with the wording of a Palestine resolution to be presented to all the delegates, discussed Silver's call for the historical rescue of the Jewish people. Moderates and non-Zionists on the committee launched a final effort to present their case. Judge Proskauer appealed to the Zionists to compromise for the sake of unity. He threatened to withdraw the American Jewish Committee from the American Jewish Conference if the Zionists persisted in pushing through a resolution supporting the establishment of a Jewish commonwealth in Palestine.[68] Dr. James Heller, a Reform rabbi and Zionist, also continued to advocate a moderate course of action. He argued that "extreme" measures would only intensify the hostile attitudes of the State Department and Foreign Office.[69]

Robert Goldman, a dedicated Zionist for over a quarter of a century, who represented the Union of American Hebrew Congregations at the conference, was also in favor of a compromise resolution. He decided to confront Silver's thesis that the best response to Hitler's extermination policies was immediately to create a Jewish state so that future persecution would be impossible. Goldman told the Palestine Committee that American Jewry faced two problems. The long-range problem was the need to create a Jewish state. The "immediate problem," he continued "is rescue; and I don't care what else you say or how you characterize it, or what you say about me for saying it, that is the immediate problem and that is the problem that we should be concerned with." Goldman insisted that the first task of American Jewry was to save their European kin and he warned that "if the long run problem which we want to project is going to interfere with the solution of the immediate problem, . . . you have no right to insist on that problem that may result in the loss of thousands and hundreds of thousands of more Jews that could otherwise be saved in the next few years." Some British and American officials, he explained, were totally opposed to increased Jewish immigration to Palestine, while others supported opening Palestine's doors as a humanitarian response to Hitler's extermination policies. If Zionists insisted on demanding statehood, Arab opposition in the entire Middle East would intensify, making it impossible for proponents of increased immigration to win their case. If this happened, hundreds of thousands of Jews would be left "in places where they can not be rescued."[70]

Proponents of Jewish statehood on the Palestine committee wasted little time before rebutting the moderates' position. Morris Rothenberg reminded the conference delegates that they were not creating a commonwealth for those Jews who were "lucky" enough to live in the United States, but for those who were "denied" and "disinherited." Louis Levinthal of the ZOA cautioned Joseph Proskauer that the British would interpret the conference's failure to endorse the commonwealth goal as a sign that Zionists had abandoned the goal of statehood.[71]

Zionists on the committee challenged Robert Goldman's position that first priority should be given to the rescue of European Jewry. Robert Szold commended Goldman for his sincerity, but warned the conference delegates that "the Jews of Palestine would feel that a blow had been delivered to them today if we here assembled deliberately refrain from holding out to them a helping hand." Hayim Greenberg, the socialist Zionist who earlier in the year had accused American Jewry of moral bankruptcy for failing to do enough to rescue those Jews facing extermination, also disagreed with Goldman's thesis. Greenberg repeated a point Silver had made in his address and argued that the right of Jews to emigrate to Palestine was linked to their right to create a state there. A campaign directed solely at opening Palestine's doors would not be successful, and he feared that a failure to clarify the political future of Palestine would only create more unrest among the country's Arab population.[72]

Emanuel Neumann delivered the most articulate and vigorous condemnation of a "rescue-first" strategy. The "immediate problem" facing the conference, he said, was not peculiar to the Jews of their day. For centuries, Jews had been in a "permanent state of emergency." He charged that Jewish leaders always concerned themselves with the "immediate problems," thereby ignoring the underlying cause of their suffering and persecution. Had Jews dealt with the problem of "homelessness" earlier, he speculated, "either a Hitler would not have arisen in our time, or, if one had, we might have had a country under Jewish control in which Jews of Germany and other lands could have been received—and received in large numbers." Neumann complained: "It has been our misfortune throughout our history that we have not been able to look ahead, to plan ahead, and to provide this radical solution." If American Jewry in 1943 failed to put an end to the long history of Jewish suffering by supporting the creation of a commonwealth in Palestine, Neumann concluded, "we shall be contemptible in our own eyes."[73]

Neumann's and Silver's argument won many more supporters than did Goldman's. With the exception of four delegates, including the representatives of the American Jewish Committee, the entire American Jewish Conference voted for a resolution demanding "the fulfillment of the Balfour Declaration, and of the Mandate for Palestine whose intent and underlying purpose, based on the 'historical connection of the Jewish people with Palestine,' was to reconstitute Palestine as the Jewish Commonwealth."[74] Proskauer responded to the Zionist victory by withdrawing the American Jewish Committee from the American Jewish Conference.[75]

The euphoric spirit of the American Jewish Conference carried over to the annual convention of the Zionist Organization of America, which was held two weeks later. ZOA President Levinthal told the convention that the American Jewish Conference had had a revolutionary impact on American Zionism. The demand for a Jewish commonwealth was no longer an idea held by Zionists; it had become the "credo" of all American Jews.[76] ZOA speakers seemed to enjoy repeating the formula so dramatically presented by Abba Hillel Silver at the American Jewish Conference. For almost two thousand years Jews had suffered through one persecution after another. Now Jews had a "rendezvous with destiny." The time had finally arrived to put an end to Jewish national homelessness, the basic cause of Jewish suffering.

Abba Hillel Silver made a triumphant appearance before the ZOA convention and announced that the American Jewish Conference proved that Zionists were not simply a party within the American Jewish community, but were *the* Jewish people. Remembering his triumph at the conference, he told the ZOA delegates: "There was real danger of conciliation, of what has come to be called 'appeasement'; there were threats made, there were dire forebodings, and the weak began to waiver, but fortunately the rank and file of the Zionist forces remained firm and strong." Receiving a standing ovation, Silver continued: "We are on the eve of a messianic era for our people. We have gone through the purging, the cleansing, the terror, the apocalyptic dread. . . . [I]t depends upon us, upon our merit, upon our desserts, whether that hour of redemption will be hastened or retarded."[77]

AMERICAN ZIONISM AND THE RESCUE OF EUROPEAN JEWRY

Besides addressing the ZOA convention, Silver spent the weeks following the American Jewish Conference reorganizing the American Zionist community's political apparatus, the American Emergency Committee for Zionist Affairs.[78] Before the American Jewish Conference, the ZOA, Hadassah, Mizrachi, and Poale Zion, fearing that a powerful AECZA would threaten their autonomy, had thwarted Emanuel Neumann's efforts to turn the body into the vanguard of political Zionism in the United States. Neumann's frustration with the impotency of the AECZA had finally led to his resignation as the organization's director in early 1943.[79]

By the summer of 1943, Zionist leaders concluded that it was necessary to revitalize the American Emergency Committee for Zionist Affairs. As early as June 1942, Chaim Weizmann had decided that Abba Hillel Silver was the "most suitable" candidate to lead Zionist political forces in the United States. Weizmann's moderate nature and policies contrasted dramatically with Silver's aggressiveness and stubborn commitment to the Biltmore program, but the future president of the state of Israel recognized Silver's charisma and talents and threw his support behind a plan to give the rabbi control of American Zionism's political machine.

On August 26, 1943, on the eve of the opening of the American Jewish Conference, Silver's opponents and supporters completed a compromise under which Silver and his rival Stephen Wise became co-chairmen of the American Emergency Committee for Zionist Affairs. The compromise also allowed Silver to assume sole leadership of the organization's all-important executive committee.[80]

Wise graciously welcomed Silver to the AECZA, saying that he "looked forward to working with him towards the fulfillment of our common aim to make Palestine a Jewish Commonwealth." Silver told the Emergency Committee that they were on the "eve of great decisions" and he confided to them that "those who know him know that his bark is worse than his bite." Under Silver's brilliant, though sometimes overbearing, leadership the AECZA was reorganized and renamed the American Zionist Emergency Council (AZEC).[81]

The AZEC claimed to represent the 95 percent of American Jewry that, it maintained, had expressed their support for a Jewish commonwealth through the American Jewish Conference. Within a few months of the conference's closing, the AZEC and Silver were seeking congressional backing for a resolution that would officially express American support for the creation of a Jewish commonwealth, while AZEC propagandists attempted to convince the American public that the establishment of a Jewish state would benefit the United States as well as the Jewish people. At the helm of the AZEC, Silver took steps to insure that American Zionists would give first priority to the "long range" problem confronting Jewry: national homelessness. However, Silver's charisma and fiery temper did not prevent some Zionists from questioning his strategy.

Rose Jacobs, a former president of Hadassah and an American representative to the Jewish Agency's Zionist Executive, wrote to Silver shortly after the American Jewish Conference to express her support of Jewish statehood. While she was pleased with the outcome of the American Jewish Conference, she also feared that it would be disastrous for Zionists to devote all their energies and resources to the commonwealth campaign. Jewish nationalists could not realistically expect to win American and British support for statehood in the near future. Therefore, Jacobs suggested that American Zionists pursue a short-term strategy of attacking British immigration restrictions to Palestine rather than stressing the goal of statehood.[82] Implicitly rejecting Silver's contention that the right of Jews to immigrate to Palestine could not be separated from their right of sovereignty, Jacobs, adopting a position taken by several AECZA members in May 1943, argued that an anti–White Paper campaign could be linked with efforts to rescue European Jewry. Thus a humanitarian plea for increased Jewish immigration to Palestine might be more effective than demanding Jewish statehood.[83]

Silver and most of the Zionist leadership nonetheless insisted on the primacy of the statehood campaign. Nahum Goldmann summarized their positions when he stated: "Thinking in terms of political reality we should fight for constructive action. We should use the fine machinery we have built up for the constructive program. Great Britain is now beginning to discuss the Near East, and there is not time first to spend six months fighting the White Paper, then to start talking about the Commonwealth."[84]

Silver and Goldmann's views triumphed within the American Zionist Emergency Council.[85] Under Silver's leadership American Zionists organized congressional and popular support for the creation of a Jewish commonwealth in Palestine. Zionist advances during the months and years that followed the August 1943 American Jewish Conference significantly contributed to the successful establishment of Israel in 1948.

Ironically and tragically, the Zionists' decision to give first priority to the creation of a Jewish commonwealth weakened American Jewish rescue efforts. Concentration on the statehood issue meant that few resources were left for the rescue campaign. Abba Hillel Silver and other Zionist leaders occupied themselves with the campaign for a Jewish state, while their talents and energies were sorely needed in the struggle to press the Roosevelt administration for rescue action. Jewish natonalist leaders were not blind to the suffering of the European co-religionists. Zionists grieved and mourned for the victims of Nazi mass murder, but they felt that other organizations, including the World Jewish Congress and the Jewish Labor Committee, should have primary responsibility to press for aid to European Jewry.[86] Zionist organizations and agencies occupied themselves with what they perceived to be a higher and more important form of rescue. The creation of a Jewish state, Zionists religiously believed, would save future generations of Jews from other Auschwitzes and Treblinkas. As a result, the extremely efficient lobby and propaganda machine fashioned by the American Zionist Emergency Council championed Jewish statehood, not the rescue of European Jewry.[87]

The ideological and political imperatives of Jewish nationalism actually forced Zionists to oppose some rescue efforts advanced by other groups. The Palestinian emissaries of the Irgun who made up Peter Bergson's Committee for a Jewish Army were the authors of several rescue plans opposed by the Zionist organizations. A month before the American Jewish Conference, Bergson and his principal associate, Samuel Merlin, organized an Emergency Conference to Save the Jewish People of Europe. At the conference the Bergsonites drew up a rescue plan and created the Emergency Committee to Save the Jewish People of Europe (ECSJPE), whose only goal was to press for the rescue of European Jewry. The writer Ben Hecht worked with the group, as did Congressman Will Rogers, Jr. (D., Cal.) and Senator Guy M. Gillette (D., Iowa). The members of the ECSJPE believed that the rescue of European Jewry superseded all other issues, reasoning that if European Jewry perished there would be little point in creating a Jewish state. Bergson remarked: "we cannot avoid the fact that our work will be determined by the fate of the European Jews. For if they perish, the Jews the world over will forever remain an international sore with no practical way for a dignified and honorable solution."[88]

The principal objective of the Bergson group was to convince the Allied governments to establish an agency to rescue the European Jews. Shortly after its establishment in July 1943, ECSJPE began building public support for a congressional resolution that it planned to have introduced by Senator Gillette and Congressman Rogers. The resolution would call on President Roosevelt to create a governmental agency of diplomatic, economic, and military experts, charged specifically with the rescue of European Jewry. Bergson supporters introduced the resolution in the House of Representatives and the Senate on November 9, 1943. It intentionally avoided making any mention of Palestine or a Jewish state. Bergson and Merlin had decided to try to avoid such politically controversial issues as a Jewish state and to present rescue to the American public as a humanitarian necessity. ECSJPE propaganda stressed that the American ideals of justice and freedom, for which American soldiers were dying, required that everything humanly possible be done to save European Jewry from destruction. The Bergsonites feared that any mention of the Jewish claim to Palestine would politicize their demands for rescue, making it easier for the Allied governments to refuse to act. Bergson and Merlin also believed that the interests of Palestine would be served by their rescue resolution, even if the Zionist program was not specifically mentioned. Eri Jabotinsky, the son of right-wing ideologue Vladimir Jabotinsky and a member of the ECSJPE explained:

> [O]nce the [rescue] commission is created it will certainly discover that Palestine is the most appropriate location for an asylum, and also that Palestine must be considered in connection with the creation of other asylums, for no country will accept several tens of thousands of Jewish refugees unless it is guaranteed that they will be removed after the cessation of hostilities. Removed where to? The commission will soon enough discover that the only answer is Palestine. The commission will probably become the central instrument in the fight for Palestine.[89]

Most American Zionists did not agree with Bergson's views. Silver, Wise, and their lieutenants feared that Zionist political efforts would be undermined by Bergson's attempts to win support from legislators and the Yiddish and American press. The American Jewish Conference and the American Zionist Emergency Council both published statements accusing the Bergson group of opportunism and stressing that Bergson did not represent the American Jewish community. Zionists also attempted to convince Bergson sympathizers to defect from the ECSJPE. Zionist representatives even met with Senator Gillette and unsuccessfully tried to convince him to support a resolution calling for the establishment of a Jewish commonwealth in Palestine instead of Bergson's rescue commission legislation.[90]

Zionist leaders could not publicly oppose the creation of a rescue agency, but they did seek to change the wording of the Bergson rescue resolution.[91] At hearings held by the House Foreign Affairs Committee, Stephen Wise, co-chairman of the AZEC, maintained that the Bergson group was not a responsible part of the Jewish community and that its program was not in accordance with the plans worked out by the legitimate American Jewish organizations. He argued that the Bergson resolution was inadequate because of the absence of any demand for free Jewish immigration into Palestine. Wise's statement angered Congressman Will Rogers, Jr., one of the cosponsors of the rescue agency bill, who responded that his resolution was specifically designed to avoid "injecting the ancient and acrimonious issue of Palestine into a resolution specifically involving relief [rescue]." Rogers shared the Bergsonite view that linking rescue and Palestine would allow Roosevelt and Churchill to treat the Jewish appeal for help as a political, not a humanitarian issue.[92]

Zionist opposition to the Bergson group continued even after January 1944, when Franklin Roosevelt established the War Refugee Board, an official United States rescue agency. During the summer of that year, Bergson and his colleagues were campaigning for the establishment of emergency refugee shelters in Palestine. Under their plan, Jewish refugees would be admitted to Palestine on a temporary basis, as a lifesaving measure. They would not have the legal right to remain in Palestine when the war ended.[93] The Bergsonites realized that Palestine was in an ideal location to grant shelter to Jewish refugees who might escape from Hungary, Romania, or Bulgaria into Turkey. The emergency refugee shelters plan, which was supported by the War Refugee Board, offered a way around the British White Paper of 1939 and its restrictive immigration policy.[94] The plan gained added relevance in mid-July 1944, when the Hungarian government offered to release all Jews with visas to Palestine. The British and American governments accepted the Hungarian offer on August 11, although they did not explain how it would be carried out. A Nazi-engineered coup in Hungary on October 14, 1944, brought an end to any hope of acting on the Hungarian proposal.[95]

American Zionists vehemently opposed the concept of Palestinian emergency refugee shelters. They feared that Bergson's plan would sabotage their efforts to get a pro-commonwealth resolution passed in Congress, which, Zionists believed, would be an important step in the ultimate and final rescue of the Jewish people. Zionist unwillingness to sacrifice this long-term goal forced them to oppose the Bergson plan and put them in the precarious position of seeming to prefer "to keep Jews out of Palestine rather than yield on the Commonwealth."[96]

As the situation of Hungarian Jewry became more precarious, Zionists cooperated in the rescue efforts of the Jewish organizations and the War Refugee Board, but they adamantly refused to endorse the establishment of emergency refugee shelters in Palestine. The very notion of Jews being labeled refugees while they

121

were in the Jewish national home was anathema to most American Zionists. AZEC spokesmen claimed that Bergson's plan was unnecessary since political and transportation difficulties would only allow a small number of Jews to leave Hungary. Those Jews who did escape could be accommodated within the White Paper limits since fourteen thousand Palestine visas were still available.[97]

Zionist opposition to emergency refugee shelters also stemmed from their conception of how a Jewish state would be created. Bergson and his colleagues were classic revolutionaries. They believed that a Jewish state would only be established through armed struggle. The Bergsonites were prepared to see Jews admitted to Palestine as refugees because they knew that the final fate of the refugees would be decided by Jewish military might. American Zionists, unlike the Bergsonites, were revolutionaries only to the extent that they wished radically to alter the historical fate of the Jewish people. However, the means to this radical end would not involve armed struggle. The entire structure of political Zionism in the United States reflected the Zionists' belief that the Jewish state could be created through diplomatic negotiations. This being the case, Zionists believed that their acceptance of Bergson's plan would weaken their bargaining position with the British and American governments. The first rule of negotiation is always to ask for more than what you want. If Zionists allowed Jews to be temporarily interned in Palestine, they would seem to be surrendering the central point on which their case was based: that Palestine was, by right, the land of the Jews. The Balfour Declaration had recognized this claim and all Zionist propaganda was aimed at convincing the world of its legitimacy.

The Zionists were ideologically and politically unable to support the establishment of emergency refugee shelters in Palestine, just as they found it impossible to give the rescue of European Jewry priority over the creation of a Jewish commonwealth. Silver and his compatriots could not distinguish between the rescue issue and the statehood issue. They seemed to be inextricably linked by the Zionist view of Jewish history. For nearly two thousand years Jews had suffered through a seemingly unending series of persecutions. Hitler's attempt to exterminate European Jewry was unique, Zionists thought, only in its dimension. Theodor Herzl had offered the Jews a chance to save themselves. Silver and his followers despairingly reasoned that the failure to achieve the Zionist dream before 1933 was a principal cause for the suffering of European Jewry. They resolved to put an end, once and for all, to the awful cycle of suffering in order to insure that future generations need not share the fate of their European ancestors. World War II, which Zionists expected would end with the redrawing of the world's boundaries, seemed to offer Jewish nationalists one last chance to achieve their goal. For the Zionists at the American Jewish Conference, failure to seize the time would be criminal.

Ironically, the Zionists' zealous commitment to solve the Jewish problem led them to underestimate significantly the very dimension of the European catastrophe. When Zionists negotiated with Allied governments, they continued to insist that a Jewish state would have to be created after the war in order to accommodate the large number of Jewish refugees who would survive Hitler's slaughter. The logic of this situation led Zionists to think in terms of the survival of European Jewry, not their eradication. American Zionists rejected Chaim Weizmann's "dangerously pessimistic" estimate of the number of Jews who would die in Hitler's Europe. Zionist convention after Zionist convention included references to the almost mystical ability of the Jews to survive persecution, and Zionist spokesmen tended to underestimate the total number of Jewish dead in their speeches. Thus, over a year after Stephen Wise's dramatic announcement that two million European Jews were dead, Abba Hillel Silver used the same figure when testifying before a congressional committee.[98] Even when the extent of the Holocaust began to be apparent near the end of the war, Zionists still insisted on focusing on the number of Jews who would survive in Europe, not on those already dead, and on the necessity of creating a Jewish state to handle the postwar Jewish refugee crisis.[99]

During 1944 and 1945, the American Zionist Emergency Council developed the experience and resources that would make it into one of the most efficient political lobbies in America. Special efforts were made to capture the loyalty of specific segments of the American population. Emanuel Neumann and his propagandists labored especially hard at convincing American liberals of the necessity for the creation of a Jewish commonwealth in Palestine. While this work progressed, the Nazi crematoriums continued to dispose of the corpses of slaughtered Jews.

V | THE AMERICAN ZIONIST LOBBY, 1943-1945: A SUMMARY AND A CASE STUDY

After their success at the American Jewish Conference in August 1943, Zionists claimed to represent over 90 percent of American Jewry. While the American Jewish Conference gave Zionists the opportunity to have "American . . . Jewry speak for us,"[1] it did not provide an effective political lobby organization capable of making the voice of American Jewry heard. This did not prove to be a serious handicap because the Conference surrendered responsibility for pro-Zionist political work to the American Zionist Emergency Council (AZEC) under the leadership of Abba Hillel Silver and Stephen Wise.[2] Zionist leaders hoped that the AZEC would prove to be a more successful public relations machine than its troubled predecessor, the American Emergency Committee for Zionist Affairs (AECZA).

Bitter factional disputes had handicapped the AECZA since its creation in 1939. The Poale Zion, Hadassah, Mizrachi, and the Zionist Organization of America feared that a powerful Zionist umbrella committee would weaken their autonomy and perhaps lower their prestige.[3] The history of the AECZA seemed to prove that the multiplicity of Jewish organizations in the United States made it difficult for the community to achieve any goal. However, by the summer of 1943, the major Zionist organizations were prepared to pool their resources and accept the discipline of an executive committee headed by Wise, the most prestigious American Jewish nationalist, and Silver, the most dynamic. While they might disagree about the political, religious, and economic nature of the reconstituted Jewish nation, American Zionist groups had agreed at the Biltmore Conference that the immediate creation of a Jewish state was

124

absolutely vital. The extermination of European Jewry, the continuing British enforcement of the White Paper, and the Zionist triumph at the American Jewish Conference, all combined to convince Jewish nationalists that they were in a life or death struggle. Either they would succeed in recreating a nation in Palestine, which would revolutionize the Jewish experience and end the long chain of catastrophes that made up their history, or they would fail, dooming Jews to centuries more of anti-Semitism and persecution.

Once they decided to cooperate in a unified political campaign, Zionist organizations found that their diversity of opinion and philosophy was an asset, not a liability. American Zionism spanned the left-right political spectrum, encompassing the orthodox religious and the anti-religious, the committed capitalist and the ardent socialist. Therefore, when Zionists sought to reach out to the general Jewish and Christian populations, they found support from a wide variety of constituencies. The religious Mizrachi, for example, specialized in working with Orthodox Jewish organizations and communities, while the socialist Poale Zion focused its attention on the American Federation of Labor (AFL) and the Congress of Industrial Organizations (CIO). Abba Hillel Silver maintained close contact with the Republican party, being especially close to Senator Robert Taft of his home state of Ohio; Stephen Wise, co-chairman of the AZEC, was an ardent Democrat, with strong ties to the party's political machine and leadership.[4]

After the American Jewish Conference, the AZEC established various committees, each geared to a particular function or aimed at a specific constituency. Louis Lipsky headed the Publications Committee, which oversaw the production of Zionist propaganda and educational material. Rabbi Milton Steinberg's Committee for Intellectual Mobilization worked with writers, academics, and artists. Hadassah's Rose Halprin ran a Zionist information campaign directed at the numerous official and unofficial groups concerned with drawing up blueprints for the postwar world. Rabbi Wolf Gold of Mizrachi headed the Committee on Contact with American-Jewish Religious Forces, primarily concerned with winning support within the Orthodox Jewish community.[5]

The Poale Zion representative on the AZEC spearheaded the formation of a committee that would maintain contact with the American labor movement. The Poale Zion had previously done this type of work independent of the larger Zionist body and it succeeded in convincing the AFL to pass a resolution "supporting the upbuilding of Palestine as a Jewish Commonwealth" at its October 1943 convention.[6]

Max Zaritsky, president of the United Hatters, Cap and Millinery Workers International Union, agreed to serve as chairman of the AZEC labor committee.[7] A Russian-born Jew, a long-time socialist, and a supporter of Franklin Roosevelt, Zaritsky established the American Labor party in 1936.[8] By April 1944, sixty Jewish labor leaders were affiliated with Zaritsky's American Jewish Trade Union

Committee for Palestine, and Zaritsky hoped that there would be "a nucleus in every city in the United States in which there is an organized Jewish trade union movement."[9]

The AZEC's national network of local emergency councils proved to be the most effective element of the Zionist public relations structure. The local committees, microcosms of the larger AZEC, were made up of representatives of all the major Zionist factions.[10] Although nominally led by Joel Gross, the AZEC's Community Contacts Committee, charged with organizing and maintaining local emergency committees, was actually directed by Rabbi Leon Feuer, a protégé of Abba Hillel Silver.[11] By the end of November 1943, Zionists had established 125 local emergency committees; the number rose to 225 by January 1944.[12]

Silver and his lieutenants on the American Zionist Emergency Council paid special attention to the organizing of Christian support groups. These Christian, for the the most part Protestant, "friends" of Zionism, were to play the critical role of demonstrating that the American and Christian values of justice, freedom, and compassion led directly to the support of Zionism and the recreation of a Jewish state in Palestine. The effort to organize such a group of Christians was older than the AZEC itself. Louis Brandeis's close friend, Judge Julian Mack, who had been a leader of American Zionism during the World War I era, organized the Chicago-based Pro-Palestine Federation of America in 1930.[13] Within a year of Mack's effort, Emanuel Neumann, then a young and promising Zionist functionary and associate of Brandeis, began enlisting prominent American politicians and public figures for a new organization, the American Palestine Committee (APC). With the cooperation of Brandeis, Neumann held a founding dinner for the APC on January 17, 1932. Vice President Charles Curtis, Assistant Secretary of State James G. Rogers, Senators Robert M. LaFollette, Jr. (R., Wisc.), William H. King (R., Utah), William E. Borah (R., Idaho), and Congressman Hamilton Fish, Jr. (R., N.Y.) supported Neumann's effort. The climax of the dinner came with the reading of a letter from President Herbert Hoover declaring his support for the Jewish development of Palestine.[14]

While its beginnings seemed to be auspicious, the American Palestine Committee was, in fact, stillborn. Largely Emanuel Neumann's creation, the organization ceased to function when he moved to Palestine later in 1932, to assume his role as American delegate to the World Zionist Executive. By mid-1941, however, Neumann had returned to the United States and Zionists faced a new crisis. Hitler controlled most of continental Europe, Rommel's Afrika Korps threatened the Suez Canal and the approaches to Palestine, and the British seemed to be adamantly committed to the White Paper policy of 1939, which threatened to ensure that Palestine would become an Arab state. Deserted by the British, Zionists looked for new allies and supporters. Louis Brandeis argued that Zionists would have to attract Christian supporters if they hoped to convince American Jewish "doubters" that Zionism was legitimate and not inimical to American interests.[15] Brandeis allowed Neumann to use his living room as a meeting place to recruit senators and representatives for a new Christian support group.[16]

Reorganized in April 1941, the new American Palestine Committee was more broadly based than its predecessor. Sixty-eight senators, two hundred representatives, several Cabinet officials, President William Green of the AFL and President Philip Murray of the CIO, and prominent Christian intellectuals, including Monsignor John A. Ryan and Dr. Henry A. Atkinson, affiliated themselves with the new organization.[17] Senator Robert Wagner (D., N.Y.) served as head of the reconstituted American Palestine Committee. Wagner, one of the premier liberals of the New Deal and World War II eras, had been close to the Zionist leadership for some time. Although truly sympathetic to the Jewish nationalist cause, his busy schedule and many commitments seem to have precluded his being any more than a figurehead leader of Christian Zionism. Rabbi Meyer Berlin of the Mizrachi Organization visited with Senator Wagner early in 1943 and reported: "My impression of Senator Wagner is that he is a fine gentleman but rather luke-warm in general political questions and knows very little about Jewish problems and Zionism, although he is the chairman of the Pro-Palestine Committee and, as I understand, delivers addresses for our cause quite willingly from time to time."[18]

Although the American Palestine Committee was nominally a Christian organization, Zionists exercised a considerable amount of control over it. Emanuel Neumann, in mid-1941, directed the Publicity Committee of the APC with the aid of such experienced Zionist workers as Arnold Israeli and Arthur Lourie.[19] The Public Relations committee of the American Emergency Committee for Zionist Affairs (precursor of the AZEC) oversaw the publication of a bulletin to be distributed to APC members, while Herman Shulman, a key AZEC staff worker, supervised the APC's 1944 membership drive.[20] Although the APC raised operating funds from its members, the Zionist organizations were also important sources of operating capital.[21]

Zionist activity in the United States increased in 1942 with the Biltmore Conference in May and with the planning for the American Jewish Conference that finally took place in August 1943. Not surprisingly, there was a corresponding increase in the organizing of Christian supporters. Neumann and other Zionist leaders, while happy with the work of the American Palestine Committee, felt that a separate organization made up exclusively of Christian clergy would allow the Sunday pulpit to become a powerful medium for transmitting the Zionist message.[22] The Christian Council on Palestine, formed in December 1942, gathered over nine hundred clergymen into its ranks within a year; by 1946 its roster approached three thousand.[23]

The American Palestine Committee, like the Christian Council, was predominantly Protestant in makeup. The failure of large numbers of Catholics to join either the APC or the Christian Council partially reflected Catholic doctrine, which saw the Jewish exile from Palestine as part of the torment that came with rejecting Jesus. Jewish wandering, Catholic tradition taught, would only end with the total conversion of the Jews to Christianity. The Catholic Church was also concerned about the fate of its Holy Land if Jews were to regain political and jurisdictional control over Palestine.[24]

As with the American Palestine Committee, Zionist officials closely directed the work of the Christian Council. Well before the actual formation of the Council, American Zionists delegated the task of organizing Christian clergy support to Rabbis Phillip S. Bernstein and Milton Steinberg. Bernstein, of Rochester, N. Y., was an excellent and logical choice for this important position given his success in bringing the Zionist message to American liberals through the *Nation* and the *New Republic*.[25]

The Christian Council listed an attractive array of Protestant clergymen and intellectuals on its letterhead. Henry A. Atkinson, secretary-general of the Church Peace Union and World Alliance for International Friendship Through the Churches, served as chairman of the council. Paul Tillich and Reinhold Niebuhr served on the council's executive committee.[26] Niebuhr, the intellectual leader of liberal Protestantism, significantly added to Zionism's prestige within the United States.[27] Professor S. Ralph Harlow of Smith College, a close friend of Stephen Wise, also was an active council participant. A veteran missionary, Harlow was a singularly unique Zionist ally, espousing the goal of a Jewish homeland while most other veterans of Middle East proselytizing campaigns identified with the Arab claims to Palestine.[28]

Christian pro-Zionists organized impressive educational campaigns. For example, the American Palestine Committee and the Christian Council on Palestine held meetings attended by more than four hundred Christian civic and religious leaders in Cincinnati on January 9, 1944. During that same week, the Christian groups sponsored 21 different meetings in St. Louis, including several for teachers, which attracted more than 4,400 educators.[29]

Christian support groups, working with and closely supervised by the AZEC, provided the Zionist public relations machine with an important weapon. In fact, American Zionists needed all the help that they could gather as they embarked on the difficult task of generating pro-Zionist support within an American public and government preoccupied with immediate wartime tasks and concerns. The threat that "dissident" Jewish organizations would challenge the Zionist claim to speak for the Jewish community significantly complicated this task.

THE ZIONIST LOBBY: COMBATING ENEMIES

The American Jewish Committee's (AJC) secession from the American Jewish Conference especially worried American Zionists. While it was not a mass-member organization, the AJC represented some of the wealthiest and most prestigious Jews of the United States. The Committee could also justly claim many impressive successes in protecting Jewish civil rights at home and abroad since its establishment in 1906.[30] With its impressive financial and political resources, the AJC might be able to block the Zionist quest for hegemony within the American Jewish community.

Abba Hillel Silver, at the helm of the AZEC, aggressively responded to the American Jewish Committee threat. He charged that the Committee's refusal to accept the decision of the democratically elected American Jewish Conference proved that non-Zionists would cooperate with Zionists only on their own terms. Silver urged that everything be done to break the influence of the American Jewish Committee.[31] Heeding an AZEC request, over half of the eighteen national organizations affiliated with the American Jewish Committee, including Hadassah, cut all ties with the group.[32]

Zionists, believing that world Jewry was involved in a battle for survival, accused the AJC of treason. By withdrawing from the American Jewish Conference, the AZEC argued, the Committee seriously undermined Jewish unity and significantly weakened the "Jewish war effort." A letter from the Council of Jewish Organizations of Bensonhurst and Mapleton (Brooklyn) is typical of the attacks on the American Jewish Committee. The Brooklyn Council chastised AJC President Joseph Proskauer for refusing to cooperate with the American Jewish Conference in protecting "our people against a future of continued horror, persecution, discrimination, and murder." The letter included a dire warning that "those who undermine the unity of our Jewish People give aid and comfort to the forces of evil by practicing their policy of 'divide and conquer.'"[33]

With all America mobilized for the war effort, the charge of giving aid and comfort to the enemy was certainly serious and powerful. Believing that only they could free the Jewish people from a 2,000-year-old tradition of persecution, Zionists realized that the AJC's opposition to the American Jewish Conference's platform threatened to do more than just challenge Zionist claims to community leadership; it might condemn future generations of Jews to the horrors of another Hitler. Given this view, the Zionist assault on the AJC is understandable and perhaps justified.

The leaders of the AJC found it difficult to resist Zionist pressure. In an attempt to maintain some leadership role in the American Jewish community, they decided that the Committee would have to undergo a drastic organizational transformation. The organization, which had always been content to restrict membership to a relatively few prominent Jews, launched a mass membership drive shortly after the American Jewish Conference. However, its struggle was futile. As American Jewry learned about the horrible extent of the Holocaust, the Zionist promise to put a "certain end" to Jewish homelessness, the principal cause of Jewish persecution, became nearly irresistible. By 1946, the AJC, finally prepared to bow to the will of American Jewry, began to cooperate with the Zionist crusade.[34]

Besides battling the AJC, the American Zionist Emergency Council devoted a considerable amount of energy to attempting to destroy the small group of Irgun representatives in the United States, led by Peter Bergson, who came to the United States shortly before the outbreak of war in Europe to raise money to support Irgun activities in Palestine. In December 1941, the Irgunists formed the Committee for a Jewish Army, believing that American public support might encourage Great Britain to organize Jewish Palestinians into a fighting force.[35]

After launching the Jewish Army effort, Bergson contacted Stephen Wise and offered to participate in a joint campaign.[36] Wise and most of the Zionist leadership considered the Irgun to be a renegade neo-fascist organization and condemned the group's refusal to accept the authority of the World Zionist Organization. As a result, Zionists refused to supply Bergson with any financial support.[37] However, American Zionists, recognizing Bergson's skills as a propagandist, were willing to cooperate on a limited basis; they proposed that the Committee for a Jewish Army would assume responsibility for publicity campaigns, while Zionist authorities would carry on all negotiations with the American and British governments.[38] David Ben-Gurion vetoed this plan, ruling out any cooperation with Bergson until he and his associates accepted the authority of the World Zionist Organization.[39]

Bergson's formation of the Emergency Committee to Save the Jewish People of Europe (ECSJPE) in July 1943 increased the tension between American Zionists and the Irgunists. The AZEC feared that the Bergson group, specialists in the use of full-page newspaper ads, would divert support and members from them. Zionists were particularly concerned about the Bergson-inspired Baldwin-Gillette resolution, which called for the establishment of a government agency to rescue the Jews of Europe but which made no mention of Palestine or Jewish statehood.[40] Appalled by what they considered to be the Bergson group's abandonment of Zionism, the American Jewish Conference on December 30, 1943, accused the ECSJPE of tricking American Jews into making financial contributions in the false belief that the committee was engaged in actual rescue work. The Conference statement also condemned the Baldwin-Gillette rescue resolution for being introduced in "complete disregard of the rescue program which is being actively pressed in Washington by representative Jewish agencies."[41]

Historians and other investigators have never found evidence to substantiate the Zionist claim that Bergson and his associates were involved in financial irregularities. Ads run by the Emergency Committee to Save the Jewish People of Europe always noted that contributions would be used to support the publicity campaign aiming to force the Roosevelt administration to adopt an aggressive rescue policy.[42] However, during the tense and dangerous years of World War II, American Zionists found it easy to believe that the "undisciplined" and "irresponsible" Bergson group was capable of almost any perfidy. A few weeks after the American Jewish

Conference assault, the American Zionist Emergency Council sent letters to American legislators and distributed press releases accusing Bergson of creating "paper" organizations that were not representative of the American Jewish community and of "acting in accordance with opportunistic impulses of the moment."[43]

As part of the AZEC's campaign against Bergson, Stephen Wise unsuccessfully attempted to convince Secretary of the Interior Harold Ickes to resign his position as Honorary Chairman of the ECSJPE.[44] Zionist leaders had more luck in securing agreements from Undersecretary of State Sumner Welles and refugee-problem expert Myron Taylor not to participate in Bergson's rescue campaign.[45] Harry Shapiro, director of the AZEC, instructed all chairpeople of the local emergency committee in May 1944 to disseminate anti-Bergson statements in their communities. Shapiro reminded the local Zionist leaders that, after securing the resignation of Bergson supporters, they should "send us their names, along with any statement which they care to make, and we will release the story to the Yiddish and Anglo-Jewish press."[46] R. J. Thomas, president of the United Auto Workers, and William Green, president of the AFL, asked that their names be withdrawn from a list of Bergson supporters shortly after the AZEC operation began. Dean Alfange, leader of New York's Labor party and one of the oldest and strongest backers of the ECSJPE, resigned from the organization in 1944.[47]

The Bergson group continued to exist in some form until Israel's creation in 1948, however they were never able effectively to challenge the claim of established pro-Zionist and Zionist organizations in the United States that they, not Bergson, represented the interests and retained the loyalty of American Jewry. Instead, Bergson and his followers remained an annoying, but perhaps healthy, stimulant for American Zionist leaders who understood that the imaginative and energetic Irgunists might find a larger audience among American Jews if the Zionists appeared to be slackening in their efforts to solve the "Jewish problem."

THE PALESTINE RESOLUTIONS

While Zionist publicists and politicians devoted considerable energy to opposing rival Jewish organizations, the main function of the AZEC was to generate pro-Zionist sentiment in the U.S. public and government. Much of the American Zionist Emergency Council's work was unspectacular and certainly unromantic. Copying the tactics of other Jewish and Christian public relations campaigns, Zionists spent much of their energies collecting endorsements from public figures. By the summer of 1945, all but seven of the nation's governors had signed an AZEC-sponsored petition calling on the president to act to "open the doors of Palestine to Jewish mass immigration and colonization and to bring about the earliest transformation of that country into a free and democratic Jewish Commonwealth."[48] The AZEC received hundreds of solicited endorsements from senators and representatives for publication in Reuben Fink's *America and Palestine*, a book that attempted to demonstrate the long-standing commitment by the U.S. government for the reestablishment of a Jewish homeland in Palestine.[49]

Zionists did not find it especially difficult to convince legislators to issue statements in support of the creation of a Jewish commonwealth. Given the insignificant number of Arab-Americans, congressmen or state representatives took no political risk when they voiced sympathy for the Zionist position. These endorsements, however easily acquired, played an important role in the political campaign for Jewish statehood. The AZEC could use even vague statements of support by American politicians to demonstrate the compatibility of American national interest and Jewish nationhood. This was important in convincing Christian Americans that there was no danger involved in supporting Zionism and was essential in winning the approval of those Jews who feared that ethnic nationalism might raise embarrassing questions about the dual loyalty of American Jewry.

As important as political endorsements were to the Zionist education campaign, the AZEC in 1944 and 1945 discovered that it could not easily transform verbal expressions of support into concrete policies. During these years the organization devoted a considerable amount of its resources to a futile attempt to win congressional support for Jewish nationalism. The resolutions the Zionists asked the Senate and the House of Representatives to consider would not commit the government to a specific course of action, but would simply express the legislature's sense that the United States should support free Jewish immigration to Palestine and the establishment there of a Jewish Commonwealth.[50]

Although seemingly devoid of any meaningful content, the resolutions were central to the Zionist program. Jewish nationalist leaders hoped that congressional action would influence the State Department to adopt a more pro-Zionist position. The State Department would then become an important ally in negotiations between Great Britain and the Zionists on the postwar status of Palestine.[51] Emanuel Neumann and Abba Hillel Silver believed that it was extremely important to introduce the resolutions in 1944, an election year, when both Democrats and Republicans, vying for Jewish votes, would be most inclined to support Jewish statehood.[52] Furthermore, it must be realized that the strategy Zionists began to pursue in 1942 led inevitably to the floor of the Congress. At the Biltmore Conference all major American Zionist groups made the creation of a Jewish commonwealth their goal, a position the representatives of the entire American Jewish community adopted at the American Jewish Conferences. The next logical step for Zionist leaders was to have the representatives of *all* Americans accept the commonwealth position. If the Senate and the House of Representatives passed the Zionist resolutions, the AZEC could claim to speak for all Americans, not only American Jewry.

Fearful that Peter Bergson's ECSJPE was preparing its own resolution for congressional approval, Zionist leaders in early 1944 decided immediately to activate their own congressional strategy. The AZEC anticipated that the Bergson-inspired resolution would, like their own, call for free, unrestricted immigration to Palestine, but would make no mention of Jewish statehood. Instead of relying on the Jewish political claim to Palestine to justify their request for free immigration, the Bergson proposal would simply argue that Palestine's geographic location made it the most practical *temporary* haven for Jews escaping from Hungary and the Balkans.[53]

Pro-Zionist legislators sponsored the Palestine resolution in the House of Representatives and the Senate. Following AZEC orders, local emergency committees solicited statements of support from hundreds of prominent Americans. The AZEC forwarded these endorsements to the House Committee on Foreign Affairs, which held hearings on the Palestine resolution in February 1944.[54]

The Zionists skillfully presented their case to the Committee on Foreign Affairs. Their statements contained few original ideas, but they articulately presented the case for Jewish statehood that Zionists had developed since the start of the war. Abba Hillel Silver condemned the British White Paper as a policy of appeasement and emphasized the vital role Palestine could play in solving the dangerous Jewish refugee problem the Allies would confront after victory.[55] Dr. Israel Goldstein, president of the ZOA, and David Wertheim, National Secretary of the Poale Zion, detailed Palestinian Jewry's contributions to the Allied war effort.[56] Hadassah President Judith Epstein's testimony focused on the many benefits the Zionists had brought to Palestine's Arabs. Stephen Wise, Wolf Gold of Mizrachi, and Emanuel Neumann reminded the representatives of the continuing murder of European Jewry. Neumann counselled the committee that by passing the Zionist resolution they could send a "word of cheer" and a message of "hope" to the Jews caught in Hitler's Europe.[57]

Prominent Christians, organized by the AZEC, assisted the Zionists at the congressional hearings. According to Senator Robert Wagner, speaking for the American Palestine Committee, the slaughter of European Jewry "demand[s] of us a statesmanlike, constructive policy which will provide a more secure and dignified future for the Jewish people in the democratic world of tomorrow."[58] Dr. Henry Atkinson, president of the Christian Council on Palestine, warned the House committee that a failure to solve the Jewish problem might allow another tyrant to use anti-Semitism to come to power and plunge the world into a third world war.[59]

For a time it seemed that the Zionists would succeed in winning Congress's support. On January 10, 1944, Isaiah Berlin, attached to the British Embassy in Washington, reported in his weekly political summary that Zionist agitation against the White Paper was "embarrassing" the Roosevelt administration. A month later he cautioned that while passage of the Palestine resolutions would not commit America to a specific course of action, "its significance should not be minimized as its passage imposes inevitable curbs on pro-Arab tendencies of Near Eastern Office of the State Department on Palestine issue."[60] To the British government's relief, the United States War Department informed Congress that passage of the pro-Zionist resolutions at that time could incite an Arab revolt in the Middle East that would undermine the Allied war effort. The House of Representatives and the Senate had little choice but to heed the War Department's warning and tabled the Palestine resolutions until the military situation in the Middle East was more secure. On March 6, Isaiah Berlin reported that the "pendulum now seems to be swinging away from the Zionists."[61] Franklin Roosevelt attempted to ease the Zionists' pain by announcing, after a visit by Rabbis Wise and Silver, that the United States did not approve and had never approved of the restrictions on Jewish immigration to Palestine imposed by the White Paper of 1939.[62] Roosevelt's Democratic party followed the lead of the Republican party and included a pro-Zionist plank in its platform.[63]

Throughout the remainder of 1944, the Zionists quietly prepared to have their resolutions reintroduced in Congress. In October, the War Department informed Senator Robert Taft that the military situation in the Middle East had substantially improved since March. With the War Department's roadblock removed, Silver and the AZEC expected that the Palestine resolutions would win easy passage. However, after the presidential elections, the State Department, at the request of President Roosevelt, convinced Congress to postpone action on the bills because of the "tense" international situation. Roosevelt, in a letter to Senator Taft, expressed his concern with avoiding an Arab massacre of Palestinian Jewry, which he feared might follow the creation of a Jewish state.[64]

The State Department's scuttling of the Zionists' lobbying campaign infuriated Abba Hillel Silver. With the support of Emanuel Neumann, he demanded that the AZEC openly attack Roosevelt for betraying his and the Democratic Party's electoral campaign pledges of support for Zionism. Stephen Wise and a majority of the AZEC members refused to accept Silver's argument. Wise, who claimed to have a close friendship with the president, maintained that Roosevelt's commitment to the Jewish cause was genuine. Many of the AZEC members understood that an attack on Roosevelt might backfire. He had not yet even begun his fourth term, and it seemed likely that the Zionists would have to deal with him for at least another four years.

After a hard-fought battle over what the Zionist response to Roosevelt should be, Silver gave up leadership of the American Zionist Emergency Council in December 1944. He would not return to the Zionist helm until July 1945. In the meantime, he and his supporters would wage an underground campaign against Wise, preparing the way for Silver's resumption of power, while the AZEC carried on its public relations campaign.[65]

The Palestine resolution fiasco proved that even an efficient and energetic public relations and lobbying organization could not easily influence a popular wartime president who was able to justify unpopular actions by citing the imperative of victory over a cruel enemy. During World War II, however, the AZEC could alleviate its frustrations over the failure to influence presidential policy by contemplating its remarkable success in achieving a position of power and prestige within the American Jewish community. In 1933, the year Adolf Hitler came to power, Zionism was just one of several competing ideologies and movements within the American Jewish community. After the American Jewish Conference, Jewish nationalists could, with much justice, claim to be the rightful leaders of the community. By V-E day in 1945, American Zionists, with their Christian allies, had made substantial progress in bringing the case of Jewish statehood to the general American public, although they were far from a decisive victory for the "hearts and minds" of the American public. Many Americans with loved ones in the armed services were little aware of the plight of European Jewry and the Zionist solution of the Jewish problem.

AMERICAN LIBERALS AND ZIONISM: A CASE STUDY

Liberalism and Zionism

Unlike many of their compatriots, American liberals seemed to be particularly sensitive to the "Jewish problem." Although they were by no means a monolithic group and could sharply disagree on many crucial factors, "liberals" during the World War II era generally shared basic values. Most espoused a creed of tolerance and opposed discrimination and persecution on the basis of race or religion. While some had flirted with isolationism in the twenties and thirties, the Japanese attack on Pearl Harbor unified them in the battle against the Axis. During the war, they devoted considerable thought to how they wished to reconstruct the world after the Allied victory. Some, like Eleanor Roosevelt, looked forward to the "internationalization" of the New Deal. Many renewed their commitment to a Wilsonian brand of anti-colonialism and anti-imperialism. Very few adopted a strictly antinationalist stance, although many who viewed nazism as an aberrant form of excessive nationalism believed that love of and commitment to nation had to be tempered with good sense. Roosevelt and Churchill's Atlantic Charter reflected a liberal sensibility in its commitment to provide all nations with "access on equal terms to the trade and raw materials . . . needed for their economic prosperity," and its "desire to bring about the fullest collaboration between all nations in the economic field, with the object of securing for all improved labor standards, economic advancement, and social security." Anthropologist Margaret Mead's 1942 ethnography of the American people, *And Keep Your Powder Dry*, ends with a blueprint for the postwar world that elaborates upon the Atlantic Charter. Mead envisioned a world of sovereign nation-states, each recognizing that its prosperity and security depended on cooperation between all nations. Republican liberal Wendell Wilkie expressed much the same view in *One World*:

> When I say that peace must be planned on a world basis, I mean quite literally that it must embrace the earth. Continents and oceans are plainly only parts of a whole, seen, as I have seen them from the air. England and America are parts. Russia and China, Egypt, Syria and Turkey, Iraq and Iran are also parts. And it is inescapable that there can be no peace for any part of the world unless the foundations of peace are made secure throughout all parts of the world.

An interest in the development of regional federations and economic unions was consistent with this world vision, which tended to equate war with unrestricted international competition and peace with economic cooperation.[66]

Partly because of their commitment to tolerance and their opposition to pseudo-scientific racism, liberals were generally more concerned about the plight of European Jewry than most of the American public. Columnist Dorothy Thompson championed the refugees' cause and attacked Nazi anti-Semitism throughout the thirties and forties.[67] The *New Republic* and the *Nation*, two of the most respected liberal periodicals of the time, sympathized with the refugees' plight and forcefully demanded that the American government take steps to prevent the extermination of European Jewry.[68]

Zionists expected liberals to become an important part of their American constituency and, as noted, went to considerable lengths to organize the liberal Christian clergy. In fact, many prominent liberals supported the Jewish national cause. Robert Wagner, the "father" of the National Labor Relations Act, championed the Zionist cause in Congress. Secretary of the Interior Harold Ickes also supported Jewish nationalism.[69]

Dr. Reinhold Niebuhr, professor of the Philosophy of Religion at the Union Theological Seminary, strongly supported the Zionist cause. A world famous Protestant theologian and philosopher, Niebuhr served as editor-in-chief of *Christianity and Crisis*, a journal committed to furthering the Christian values of humanism and tolerance in the political world, sat on the editorial board of the *Nation*, and was a member of the pro-Zionist American Palestine Committee. Many American Zionists, perhaps surprised that a leading Christian thinker would join their crusade, admired Niebuhr. In September 1941, the minister received a tumultuous ovation when he told the annual convention of the Zionist Organization of America that "justice" demanded that the Jews have a homeland.[70]

In February 1942, nine months before the American public learned about the continuing Holocaust in Nazi-occupied Europe, Niebuhr wrote a two-part essay for the *Nation*, "Jews After the War." Taking a position that David Ben-Gurion and Abba Hillel Silver would popularize at the Biltmore Conference two months later, he told the liberal readers of the *Nation* that the defeat of Hitler would not solve the problems of the Jewish people. Because the war would leave "millions" of Jews homeless and "disinherited," the world would have to provide the Jews with a post-war home. Declaring it "a scandal that the Jews have had so little effective aid from the rest of us," the theologian launched a devastating attack against unnamed liberals who, he claimed, incorrectly evaluated the Jewish problem.

Niebuhr condemned the tolerance of many American liberals, which was "based upon a false universalism which in practice develops into a new form of nationalism." There was a "partly unconscious" element of "cultural imperialism" in a tolerance that welcomed and expected "a complete destruction of all racial distinctions." Assimilation, he noted, was a "painless death," but it was "death nevertheless."

Jews, Niebuhr maintained, had a unique position in the American melting pot. While other ethnic groups could allow themselves to assimilate because their "collective will to survive" was "engaged" and "expressed" in their native homeland, Jews, a people without a country, would lose their collective identity if they chose to assimilate into liberal and tolerant America.

Zionism expressed the "national will" of Jewry to live. Liberals in particular and the Allied world in general must accept the Zionist program, which was "correct in principle, however much it may have to be qualified in application." Niebuhr explained that "every race finally has a right to a homeland where it will not be 'different,' where it will neither be patronized by 'good' people nor subjected to calumny by bad people."[71]

Many American liberals, like Niebuhr, sympathized with the suffering Jews of Europe, but not all followed him into the Zionist ranks. The editors of the *Nation*, who published Niebuhr's pro-Zionist articles, and their colleagues at the *New Republic* did not endorse the establishment of a Jewish state in Palestine. After the beginning of the Arab revolt in Palestine in 1936 both of these prestigious liberal journals opened their pages to liberal supporters and critics of the Zionist enterprise. Both journals appreciated the work of the Yishuv in resettling Jewish refugees, but they also were genuinely concerned and troubled by Arab opposition to Jewish settlement.[72]

Some American liberals questioned whether Palestine could become either a Jewish state or a mass haven for refugees. In November 1940, Henry Wallace, the newly elected vice president, told one prominent Zionist to consider using Brazil as a haven for Jewish refugees because Palestine was only a little land with limited natural resources.[73] Six months later, Wallace argued that Palestine could not be a solution for the refugee problem because the Holy Land had already reached its population "saturation" point. Solomon Goldman, president of the Zionist Organization of America, feared that most American officials shared Wallace's view.[74]

In the early years of World War II, as Zionist activities in the United States intensified, Jewish nationalists decided to confront the fears of Henry Wallace. An American Christian stood at the center of the new Zionist strategy. Dr. Walter Clay Lowdermilk, one of America's leading soil conservationists and assistant chief of the United States Agriculture Department's Soil Conservation Service, visited the Middle East in 1938 and 1939, on an official study of land use in the region.[75] As he traveled through the Middle East, he despaired to see the "repugnant evidences of deadly soil erosion superseding the results of skill and land use during previous centuries."[76] Lowdermilk's mood brightened when he discovered the three hundred Jewish settlements of Palestine, where he found refugees from European persecution defying all hardship and "applying the principle of cooperation and soil conservation to the old Land of Israel."[77] His experience in Palestine moved Lowdermilk to suggest that an eleventh commandment be added to the ancient ten. Speaking on Palestine's radio network in June 1939, the American soil conservationist proclaimed: "Thou shalt inherit the holy earth as a faithful steward conserving its resources and productivity from generation to generation. . . . If any shall fail in this stewardship of the land, thy fruitful fields shall become . . . wasting gullies and thy descendants shall decrease and live in poverty or perish from the face of the earth."[78]

Lowdermilk's enchantment with the Jewish pioneers and his conviction that continued scientific development would allow Palestine to absorb millions of Jewish refugees, attracted the attention of American Zionists. Emanuel Neumann contacted Lowdermilk and happily discovered that the soil conservationist was willing to write a book about Palestine's development prospects.[79] Zionist leaders agreed to provide Lowdermilk with technical and financial assistance and assumed responsibility for finding a suitable publisher for the planned volume.[80]

Lowdermilk's plan for a huge irrigation and hydroelectric project in the Jordan Valley fascinated Neumann.[81] The project would be modeled on the New Deal's Tennessee Valley Authority and would accordingly be named the Jordan Valley Authority (J.V.A.). Lowdermilk informed Neumann that the J.V.A. would allow five million Jewish refugees to settle in Palestine.[82] With this prospect in mind, Neumann took steps to begin planning for the eventual construction of the J.V.A. project.[83]

Even before the publication of his book, Lowdermilk was playing an important role in the Zionist campaign. He appeared as a witness before the House Committee on Foreign Affairs in February 1944, testifying on Palestine's ability to absorb a great number of Jewish refugees without displacing the Arab population.[84] Zionists used Lowdermilk's work to argue that the creation of a Jewish state in Palestine would be practical as well as just. Emanuel Neumann expected that liberals would be particularly impressed by Lowdermilk. The J.V.A. offered, Neumann remarked, "a new approach to the problem of Palestine and one that is peculiarly suited to the American mind." It would "attract wide support on the part of many who would naturally resent a direct political approach. Politically speaking, it may be regarded as a flanking movement of a most promising character — one of the most significant contributions ever made to Political Zionism."[85]

According to an agreement Neumann negotiated with Harpers Brothers, Lowdermilk's publisher, the American Zionist Emergency Council financed a promotional campaign for *Palestine: Land of Promise.* [86] The AZEC arranged for magazines and newspapers to print reviews.[87] George W. Norris, the "father" of the T.V.A., bestowed his blessings on the Jordan Valley Authority in the *Nation.*[88] Within a year, *Palestine: Land of Promise* went through seven printings, producing a total of sixteen thousand copies. Zionists distributed fifteen hundred gratis copies to congressmen, government officials, educational and religious leaders, journalists, diplomats, and state and local politicians.[89] By the end of 1945, the text appeared in Hebrew and Spanish translations, while the *Jewish Morning Journal* printed a serialized Yiddish version of the book.[90]

Lowdermilk's success delighted Zionist leaders. At Stephen Wise's suggestion, the American Palestine Committee organized a large testimonial dinner in the soil conservationist's honor.[91] The Mutal Broadcasting System broadcast portions of the testimonial including a call for a Jewish state. Prominent public officials attended the dinner including T.V.A. chairman David Lilienthal and Undersecretary of the Interior Abe Fortas. Neumann wrote that the continued "propagandization" of the Jordan Valley Authority scheme would "not only win new friends for our movement in areas in which we have very few friends, but will . . . offset the questions as to the absorptive capacity of Palestine with which we are continuously confronted."[92]

By November 1942, Zionists had undertaken substantial steps to win the support of liberal America. Reinhold Niebuhr had presented an elaborate pro-Zionist argument aimed specifically at a progressive audience. Walter Lowdermilk's work seemed to be especially promising. At the end of November, however, a tragic outside event interjected itself into the Zionist-liberal relationship when Americans learned about the Nazis' systematic extermination of European Jewry.

Liberals, Zionists, and the Rescue of the European Jews

Unlike many Americans, liberals quickly acknowledged and bemoaned what Alfred Kazin termed "our silent complicity in the massacre of the Jews."[93] The

New Republic reported in its December 7th edition that Hitler considered the "annihilation" of the Jews the most important Nazi goal.[94] Two weeks later, the journal published a long article on the Holocaust written by Varian Fry. A journalist and frequent contributor to the *New Republic* (he would later serve on the magazine's editorial board), Fry had worked for thirteen months in Vichy France, legally and illegally aiding Jews to escape Hitler's reach.[95] In his essay, Fry, remembering the false atrocity stories of World War I, acknowledged that it was difficult to believe the stories of systematic slaughter. But convinced that the terrible news was true, he urged Franklin Roosevelt to publicly threaten to punish individuals participating in the extermination and suggested that the United States offer asylum to those few Jews who could escape Europe.[96]

On December 19, 1942, the *Nation's* editors recommended that the Vatican intercede on the Jews' behalf and that Franklin Roosevelt condemn the Nazi murders.[97] By the end of February 1943, the magazine was charging the Allied governments with near complicity in European Jewry's demise. The Jews, an editorial stated, needed more help and less pity, "for when definite measures are proposed to help the victims . . . the State Department and the British Foreign Office, though ever so politely, turn away."[98] In March, Freda Kirchwey, the publisher and chief editor of the *Nation*, warned that an Allied victory might not save European Jewry. "It is not fantastic to believe that even when Hitler is overthrown, he will find profound compensation in leaving behind him a Europe 'cleansed' of the hated Jew." If the Jew perished, the United States would be guilty of abetting the Nazi murders in their heinous crime. Kirchway mourned: "If we had behaved like humane and generous people instead of complacent, cowardly ones, the two million Jews lying today in the earth of Poland . . . would be alive and safe. And other millions yet to die would have found sanctuary. We had it in our power to rescue this doomed people and we did not lift a hand to do it."[99]

Zionists attempted to shape the liberal response to the Holocaust. During January and February 1943, the *Nation* published a series of four articles by Zionist publicist Rabbi Philip S. Bernstein. The first essay appeared less than two months after news of the Holocaust reached the American public.[100] Repeating a standard Zionist argument, Bernstein noted that while the Jews were the "worst victims of the war," anti-Semitism endangered all Europeans. For centuries tyrants had used Jew hatred to maintain the loyalty of the masses and to justify conquest. He warned that a peace treaty that did not provide a solution for the Jewish problem could not effectively ensure peace and stability in Europe. Jews would again become the first victims of would-be dictators and conquerors.

Bernstein's second essay focused on European Jewry's "frightful dilemma."[101] Allied victories would not necessarily lead to Jewish salvation. Every German defeat seemed to infuriate the Nazis who then "perpetrated new pogroms." Recognizing that only England and the United States had the resources and power to prevent the Jews' destruction, Bernstein proposed a seven-point Allied rescue plan, calling on Great Britain to open Palestine's doors to at least the number of refugees allowed under the White Paper. The Allies, he demanded, should also allow stateless and Palestinian Jews to form Jewish military units and should immediately announce that the Jews "will have a hearing in the councils of the United Nations."

The magnitude of Hitler's persecution horrified Bernstein, but he refused to label the attempted extermination of European Jewry an "aberration" born in the mind of a mad dictator. Rather, in a third article,[102] anticipating the major theme of Abba Hillel Silver's epic address to the American Jewish Conference, Bernstein argued that the mass murder was "the logical culmination of the whole history of the Jews in Europe." To escape the threat of postwar pogroms, Jews, particularly the East Europeans who had little contact with their Christian neighbors, would have to emigrate. He regretfully reported that there was little support for opening the doors of the United States to Jewish refugees. Many Americans expected that the country's postwar capacities and resources would be severely strained by the need to absorb millions of returning soldiers. While he hoped for an eventual liberalization of the American immigration quotas, Bernstein suggested that large-scale Jewish immigration to Palestine would be a bold and practical solution to the Jewish problem.

Bernstein concluded his series of essays with a powerful defense of Zionism that glorified Jewish accomplishments in Palestine.[103] Most Palestinian Jews were farmers and workers, not merchants and middlemen like their Diaspora ancestors and brethren. Americans could identify with these "new Jews" who had "much in common with the frontiersmen who cleared the wilderness and built the first settlements on the North American continent." An attachment to Palestine's soil gave Jews there "a quiet strength and courage denied to the harried restless Jews in Europe."

Bernstein, like most Zionists, believed that only a few American Jews would choose to settle in Palestine. Nevertheless, he announced that Palestine could still help ensure the security and safety of American Jewry. Every European Jew who went to the Holy Land reduced the pressure on the United States to settle refugees within its own borders. This pressure, Bernstein warned, threatened to incite anti-Semites within the United States.

Aiming his comments at his liberal audience, Bernstein maintained that the Zionist development of Palestine benefited the native Arab population, and he cited the work of Lowdermilk to prove that millions of Jews could settle in the Holy Land without displacing any Arabs. He asserted, however, that Zionism would still be justified even if some Arabs were displaced. Jews needed Palestine more than the Arabs did, for there was "no Arab problem in the sense that there is a Jewish problem." The Arabs did not have to fear brutal extermination, and they possessed more land than they could possibly settle.

141

Eleven weeks after the final installment of his *Nation* series, Bernstein's appeal to American liberals appeared in abridged form in the *New Republic*.[104] He repeated many of the points he made in the earlier series and wrote that "it would be an injustice to the Arabs not to expose them to the inspiration and the example of Jewish social idealism and scientific progress in Palestine."

The continuing murder of European Jewry seemed to strengthen Bernstein's argument. As the Nazi extermination plan progressed, liberal concern for European Jewry began to dwarf consideration of Zionism's perceived drawbacks. The Arab population of Palestine was not forgotten, but secular liberal journals began to demand that Britain disregard Arab opposition of Jewish settlement and allow any Jew who could escape into Palestine.

The *New Republic* printed a nineteen-page special rescue supplement in August 1943.[105] The journal asked Americans to realize that "the fate of the Jewish people is one of the issues of the war."[106] If World War II was to be a crusade for peace and humanitarian idealism and not a struggle for national power, the United States had to attempt the rescue of European Jewry. The *New Republic*'s editors suggested many steps to alleviate Jewish suffering in Europe and paid particular attention to Palestine's central role in any rescue strategy. One article asserted that due to the hard work of Zionist pioneers, the Holy Land could provide homes for at least two million refugees, if only the British would reverse their inhumane White Paper policy. The essay acknowledged, however, that the final decision on Palestine's political future would have to await the war's conclusion.[107]

Arab-Americans tried, with difficulty, to argue against unrestricted Jewish immigration to Palestine. In a letter to the *New Republic*, Jabir Shibli of the State College of Pennsylvania accused Jewish nationalists of being "more interested in the conquest of Palestine from the Arabs . . . than they are in saving the Jews from Nazi persecution." The Palestine Zionist was an "alien" who used British power to master Palestine, an Arab land. The persecution of Jewry was a "disgrace," he conceded, and everyone had to be willing to sacrifice to put an end to European Jewry's suffering. Palestine, however, had already done its humanitarian duty by absorbing nearly five hundred thousand Jewish refugees. Any further growth in Zionist strength in Palestine, he feared, would hinder legitimate Arab aspirations for "independence" and "unification."[108]

Arab nationalists in the United States were not formidable opponents to the American Zionist campaign for liberal support. However, even as the Zionist education campaign continued in full force, some influential American liberals began to adopt positions on the Jewish problem that potentially threatened the successful establishment of a Jewish state in Palestine. Most disturbingly for Zionists, several liberals seemed to be attracted to the "heretical" ideas of Peter Bergson.

Although the Palestinian Irgun was a right-wing organization, Bergson and his Irgun associates won a surprising level of support from American progressives.

Dean Alfange, a New York Labor party leader, served as co-chairman of the Emergency Committee to Save the Jewish People of Europe (ECSJPE) until his resignation in the summer of 1944. The presidents of the American Federation of Labor and the Congress of Industrial Organizations gave at least nominal support to the Bergson rescue committee. The *New York Post*, at that time a strong supporter of liberal and left-wing causes, was the ECSJPE's closest media ally. Bergson maintained a very cordial relationship with Ted Thackrey, the *Post*'s managing editor, and the newspaper, in turn, strongly endorsed the program of the ECSJPE. When the Zionist establishment launchd a concerted attack against the Bergsonites in 1944, the *Post* carried an extremely favorable feature story on Bergson.[109]

Other prominent liberal journals never embraced the ECSJPE with the same warmth as the *New York Post*. In fact, a March 1943 *New Republic* editorial sharply criticized the Irgun's brand of right-wing Zionism without specifically naming Bergson and his organization.[110] Despite this, the "Bergson Boys" (as their opponents called them) managed to have some input into the magazines that both reflected and helped to mold liberal thought.

The ECSJPE made extensive use of full-page newspaper and magazine advertisements. During World War II the organization ran many advertisements in liberal journals. These ads, some written by Hollywood script writer Ben Hecht, caught the public's attention with such stirring headlines as: "HITLER'S ENEMY NO. 1 *MUST BE RECOGNIZED* AS OUR ALLY NO. 1"; "HOW WELL ARE YOU SLEEPING?"; "TIME RACES DEATH–WHAT ARE WE WAITING FOR?"; "ONE VICTORY FOR HITLER?"[111]

Many American liberals, like the Bergson group, were primarily concerned with the immediate rescue of European Jewry. They recognized Zionist leaders as legitimate representatives of American Jewry, but naturally found themselves attracted to certain aspects of the ECSJPE's program.

On November 9, 1943, Congressmen Will Rogers, Jr., and Joseph B. Baldwin and Senator Guy M. Gillette, all supporters of Peter Bergson, introduced congressional resolutions calling for the creation of a United States Commission to Save the Jewish People of Europe. The Zionist-dominated American Jewish Conference charged that the resolutions were introduced in "complete disregard" of the rescue programs of "representative" Jewish organizations.[112] In spite of this formidable opposition, the *Nation*'s editorial staff saw fit to support the rescue agency resolution. The journal attacked the American government's inaction and callousness toward the murders in Europe and asked Congress to establish an agency that would "help save the stateless Jews of occupied Europe who have no government to speak for them."[113]

On several other occasions, liberal positions coincided with those of the Bergson Boys and conflicted with the interests of the American Zionist establishment. The American Zionist Emergency Council had its own set of resolutions introduced in Congress in early 1944. If passed, they would have expressed the legislature's support for the creation of a Jewish commonwealth. The *New York Post*, reflecting Bergson's view, opposed the Zionist resolutions because they politicized the rescue issue.[114] The editors of the *New Republic* endorsed the *Post* and recommended that the resolutions be modified to ask only for a "temporary refuge" in Palestine for those Jews whose "alternative" was death. Because the temporary refuge proposal would not affect the Holy Land's future political status, the liberal editors confessed, "We don't see how even the Arabs or the War Department can legitimately object to this action."[115]

Bergson and his colleagues spent the summer of 1944 campaigning for the establishment of emergency refugee shelters in Palestine. Under their plan, Jewish refugees admitted to the shelters would have no legal right to remain in Palestine once the war ended.[116] The emergency shelter scheme offered a way around Britain's restrictive immigration policy, but American Zionists vehemently opposed it. The idea of Jews being treated as refugees in their "national home" was too painful for Jewish nationalists.[117] The *Nation*'s Freda Kirchwey, however, could contemplate the possibility without great anguish.[118]

Liberals and Binationalism

Liberal deviation from the rescue strategy of pursuing Jewish statehood troubled Zionist leaders. The tendency of some liberals to adopt the binationalist cause when they became interested in a Palestinian solution to the Jewish problem further disturbed Jewish nationalists.

The idea of a binational Arab-Jewish state in Palestine did not originate in the forties. In 1925, Brith Shalom, a Palestinian Jewish organization, advocated the creation of a state where Jews and Arabs would share power equally. Each people would be guaranteed equal rights and cultural autonomy. Brith Shalom never attracted many members, but it included some of Palestine's leading intellectuals. The remarkable Judah Magnes led the organization. An American by birth, a Reform rabbi by vocation, and a nonconformist by inclination, Magnes pioneered community work among East European Jewish immigrants crowded into New York's Lower East Side. His pacifism compromised his position as a communal leader during the patriotically intolerant days of World War I. Shortly after the armistice, Magnes moved to Palestine, becoming chancellor of the Hebrew University in Jerusalem.[119]

Most American Zionists opposed the binational state idea. Their hostility intensified after May 1942, when Zionist leaders at the Biltmore Hotel decided that their common goal would be the immediate postwar establishment of a Jewish commonwealth in Palestine. When Magnes resuscitated the defunct Brith Shalom organization (now to be called Ihud) in the early forties, Jewish nationalist leaders prepared to do battle with him.[120]

Magnes presented his program to American liberals at the end of 1944, in a long letter published in the *Nation*.[121] His concept of a binational state linked to a larger regional federation appealed to liberals concerned with regionalism and internationalism. With an insight that proved to be all too prophetic, Magnes warned that any attempt to turn Palestine into either an Arab or Jewish state would lead to war. If bloodshed was to be avoided, large numbers of Jews would have to be allowed into Palestine, and Arab fears of being dominated by a Jewish majority would have to be allayed. A binational state was the logical solution to this perplexing riddle. In such a state, to be based loosely on the Swiss model, Arabs and Jews would share political power and each group would be assured of equal rights. Magnes proposed that an additional half-million Jews be allowed to enter Palestine. This influx would give the half-million Jews already in Palestine numerical parity with the country's million Arabs. He stipulated, however, that the Jewish rate of entrance should be determined by the economic absorptive capacity of Palestine. After this initial influx of Jews, immigration would continue at a pace designed to offset the higher Arab birthrate. Thus, neither Arabs nor Jews could hope to achieve a majority in the state. Arab fears of being dominated by Jews would be further assuaged by the creation of a larger union (or federation) of binational Palestine, Transjordan, Syria, and Lebanon. Magnes believed that this program would provide both Arabs and Jews with a sense of security and that the binational framework would allow both peoples to build bonds and mutual trust.

The Zionist leadership wasted little time in countering Magnes's presentation.[122] Attorney Bernard Joseph, a Jewish Agency adviser, called the binational scheme "unrealistic." In a letter to the *Nation*, he argued that giving Jews and Arabs equal political power in Palestine would only result in continual stalemate, while the other Arab nations would probably refuse to join the federation that Magnes proposed.[123] Magnes's concern with Jewish immigration to Palestine, Joseph wrote, ignored the major issue, which was to give every Jew who desired it, the right to enter the Holy Land by putting an end to the national homelessness of the Jewish people. Magnes's second major error was to base his program on fear of the Arabs. Arab disapproval or protest should not be allowed to interfere with a just solution to the Jewish problem because the conflict was not between the Jews and Arabs of Palestine, but between the Jewish and Arab peoples. The Arabs already had six independent countries, why couldn't the Jews have at least one? Most Arabs opposed binationalism, Joseph concluded, and Jews would also refuse to support Magnes, who, in spite of living in Palestine for more than two decades, still failed to understand its Jewish community.

Despite the Zionist attack on Magnes, binationalism succeeded in winning some American support. The binational idea's foundation on the ideals of tolerance and cooperation especially appealed to American liberals who hoped that it would militate against the dangers of excessive nationalism. The plan to link Palestine to a larger Middle Eastern federation attracted those liberals who, as late as 1945, continued to look forward to a postwar world reconstructed on the cornerstones of regionalism and internationalism.

Former Undersecretary of State Sumner Welles was among the few State Department veterans to sympathize with the suffering of European Jewry and the goals of the Zionist movement. In *The Time for Decision*, published in 1944, Welles supported the creation of a Jewish National Home in Palestine and expressed great confidence in the leadership abilities of Chaim Weizmann.[124] But Welles also wrote that he was convinced that a solution to the Arab-Jewish problem would be found "along the lines proposed by Judah Magnes." Welles suggested that an international organization (the United Nations) temporarily supervise the regional federation Magnes proposed to create.[125]

The editors of the *New Republic* also believed that the binational solution would provide a basis for Jewish-Arab compromise and peace. The magazine called a rumored Arab compromise offer in the winter of 1945, the "most interesting and important development in Palestinian racial relations in a long time." Under the plan, reportedly proposed by Arab foreign ministers, enough Jews would be allowed into Palestine to create numerical parity with Moslems in the country. The balance of power would be held by Palestine's small Christian Arab population. The *New Republic* conceded that Zionists who insisted on the creation of a Jewish state would object to the Arab proposal, however the magazine found hope in the plan's striking similarity to Judah Magnes's binational state proposal.[126]

I. F. Stone, a prominent liberal journalist and long-time Washington editor of the *Nation*, also supported binationalism. Stone, however, was not an early follower of Magnes. In fact, his adoption of the binational state idea came after he had seemingly adopted the Jewish state solution. Writing about the Jewish problem in March 1944, Stone carefully avoided any mention of statehood in Palestine and expressed support only for the creation of a nondefined "Jewish national home." He charged that British and American foreign policy makers opposed Zionism because they feared that Jewish settlement of Palestine would lead to a war that could jeopardize the continued flow of Middle Eastern oil. He believed, as did many Zionists, that the State Department and Foreign Office preferred to deal with neo-feudal Arab leaders who did not represent the best interests of their people rather than with the Jews of Palestine who were committed to democracy and anti-colonialism. English and American selfishness had deadly consequences, he explained, as both governments attempted to appease the Arabs by restricting immigration to Palestine while the Jews of Europe, a people without a refuge, continued to be shipped to Nazi slaughterhouses.[127]

Soon after World War II, Stone's opinions underwent a metamorphosis when he visited Palestine and personally confronted the Arab-Jewish conflict. He risked displeasing American Jewry and wrote back to the States that "we have been carrying on a campaign in America on the basis of half-truths." Zionists were correct in claiming that there was room in Palestine for millions of Jewish refugees and that the Arab population had progressed because of Jewish settlement. But, Stone warned, no Jew he talked to could identify an Arab who wanted to live in a Jewish state. This was not surprising, he noted, because "it should not be hard to understand the natural dislike of any human being for being ruled by another people or his unwillingness to trust himself to such rule." At the beginning of his stay in Palestine, partitioning Palestine into separate Arab and Jewish states seemed to be the only practical solution to this dilemma. Carefully noting the arguments Zionists would use against partition, Stone argued:

> I know there are other Arab states, while there is only one possibility for a Jewish state; I know that proposals to divide Palestine into two national states, put forward several times by Jewish sources, have fallen on stony ground. Nevertheless, despite present public utterances by the leadership of both sides, I think that a division on these lines . . . is ethically right and politically feasible and would be acceptable to a great majority of Jews and Arabs if it were imposed from above by Anglo-American or United Nations decision.[128]

When he left Palestine, Stone declared that he no longer favored the creation of a Jewish state. He had discovered a major defect in Jewish nationalist ideology, which he identified as a "failure to take into account the feelings and aspirations of the Palestinian Arab." While Zionists had not hurt the Arabs, they had made them feel excluded. He happily reported though that relations between Jews and Arabs were not as bad as he had first thought and that the Arab "does not fear the Jew, . . . he fears being dominated by him." If this fear could be allayed, Jewish and Arab cooperation would develop and mature. Stone concluded that the fairest solution to the Palestine problem was to establish a binational state that would exist within a larger Middle Eastern federation.[129]

I. F. Stone, Sumner Welles, and some other American liberals who were extremely concerned with the plight of European Jewry, found it difficult to fully accept the Biltmore formula of Jewish statehood. Even while agreeing to a Palestinian solution of the Jewish problem, they could not totally forget that another people claimed the Holy Land as their own. The war against fascism was for many liberals a fight against the excesses of nationalism. The future world that they were sacrificing for would be based on cooperation not competition, justice not strength, tolerance not hate, and pluralism not ethnocentrism. The concept of a binational state allowed some liberals to express their concern for European Jewry while maintaining their tolerant stance of internationalism.

Weaning American liberals away from their neo-universalist convictions was not an easy task for American Zionists. Individuals like I. F. Stone were often stubborn, and Zionist influence on them was always limited. However, the liberal tendency to flirt with binationalism on the one hand and to accept Bergsonite positions on the other did not cripple efforts to build support for Jewish nationalism. The American Zionist Emergency Council continued to denounce the Magnes plan, and Zionists continued to link the rescue of European Jewry with the need for a Jewish state. The bond connecting salvation from Hitler's hell with Jewish Palestine was extremely effective when personalized, as it was in a September 1944 essay written by Gerold Frank.

Frank, a professional journalist and occasional contributor to the *Nation*, was sympathetic to Zionism and maintained close contact with American Zionist organizations. While visiting Palestine, Frank met with Jewish children who had escaped the Nazi deathtrap. Many were the sole surviving members of their families and their tales, as related by Frank, were horrifying. The children owed their lives, he explained, to the executive branch of the Zionist movement, the Jewish Agency for Palestine, which had negotiated the children's rescue. While most of the world reluctantly accepted refugees, the Jewish community of Palestine enthusiastically welcomed the European survivors. Palestine gave these demoralized and despondent victims of Hitler's persecution a new sense of purpose, mission, and self-worth.[130]

Shortly after the publication of Frank's article, Rabbi Stephen S. Wise also centered an appeal to American liberals around the Holocaust. In common with other Zionists, Wise linked the extermination of European Jewry with the need for a Jewish state, but his approach differed from that of Frank and previewed a theme that would be used much more widely by Jewish nationalists after the war's end. Attempting to come to terms with the awful dimensions of the Holocaust, the rabbi argued that Jewish statehood was not simply a means to the rescue of the Jewry, but was a form of just reparation for the heinous crimes committed against his people.

In an address to a conference organized by the *Nation*, Wise proclaimed that the United States as well as Germany had to accept responsibility for Hitler's genocide. Washington was guilty of "assenting" to Hitler's persecution of the Jews, he said, "as witnessed . . . by the non-organization in any real sense of rescue and of migration." He applauded the work of the War Refugee Board established by Franklin Roosevelt in January 1944, but he realistically noted that even that measure was "too little and . . . too late." Great Britain too must also accept its fair share of the blame for cruelly putting Palestine, which could have been a haven for the oppressed, off limits. Speaking for the remnants of the Jewish people, Wise asked the Allies, at the war's conclusion, to allow the Zionists to establish a commonwealth in Palestine. "My people," he implored, "deserve reparation from a Christian world if there be a Christian world."[131]

In the years after World War II, Wise's argument would prove to be an important factor in Zionism's success. During the war, American Zionists had made significant progress in their campaign to win liberal support for Jewsh statehood. Liberals were more aware than most Americans of Hitler's persecution of European Jewry. When the Nazis moved from discrimination and expropriation of wealth to genocide, progressive-minded Americans suffered mental anguish. In a world filled with war and horror, Jews seemed to be suffering much more than most. Believing that the war against Hitler was a crusade in defense of progressive and humanitarian values, many liberals wanted the Allies to do something to save those awaiting slaughter. To do less would nullify the Allies' claim to be fighting for mankind.

Increased liberal concern for Jewry's sad plight coincided with the Zionists assumption of American Jewish community leadership. Zionist organizations claimed to be the legitimate representatives of American and European Jewry, and liberal opinion makers accorded them increased respect. Liberal concern for Palestine's Arab population continued, but it was generally superseded by a wish to provide Jewish refugees with at least one haven.

Zionists, however, did not succeed in gaining full liberal support during World War II. I. F. Stone, for example, agreed that Palestine had a role to play in the Jewish future, but he opposed the establishment of a Jewish state. Other liberals questioned the Zionist claim that Jewish statehood was inextricably linked to the rescue and salvation of European Jewry. Two months after V-J Day, a *New Republic* editorial demanded that all the survivors of the Nazi death camps be allowed into Palestine.[132] The editorial also argued that Zionist demands for a Jewish state complicated the job of getting the refugees to Palestine. The article bluntly concluded:

> The editors of the *New Republic* are not and cannot be Zionists. They believe that the Zionists ill serve the cause of human decency when they raise the issue of Jewish nationalism and a Jewish state in Palestine. Nor are they impressed by Arab nationalism. . . . all of these matters are secondary to the immediate and practical job of bringing the Jews of Europe—those who want to go—to the only place where they are really welcome, Palestine.

After receiving angry letters complaining about its editorial, the *New Republic* acknowledged that the British and Arabs "ill serve the cause of human decency" by using the Jewish survivors of Nazism as a "political football." But the journal maintained that, just because Arab nationalism and British imperialism were wrong, did not mean that the "Zionist demand for a Jewish state is right." Reasserting their position, the editors wrote: "From the liberal point of view, nationalism—the

Zionists do not deny their nationalist objectives—and sovereign independence are hardly adequate solutions in the modern world, regardless of whether they are advocated by nascent nationalists like the Zionists or articulate Arab elements or by dying nationalists like our own isolationists or British imperialists."[133]

VI

THE TRIUMPH OF
AMERICAN ZIONISM

AMERICAN ZIONISTS CONFRONT THE POSTWAR WORLD

Adolf Hitler's suicide in April 1945 and the American Army Air Corps' bombing of Hiroshima and Nagasaki in August brought World War II to a close. On V-J Day thousands of Americans celebrated the end of a long and costly conflict. American Zionists joined in the rejoicing, but they understood that their war was far from over. By the summer of 1945, Zionists could legitimately claim to be the leaders of America's five million Jews. The Zionist Organization of America and Hadassah, the two largest American Zionist groups, claimed a combined membership of 315,000. Nearly half a million American Jews belonged to some form of Zionist organization.[1] Segments of the general American public, the targets of a steady stream of Zionist produced propaganda, were beginning to acknowledge the justice and logic of Jewish nationalism. The Jewish state, however, still did not exist, and the British authorities at the end of the war remained firm in their opposition to the Zionist program.

Several new and important factors confronted American Zionists after the surrender of the German and Japanese forces. On the domestic political front, Zionists found themselves confronting a new American president. On April 12, 1945, as Allied armies were advancing through Germany, Franklin Roosevelt died of a cerebral hemorrhage. Stephen Wise forwarded the American Zionist Emergency Council's condolences to the president's widow. Wise considered Roosevelt to be a friend and believed that he "deeply sympathized with my people and their aspirations." The elderly rabbi found it impossible to blame the president for American policies that injured the Zionist cause. To associates and subordinates he explained that the "anti-Zionist" State Department

151

was not following Roosevelt's directives, that "he plans and recommends one course; they execute another."[2]

Other Zionist leaders did not share Wise's dismay at Roosevelt's passing. Publicly, they expressed their sorrow, acknowledging Roosevelt's greatness as a leader during depression and war. Privately, they realized that the Zionist task would be eased by his passing. Nahum Goldmann admired Roosevelt as a humanitarian but recognized that the president's commitment to political Zionism and the creation of a Jewish state was weak. Emanuel Neumann, unlike Stephen Wise, believed that the State Department's anti-Zionist bias reflected Roosevelt's position and reported that Abba Hillel Silver was "thoroughly disillusioned and disgusted with the tactics of the White House and the State Department."[3]

During his presidency Roosevelt was an obstacle for American Zionists. Shortly before his death, Roosevelt, returning from the Yalta conference, stopped in Cairo to confer with Saudi Arabia's ruler Ibn Sa'ud. After the meeting, Roosevelt, to the dismay of Zionist leaders, commented: "I learned more about the whole problem, . . . the Jewish problem, by talking with Ibn Sa'ud for five minutes than I could have learned in an exchange of two or three dozen letters." Despite their concern, there was little that Zionists could do to Roosevelt. His overwhelming popularity with American Jews made any Zionist threat of political retaliation appear empty if not ludicrous. This immunity from attack was not transferred with the White House to Roosevelt's successor. Harry Truman, who had not forged strong ties to the Zionist organizations during his political career, attempted to devise a Palestine policy that would satisfy some of the demands of the Jews, Arabs, and British. To his dismay he found himself under intense attack from a Zionist community that now discovered itself free to unleash all its impressive political weapons against the White House's occupant.[4]

Zionists also found themselves confronting a new power alignment in the Congress following the elections of 1946. After more than a decade of Democratic domination, Republicans gained control of the Senate and House of Representatives. This development increased the importance of Abba Hillel Silver within the Zionist leadership, as he was one of the few American Jewish leaders to have intimate contacts with the national leadership of the Republican Party. Silver was on particularly good terms with Senator Robert Taft from his home state of Ohio.[5]

American Zionists also found a new political leadership in London after World War II. In the summer of 1945, to the surprise of the world, the British Labor party succeeded in gaining a majority in Parliament. Clement Attlee took Winston Churchill's place at 10 Downing Street, and Ernest Bevin assumed command of the Foreign Ministry. At first, Zionists assumed that the Labor party would support the creation of a Jewish state. As an opposition party, Labor had supported the Zionist program and had opposed the White Paper of 1939. To the chagrin of American and world Zionists, however, Labor leaders abandoned their pro-Zionist position once they assumed control of Parliament, and the new cabinet announced that it would continue to restrict Jewish immigration to Palestine.[6]

American Zionists were at least able to confront the postwar situation with a united leadership dedicated to vigorous action. Near the end of 1944, tensions within the top echelons of the American movement had threatened to destroy Zionist unity. Abba Hillel Silver was a talented political leader. His colleagues respected his gifts, but many found it impossible to like the man. Silver's fiery temper and lack of personal charm disturbed many of his associates. After becoming cochairman of the AZEC in August 1943, Silver and Nahum Goldmann, the director of the Washington office of the Jewish Agency, squared off in a bitter jurisdictional dispute over who would have authority for carrying on Zionist diplomatic work in America. Although there was little love lost between Silver and Goldmann, their differences seemed trivial when compared to the tenuous relationship that existed between Silver and Stephen Wise. Following the American Jewish Conference, the two leaders of the AZEC were able to work out a viable but uneasy partnership. By the end of 1944, however, the two rabbis found themselves moving in entirely different directions. Silver, a Republican, believed that Wise's allegiance to Franklin Roosevelt undermined the effectiveness of the American Zionist lobby. Wise trusted Roosevelt's decency and refused to sanction Silver's attacks on the president and his administration. In December 1944, the two chairmen of the AZEC resigned their posts. Wise, supported by the leadership of Hadassah and Poale Zion as well as by Israel Goldstein, president of the Zionist Organization of America, then assumed the undivided leadership of the AZEC.[7]

Silver and his loyal lieutenant Emanuel Neumann left the AZEC but did not turn their backs on the Zionist movement. With their followers, Neumann and Silver began to gather support for Silver's return to power. Realizing that a large portion of the Zionist rank and file remained loyal to Silver and that his political skills and energy were irreplaceable, the AZEC welcomed him back as its leader in July 1945. During the postwar years Silver forged a strong alliance with David Ben-Gurion, who in 1946 finally succeeded in ousting Chaim Weizmann to become the undisputed leader of the international Zionist movement. The two men, one a socialist pioneer, the other a Republican rabbi, would engineer and execute a militant campaign that succeeded in establishing the State of Israel in May 1948.[8]

Before the Jewish state could be created, American Zionists had to deal with one of the most tragic results of World War II. Following the German surrender, it became apparent that the Nazi murder machine had been more efficient than anyone had expected. Of the nearly 3.5 million Polish Jews alive when German armies invaded their country in 1939, a mere fifty thousand survived to see the defeat of their tormenters. Only 14 percent of the Jews of Holland were alive on V-E Day. The Jews of Hungary, a German satellite state, were "lucky" enough to be among the last Jewish communities dispatched to the extermination camps.

They suffered a mortality rate of 50 percent. Postwar studies revealed that Hitler's henchmen had murdered between five and six million Jewish men, women, and children.[9]

The magnitude of the Nazi slaughter did not cause Zionists to question the policies they had pursued during the war. Shortly before V-E Day, even as the shocking number of Jewish dead was becoming ever more apparent, David Ben-Gurion lamented that, had a Jewish state in Palestine existed, the Nazis would never have exterminated European Jewry. Almost two years earlier, Emanuel Neumann and other American Zionists had made the same point at the American Jewish Conference. Senator Robert Wagner, a staunch Zionist ally, explained that the death of six million Jews was "a tragic and conclusive demonstration of the necessity for a Jewish Homeland."[10]

Judith Epstein, president of Hadassah, believed that Zionist efforts in Palestine had eased the pain of European Jewry during their imprisonment and torture. Shortly after meeting with some death camp survivors, Epstein told an American Zionist audience that:

> They had not been afraid to die because they knew that life was good and because they believed life was worth living with dignity and with beauty . . . and what made life beautiful? The fact that there was a Palestine; that the Jews could look forward if not to personal happiness, to future happiness for their descendants, that there would be a collective Jewish future which was well worth dying for.

Other American Zionists shared Epstein's view that Hitler's Jewish victims were casualties in a war being fought for Jewish survival. In November 1945, the entire annual convention of the ZOA stood in a moment of silent tribute "as a mark of respect for those who suffered and died in the cause of freedom—our cause." American Zionists, believing themselves engaged in a holy crusade to change the course of Jewish history, knew that in all wars, soldiers fell. The Jewish nation, just like the Allied nations, had to be willing to make huge sacrifices in the struggle against tyranny. Thus, American Zionists tended to perceive of the Holocaust victims as fallen soldiers of a great Zionist army.[11]

THE DISPLACED PERSONS

While the soldiers of other armies demobilized and went home, those Jews who managed to outlive the Third Reich began to contemplate just where their homes were. Many made their way back to their cities and towns and began the slow process of rebuilding their lives. Only some managed to succeed in this painful task. The war left Europe's economy in ruins and many Jewish survivors found it difficult to support themselves. Jews often found their homes occupied by Christian families and sometimes survivors encountered intense anti-Semitism. One day in the summer of 1946, a young boy in the Polish town of Kielce accused local Jews of having kidnapped him and claimed that the Jews were killing Christian children. The citizens of Kielce responded to this charge by murdering forty-one Jews who had somehow managed to survive Hitler's extermination program.[12]

Allied occupation armies in Germany established camps for those Jews who could not create new lives for themselves. These refugee centers, sometimes located on the sites of former Nazi concentration camps, also housed Jews who had not even attempted to return to their old homes. Many of the survivors of the extermination camps, suffering from starvation and disease, required long periods of care and recuperation. The psychological wounds endured by these people were often even more severe than the physical, and many understandably wanted to escape from the scene of their suffering.

The Jewish displaced persons (DPs) cared for in the American, British, and French zones of occupied Germany numbered about a quarter of a million by the end of 1946. They created serious problems for the occupation authorities who had to provide them with food, clothing, and medical care. Aside from a financial burden, the DPs also were a political problem for Great Britain and the United States. The DPs, like the Jewish refugees of the prewar period, were in need of a home, and few nations in the world seemed to be willing to welcome them. London, after the war, continued to believe that supporting the Zionist development of Palestine would undermine British imperial interests, and thus maintained that the DPs could not find a home in Palestine. Restrictionist sentiment in the U.S. Congress remained strong after the end of World War II, and many Americans expected a dramatic increase in the unemployment rates as discharged soldiers attempted to re-enter an economy making the difficult adjustment to peacetime. The massive influx of DPs would only intensify the competition for jobs.[13]

Despite these difficulties, the Jewish displaced persons did not constitute as grave a problem as Zionists had anticipated. During the war Zionist strategists assumed that European Jewry would play a crucial role in their postwar campaign. Zionists expected world opinion to support the creation of a Jewish state in Palestine for practical, not humanitarian, reasons. Millions of homeless Jews, wartime Zionist propaganda had predicted, would threaten the political stability of postwar Europe and might even serve as a vehicle for new demagogues to gain power. But the relatively small number of Jewish DPs did not jeopardize the political equilibrium of postwar Europe.

Although the small number of Jewish survivors did not threaten the stability of Europe, the DPs did significantly contribute to the establishment of Israel in

1948. Wartime Zionists, as events would prove, had not only overestimated the extent of the postwar Jewish problem, but had to some extent underestimated the sympathy and compassion that the Christian world would extend to those who endured the Nazi horror.

Revelations about the true nature of Nazi atrocities disturbed the American public, which had largely ignored or disbelieved wartime reports about German brutality. General Dwight Eisenhower, the Supreme Allied Commander, asked Washington to dispatch a select committee to inspect the death camps because he did not want anyone to doubt the validity of his reports. Edward R. Murrow, in a moving radio address, stood in the middle of a Nazi concentration camp and begged his audience to believe the nightmarish scene he described. On April 30, 1945, *Newsweek* published photographs of the liberated Buchenwald concentration camp, and on May 12, the *New Yorker* carried a short, but graphic account of Nazi atrocities against the Jews. The more scholarly audience that read the *Annals of the American Academy of Political and Social Science* learned about Nazi extermination practices in Holland, while the *Presbyterian*, a leading Protestant periodical in October 1945, expressed its horror at the extermination of European Jewry and concluded that the establishment of a Jewish state in Palestine would be just compensation for their suffering. Public opinion polls revealed that the American public wanted to do something to relieve the suffering of the Holocaust survivors, but most were not yet willing to liberalize United States immigration quotas, particularly for Jews whom many still regarded somewhat critically. Americans seemed to be searching for some solution to the refugee crisis that would not call on them to make any significant sacrifice.[14]

Zionists hoped that "Christian guilt" could be directed in the interest of Jewish statehood. Zionist propagandists accused the Allies of complicity in Hitler's murders. They argued that the world could begin to pay for its sins by establishing a Jewish state in Palestine. By presenting Jewish statehood as the only suitable compensation for the Holocaust, Zionists were able to abandon the argument that Jewish survivors would undermine the stability of the continent and possibly be the cause of yet another world war.

In September 1945, Senator Robert Wagner remarked that it was "heartbreaking" to calculate how many lives might have been saved had Palestine's doors been open to Jewish refugees. The "small remnant" of European Jewry that survived, Wagner continued, only sought to leave Europe. Whether they would be allowed to enter Palestine was not only a question of importance for Jews, but for all Americans. Palestine was "the crucible in which will be tested the ability of the powerful to deal faithfully with the weak."[15]

Other Zionist spokesmen went beyond Wagner's restrained position and indicted the Allied powers as accessories in the extermination of European Jewry. Abba Hillel Silver told a Zionist audience near the end of 1945 that "our six million

dead are a tragic commentary on the state of Christian morality and the respon-
siveness of Christian conscience." Had Great Britain and the United States been
willing to grant Jewry the same "temporary refuge" accorded to prisioners of war,
many lives might have been saved.[16]

Zionist leaders contrasted the indifference of the Allies toward the Holocaust
with the courageous efforts of Palestinian Jewry to rescue their suffering co-
religionists. Spokesmen specifically praised the efforts of thirty-two Jewish volunteers
who parachuted into Bulgaria, Hungary, Slovakia, Italy, and Yugoslavia to organize
resistance and rescue efforts. Axis soldiers captured and executed seven of these
agents. The martyrs included Channa Senesh, a young Hungarian-born girl from
Kibbutz S'dot Yam, and Enzo Sereni, who had been a leading Italian Zionist.[17]
Remembering the parachutists, Israel Goldstein asked, "Who was it that dared
at the risk of life to bring succor . . . to thousands of Jews trapped in Nazi occupied Europe during the war?" While the United Nations hesitated and the Jewish relief organizations of the United States waited for authorizations before acting,
the "sons of the Yishuv found a way by unconventional methods to help thousands
and to rescue hundreds." Chaim Weizmann also praised the handful of courageous
Palestinian volunteers, remarking that had their determination been matched by
the United Nations, Hitler's murderous campaign might have been halted. Weizmann explained, "I am not prepared to say that we could have saved all the millions, but it might have saved hundreds of thousands."[18]

Jewish nationalists singled out Great Britain, the Mandatory Power in Palestine,
for special attack. Morris Rothenberg, a former president of the ZOA, charged
that "tens of thousand of Jews now in nameless graves, whom Palestine might have
saved but for the inhuman enforcement of the infamous and illegal White Paper,
point an accusing finger at Great Britain for what is now happening in Palestine."
Even Chaim Weizmann, who more than any other Zionist leader admired the English
and their traditions, believed that had it not been for the White Paper, many Jews
might have been able to flee to Palestine and escape deportation and extermination.[19]

Nothing could bring the dead back to life, but England and America could
begin to make up for their crimes by satisfying the demands of those few lucky
Jews who survived Hitler's inferno. Zionists in the United States argued that these
demands included the opening of Palestine's doors to free Jewish immigration and
the creation there of a Jewish state. Louis Levinthal of the ZOA wrote: "Historic
justice demands that atonement be made for the needless death of multitudes
of innocent victims of bureaucracy and red tape. Historic justice demands the fulfillment, at long last, of the Balfour Declaration and the Mandate."[20]

American Zionists effectively used the plight of the Jewish displaced persons
in Europe to arouse feelings of concern and guilt in the American public. Felix
Frankfurter, who had largely withdrawn from Zionist activities after being appointed
to the Supreme Court, in a rare public statement cited the urgent need of Jewish

DPs for a home, which only Palestine could provide.[21] In April 1946, a little less that one year after Adolf Hitler's suicide, a moving portrait of the DP dilemma appeared in the *New Republic*. Gerold Frank, a journalist with close ties to the American Zionists, reported that the Jewish survivors of Hitler's death camps detested Europe and distrusted the world. Only the hope of going to Palestine kept the survivors from going mad. The DPs understood that in the Jewish Holy Land they would be "wanted by those among whom they live." He warned that if the English and Americans prevented the survivors from casting "off the stigma of an inferior race," they might respond with a violent burst of vengeance and despair. The DPs would accept no answer to their plight other than Palestine, for "they are convinced that their only hope is to begin life anew on their own soil."[22]

Individuals and institutitons who had not been strongly committed to the cause of Jewish statehood helped the Zionists to publicize the DP problem. Henry Wallace was convinced "that there will never be peace in the world until justice is done to the Jew." The former vice president supported the complete opening of Palestine's doors to Jewish survivors.[23] Eleanor Roosevelt, who had refused to throw her support behind the Zionists during the war, was moved by the DPs' condition and urged that they be allowed to enter Palestine. She suggested that the United States should unequivocally tell the Arabs that "we intend to protect Palestine."[24] The editors of the *New Republic* also urged the Truman administration to support large-scale Jewish immigration to Palestine.[25]

I. F. Stone accompanied a group of Jewish refugees on their attempt to illegally enter Palestine and published a series of articles describing his journey in the New York liberal daily *PM*. Stone vividly described the determination of the survivors to reach Palestine and the courage and idealism of the young Palestinians who operated the modern "underground railroad."[26] Stone reported: "The 'pull' toward Palestine I heard expressed again and again, not only from the young Khalutsim on the train, but from older folk who would say, 'I'm not a Zionist, I'm a Jew. That's enough. We have wandered enough. We have worked and struggled too long on the lands of other peoples. We must build a land of our own.'"[27]

The *Nation* and its publisher Freda Kirchwey played an active role in publicizing the contribution Palestine could make to the solution of the DP problem. In May 1947, the *Nation* published a special supplement on the Palestine problem. If the DPs were not allowed to enter Palestine, the journal told its readers, there was virtually nowhere else for them to turn. The United States, which could provide a secure future for the European Jews, was virtually off-limits as a result of immigration restriction quotas. Even if America's doors were opened, it was not certain that the Jewish survivors would accept an offer of hospitality. When asked to list a preferred location of resettlement other than Palestine, hundreds of DPs reportedly responded, "the crematorium."[28]

In their campaign to confront the American public with the Jewish problem,

Zionists received help from a most unexpected source – the American government. Harry Truman, shortly after taking possession of the White House, found himself under Zionist pressure to support mass Jewish immigration to Palestine. Media coverage of the DP issue focused attention on the Army's allegedly incompetent and insensitive treatment of Displaced Persons, leading Secretary of the Treasury Henry Morgenthau, Jr., to call for the creation of a special cabinet-level committee to wrestle with the refugee dilemma. Truman opposed Morgenthau's suggestion, but did agree to send a special delegation to Europe to investigate the treatment of the DPs.[29]

Truman, Morgenthau, and the State Department agreed that the American delegation should be led by Earl G. Harrison, a lawyer who had had a distinguished career as a government official and law school dean. The Harrison delegation, including Patrick M. Malin of the Intergovernmental Committee on Refugees, Herbert Katzski of the War Refugee Board, and Dr. Joseph J. Schwartz of the American Jewish Joint Distribution Committee, left the United States in July 1945. Harrison's selection to head the group disturbed Stephen Wise, who had hoped that James G. McDonald, the past chairman of the Intergovernmental Committee on Refugees, would be assigned the task. Harrison, unlike McDonald, had few ties to American Zionist leaders and organizations and could not be relied on to make a report that would be favorable to the Jewish nationalist cause. As events would prove, Wise's concern was unwarranted.[30]

Harrison's final report filtered through the Washington bureaucracy in last August 1945. The report documented the inadequate living conditions and diet supplied to the DPs by American authorities and the United Nations Relief and Rehabilitation Administration (UNRRA). The Harrison group reported that the great majority of Jewish DPs wished to be resettled in Palestine. Harrison and his associates recommended that British immigration policies be revised to allow for the entrance of the DPs into Palestine, and Harrison threw his support behind a Jewish Agency request for British permission to allow one hundred thousand DPs immediately to enter the Holy Land.[31]

The Harrison report seemed to offer official, nonpartisan confirmation of many of the claims being made by Zionist spokesmen. Zionists seized on the Harrison report, and the demand for the immediate settlement of one hundred thousand Jews in Palestine became one of their most employed slogans. I. F. Stone wrote that Harrison had left the United States unsympathetic to the Zionist cause, but in Europe had found that the Nazis had succeeded in spreading anti-Semitism throughout the territories they once occupied. As Zionists claimed, the Jewish survivors "want to go home as others are going home, and this for most of them means going to Palestine."[32]

Harry Truman also threw his support behind the Harrison proposal. The president might have been truly affected by the terrible situation of the DPs, but he also saw good political reasons for favoring the entrance of one hundred thousand Jews into Palestine. He hoped that this action would pacify the Zionist lobby without distressing British and Arab leaders who would realize that the president's actions fell far short of endorsement of the creation of a Jewish state. Unfortunately for Truman, his calculations proved to be faulty. British Foreign Minister Bevin angrily denounced the president for meddling in London's affairs. Arab leaders were dismayed by what they perceived to be Truman's pro-Zionist position, while American Zionists continued to pester the White House, demanding presidential support for Jewish statehood.[33]

During the long and often depressing years between V-E Day and the establishment of Israel in 1948, the DP problem strengthened the resolve and revived the morale of Zionist activists in the United States, as it won new supporters for the Jewish nationalist cause. In April 1946, shortly after visiting several DP camps, one prominent AZEC official, clearly upset by the suffering he witnessed, privately remarked that "the despair of people standing around in camps with nothing to do and no place to go is heartbreaking to witness. There is no other stand than to be firm Zionists."[34]

ZIONISM AS ANTI-IMPERIALISM

The misery of the DPs stiffened the resolve of Jewish nationalists but posed serious problems for the Arabs and their supporters. As sympathy for the DPs developed into increased pro-Zionist sentiment within the American public, anti-Zionist spokesmen faced the difficult problem of responding to the Holocaust. Samir Shamma, an Arab lobbyist in Washington, told the editors and readers of the *New Republic* that all Arabs condemned the Nazi extermination of European Jewry as an "abhorrent crime." Arabs, however, regarded "it as most unfair to suggest that the problem of the persecuted Jews be solved by persecuting another nation, the Arabs of Palestine." C. A. Hourani, an associate of Shamma's, argued that the DP problem had to be considered separately from the future development of Palestine. Both Hourani and Shamma maintained that the Jewish survivors had to be resettled somewhere else other than Palestine.[35]

The Arab position, as presented by Shamma and Hourani, seemed to have some validity. The refugee crisis, as they claimed, was a "global humanitarian problem." The Germans and their Axis allies were guilty of the murder of six million European Jews. The United States and Great Britain callously refused to undertake large-scale rescue efforts and could be justly branded accomplices in the Nazi crimes. But why should the Arabs of Palestine be asked to pay for the misdeeds of others?[36]

The men and women guiding the American Zionist movement in the postwar period understood that they were competing with Shamma and Hourani in a struggle to capture American public opinion. Zionists, Emanuel Neumann understood, had an advantage because "through our far-flung organization we have roots and units in every community in the land." Still, the Arab lobby, which Zionists estimated to have an operating budget of three quarters of a million dollars, seemed to be a powerful enemy. Clearly some response had to be made to the Arabs' claim that they were not responsible for the plight of European Jewry.[37]

The failure of the Arab states to rigorously support the Allied cause during World War II provided Zionist spokesmen with some valuable ammunition. British attempts to appease the Arabs had failed miserably. As Rommel's troops approached the Suez Canal, concerned British officials incarcerated pro-Nazi sympathizers including Anwar Sadat, a young nationalist leader. Few Arab Palestinians joined the thousands of young men of the Yishuv in volunteering for British military service. At the end of April 1941, at the height of an Afrika Korps offensive, anti-British elements of the Iraqi Army attempted a coup d'etat. Haj Amin al-Husseini, the Grand Mufti of Jerusalem, who had led the Arab uprising in Palestine in 1936, participated in the Iraqi revolt. When the British-officered Arab Legion of Transjordan crushed the pro-Nazi coup, the Mufti found refuge in Berlin where he made propaganda broadcasts for the Hitler regime.[38]

During and immediately after the war, Zionist propaganda emphasized the dismal Arab war record. In late October 1945, Eliahu Ben-Horin, a Palestinian journalist connected to the AZEC, condemned wartime pro-Nazi Arab sympathizers. He told a liberal American audience that even after Hitler's fall, Arab leaders remained unrepentant, while the Allies had taken no action against the Nazi collaborators. AZEC leader Abba Hillel Silver and ZOA President Israel Goldstein also publicly denounced the Mufti of Jerusalem as a Nazi war criminal.[39]

In early 1946, the Mufti, who had been in the custody of French authorities, escaped and fled to Cairo. The American Zionist Emergency Council feared that British authorities, in a further attempt to appease Arab public opinion, would permit the Mufti to return to Palestine. The AZEC Executive Committee decided to fight this possibility with an aggressive publicity campaign that would document the Mufti's pro-Nazi activities. Eliahu Epstein, chief of the Jewish Agency's Arab Department, published a devastating attack on the Mufti in the *Nation*. According to Epstein, the Mufti was not only guilty of collaborating with Nazi attempts to ferment revolts in the Middle East, but had also played a part in the extermination of European Jewry. The Nuremberg judges, the article said, possessed an affidavit from Rudolf Kastner, the former chairman of the Budapest Jewish Council, who reported that a high-ranking Gestapo official had told him that the Mufti had encouraged Hitler to murder all of Europe's Jews.[40]

The American Zionist Emergency Council argued that the Mufti's responsibility for the extermination of European Jewish constituted a "crime against humanity" and insisted that he be tried as a major war criminal at Nuremberg. The State Department refused to accept the Zionist position and also resisted persistent requests for the United States government to publish the documents that incriminated the Mufti in the liquidation of European Jewry. The AZEC therefore used its own formidable information apparatus to bring the "facts" to the American media and public.[41]

Arab attempts to respond to the Zionist charge were not particularly effective. Kahil Totah, executive director of the Institute of Arab American Affairs, attempted to put the Mufti's activities into historical perspective. There had been many examples of alliances between nations and groups based on shared interest not principle. The American revolutionaries of the eighteenth century had fought Great Britain with the assistance of the despotic government of France; Communist Russia under Stalin had even forged a short-lived alliance with Hitler's Germany. According to Totah, the Mufti, an ardent Arab patriot, had cooperated with the Nazis because he believed a German victory would facilitate the liberation of Palestine from British imperial control. The Mufti was a patriot, Totah said, not a Nazi.[42]

Historians of the Holocaust have found no substantial evidence to link the Mufti with Hitler's decision to liquidate European Jewry. However, in the late 1940s, Zionists and their supporters could find little reason to doubt the charge. They could still vividly remember the bloody and murderous attacks of the Mufti's followers during the bitter 1936 civil war in Palestine. For Zionists it seemed reasonable that the Mufti, whom they believed was a rabid anti-Semite, would transfer his hatred of the Yishuv to the Jews of Europe. Not coincidentally, the attacks on the Mufti and other Arab Nazi sympathizers and collaborationists, effectively countered the claims of Arab lobbyists that they were being asked to pay the penalty for a European-engineered crime.[43]

The attacks on the Mufti were part of a larger pro-Zionist education campaign aimed at portraying the Arab leaders of the Middle East as reactionary despots intent on destroying the progressive Jewish experiment in Palestine. Several months before the end of the war, Stephen Wise, Nahum Goldmann, Hayim Greenberg, Rose Halprin, and the other members of the American Zionist Emergency Council determined that if a Jewish state were to be created, "the idea that the Arabs consent must be obtained . . . must be broken down." Accordingly, they decided that AZEC propaganda should stress that the Arabs represented "a reactionary element in the Middle East."[44]

Shortly after the meeting of American Zionist leaders, publicist Eliahu Ben-Horin wrote that "Arab social philosophy and the existing forms of Arab society are in harmony with the Nazi-Fascist system rather than with our democratic ideas." The Arab rulers of the Middle East, the last remaining bulwarks of feudalism in the world, "fight bitterly against any democratic or civilizing innovation." Meanwhile, Ben-Horin complained, Britain and America continued to support Arab leaders who consistently undermined any possibilities for Arab-Jewish rapprochement in Palestine. The Mufti, for example, had killed many progressive Arabs who "regarded sympathetically the social-economic progress brought to Palestine by Jewish-Zionist enterprise."[45]

Besides attacking Arab leaders as reactionary despots and anti-Semites, American Zionists pressed the point that the Arab masses were unwilling to follow them. Abba Hillel Silver maintained that the "fellaheen," the peasant class of Palestine, bore no responsibility for the anti-Zionist propaganda emanating from the Middle East. The Arab peasant was not "concerned" about the Jewish settlement of Palestine, while "the feudal lords" of the Arab world, knowing "that the establishment of the Jewish homeland means the end of their feudal regime," attempted to destroy the Zionist experiment. Jewish settlement of Palestine had significantly improved the lives of the Arab population. Citing the work of Walter Clay Lowdermilk, Silver maintained that Palestine could easily accommodate three or four million people. Jews, Moslems, and Christians could all share a prosperous life in a Palestine modernized by Zionist investments of money and sweat.[46]

In May 1947, as the United Nations began to consider the question of Palestine, Silver again attacked the validity of Arab national claims to Palestine. The League of Nations Mandate for Palestine, Silver told a group of reporters, had specifically recognized the "historical connection of the Jewish people with Palestine." Silver pointed out that the document made "no mention of the establishment of an Arab National Home." The loss of Palestine would not deny the Arabs of the Middle East autonomy and independence. Zionists, Silver insisted, supported the national aspirations of the Arab people. During the years between 1920 and 1947, Arabs had established five Arab states in the Middle East, which occupied over a million square acres of land. All that the Zionists asked for was "a little notch" of the vast Middle East.

Silver's comments reflect his and other Zionists' simplistic view of Arab nationalism. No attempt was made to distinguish between the national aspirations of Syrians, Egyptians, Iraqis, and Palestinians. When one reporter raised the issue of the Arab claim to Palestine based on centuries of residence, Silver responded:

> There has never been an Arab country called Palestine. There has never been an Arab government in Palestine. Palestine has been for centuries now a province within the Turkish Empire. The statesmen of the world at the time that they issued the Mandate fully understood the . . . background of Palestine and the historical connections of the Jewish people with Palestine.[47]

Zionist depictions of Arab society and Arab nationalism after World War II were in most ways similar to the portraits they presented to the American public during the 1930s. During both periods, Zionist spokesmen essentially attempted to deny that there was any basic conflict between the goals of the Jewish settlers in Palestine and the aspirations of the land's Arab majority. Believing that increased prosperity and better health care could win the loyalty of Palestine's non-Jewish population, Zionists blamed tensions and unrest in the country on unscrupulous leaders committed to protecting their own selfish interests. Zionism, as Silver explained, frightened the Arab leaders of the Middle East because it was importing "irresistible democratic influences which are bound to penetrate to the periphery."[48]

In one respect however, postwar Zionist explanations of political conditions in Palestine did differ from those made earlier. Before World War II, most influential Zionists in the United States were sparing in their condemnation of Great Britain and its policies. Zionists often had held unenlightened colonial administrators, not the London cabinet, responsible for unsatisfactory conditions in Palestine. As relations between Jews and Britain strained following the Arab revolt in 1936, Zionists began to direct their criticism directly at Whitehall and Parliament. Even then, Zionists continued to hope that a change in Britain's political leadership would result in the resumption of a pro-Zionist policy. Essentially, Zionists then believed that a community of interest existed between themselves and the "justice-loving" British people. During World War II, Zionists grew disillusioned with the British, who seemed to be doing little to save European Jewry from Hitler's henchmen. After the war, Zionists increasingly asserted that imperial self-interest dictated British policy in Palestine. Jewish nationalists came to portray themselves as the victims of a partnership between British imperialists and Arab reactionaries.

Frank Gervasi's *To Whom Palestine?* (1946), published with the assistance of the AZEC, reflected the Zionists' belief that the British and Arabs were conspiring against them. Although not a Jew, Gervasi had become strongly attracted to the Zionist cause. He felt compelled to tell the story of Jewish Palestine because, during the war, "I'd seen Jews die alongside Catholics and Protestants and Orthodox Greeks, and their blood, I assure you, is uniformly red. I didn't see any Arabs die in freedom's cause."[49]

Great Britain's Palestine policy, Gervasi wrote, was just one element of a larger strategy designed to secure British hegemony in the Middle East. The British government believed that yielding to Zionist demands in Palestine would exact "a price in prestige and power in the Levant out of all proportion to what it would gain by the creation there of a new independent state." In seeking to maintain the imperial status quo in Palestine and the Middle East, British officials found it easy to forge an alliance with the Arab leaders of the region, who also felt "the pressures gestating within their society." For both the reactionary Arab leader and the British colonial official, the Jews represented "a force of change and progress" that threatened to upset their domination of the Arab masses.[50]

Non-Jewish Zionist spokesmen, in particular, seemed to be eager to attack "perfidious Albion" and also attempted to portray the Jews of Palestine as victims of

British imperialism and Arab reaction. Bartley Crum, a liberal Republican busi-
nessman, was an American representative on the Anglo-American Commission
of Inquiry established in 1946 to investigate the question of Palestine. Crum was
sympathetic to the Zionists' goals and in 1947 published an account of the commission's activities. He remembered that:

> Albert Einstein had pointed out that the English had two interests; raw materi-
> als for industry and oil. Large landowners, he said, found themselves in a
> precarious situation because "they fear they will be gotten rid of. The British
> are always in a passive alliance with these land possessing owners." People
> who are ruled, he pointed out, "will accept rule as long as they . . . know no
> better, but as soon as they realize that serfdom is not preordained, they begin
> to resist. . . ." Neither rulers nor landlords wish this, for it means the end of
> their privileged status; thus the "passive alliance" cited by Einstein.

James McDonald, another American Christian friend of Zionism, concurred with
Crum's view, noting "the British natural sympathy with the static Arab civilization
and resentment at the pushing dynamic Jewish conception of what Palestine should
be."[51]

Zionist portrayals of themselves as the victims of British imperialism reached
a sympathetic American audience. A Gallup poll taken in December 1945 found
that 76 percent of those Americans who followed events in Palestine favored allowing Jews to settle there. Only one percent believed that Great Britain should determine the rate of settlement, and one additional percent believed that the Arabs
should decide how many Jews entered Palestine. A second public opinion poll
in early 1946 found that 33 percent of those Americans who kept abreast of
events in Palestine believed that the British were primarily to blame for disorders
there. Twelve percent blamed the Jews; 10 percent the Arabs. By August 1946,
38 percent of knowledgeable Americans believed that British authorities treated
Arabs better than Jews in Palestine. Only 7 percent believed that Jews received
preferential treatment.[52]

Liberal Americans seemed to be particularly willing to believe that British actions in Palestine were unjustly motivated by selfish interests. Freda Kirchwey,
publisher of the *Nation*, wrote in November 1945 that there was no contradiction
between the shooting of nationalists in Java and the British support of Arab nationalists in the Middle East. Both policies were attempts "to suppress those elements which threaten the dominance of the ruling groups to whom the Colonial
Office looks for cooperation in maintaining British control." A tour of Europe and
the Middle East in the summer of 1946 strengthened Kirchwey's belief that British
opposition to Zionism was motivated only by imperial concern. The Jewish development of Palestine, she observed, was bringing progress to the region and threatened
to topple the Arab feudal leaders on whom British rule depended. Kirchwey

urged President Truman to reject British imperialist policies and pursue a new, more progressive strategy in the Middle East. I. F. Stone, like Kirchwey, believed that as the Jewish community of Palestine grew it would "continue to dissolve feudal Arab relationships, to raise living standards, and to make reform inevitable." Stone, a supporter of the creation of a binational Arab-Jewish state in Palestine, believed that the Arabs and the Jews were both victims of British imperialism. He believed that "a Palestine settlement beneficial to both Jews and Arabs is possible any time the British government wants it."[53]

While American Zionists waged a campaign against British imperialism, they also sought to prove that American support of Jewish Palestine would further this nation's interests in the developing cold war with the Soviet Union. Eliahu Ben-Horin, the Zionist publicist, told Americans that they were being tricked by Arab leaders who threatened to ally themselves with the Soviet Union if the United States supported the establishment of a Jewish State. The reactionary Arab elite, Ben-Horin wrote, might not be "learned gentlemen," but they understood that the Soviets advanced their interests by destroying "political reaction" and "social-economic backwardness." Stalin himself, always the opportunist, understood that a partnership with the Arabs was impossible and was instead beginning to adopt a pro-Zionist line in order to portray himself as the friend of progress and justice. American pro-British policies, Ben-Horin warned, actually benefited Moscow because "the conviction is spreading that the Soviet Union is the true bearer of progressive ideas and that Britain—now joined by America—upholds diehard conservatives and reaction." Washington could avoid this propaganda defeat by unequivocally giving its support to the cause of Jewish statehood. The Arab states of the Middle East would have no alternative but to support the United States, the only nation in the world willing to give generous oil royalties without getting "anything important" in return. The Arabs would remain loyal allies, Ben-Horin concluded, "as long as America remains the richest and least imperialistic power in sight."[54]

THE ANGLO-AMERICAN COMMITTEE

While Zionists attempted to influence Allied foreign policy, the British and American governments grappled with the difficult problem of Palestine. Zionist leaders understood that the political development of the Middle East and particularly Palestine was just one of the major issues the Western powers had to consider in their effort to establish a peaceful and secure postwar world. Clearly, as the cold war deepened, Western interests required the development of a Palestine plan that would prevent political instability in the geographically strategic and oil rich Middle East. The size of the Arab population of Palestine, its tradition of violent opposition to Jewish settlement, and the anti-Zionist positions of important Arab states like Egypt and Transjordan made it politically impossible for Washington to support the establishment of a Jewish state in all of Palestine. Realistically, Zionists had to be willing to accept some territorial compromise and had to begin to consider the kind of concessions they would be willing to make in exchange for American support of Jewish sovereignty.

Any discussion by Zionist leaders of the future Jewish state's boundaries was bound to be difficult and fiery. In 1937 and 1938, the possible partition of Palestine had bitterly divided the Zionist community in the United States. The brutal destruction of six million Jews psychologically prepared most American Zionists to surrender some part of the historic Jewish homeland in return for sovereignty and security, but the actual terms of the Zionist position on Palestine's partition was a source of bitter Zionist debate in the years between V-E Day and the establishment of Israel in 1948.

In November 1945, London and Washington announced the formation of an Anglo-American Committee of Inquiry Regarding the Problems of European Jewry and Palestine. The Anglo-American committee explored various plans for the resettlement of Jewish displaced persons and studied the part Palestine could play in the rehabilitation of the death camp survivors.

The creation of the Anglo-American Committee of Inquiry (AACI) temporarily divided the Zionist leadership in the United States. Abba Hillel Silver was enraged by the proposal to investigate Palestine's role in the solution of the refugee problem, although he distinguished between the motives of Harry Truman and Ernest Bevin. Truman, Silver explained, had been genuinely moved by Earl Harrison's description of the DPs plight, but was being manipulated by the British into accepting an investigation instead of action. Bevin's support to the AACI, on the other hand, reflected his basic desire to "liquidate" the Jewish national home in Palestine. Believing that Jews should not cooperate in their own destruction, Silver proposed that the Zionist leadership announce that they would not accept and would not be bound by the decisions of the AACI. Several prominent Zionists lent their support to Silver's radical position. Gedalia Bublick, the Mizrachi representative on the American Zionist Emergency Council, announced that his organization would refuse to cooperate with the AACI. Emanuel Neumann condemned the AACI as a "deadly trap" aimed "to enmesh America in the toils of British policy." It was the duty of all Zionists, he continued, to discredit the committee even before it completed its mission.[55]

Other Zionist leaders approached the Anglo-American committee suspiciously, but favored cooperation with the British and American investigation. Stephen Wise, always more cautious than Silver and Neumann, counseled against a hasty rejection of the AACI. The leadership of Hadassah strongly supported Zionist cooperation with the investigative body in order to insure that the committee was given access to the "right information."[56]

The Zionist leaders of Palestine and Great Britain supported the moderate position advanced by American Hadassah. They reasoned that the American public would interpret a rejection of the AACI as an act of extremism. This would undermine the work of the movement's publicists who contrasted the noncompromising, aggressive Arab opposition to Zionism with Jewish nationalists' willingness to pursue negotiations and compromise. Zionists also understood that the military forces of the Yishuv were not strong enough to drive the British from the Middle East. A diplomatic solution to the Palestine problem was their only alternative. Even those Americans who had attacked the AACI finally decided to abide by the decision of the World Zionist leadership and cooperated with the Anglo-American investigation.[57]

After spending months collecting testimony and data, the AACI issued its final report in May 1946, unanimously calling for the abandonment of the White Paper restrictions on immigration to Palestine so that one hundred thousand Jewish DPs could immediately settle there. While they supported Jewish immigration to Palestine, the AACI members opposed the creation of either a Jewish or an Arab state. Instead, they looked forward to the eventual sharing of political power by Jews and Arabs and the creation of a unified Palestinian nation in which neither Jews nor Arabs would dominate. Realistically recognizing that their plan could not be implemented while a near state of war existed between Palestinian Arabs and Jews, the committee recommended that Britain continue to control the Palestine territory until a climate of peace and cooperation could be restored.[58]

Nahum Goldmann, the head of the Jewish Agency's Washington Office, admitted that the AACI's report was "at best a very poor statement of non-Zionism." However, he continued, Zionists should disregard the AACI's refusal to endorse Jewish statehood and should concentrate on winning implementation of the committee's call for increased Jewish immigration to Palestine. Elimination of British immigration restriction to Palestine would strengthen the Jewish position in the Holy Land and would allow the Zionists to save the lives of at least one hundred thousand DPs.[59]

Emanuel Neumann accused Goldmann of dangerous defeatism. He agreed that the immediate task for Zionists was to have the American government implement the "100,000 recommendation," but he warned against ignoring the implications of the Anglo-American committee's recommendations for the political development of Palestine. Believing that Jewish nationalists should continue their public demands for the establishment of a Jewish state in all of Palestine, Neumann declared: "We must fight for the positive part of the Report, but we must also fight against the negative aspects."[60]

Neumann's position prevailed within the American Zionist Emergency Council largely because of the strenuous support of Abba Hillel Silver and David Ben-Gurion, who arrived in the United States for a short visit in May 1946. Ben-Gurion agreed that Zionists should work for the implementation of the AACI's proposal for mass immigration to Palestine while attacking the group for not supporting the creation of a Jewish state in all of Palestine. Accordingly, the American Jewish Conference applauded the AACI's criticism of the British White Paper immigration restriction as a "posthumous victory" for the millions of dead Jews who might have been saved from Hitler had it not been for the White Paper. At the same time, it objected to the AACI's proposal for continued British control of Palestine, branding it "unrealistic" and "unfortunate."[61]

Zionist leaders could have avoided their acrimonious debates over how to respond to the proposals made by the AACI. Silver, Ben-Gurion, and Neumann probably would have been amused to know how much the AACI's report angered Britain's Labour party government. While Zionists rebelled against the report's failure to endorse Jewish statehood, British leaders fumed about the AACI's refusal to sanction London's Palestine policies. When Prime Minister Clement Attlee and Foreign Secretary Ernest Bevin proposed establishing the Anglo-American Inquiry Committee, they expected that the investigators would conclude that the tenuous nature of Arab-Jewish relations in Palestine made large-scale refugee resettlement impractical if not impossible. The AACI's repudiation of Britain's immigration restriction policies and suggestion that one hundred thousand Jews be allowed to enter Palestine shocked British authorities, who quickly asked Washington to postpone official publication of the committee's report. President Truman's refusal to accede to London's request and his public endorsement of the AACI's report on May 1, 1946, enraged Bevin and Attlee. They quickly maneuvered to soften the impact of Truman's action, announcing that Britain could not assume sole responsibility for acting upon the committee's findings. Bevin and Attlee correctly calculated that Truman's support for increased Jewish immigration to Palestine was motivated by his desire to solve the refugee problem cheaply. They knew that the president was unwilling and unable to commit the United States to share the responsibility for putting the AACI proposals into effect, particularly if this entailed dispatching American troops to Palestine to pacify the Arabs who could be expected to respond violently to the influx of large numbers of Jews to the Holy Land. Bevin's infamous remark that Truman supported Jewish immigration to Palestine because he did not want too many of them in New York was crude, but it accurately described the self-serving nature of the Truman administrations's support for a humanitarian policy that entailed little or no expense for Washington.[62]

While the politicians attempted to devise a plan for Palestine that would be acceptable to Jews and Arabs as well as serve British and American national interests, the Jewish community in Palestine struggled for control of the Holy Land. In liberated Europe, emissaries from the Haganah, the Jewish underground army in Palestine, and former Jewish partisans prepared the survivors of Hitler's death camps to participate in the struggle against Great Britain. The Hagannah men were especially active in the displaced persons camps, raising the morale of the survivors by describing the lives of dignity and freedom they would one day lead in a Jewish Palestine. Periodically, the Palestinian emissaries transported large groups of homeless Jews to European ports and onto ships, which then attempted to reach Palestine. Only a few of these antiquated vessels, often christened for the occasion with the names of Zionist heroes, succeeded in delivering their passengers to freedom. Usually, British air or naval units intercepted and boarded the ships, interning their refugee cargo in the Atlit detention camp, about ten miles south of Haifa. The leaders of the Haganah and the Jewish Agency did not consider the detentions a defeat because they realized that "illegal immigration" (as the British authorities dubbed it) was a most efficient means of undermining British strength in Palestine. To close off Palestine's shores to the hapless Jewish refugees, London had to maintain a huge and costly military presence in the Middle East, which significantly added to Britain's severe economic crisis at the end of World War II. Each illegal immigrant ship captured also kept the plight of the displaced persons and Palestine in the press and seemed to highlight the immorality and inhumanity of Britain's immigration policies, which prevented Hitler's victims from returning "home."[63]

In mid-1946 the Haganah high command decided to escalate their struggle against British immigration restriction and anti-Zionism. Following the lead of Menachem Begin's Irgun, which had been waging an underground war against the British since 1944, the Haganah secret radio network threatened the British with a campaign of sabotage unless London lowered Palestine's immigration barriers. On the night of June 17, 1946, soldiers of the Palmach, the shock troops of the Haganah, blew up key railway lines and bridges, totally distrupting Palestine's transportation system. The Holy Land seemed to be on the brink of open and total warfare.[64]

If Zionist leaders expected to achieve a military victory over the British, they were sadly mistaken. On Saturday, June 29, British military and police units conducted a massive sweep through Jewish Palestine, uncovering and seizing arms caches and arresting over two thousand members of the Yishuv. Most of the Jewish Agency's leadership found themselves jailed; fortunately, David Ben-Gurion, chairman of the Jewish Agency, was temporarily out of the country and avoided arrest. The British agreed to release the Zionist leaders only after they pledged to abandon military action and pledged their cooperation in the suppression of the Irgun. The discovery of a large arms depot on Kibbutz Yagur particularly worried Zionist leaders who feared that the British police action would leave the Yishuv unarmed and open to Arab attack. Zionist concern deepened when the British announced in August 1946 that "illegal immigrants" would no longer be interned in Palestine but would be transported to prison camps on the island of Cyprus. London hoped that the displaced persons in Europe would refuse to challenge the British blockade once they knew that they could not even look forward to incarceration in the Holy Land.[65]

THE AMERICAN ZIONIST STRUGGLE OVER PARTITION

The intensity and efficiency of Great Britain's repressive measures in Palestine left the Zionist leadership in disarray. Nahum Goldmann was convinced that the Zionists would have to minimize their demands drastically if they were to avoid total defeat. Goldmann's concerns were deep-rooted. As early as May 1946, when the AACI's report was published, he had attempted to convince his fellow Zionist leaders that they had no alternative but to ask Great Britain and the United States to partition Palestine into Jewish and Arab states. In 1946 there were still less than six hundred thousand Jews in Palestine who were outnumbered by nearly two million Arabs. Goldmann knew that a Jewish state could only be established in Palestine when Jews achieved majority status in the land. Goldmann determined that it was impossible for Jews to become a majority in the Holy Land because the British would never be willing to jeopardize their strategic interests in the Middle East by opening Palestine's doors to large-scale Jewish immigration. The only viable Zionist plan, Goldmann argued, was to propose the partition of Palestine. He recommended that Jewish nationalists present the proposal as an ultimate compromise and plead with Washington and London that this statesmanlike act deserved acceptance. Goldmann acknowledged that a Jewish state in a partitioned Palestine would be small, but it would also be autonomous. The Zionists would finally be free of British control and would have the power to establish their own immigration policy.[66]

Goldmann's position had little support in the summer of 1946. Most Zionist leaders in the United States and Palestine believed that any partition proposal would have to be initiated by Great Britain. They shrewdly calculated that a Zionist partition proposal would seriously weaken their negotiating position because Britain would not accept the Zionist plan as a legitimate compromise. Instead, the Zionist request would become the starting point for negotiations, the outcome of which would surely be less satisfactory than the plan originally put on the table by Jewish nationalist leaders.[67]

Following the British arrest of Jewish Agency leaders on June 29, 1946, Goldmann again tried to advance his views on partition. On July 11, the *New York Times* reported that Zionist leaders were contemplating an appeal to the United Nations and that they had reluctantly determined that partition was the only practical solution for the Palestine problem. The *Times* noted that the Zionist spokesman on partition asked to remain anonymous, yet the careful reader could determine that Goldmann was the source. His was the only name mentioned in the article and the *Times* reporter credited him with providing details about Zionist plans regarding the U.N. Goldmann's partition plan, as outlined in the newspaper, was detailed and precise. One-third of Palestine, with the largest concentration of Arabs, would be ceded to Transjordan, while the remaining two-thirds would become a Jewish state.[68]

From the perspectives of Abba Hillel Silver and Emanuel Neumann, Goldmann's leak to the *Times* could not have come at a less opportune time. The day after the newspaper report, Ambassador Henry F. Grady brought an American delegation to London to confer with his English counterpart, Herbert Morrison, about devising a plan to act on the proposals of the Anglo-American Committee of Inquiry. Although Morrison and Grady conducted their discussions in secret, details of their negotiations quickly reached the press. Long before the official announcement of their plan on July 31, Zionist leaders in the United States knew that Morrison and Grady proposed to divide Palestine "into Arab, Jewish and British provinces, with full control over the entire country to be vested in the central British administration." Silver, who had been angered by Goldmann's flirtation with partition, quickly went to Washington where he convinced Goldmann to join him in denouncing the Morrison-Grady proposals. Under Silver's skillful leadership, the American Zionist Emergency Council generated enough public pressure to force President Truman to reject the Morrison-Grady proposal.[69]

Goldmann's willingness to cooperate with Silver did not reflect any change in his attitude on partition. In early August, while Silver remained in the United States to coordinate opposition to the Morrison-Grady plan, Goldmann traveled to Paris for strategic and tactical discussions with leaders of the Jewish Agency and the Zionist Executive who had escaped arrest and internment by the British. Goldmann was able to overcome the suspicions of David Ben-Gurion and Moshe Sneh (the commander of the Haganah who had escaped arrest in Palestine) and won their permission to go to Washington to make one more attempt to win American support for Jewish statehood. The Zionist leadership instructed Goldmann to convey to President Truman the Zionist Executive's total objection to the Morrison-Grady scheme, but also its willingness to discuss a partition plan that would establish a "viable Jewish state" in part of Palestine. Goldmann was to request that immigration of one hundred thousand Jews to Palestine begin at once and that the Jewish leaders of Palestine immediately be granted full administrative and economic autonomy in the part of Palestine destined to become a sovereign Jewish state. The Paris meeting specifically wanted Truman's assurance that Zionists would be allowed to determine the rate of immigration into the designated Jewish territory even before formal statehood was declared.[70]

Goldmann knew that he could not expect to have the full support of the American Zionist leadership for his mission to Truman. At the Paris meeting, Israel Gold-

stein, a nonvoting observer from the Zionist Organization of America, had refused
to endorse the partition scheme. Goldmann could expect Abba Hillel Silver to fight
any attempt to discuss the division of Palestine before any concrete partition plan had
been proposed by Great Britain or the United States. Silver had even opposed holding
the Zionist Executive meeting in Paris and had refused to attend because he believed
that the entire Zionist leadership should be in Washington lobbying against the
Morrison-Grady plan. Ironically, Goldmann was able to use Silver's absence from
Paris to divert the Rabbi's attention away from his partition scheme.

At a meeting of the AZEC's executive committee on August 7, Silver described
his understanding of what Goldmann's instructions were. Basing his analysis on
sketchy information, Silver explained that Goldmann would convey the Zionist Executive's rejection of the Morrison-Grady plan to Truman and would demand the
immediate implementation of the AACI's proposal that one hundred thousand DPs
be transported to Palestine. If Truman then proposed partition as a compromise
solution to the Palestine quandary, Silver acknowledged that Goldmann had the
authority to begin negotiations. Goldmann, who had just returned from Europe
and was attending the AZEC meeting, announced that Silver's understanding of
the Paris decision was correct, even though Goldmann knew that he not Truman
would propose the partition compromise.[71]

Goldmann next turned his attention to winning the Truman administration's support for the partition of Palestine, but he was far less successful in influencing
Truman than he was in tricking Silver. He met with Acting Secretary of State Dean
Acheson several times, but was never able to see President Truman, and he found
it impossible to convince the administration to abandon Great Britain and to take
the lead in championing a Zionist partition plan.[72]

When Silver discovered Goldmann's activities, he was furious, but reluctantly
concluded that the best had to be made of a terrible situation. He told the AZEC:

> It is clear that as of the moment the entire demarche of the [Jewish] Agency
> has been a failure. The American government did not advance the partition
> proposal as its own, and the British Government has refused to accept it as
> a basis of discussion. As to our own position, whether we like it or not, we
> have to recognize it as a fact that the partition proposal has been put forward
> officially in the name of the movement and once made, there is no way at
> the moment for us to go behind or around it. If we are the continue to carry
> on any political work in Washington we cannot ignore these official proposals
> made by the Jewish Agency. They are now the maximum that we can ask for
> and the minimum that we can accept. We must fight hard to make sure that
> we at least *get* that which has been asked for, and it will not be easy.

Silver discovered, however, that he, like Goldmann, could find little official support for partition in either Washington or London. He concluded that the Jewish

Agency's partition initiative had been a total disaster, and he resolved to put a final end to any premature discussion of Palestine's division. His opportunity came in December 1946 when representatives of the entire Zionist movement convened in Basel, Switzerland, for the first World Zionist Congress of the postwar era.[73]

The Zionists' choice of Basel was most appropriate as the city had hosted the very first Zionist Congress organized by Theodor Herzl in 1897. The delegates arriving in 1946 did not share the optimism and enthusiasm of their counterparts who had heard Herzl's historic call for Jewish emancipation and independence. The extermination of six million Jews and the opposition of Great Britain to Jewish statehood angered all the Zionists at Basel. Their discussions promised to be long and acrimonious.

Debates about the wisdom of both Zionist policies and leaders dominated the deliberations of the World Zionist Congress. Abba Hillel Silver, David Ben-Gurion, and their followers ferociously attacked Nahum Goldmann and Chaim Weizmann, claiming that their lack of intestinal fortitude had seriously undermined the Zionist position. Goldmann, who was frequently involved in controversy and who was endowed with a powerful ego, does not seem to have been very hurt by the criticisms of his associates. He later remembered: "My friends in the [Zionist] Executive held back somewhat and did me the honor of letting the opponents of partition concentrate their fire on me. I mention this in no spirit of complaint; on the contrary, I sometimes enjoy being the target of attack in fair debate." Weizmann, who was nearing the end of his life and who possessed a far more gentle soul than Goldmann, found it much more difficult to tolerate attack. His autobiography, which graphically chronicles his decades of service to the Zionist cause, barely mentions his painful experience at Basel.[74]

At first, it seemed as if Weizmann would survive the onslaught of his opponents and continue to play a leadership role within the Zionist movement. On December 10, congress delegates honored Weizmann by naming him president of the World Zionist Congress. Although the congress president actually exercised little power, the overwhelming vote for Weizmann indicated that the "father of the Balfour Declaration" still held the support and respect of many within the movement. While forty-eight Zionist delegates opposed Weizmann's selection, approximately four times that many supported his elevation.[75]

In a fifty-minute address to the congress, Weizmann attempted to explain why the Jewish Agency had taken the initiative in proposing partition as a solution to the Palestine quandary. His listeners might very well have experienced a sense of déjà vu while listening to Weizmann. His position on the partition of Palestine in late 1946 closely resembled his response to the Peel Commission report of 1937. On both occasions Weizmann reasoned that the plight of the Jewish people and inadequate support from Great Britain made it imperative for Zionists to sacrifice territory for autonomy. Nineteen months after V-E Day, Weizmann's appeal seemed to have much merit. Congress delegates could still vividly remember the newsreel film of liberated Nazi concentration camps and the horrible images they captured. Many of the emancipated survivors of those camps were incarcerated in Cyprus detention camps. Their dream of reaching Palestine and the continuing British resolve to keep them out of the Holy Land lent support to Weizmann's claim that Zionist leaders had to take immediate and extraordinary measures to create a Jewish state in at least part of Palestine.[76]

Weizmann's oration moved many of the delegates at the World Zionist Congress and they frequently interrupted his address with applause. Nahum Goldmann, of course, also supported Weizmann and shared his views on partition. Stephen S. Wise, who had bitterly opposed Weizmann during the Peel Commission controversy, now came to the defense of his former adversary. Although he was not a strong supporter of the Weizmann-Goldmann partition strategy, Wise sympathized with Weizmann's personal plight because it closely resembled his own. Wise, like Weizmann, was struggling to survive the attacks of Silver and his supporters who accused the elderly rabbi of undermining their attempts to forge links with the Republican party.[77]

Weizmann's prestige, Nahum Goldmann's cleverness, and Stephen Wise's fighting spirit were not sufficient to defeat the followers of Ben-Gurion and Silver. Emanuel Neumann, Silver's long-time friend and loyal lieutenant, organized a block of delegates at Basel to oppose Weizmann's leadership and Goldmann's tactics of partition. Neumann's coalition transcended party organization; at its core were two-thirds of the ZOA representatives and the delegates of the Mizrachi (religious) and Revisionist (right-wing) parties, which were deeply opposed to Weizmann and any premature discussion of partition. Neumann also relied on the support of most of the Labor Zionist delegates who could be counted on to vote against Weizmann out of loyalty to Ben-Gurion. He also attempted to win the allegiance of as many of the Hadassah delegates as possible, though this proved to be difficult because most disliked and disapproved of Silver's vicious attacks on Goldmann, Weizmann, and particularly Wise.[78]

While Neumann quietly worked to recruit allies at Basel, his comrades used the congress proceedings as a forum to launch their attacks and articulate their views. On December 10, David Ben-Gurion, who had reservedly endorsed Nahum Goldmann's partition tactics earlier in the year, delivered a long political report to the congress. He unequivocally announced that he would oppose any Zionist overture to Great Britain that proposed to partition Palestine into Jewish and Arab states. Responsible Zionist governing bodies should not even discuss the desirability of dividing Palestine until Great Britain formally presented such a proposal.[79]

As was often the case, Abba Hillel Silver made one of the most effective presentations at the World Zionist Congress. The ideas Silver articulated were not original; almost any of Goldmann's American Zionist adversaries could have made them. However, few could have delivered the message with the same force and eloquence.

Silver's speech reflected his cynical and probably accurate belief that morality and justice would never dictate how Christian governments and leaders responded to Jewish needs. Whereas his arch rival Stephen Wise had devoted his career to fostering Jewish and Christian dialogue and conciliation, Silver by 1946 had determined that Christian society was fundamentally anti-Semitic. Jewish Agency leaders, Silver explained, had overestimated the humanity of the British authorities when they endorsed Nahum Goldmann's partition plan believing that this "supreme sacrifice" would evoke a generous response. They should have realized that

> This is not the spiritual climate of our age. If sacrifices could move the hearts of Governments today, the leaking hulks which are transporting our storm-tossed refugees would not be turned away with their cargo of human misery from the shores of Palestine to detention camps in Cyprus. The sacrifice of six million of our people did not move the British Government to deviate by an iota from its illegal and immoral action which shut the one real haven of refuge against their possible rescue.

In the "real" world, governments recognize sacrifices as signs of weakness. The "surest way" for Zionists not to "get" partition was to propose the division of Palestine to the great powers, for Washington and London understood the rules of negotiations, which the Jewish Agency had forgotten: You always ask for more than what you want. When Goldmann made his partition offer, "it became the Jewish solution, and therefore, unavailable as a compromise solution." Silver urged his audience to realize that "every eloquent speech made at this Congress in favor of partition is a nail driven into its coffin." Truman and Bevin would propose "sound and just" solutions to the Palestine problem if Zionists did not lose their "nerve" and if they courageously and determinedly exerted political pressure on the White House and 10 Downing Street. In the future, Silver counseled, all Zionist spokesmen should insist on the establishment of a Jewish state in an "undivided" Palestine.[80]

Silver and Ben-Gurion's arguments, combined with Neumann's skillful negotiations, successfully convinced a majority of the World Zionist Congress to reject the Weizmann-Goldmann position. The delegates at Basel voted to give Ben-Gurion and Silver total control of charting the Zionist political course. After defeating Weizmann decisively, Ben-Gurion asked the congress to pay tribute to the long service and accomplishments of the elderly Zionist leader. Ben-Gurion's praise for the architect of the Balfour Declaration was actually a eulogy. Weizmann left Basel powerless, although he would continue to play a limited role in Zionist affairs. Wise returned to the United States a bitter man and announced that he was resigning from his role as leader in the Zionist Organization of America because he could not support Abba Hillel Silver's extremist tactics and demands for the creation of a Jewish state in an undivided Palestine.[81]

THE TRIUMPH OF AMERICAN ZIONISM

Events following the Basel congress proved the validity of Silver's political analysis. The British Labour government, as Silver had accurately perceived, was firmly committed to pursuing an anti-Zionist policy. Foreign Secretary Ernest Bevin was simply unprepared to accept the establishment of a geographically viable and fully sovereign Jewish state, and he rejected every Zionist attempt to initiate a compromise solution to end the struggle for Palestine. Therefore, after the Zionist Congress, Jewish nationalists pursued a two-pronged campaign. Publicly, Silver and other Zionist orators repeatedly stated that their goal was to achieve full Jewish control over all of Palestine, while Jews in Europe and Palestine persevered in a much more grueling and demanding conflict. Zionist agents in Europe, under the command of Jewish leaders in Palestine, continued to assault the British blockade of the Holy Land with boatloads of Jewish refugees. Meanwhile, the renegade Jewish terrorist organizations, the Irgun and the Stern Gang, which refused to accept Ben-Gurion's authority, attacked military installations in Palestine and assassinated British officials.[82]

The Zionists' aggressive war of words and deeds achieved results within an astonishingly short period of time. On February 14, 1947, a weary and frustrated British government announced that it would allow the United Nations to resolve the Palestine problem. In the United States, Silver's championing of an extreme Zionist platform was actually helping to build up American support for the partition of Palestine. The extermination of six million Jews and the DPs' plight troubled Americans, who could also admire the stubborn determination of the survivors of Hitler's death camps to reach their "homeland" in Palestine. Still, they knew that Palestine was a contested territory and that Arabs were equally as willing to kill and be killed for its possession. By posing as an "extremist," Silver allowed Americans to weigh his position against that of militant Arab Palestinian nationalists. The partition of Palestine seemed to be a reasonable and practical compromise.[83]

The key to this strategy, for Zionists, was not to adopt the partition formula too quickly. Silver understood that it was critical for world opinion to believe that, in accepting partition, the Zionists were making a sacrifice, not winning a victory.

The final act of the partition drama was staged before the United Nations. The General Assembly opened its debate on Palestine in April 1947 and decided to send a special committee to the Middle East to investigate the situation and devise proposals to be submitted for approval by the whole assembly.[84]

177

After visiting Palestine, the eleven-nation committee submitted two reports to the General Assembly. A minority report submitted by the representatives of India, Iran, and Yugoslavia essentially called for the cantonization of Palestine into Arab and Jewish semi-autonomous regions united under a federal government. The majority proposal, made by the representatives of Canada, Czechoslovakia, Guatemala, the Netherlands, Peru, Sweden, and Uruguay, called for the partition of Palestine into Arab and Jewish states.[85]

The majority partition proposal was precisely what Zionist leaders had been waiting for. A suggestion for dividing Palestine was now being initiated by a responsible political body, not by the Zionists themselves. According to Silver and Neumann's conception of how the diplomatic game was played, it was now time for the Zionists reluctantly but nobly to accept the division of the Holy Land. Coincidentally, the task fell to Abba Hillel Silver, the only American on the Zionist delegation that had been invited by the United Nations to participate in the proceedings.

Silver played his part beautifully, beginning his address with a strong attack on the legitimacy of Palestinian nationalism. There had never been a "politically or culturally distinct" Arab nation in Palestine, Silver claimed. In fact, the Arabs who took possession of Palestine in 634 A.D. had "held sway" for only 437 years before the region was conquered by "non-Arab peoples," including the Kurds, Crusaders, and Turks. In contrast, Silver continued, "by the time the Arabs conquered Palestine . . . the Jewish people had already completed nearly two thousand years of national history in that country, during which time they created a civilization which decidedly influenced the course of mankind." Repeating a common theme of Zionist propaganda, Silver claimed that the Zionist return to Palestine harmed no one. For the Arabs of Palestine, Jewish settlement brought economic and social progress. Zionism was not even a threat to Arab nationalism, Silver continued, pointing out that "the Arabs possess today independent monarchies in Saudi Arabia, Yemen, Egypt, Iraq, and Transjordan, and independent republics in Syria and Lebanon." All the Jews desired was to return to their homeland, which occupied a mere ten thousand square miles of the vast Middle East.

After presenting the reasons why the Zionists could justly claim control of all of Palestine, Silver turned his attention to the two proposals before the General Assembly. The minority report of the Palestine committee, calling for the creation of an independent Federal State of Palestine consisting of two semi-autonomous regions, was totally unacceptable to the Zionist movement. The Arab majority of Palestine would never allow large-scale Jewish immigration to Palestine, thereby condemning the Jews of the nation to permanent minority status. Silver said, "The plan entails for the Jews all the disadvantages of partition—and a very bad partition geographically—without the compensating advantages of a real partition: statehood, independence and free immigration."

The majority report calling for the partition of Palestine was clearly not in the spirit of the framers of the Balfour Declaration, who Silver claimed intended to create a Jewish state in all of Palestine. To propose partition was to ask the Jewish people to make a "very heavy sacrifice," but the Zionist movement was willing to pay this price because "the proposal makes possible the immediate re-establishment of the Jewish State, an ideal for which our people ceaselessly strove through the centuries, and because it ensures immediate and continuing Jewish immigration which, as events have demonstrated, is possible only under a Jewish State." Then, attempting to prove that the Zionist leadership was capable of great statesmanship and maturity, in comparison to Arab nationalist leaders who had never been willing to compromise, Silver said the Zionists would also accept partition "as our contribution to the solution of a grave international problem and as evidence of our willingness to join with the community of nations in an effort to bring peace at last to the troubled land which is precious to the heart of mankind." There were limits to sacrifice, however. The Jews would only accept partition with the understanding that the Jewish state would be fully sovereign and would have full control over its own immigration policy. Silver summed up the Zionist position succinctly:

> We have builded a nation in Palestine. That nation now demands its independence. it will not be dislodged. Its national status will not be denied. We are asked to make an enormous sacrifice to attain that which, if uninterfered with, we would have attained long ago. In sadness, and most reluctantly, we are prepared to make this sacrifice. Beyond it we cannot, we will not go.[86]

After additional debate and deliberation, the General Assembly decided to accept the majority report and partition Palestine into Jewish and Arab states. The U.N. vote was quite impressive, particularly given the fact that both the United States and the Soviet Union both opted to support the creation of a Jewish state. The Soviet Union's vote to create a Jewish state was probably the result of Stalin's shrewd calculations. The Soviets, who had always been hostile to Zionism, recognized that by voting to create a Jewish state they would be promoting the decline of the British Empire in the Middle East while they received credit for supporting a measure that many in the United States considered just and humane.[87] Washington's support of Jewish statehood, on the other hand, was the result of the long, hard political and propaganda struggle of American Zionists.

It was a bittersweet victory for American Zionists. In 1933 they were just a small, beleaguered segment of the American Jewish community. The rise of Hitler had rejuvenated their movement. Responding to the plight of their co-religionists, American Zionists provided the financial and political support necessary to bring large numbers of refugees to Palestine. The Zionists' ability to provide a practical solution to the refugee crisis brought the movement great prestige and respect among American Jews who were anguished and concerned by Nazi anti-Semitic policies. An Arab revolt and increasingly hostile British policies convinced American Zionists that to provide a haven for refugees they would first have to insure the security of Jewish Palestine. Believing that they were waging a war for the survival of the Jewish people, Zionists set out to unite the American Jewish community in a statehood campaign as the first important step to winning the support of the Roosevelt administration. In this context, learning about Hitler's extermination of European Jewry only served to convince American Zionists that their path was correct. Abba Hillel Silver's passionate and eloquent claim that the Nazi extermination program was the latest link in a chain of anti-Semitism that could only be broken by the end of Jewish homelessness, not only expressed the view of most American Zionists, it captured the attention of concerned American Jews who were in agony over the seemingly insurmountable task of rescuing European Jewry. They flocked to the Zionist movement believing, like Silver, that Zionism was the ultimate form of rescue. Together with Silver and other Zionist leaders they worked and sacrificed to gain American public and political support. Tragically, their victory came only after the murder of six million Jews.

Almost all American Zionists could take some credit for Israel's creation. Emanuel Neumann and Abba Hillel Silver had skillfully constructed an efficient public relations machine and had astutely developed an aggressive and tough strategy. Stephen Wise's charm and good works had steadily won support for Zionism from Jews and Christians and gave Zionists an important link to the Democratic party. In spite of their dislike for each other, Neumann, Silver, Wise, and Goldmann made an effective team. The "extremists" provided the force and attempted to influence American policymakers with a stick, while the moderates were always available to mend fences and extend sympathy to Truman and his administration.

The United Nations vote did not end the struggle for Palestine. Other political battles remained to be fought as elements within the State Department unsuccessfully attempted to postpone Jewish independence, which was scheduled for mid-May 1948. Egypt, Transjordan, Syria, and Lebanon responded to David Ben-Gurion's declaration of independence by launching a full-scale military invasion against the new Jewish state of Israel. That long bloody war did not end with a peace settlement, but with an armistice. More conflict was to follow.

CONCLUSIONS

For world Jewry, the decade and a half between 1933 and 1948 was traumatic and cataclysmic. The persecution of German Jewry that began with Adolf Hitler's rise to power in 1933, ended with the annihilation of six million Jews. While Germany was primarily responsible for the Holocaust, the democratic governments of the United States and the United Kingdom must be considered at least accomplices in genocide. Franklin D. Roosevelt, a liberal and humane leader, rescued his country from the despair caused by a massive economic failure and saved the world from the threat of fascist domination, but did practically nothing to deliver six million men, women, and children from the hands of their executioners. While the Jews perished in Nazi death camps, the Roosevelt administration persistently, if politely, resisted appeals from Jewish leaders for salvation. The record of Winston Churchill's government is perhaps even bleaker than that of Roosevelt's. Fully aware of the fate of Jews trapped in Nazi-occupied Europe, Great Britain refused to open the doors of Palestine to those few who might have been able to escape from the clutches of their murderers if only a safe haven had existed.

The Allied victory over the Axis in 1945 did not end the plight and suffering of the pitifully small number of European Jews who had somehow managed to survive the war. For many of the survivors, the war's end did not bring freedom, but only a reprieve from the threat of immediate annihilation. Homeless and stateless, many of the postwar survivors continued to live in the former Nazi concentration camps, cared for by the American GIs and British "Tommies" who had replaced the SS guards.

Most of the survivors refused to allow themselves to sink into a state of deep and permanent mental depression. Soon after the war, many began the painful task of resconstructing their lives and of creating new families to re-place those extinguished by the Nazis. With the help of Palestinian Jewish emissaries, the one-time concentration camps became Zionist training centers where the sur-vivors prepared themselves for a new life in Palestine. With the establishment of the State of Israel in May 1948, the homelessness of many of the survivors ended. Some of those who had escaped death in Auschwitz and Treblinka fell on battle-fields in the Galilee and Negev, fighting to ensure the existence of a state that they hoped would protect future generations of Jews from suffering the same fate as the martyred six million. Most of the survivors who came to Israel in 1948 lived to see their children reach maturity in a modern Jewish state which had, in spite of numerous wars and economic crises, become a regional superpower.

American Zionists shared in the experiences of their European co-religionists. Although they personally did not have to endure deportation to death camps, American Zionists were painfully aware of what was occurring in the Nazi murder factories. Many had relatives in occupied Europe, and all felt a real responsibility to combat the Nazi forces of extermination. The leaders of the Zionist movement in the United States were all too aware of the reluctance of American and British officials to deal decisively with the "Jewish problem."

In spite of the great hardships they endured, the period between 1933 and 1948 ended triumphantly for American Zionists. In 1933, American Zionism was just one of several movements competing for the loyalty of American Jewry. At the helm of disorganized, financially and numerically weak organizations, few of the leaders of American Zionism expected to witness the triumph of Jewish na-tionalism within their lifetimes.

The fight against Hitler radically transformed American Zionism. During the decade of the thirties, the ability of American Zionists to present Palestine as a practical solution to the European refugee crisis resulted in a steady increase in the power and prestige of Jewish nationalism in the United States. During World War II, the Zionist claim to hold the ultimate solution to the problem of anti-Semitism captured the imagination of American Jews struggling to comprehend and respond to the Holocaust. In remarkably large numbers, American Jews enlisted in the Zionist crusade to create a Jewish state that would finally end the problem of Jewish homelessness, which they believed was the basic cause not only of the Holocaust but of all anti-Semitism. By 1943, American Zionists had achieved a commanding position within the American Jewish community.

Having won the competition for the allegiance of American Jewry, Zionists set out to turn their movement into a powerful political force. By the end of World War II, American Zionist organizations had not only succeeded in vanquishing opposing Jewish groups, but had also created the machinery necessary to gain influence in Washington. The fight for American political support was a difficult one, but at the crucial November 1947 United Nations deliberations on the future of Palestine, the United States supported the establishment of a Jewish state in the Holy Land. American Zionists could justly claim some of the credit for the successful establishment of the State of Israel in May 1948.

The triumph of American Zionism entailed great cost and sacrifice. Unlike their comrades in Palestine, no American Zionist had to endure combat to create Israel. However, the leaders and rank and file of the American Zionist movement contributed generously to the Jewish nationalist cause. American fund raisers provided much of the necessary capital to build and defend the Jewish state. Considerable amounts of energy and time went into generating the American political and popular support for Zionism that was vitally important to Israel's creation. While American Zionists were aware of their sacrifices, few if any realized that the Zionist success in America exacted a far more tragic cost.

After learning in late 1942 about Hitler's program to exterminate European Jewry, American Zionist leaders decided that their primary task had to be the building of support for the immediate establishment of a Jewish state in Palestine. Their decision did not reflect a callousness about or disinterest in the terrible fate of the European Jews. Rather, American Zionists believed that there was nothing unique about Hitler's plan for genocide. It simply seemed to be the latest of a long series of anti-Semitic persecutions that had plagued the Jewish people since their exile from the Holy Land by the forces of the Roman Empire. Believing that Jewish homelessness was the basic cause of all anti-Semitism, American Zionists resolved to put a final end to Jewish statelessness. The failure of previous generations to accomplish this task, Zionists believed, was partly responsible for the tragic situation of European Jewry. If Zionists failed to create their state, future generations of Jews would surely follow in the path of the Jews being deported to Auschwitz.

Sadly, the American Zionists' calculation was faulty. The existence of a Jewish state in Palestine during the 1930s probably would have provided many Jewish refugees with a haven and might have been able to offer salvation to the Jews marked for annihilation by the Nazis. However, once the Nazis embarked on their program of genocide, the American Zionist decision to make the establishment of a Jewish state their primary goal handicapped any attempt to build a powerful lobby to force the American government to undertake the rescue of European Jewry. Powerful and talented leaders like Abba Hillel Silver gave their energies to Zionism, not the immediate rescue of the Jews of Europe. The American Zionist Emergency Council, an efficient and successful political lobby and public relations machine, devoted little of its resources to the rescue of European Jewry. Finally, the Zionist insistence on including a demand for Jewish statehood in any proposal to aid European Jewry, politicized the rescue issue, and made it impossible to appeal for American aid on purely humanitarian grounds.

While we can criticize the policies of American Zionists, it is important to remember that Adolf Hitler is primarily responsible for the murder of six million

Jews. To some extent, the Nazi persecution of European Jewry is also responsible for the political turmoil in the Middle East that followed Israel's creation.

In 1933, the year Hitler gained power in Germany, few Zionist leaders expected to live to see the establishment of a Jewish state in Palestine. The Zionist settlement of the Holy Land was to be carried out slowly and judiciously. With time on their side, Zionists wanted to ensure the careful and scientific creation of an economic and social base in Palestine that could effectively support larger numbers of Jewish settlers. Time might also have allowed Zionists to come to an accommodation with the Arabs of Palestine who feared that Zionist settlement would displace them and turn them into second-class citizens in their own land.

The terrible plight of European Jewry upset Zionist plans and made it impossible to reach any agreement with the Arabs. As the Zionists began to bring Jewish refugees to Palestine, the Palestinian Arabs revolted in defense of their own national interests. Zionists, primarily concerned with providing a home for the Jewish refugees and fearing a British betrayal, could not respond to the Arab protests with understanding. Instead, they responded to the Arab revolt with armed force and sought to insure their own claim to Palestine.

The British abandonment of a pro-Zionist policy in 1939 and the Nazi extermination of European Jews that began in June 1941 finally convinced Zionists in the United States and Palestine that Jews must achieve immediate independence in Palestine. This understandable conclusion based on an accurate understanding of the dangers they faced not only hampered the establishment of a powerful pro-rescue lobby in the United States, but also guaranteed that the conflict with Palestine's Arab population would continue. During World War II and the immediate postwar years, Zionists increasingly came to link the Arabs with the Nazi and the British forces that were seeking to prevent the establishment of a Jewish state. Sadly, in the eyes of American Zionists, the Arabs were steadily being transformed from a people with whom an accommodation would have to be made into a mortal enemy who had to be defeated. This is the legacy we still live with today.

NOTES

Note: The following abbreviations are used:
ZAL Zionist Archives and Library, New York City.
AHSMA Abba Hillel Silver Memorial Archives, The Temple, Cleveland, OH.

INTRODUCTION

1. Greenberg's essay, "Bankrupt," can be found in Marie Syrkin, ed., *Hayim Greenberg Anthology* (Detroit: Wayne State University Press, 1968), pp. 192–203.

2. Arthur Morse, *While Six Million Died: A Chronicle of American Apathy* (New York: Random House, 1968); David S. Wyman, *Paper Walls: America and the Refugee Crisis, 1938–1941* (Amherst: University of Massachusetts Press, 1968); Henry Feingold, *The Politics of Rescue: The Roosevelt Administration and the Holocaust 1938–1945* (New Brunswick, NJ: Rutgers University Press, 1970); Saul S. Friedman, *No Haven for the Oppressed: United States Policy Toward Jewish Refugees 1938–1945* (Detroit: Wayne State University Press, 1973). David S. Wyman, *The Abandonment of the Jews: America and the Holocaust 1941–1945* (New York: Pantheon, 1984) is a recent and important addition to this literature.

3. Samuel Halperin, *The Political World of American Zionism* (Detroit: Wayne State University Press, 1961), p. 327.

4. Halperin, *Political World of American Zionism*, p. 327.

5. In particular, see Melvin Urofsky, *American Zionism from Herzl to the Holocaust* (Garden City, NY: Anchor Press, 1975); Urofsky, *We are One!: American Jewry and Israel* (Garden City, NY: Anchor Press, 1978); Yonathan Shapiro, *Leadership of the American Zionist Organization 1897–1930* (Urbana: University of Illinois Press, 1971); Marnin Feinstein, *American Zionism 1897–1904* (New York: Herzl Press, 1965); Zvi Ganin, *Truman, American Jewry and Israel, 1945–1948* (New York: Holmes & Meier, 1979); Peter Grose, *Israel in the Mind of America* (New York: Alfred A. Knopf, 1983); Michael J. Cohen, *Palestine and the Great Powers 1945–1948* (Princeton: Princeton University Press, 1982); John Snetsinger, *Truman, the Jewish Vote and the Creation of Israel* (Stanford: Hoover Institution Press, Stanford University, 1974).

CHAPTER I

1. The best biographies of Herzl are Alex Bein, *Theodor Herzl: A Biography*, trans. Maurice Samuel (New York: Atheneum, 1962, reprint 1970); Amos Elon, *Herzl* (New York: Holt, Rinehart & Winston, 1975). Herzl's *The Jewish State* has been reprinted many times. For an easily accessible

version, see Arthur Hertzberg, ed., *The Zionist Idea: A Historical Analysis and Reader* (New York: Atheneum, 1959, reprint 1973), pp. 204–26.

2. On Pinsker, see Hertzberg, *Zionist Idea*, 178–98; Walter Laqueur, *A History of Zionism* (New York: Holt, Rinehart & Winston, 1972), pp. 70–75.

3. Laqueur, *History of Zionism*, pp. 103–9.

4. *Ibid.*, pp. 107–8, 162–66, 481–84; Chaim Weizmann, *Trial and Error: An Autobiography* (New York: Schocken Books, 1949, reprint 1966), pp. 43–54.

5. Laqueur, *History of Zionism*, chap. 6.

6. *The American Jewish Year Book 5690, Oct. 5, 1929 to Sept. 22, 1930*, vol. 31 (Philadelphia: Jewish Publication Society of America, 1929), p. 274; Melvin Urofsky, *American Zionism: From Herzl to the Holocaust* (Garden City, NY: Anchor Press, 1975), p. 104; Laqueur, *History of Zionism*, pp. 481–84; Samuel Halperin, *The Political World of American Zionism* (Detroit: Wayne State University Press, 1961), pp. 65–71; Maier Bryan Fox, "American Zionism in the 1920s," Ph.D. diss., George Washington University, 1979, pp. 231–36; Naomi W. Cohen, *American Jews and the Zionist Idea* (New York: Ktav Publishing House, 1975), p. 7.

7. *American Jewish Year Book 5690*, vol. 31, p. 270; Urofsky, *American Zionism*, pp. 103–4; Laqueur, *History of Zionism*, chap. 6; Halperin, *Political World of American Zionism*, pp. 159–62, 173–75; Fox, "American Zionism in the 1920s," pp. 253–73.

8. *Palestine Department of Migration Annual Report, 1934* (Jerusalem: 1935), p. 13; Martin Gilbert, *Exile and Return: The Struggle for a Jewish Homeland* (Philadelphia: Lippincott, 1978), chaps. 12 & 13; Alan R. Taylor, *Prelude to Israel: An Analysis of Zionist Diplomacy 1897–1947* (New York: Philosophical Library, 1959), chap. III

9. Laqueur, *History of Zionism*, chap. 7.

10. *American Jewish Year Book 5696, Sept. 28, 1935 to Sept. 16, 1936*, vol. 37 (Philadelphia: Jewish Publication Society of America, 1935), p. 333; Urofsky, *American Zionism*, pp. 357–58 n.; Halperin, *Political World of American Zionism*, 320; Fox, "American Zionism in the 1920s," pp. 240–43.

11. For the best histories on the early American Zionism, see Urofsky, *American Zionism;* N. Cohen, *American Jews and the Zionist Idea*, chaps. 1, 2, 3; Marnin Feinstein, *American Zionism, 1884–1904* (New York: Herzl Press, 1965); Yonathan Shapiro, *Leadership of the American Zionist Ogranization, 1897–1930* (Urbana: University of Illinois Press, 1971).

12. *American Jewish Yearbook 5690*, vol. 31, p. 290. There is a vast amount of literature on the Brandeis-Weizmann feud. For examples see: Urofsky, *American Zionism*, chap. 7; Laqueur, *History of Zionism*, pp. 458–62; Weizmann, *Trial and Error*, pp. 248–50, 265–78; Ben Halpern, *The Idea of a Jewish State*, 2d ed. (Cambridge: Harvard University Press, 1969), pp. 183–88; Peter Grose, *Israel in the Mind of America* (New York: Alfred A. Knopf, distributed by Random House, 1983), pp. 72–82; Ben Halpren, *A Clash of Heroes: Brandeis, Weizmann and American Zionism* (New York: Oxford University Press, 1987).

13. American contributions to the two major Zionist philanthropic funds, the Keren Hayesod and the Keren Kayemeth, shrunk after the onset of the depression. This was particularly serious because American Jews had traditionally provided 50 percent of the income of these international funds. Stenographic transcript of the thirty-sixth convention of the ZOA, July 1–4, 1933, p. 23, ZAL (hereafter: Transcript of the 1933 ZOA Convention). Also see Chaim Weizmann to Felix Warburg, Dec. 24, 1932, letter #328 in *The Letters and Papers of Chaim Weizmann*, Series A, vol. XV, ed. Barnet Litvinoff, (New Brunswick, NJ: Transaction Books, Rutgers University, 1978).

14. See Minutes of Hadassah National Board Meetings, Jan. 26, 1932; Feb. 9, 1932; Feb. 23, 1932; May 10, 1932; Nov. 6, 1932, Hadassah Papers, ZAL.

15. *Ibid.*, May 31, 1932.

16. *Ibid.*, Aug. 3, 1932; Nov. 6, 1932.

17. *Ibid.*, Dec. 21, 1932; Feb. 1, 1933; Mar. 19, 1933; Apr. 19, 1933; July 26, 1933.

18. For an impressively extensive analysis of Nazi anti-Semitic policies, see Raul Hilberg, *The Destruction of the European Jews*, 2d ed., 3 vols. (New York: Holmes & Meier, 1985).

19. Transcript of the 1933 ZOA Convention, p. 16.

20. *Ibid.*, pp. 62–64.

21. Urofsky, *American Zionism*, pp. 369–70.

22. Bernard Wasserstein, *Britain and the Jews of Europe 1939–1945* (New York: Oxford University Press, 1979), p. 6; David S. Wyman, *Paper Walls: America and the Refugee Crisis, 1938–1941* (Amherst: University of Massachusetts Press, 1968), pp. 27–30; Mark Wischnitzer, *To Dwell in Safety* (Philadelphia: Jewish Publication Society of America, 1948), p. 178.

23. Ari J. Sherman, *Island Refuge: Britain and Refugees from the Third Reich* (London: Elek, 1973), pp. 40–55; Wischnitzer, *To Dwell in Safety*, pp. 182–83.

24. Wyman, *Paper Walls*, pp. 33–34; Wasserstein, *Britain and the Jews of Europe*, p. 7; Arieh Tartakower and Kurt R. Grossman, *The Jewish Refugee* (New York: Institute of Jewish Affairs of the American Jewish Congress and the World Jewish Congress, 1944), pp. 130–42, 217–22. Sherman, *Island Refuge*, is the most extensive analysis of British immigration policy during the prewar period.

25. U.S. Department of Labor, *Annual Report of the Commissioner General of Immigration–1932* (Washington, DC: U.S. Government Printing Office, 1932), p. 16; Wyman, *Paper Walls*, p. 221.

26. Wyman, *Paper Walls*, pp. 3–4; Arthur Morse, *While Six Million Died* (New York: Random House, 1968), pp. 139–40; Henry L. Feingold, *The Politics of Rescue: The Roosevelt Administration and the Holocaust, 1938–1945* (New Brunswick, NJ: Rutgers University Press, 1970), p. 16; Saul S. Friedman, *No Haven for the Oppressed: U.S. Policy Toward Jewish Jewish Refugees, 1938–1945* (Detroit: Wayne State University Press, 1973), p. 22.

27. Wise and Bernard Deutsch Memorandum, Apr. 38, 1933, Brandeis Records, Microfilm Roll #22, ZAL.

28. Hull to Frankfurter, May 6, 1933, Brandeis Records, Microfilm Roll #22, ZAL.

29. Brandeis to Wise, May 11, 1933, Brandeis Records, Microfilm Roll #22, ZAL.

30. Wyman, *Paper Walls*, pp. 168–69, 221.

31. Melvin I. Urofsky, *A Voice that Spoke for Justice: The Life and Times of Stephen S. Wise* (Albany: State University of New York Press, 1982), pp. 302–7.

32. Charles H. Stember et al., *Jews in the Mind of America* (New York: Basic Books, 1966), p. 145.

33. *Ibid.*, p. 56.

34. *Ibid.*, p. 54.

35. *Ibid.*, pp. 131, 138.

36. Wyman, *Paper Walls*, pp. 14–23; Donald S. Strong, *Organized Anti-Semitism in America: The Rise of Group Prejudice During the Decade 1930–1940* (Washington, DC: American Council on Public Affairs, 1941); Alan Brinkley, *Voices of Protest: Huey Long, Father Coughlin and the Great Depression* (New York: Alfred A. Knopf, 1982), pp. 269–73.

37. Wyamn, *Paper Walls*, chap. 4; Feingold, *Politics of Rescue*, pp. 148–55; Morse, *While Six Million Died*, chap. XIV; Friedman, *No Haven for the Oppressed*, chap. 4.

38. Weizmann to Louis Lipsky, n.d. (May 1933?), letter #369 in *Letters and Papers of Chaim Weizmann*, Series A, vol. XV.

39. Transcript of the 1933 ZOA Convention, pp. 1–4.

40. Wise's address can be found in *Ibid.*, pp. 58–72.

41. *Ibid.*, p. 76.

42. Michael Traub, "Tempo of Palestine," *Jewish Frontier*, Feb. 1933, pp. 25–26. Also see Hayim Greenberg, "Profiteers Discover Palestine," *Jewish Frontier*, Mar. 1935, pp. 20–22.

43. Transcript of the 1933 ZOA Convention, pp. 47–48.

44. *Ibid.*, p. 142.

45. *Ibid.*, pp. 48, 256.

46. Emanuel Neumann's address can be found in *Ibid.*, pp. 84–115.

47. *Ibid.*, pp. 127–28.

48. The resolution can be found in *Ibid.*, pp. 73–75.

49. *Ibid.*, p. 43.

50. *Ibid.*, pp. 101–2, 113.

51. *Ibid.*, pp. 69–70.

52. Szold to Harry Friedenwald, Oct. 19, 1933, Brandeis Records, Microfilm Roll #22, ZAL.

53. Wise to Brandeis, Apr. 5, 1933, Brandeis Records, Microfilm Roll #22, ZAL; *Palestine Department of Migration Annual Report, 1937* (Jerusalem: 1938), p. 14.

54. Szold's comments can be found in Minutes of Hadassah National Board Meeting, Nov. 27, 1933, Hadassah Papers, ZAL.

55. Lipsky to McDonald, Nov. 28, 1933, McDonald Papers, General Correspondence File #13, Lehman Library, Columbia Univ.; Brandeis to J. W. Mack, Sept. 27, 1933, in *Letters of Louis D. Brandeis*, vol. V, ed. Melvin Urofsky and David Levy (Albany: State University of New York Press, 1971), pp. 521–22.

56. Brandeis to Bob (Szold), Nov. 19, 1933, Brandeis Records, Microfilm Roll #22, ZAL; Ben-Gurion to Felix Frankfurter, Dec. 8, 1933, Brandeis Records, Microfilm Roll #22, ZAL; Brandeis to Ben-Gurion, Jan. 25, 1934, in *Letters of Louis D. Brandeis*, vol. V, pp. 531–32. Also see, Ben-Gurion to Brandeis, Jan. 5, 1934, in *Letters of Louis D. Brandeis*, vol. V, p. 533.

57. *Palestine Department of Migration Annual Report, 1934* (Jerusalem: 1935), p. 12; *1935* (Jerusalem: 1936), p. 10; *1937* (Jerusalem: 1938), p. 14.

58. Wise to Brandeis, Apr. 5, 1933, Brandeis Records, Microfilm Roll #22, ZAL.

59. Szold to Brandeis, Apr. 19, 1933, Brandeis Records, Microfilm Roll #22, ZAL.

60. *American Jewish Yearbook 5695, Sept. 10, 1934 to Sept. 27, 1935*, vol. 36 (Philadelphia: Jewish Publication Society of America, 1934), pp. 350–51.

61. Minutes of Hadassah National Board Meeting, Feb. 26, 1934, Hadassah Papers, ZAL.

62. *Ibid.*, Mar. 21, 1934.

63. *Ibid.*, Apr. 25, 1934.

64. *Ibid.*, May 3, 1934.

65. Morris Rothenberg's address can be found in the Stenographic Transcript of the thirty-seventh ZOA Convention, July 1–3, 1934, pp. 4–57, ZAL (hereafter: Transcript of the 1934 ZOA Convention).

66. Louis Lipsky's address can be found in *Ibid.*, pp. 73–95.

67. Robert Szold's address can be found in *Ibid.*, pp. 96–105.

68. *Ibid.*, pp. 48–49.

69. *Ibid.*, pp. 48–57.

70. *Ibid.*, pp. 108–14.

71. *Ibid.*, pp. 212–19.

72. *Ibid.*, p. 77.

73. Lewisohn's address can be found in *Ibid.*, pp. 119–43.

74. Friedland's address can be found in *Ibid.*, pp. 189–98. Also see the addresses of Maurice Samuel, pp. 143–59; Dr. S. Margoshes, pp. 198–204; and Dr. Greenberg, pp. 220–24.

75. Rosenblatt's address can be found in *Ibid.*, pp. 292–303.

76. Silver, "A Happier New Year," Sept. 19, 1934, *Jewish Daily Bulletin* articles, Silver Papers, MSS. and Typescripts File #34–17, AHSMA.

77. See Robert Svold's comments on Palestine in Szold to Brandeis, Apr. 21, 1935, Brandeis Records, Microfilm Roll #24, ZAL.

78. Rothenberg to Brandeis, Nov. 21, 1934, Brandeis Records, Microfilm Roll #23, ZAL. Also see Rothenberg to Brandeis, Dec. 28, 1934, on the same microfilm roll.

79. For descriptions of the conference, see *New York Times*, Jan. 21, 1935, p. 6; *Washington Post*, Jan. 21, 1935, p. 13, and Jan. 22, 1935, p. 15.

80. See Morris Rothenberg address in Stenographic Transcript of the thirty-eighth ZOA Convention, June 30–July 2, 1935, pp. 26–27, ZAL (hereafter: Transcript of the 1935 ZOA Convention); Joseph Saslaw to Brandeis, Jan. 25, 1935, Brandeis Records, Microfilm Roll #24, ZAL. Also see "A Rabbinical Statement Regarding Labor Palestine," *Jewish Frontier*, Feb. 1935, pp. 32–34.

81. On B'nai B'rith, see Halperin, *Political World Of American Zionism*, pp. 144–47; *American Jewish Year Book, 5696*, vol. 37, pp. 287–88. On the American Jewish Committee, see Naomi W. Cohen, *Not Free to Desist: The American Jewish Committee, 1906–1966* (Philadelphia: Jewish Publication Society of America, 1972); Stuart Knee, *The Concept of Zionist Dissent* (New York: R. Speller, 1979), chap. IV.

82. Howard R. Greenstein, *Turning Point: Zionism and Reform Judaism* (Chico, CA: Scholars Press, 1981); Neutrality Resolution quoted in *Ibid.*, p. 29; Knee, *Concept of Zionist Dissent*, chap. III; Halperin, *Political World of American Zionism*, pp. 71–79; Michael A. Meyer, *Response to Modernity: A History of the Reform Movement in Judaism* (New York: Oxford University Press, 1988), pp. 293–95, 326–32.

83. For expressions of this view, see "Plain Words On the Mandate," *Jewish Frontier*, Feb. 1935, pp. 6–7; "Solution by Surrender," *Jewish Frontier*, Mar. 1935, pp. 6–7.

84. Oswald Garrison Villard, "Russia and the Jews," *Nation*, Aug. 28, 1935, p. 231.

85. "Futile Search for Territories," *Jewish Frontier*, Sept. 1935, p. 4.

86. Silver, "Ersatz," Jan. 6, 1935, *Jewish Daily Bulletin* articles, Silver Papers, MSS. and Typescripts File #34–17, AHSMA.

87. *American Jewish Yearbook 5696*, vol. 37, p. 332; Israel Goldstein to Brandeis, Aug. 26, 1935, Brandeis Records, Microfilm Roll #24, ZAL.

88. Abraham Goldberg quoted in Transcript of the 1935 ZOA Convention, pp. 226–34.

89. Joan Dash, *Summoned to Jerusalem: The Life of Henrietta Szold* (New York: Harper & Row, 1979), chap. VI; Irvin Fineman, *Woman of Valor: The Life of Henrietta Szold 1860–1945* (New York: Simon and Schuster, 1961), pp. 357–95; Urofsky, *American Zionism*, p. 397.

90. Minutes of Hadassah National Board Meeting, May 3, 1934, Hadassah Papers, ZAL; Mrs. Edward Jacobs to Brandeis, June 17, 1935, Brandeis Records, Microfilm Roll #24, ZAL.

91. Jacobs to Brandeis, Oct. 31, 1935, Brandeis Records, Microfilm Roll #24, ZAL; Minutes of Hadassah National Board Meeting, Oct. 23, Nov. 27, Nov. 28, 1935, Hadassah Papers, ZAL.

92. Jacobs to Brandeis, Oct. 31, 1935, Brandeis Records, Roll #24, ZAL; Minutes of Hadassah National Board Meeting, Nov. 27, 1935, Hadassah Papers, ZAL; Weizmann to Hexter, Nov. 20, 1935, and Nov. 24, 1935, letters #76, #79 in *Letters and Papers of Chaim Weizmann*, Series A, vol. XVII.

93. Jacobs to Brandeis, Oct. 31, 1935, and Nov. 14, 1935, Brandeis Records, Microfilm Roll #24, ZAL.

94. Minutes of Hadassah National Board Meeting, Nov. 28, 1935, Hadassah Papers, ZAL; Weizmann to Hexter, Nov. 24, 1935, letter #79 in *Letters and Papers of Chaim Weizmann*, Series A, vol. XVII; also see editorial note on p. 65. On the controversy over Youth Aliyah, also see Marlin Levin, *Balm in Gilead: The Story of Hadassah* (New York: Schocken Books, 1973), pp. 120–29.

95. Minutes of Hadassah National Board Meeting, Apr. 19, 1936, and Dec. 19, 1936, Hadassah Papers, ZAL; Donald H. Miller, "A History of Hadassah 1912–1935," Ph.D. diss., New York Univ., 1968, p. 320; Levin, *Balm in Gilead*, pp. 129–35.

96. Transcript of the 1933 ZOA Convention, pp. 15–46, 58–72, 276–77.

97. Minutes of Hadassah National Board Meeting, May 3, 1933, Hadassah Papers, ZAL. But for some reluctance of Hadassah leaders to cooperate, see minutes of Nov. 8, 1933, and Apr. 11, 1934.

98. For example, see Morris Rothenberg's address in Transcript of the 1933 thirty-sixth ZOA Convention, p. 42, and Transcript of the 1935 ZOA Convention, p. 34.

99. For more on Wise's remarkable career, see Urofsky, *A Voice that Spoke for Justice.*

100. On the boycott, see Moshe Gottlieb, *American Anti-Nazi Resistance 1933–1941* (New York: Ktav Publishing House, 1982); Gottlieb, "The Anti-Nazi Boycott Movement in the United States: An Ideological and Sociological Appreciation," *Jewish Social Studies* XXXV (July–Oct. 1973): pp. 198–227.

101. Minutes of Joint Meeting, Hadassah National Board and Junior National Board, Apr. 16, 1934; Minutes of Hadassah Summer Executive Meeting, n.d. (1934), Hadassah Papers, ZAL.

102. Transcript of the 1934 ZOA Convention, pp. 323–24; "Hitler's War of Extermination," *Jewish Frontier*, Sept. 1935, pp. 4–5.

103. Brandeis to Wise, Sept. 18, 1933, *Letters of Louis D. Brandeis*, vol. V, pp. 520–21; Memorandum of Strook, Waldman, Kallen, and Wise meeting with Brandeis, May 15, 1934, Brandeis Records, Microfilm Roll #23, ZAL.

104. "Abstract of an Address on the Boycott of Nazi Germany," delivered at the Hotel Pennsylvania, Jan. 3, 1934, Silver Papers, MSS. and Typescripts File #34–7, AHSMA.

105. Silver, "Relief Is Not Enough," Feb. 12, 1934, *Jewish Daily Bulletin* articles, Silver Papers, MSS. and Typescripts File #33–13, AHSMA. For additional information on Silver and the boycott, see his *Jewish Daily Bulletin* articles: "On the Alert!," Apr. 8, 1934; "Yorkville is Not Yet America," Oct. 28, 1934.

106. On the Haavara Agreement, see Edwin Black, *The Transfer Agreement: The Untold Story of the Secret Agreement Between the Third Reich and Jewish Palestine* (New York: Macmillan, 1984); Gottlieb, *American Anti-Nazi Resistance*, pp. 88–91.

107. Friedman, *No Haven for the Oppressed*, pp. 75–76.

108. Silver, "The Line of Confusion and the Plummet of Emptiness," April 22, 1934, *Jewish Daily Bulletin* articles, Silver Papers, MSS. and Typescripts File #33–13, AHSMA.

109. Silver, "Orange Juice," Nov. 4, 1934, *Jewish Daily Bulletin* articles, Silver Papers, MSS. and Typescripts File #34–17, AHSMA.

110. Transcript of the 1935 ZOA Convention, pp. 304–29.

111. Black, *The Transfer Agreement*, pp. 334–43.

112. Minutes of Hadassah National Board Meeting, May 20, 1936, Hadassah Papers, ZAL.

CHAPTER II

1. *Palestine Department of Migration Annual Report, 1934* (Jerusalem: 1935), p. 13; *1935* (Jerusalem: 1936), p. 10; *1936* (Jerusalem: 1937), p. 9.

2. Yehoyada Haim, *Abandonment of Illusions—Zionist Political Attitudes Toward Palestinian Arab Nationalism, 1936–1939* (Boulder, CO: Westview Press, 1983), pp. 5–6; Ben-Gurion to Frankfurter, Dec. 8, 1933, Brandeis Records, Microfilm Roll #22, ZAL. Also see Emanuel Neumann's minutes of a discussion with Ben-Gurion on Feb. 23, 1933, Brandeis Records, Microfilm Roll #22, ZAL. For an interesting analysis of Ben-Gurion's developing views on the Arabs, see Shabtai Teveth, *Ben-Gurion and the Palestinian Arabs: From Peace to War* (New York: Oxford University Press, 1985).

3. Felix Frankfurter, "The Palestine Situation Revisited," *Foreign Affairs* 9 (April 1931): pp. 409–34.

4. Hayim Greenberg, "Jew and Arab," *Jewish Frontier*, December 1934, pp. 23–24.

5. Stenographic transcript of the thirty-sixth ZOA Convention, July 1–4, 1933, p. 78, ZAL (hereafter: Transcript of the 1933 ZOA Convention).

6. Minutes of Hadassah National Board Meeting, Mar. 1, 1934, Hadassah Papers, ZAL. Also see Dr. Jonas S. Friedenwald to Brandeis, Mar. 3, 1938, Brandeis Records, Microfilm Roll #22, ZAL.

7. Emanuel Neumann, *In the Arena* (New York: Herzl Press, 1978), p. 121; Minutes of Hadassah National Board Meeting, Mar. 21, 1933, Hadassah Papers, ZAL.

8. Neumann, *In the Arena*, p. 123.

9. *Ibid.*, p. 123; Brandeis to Szold, July 11, 1932, in *Letters of Louis D. Brandeis*, vol. V, ed. Melvin Urofsky and David Levy (Albany: State University of New York Press, 1971), pp. 506–7.

10. Neumann, *In the Arena*, chap. 11, pp. 131–34, 325–30.

11. Neumann to Wise, Jan. 26, 1933, Stephen S. Wise Papers, Box 128, File 8, American Jewish Historical Society, Waltham, MA (hereafter: Wise Papers).

12. Many copies of this document exist. See Brandeis to Neumann, Jan. 27, 1933, Wise Papers, Box 128, File 8; *Letters of Louis D. Brandeis*, vol. V, pp. 513–14; Brandeis Records, Microfilm Roll #21, ZAL; Neumann, *In the Arena*, p. 130. Chaim Weizmann, however, was not pleased with Neumann's activities and feared that they might injure Zionist relations with Great Britain. See Weizmann to Arlosoroff, Jan. 31, 1933, letter #340 in *Letters and Papers of Chaim Weizmann*, Series A., vol. XV, ed. Barnet Litvinoff (New Brunswick, NJ: Transaction Books, Rutgers University, 1978).

13. Transcript of the 1933 ZOA Convention, pp. 101, 102, 113, 268–69, 275–76.

14. Neumann, *In the Arena*, pp. 133–34; Neumann to Franfurter, July 20, 1933, Felix Frankfurter Papers, Box 86, Microfilm Roll #2, Library of Congress, Washington, DC (hereafter: Frankfurter Papers).

15. Frankfurter to Neumann, July 22, 1933, Frankfurter Papers, Box 86, Microfilm Roll #2.

16. James N. Rosenberg to Felix Warburg, Mar. 19, 1934, Brandeis Records, Microfilm Roll #22, ZAL; Neumann to James N. Rosenberg, Mar. 22, 1934, Brandeis Records, Microfilm Roll #22, ZAL; Abba Hillel Silver, "Enlarge the Place of Thy Tent!," *Jewish Daily Bulletin*, Jan. 7, 1934, Silver Papers, MSS. and Typescripts File #3–13, AHSMA.

17. Frankfurter, "Memorandum of Interview with Sir Philip Cunliffe-Lister," June 28, 1934, Frankfurter Papers, Box 88, Microfilm Roll #4.

18. Stenographic Transcript of the thirty-eighth ZOA Convention, June 30–July 2, 1935, pp. 407–8, ZAL.

19. Jacob C. Hurewitz, *The Struggle for Palestine* (New York: Schocken Books, 1950, reprint 1976), chap. 4; Y. Porath, *The Palestinian Arab National Movement: From Riots to Rebellion* (London: F. Cass, 1977), chaps. 4 & 5; Ann M. Lesch, *Arab Politics in Palestine 1917–1939* (Ithaca, NY: Cornell University Press, 1979), pp. 67–75.

20. Howard M. Sachar, *A History of Israel: From the Rise of Zionism to Our Time* (New York: Alfred A. Knopf, 1976), pp. 196–201; Hurewitz, *Struggle for Palestine*, pp. 67–68; Haim, *Abandonment of Illusions*, p. 33–35; "No Immigration Ban, Says Thomas," *New Palestine*, May 8, 1936, p. 1. Porath's description of this stage of the Arab revolt is quite detailed, see Porath, *The Palestinian Arab National Movement*, chap. 5.

21. Michael J. Cohen, *Palestine: Retreat from the Mandate: The Making of British Policy, 1936–45* (New York: Holmes & Meier, 1978), chap. 2; Hurewitz, *Struggle for Palestine*, pp. 69–72; Haim, *Abandonment of Illusions*, pp. 39–40.

22. Brandeis to Szold, Oct. 5, 1936, Brandeis Records, Microfilm Roll #25, ZAL; Haim, *Abandonment of Illusions*, pp. 46–49. The Irgun, a small group of Revisionist Zionist activists, rebelled against the "self-restraint" policy of Yishuv authorities and waged their own war of counterterror against Palestinian Arabs.

23. Not all Jews were willing to contribute to Jewish self-defense. Felix Warburg, a wealthy assimilated Jew, refused Stephen Wise's request for financial aid. Wise to Brandeis, May 5, 1936, Brandeis Records, Microfilm Roll #25, ZAL.

24. *New York Times*, May 31, 1936, p. 14.

25. *Ibid.*, June 8, 1936, p. 12; June 10, 1936, p. 22. For the same position, see "The Disturbances in Palestine," *New Palestine*, Apr. 24, 1936, p. 4.

26. Wise to Brandeis, May 5, 1936, Brandeis Records, Microfilm Roll #25, ZAL; Minutes of Hadassah National Board Meeting, June 17, 1936, Hadassah Papers, ZAL.

27. *New York Times*, Apr. 21, 1936, p. 22.

28. Albert Viton, "Why Arabs Kill Jews," *Nation*, June 3, 1936, pp. 708–9. Also see H. N. Brailsford, "Storm Over Palestine," *New Republic*, July 1, 1936, pp. 230–32.

29. William Ernest Hocking, "Misconceptions About Palestine," *Christian Century*, July 1936, pp. 930–32. Also see William Hocking letter to the editor, *New York Times*, June 14, 1936, sec. IV, p. 9. See Hocking's obituary in *New York Times*, June 13, 1966, p. 39.

30. *New York Times*, June 28, 1936, sec. IV, p. 9. On the history of Arab-American anti-Zionism, see Stuart E. Knee, *The Concept of Zionist Dissent in the American Mind 1917–1941* (New York: R. Speller, 1979), chap. VIII.

31. *New York Times*, May 18, 1936, p. 16.

32. *Ibid.*, May 26, 1936, p. 10.

33. "Page Albert Viton," *Jewish Frontier*, July 1936, pp. 5–6; Syrkin's letter can be found in *Nation*, June 24, 1936, p. 822.

34. Maurice Samuels, "The Intellectual Dilemma," *Jewish Frontier*, November 1936, pp. 35–37.

35. Hayim Greenberg, "Arab Nationalism," *Jewish Frontier*, June 1936, pp. 18–20.

36. Albert Viton, "The Fate of Zionism," *Nation*, Dec. 19, 1936, pp. 725–28; Viton, "A Solution for Palestine," *Nation*, Dec. 26, 1936, pp. 756–58.

37. Philip Bernstein, "Promise of Zionism," *Nation*, Jan. 2, 1937, pp. 12–15.

38. "Letters to the Editors," *Nation*, Jan. 16, 1937, pp. 307–8.

39. Wise to Bernstein, Jan. 6, 1937, Wise Papers, Box 44, File 5; "*The Nation's* New Policy," *Jewish Frontier*, Jan. 1937, pp. 2–3; "Viton Statistics," *Jewish Frontier*, Jan. 1937, p. 2. Also see "*The Nation* Discusses Palestine Again," *New Palestine*, Jan. 1, 1937, p. 4.

40. *New York Times*, July 21, 1936, p. 5. On the Peel Commission's investigation, see Joan Peters, *From Time Immemorial: The Origins of the Arab-Jewish Conflict Over Palestine* (New York: Harper & Row, 1984), pp. 302–12; Martin Gilbert, *Exile and Return: The Struggle for a Jewish Homeland* (Philadelphia: Lippincott, 1978), pp. 164–77.

41. American Zionist leaders did make their feelings known to officials who appeared before the Peel Commission. Wise to Brandeis, July 8, 1936, Brandeis Records, Microfilm Roll #24, ZAL; Brandeis to Julius Simon, July 31, 1936, Brandeis Records, Microfilm Roll #25, ZAL; Brandeis to Robert Szold, Sept. 5, 1936, *Letters of Louis D. Brandeis*, vol. V, pp. 577–81.

42. Hexter Testimony, *Palestine Royal Commission, Minutes of Evidence Heard at Public Sessions* (London, 1937), p. 114–32 (hereafter: *Royal Commission Minutes*). A copy can be found at the Zionist Archives and Library.

43. Ben-Gurion Testimony, *Royal Commission Minutes*, pp. 288–91.

44. Weizmann Testimony, *Royal Commission Minutes*, pp. 30–40; Weizmann, *Trial and Error: The Autobiography of Chaim Weizmann* (New York: Schocken Books, 1949, reprint 1966), pp. 384–85; Norman Rose, *Chaim Weizmann: A Biography* (New York: Viking, 1986), pp. 316–18.

45. Totah Testimony, *Royal Commission Minutes*, pp. 351–57.

46. Mufti's Testimony, *Royal Commission Minutes*, pp. 292–99.

47. Wise to Warburg, Mar. 8, 1937, Brandeis Records, Microfilm Roll #26, ZAL.

48. "The Two-Faced Policy Controversy," *New Palestine*, Nov. 13, 1936, p. 4.

49. Gabriel Sheffer, "Political Considerations in British Policy-Making on Immigration to Palestine," *Studies in Zionism*, no. 4 (Autumn 1981): pp. 258–72.

50. Minutes of Hadassah National Board Meeting, Feb. 17, 1937, Hadassah Papers, ZAL; Hurewitz, *Struggle for Palestine*, p. 72.

51. "The Immigration Schedule," *Jewish Frontier*, Dec. 1936, p. 5.

52. "Rejected," *Jewish Frontier*, June 1937, p. 3; Hurewitz, *Struggle for Palestine*, p. 72.

53. Arthur Lourie to Stephen Wise and Louis Lipsky, Apr. 4, 1937, Brandeis Records, Microfilm Roll #26, ZAL; Weizmann, *Trial and Error*, pp. 385–87; Rose, *Chaim Weizmann*, pp. 319–20.

54. Dr. Samuel Margoshes, editor of the Yiddish daily newspaper *The Day,* was one of the few Zionists to defend partition. He acknowledged that the division of Palestine was bad, but he argued that it was better than any other British action that could be expected. Margoshes editorial, *The Day,* Apr. 19, 1937, Brandeis Records, Microfilm Roll #26, ZAL.

55. "Hadassah Petition to the U.S. Secretary of State and the British Ambassador in the U.S.— May 1937–Passed at the HADASSAH SPRING CONFERENCE," attached to Minutes of Hadassah National Board Meeting, May 11, 1937, Hadassah Papers, ZAL.

56. Greenberg, "Balkanization of Palestine," *Jewish Frontier,* May 1937, pp. 12–14.

57. "Cantonization–An Experiment in Geographic Surgery," *Jewish Outlook,* May 1937, p. 4.

58. "Rejected," *New Palestine,* Apr. 30, 1937, p. 4. Also see "Why Ignore Transjordan," *New Palestine,* May 7, 1937, p. 4.

59. Minutes of Hadassah National Board Meeting, June 2, 1937, Hadassah Papers, ZAL.

60. Szold to Brandeis, June 10, 1937, Brandeis Records, Microfilm Roll #26, ZAL.

61. Wise's address can be found in the Stenographic transcript of the fortieth ZOA Convention, June 1937, pp. 2–24, ZAL (hereafter: Transcript of 1937 ZOA Convention). Also see Wise's comments on pp. 253–59.

62. Robert Szold's address can be found in *Ibid.,* pp. 31–39.

63. Lipsky's address can be found in *Ibid.,* pp. 61–76.

64. Morris Rothenberg's address can be found in *Ibid.,* pp. 412–18.

65. Senator Wagner's address can be found in *Ibid.,* pp. 402–7.

66. Silver's address can be found in *Ibid.,* pp. 96A–111.

67. *Ibid.,* pp. 43–44, 47–50; Szold to Brandeis, June 30, 1937, Brandeis Records, Microfilm Roll #26, ZAL.

68. Szold to Brandeis, June 30, 1937, Brandeis Records, Microfilm Roll #26, ZAL; "Memorandum of Overseas Telephone Talk with Weizmann," June 28, 1937, Frankfurter Papers, Box 86, Microfilm Roll #2.

69. Weizmann to Frankfurter, June 29, 1937, Frankfurter Papers, Box 86, Microfilm Roll #2.

70. Weizmann to Frankfurter, June 29, 1937, Frankfurter Papers, Box 86, Microfilm Roll #2. This letter is different from the one cited in the previous footnote.

71. *Palestine Royal Commission Report* (London: 1937), pp. 113, 128–30.

72. *Ibid.,* pp. 110–11, 144, 363.

73. *Ibid.,* pp. 2–3.

74. *Ibid.,* pp. 380–93.

75. *Ibid.,* p. 375.

76. *Ibid.,* p. 306–7.

77. M. Cohen, *Palestine: Retreat from the Mandate,* pp. 32–34; *Palestine Statement of Policy* (London: July 1937).

78. *Parliamentary Debates* (Commons), 5th ser., vol. 326 (1937): Tom Williams, cols. 2337–50; Archibald Sinclair, cols. 2264–74; Winston Churchill, cols. 2329–33. Also see Gilbert, *Exile and Return,* p. 182; M. Cohen, *Palestine: Retreat from the Mandate,* pp. 34–38; Hurewitz, *Struggle for Palestine,* p. 76; Norman A. Rose, *The Gentile Zionists: A Study in Anglo-Zionist Diplomacy, 1929–1939* (London: F. Cass, 1973), pp. 130–40; Joseph Gorny, *The British Labour Movement and Zionism 1917–1948* (London: F. Cass, 1983), pp. 129–39.

79. "American Zionist Leaders Comment on Report," *New Palestine,* July 12, 1937, pp. 1, 3; Wise to Brandeis, July 5, 1937; Wise to Zioniburo, London, July 3, 1937; Brandeis (?) to Friedenwald, July 12, 1937; Mack to Brandeis and Frankfurter, July 12, 1937, all in Brandeis Records, Microfilm Roll #26, ZAL. Hayim Greenberg, "'Jewish State' Examined," *Jewish Frontier,* Aug. 1938, pp. 4–7. Also see Abraham Revusky, "Facts About Palestine," *Jewish Frontier,* Aug. 1938, pp. 7–10; Brandeis to Robert Szold, July 12, 1937, in *Letters of Louis D. Brandeis,* vol. V, pp. 590–91.

80. Brandeis to Szold, July 12, 1937, in *Letters of Louis D. Brandeis*, vol. V, pp. 590–91; Szold to Brandeis, July 21, 1937, Brandeis Records, Microfilm Roll #26, ZAL.

81. Weizmann, *Trial and Error*, p. 386; Walter Laqueur, *A History of Zionism* (New York: Holt, Rinehart & Winston, 1972), p. 518; Hurewitz, *Struggle for Palestine*, p. 77, Rose, *Chaim Weizmann*, pp. 325–27. See reprints of Weizmann's address in "The Zionist Congress Debates," *Jewish Frontier*, Sept. 1937, pp. 22–25; "A Basis for the Growth of Jewish Life," *New Palestine*, Sept. 3, 1937, pp. 4–5.

82. Mack to Brandeis and Frankfurter, Aug. 6, 1937, and Szold to Mack, Aug. 16, 1937, both in Brandeis Records, Microfilm Roll #26, ZAL. Also see: Melvin Urofsky, *A Voice That Spoke for Justice* (Albany: State University of New York Press, 1982), pp. 286–87; *New York Times*, Aug. 9, 1937, p. 5; "Answer to Britain is 'Non Possumus,'" *New Palestine*, Sept. 3, 1937, pp. 5–6.

83. Szold to Mack, Aug. 16, 1937, Brandeis Records, Microfilm Roll #26, ZAL. Szold's analysis was essentially correct. Ben-Gurion's criticism of the Peel Plan had been half-hearted. In a letter to his son, he wrote: "A Partial Jewish state is not the end, but only the beginnning. . . . We shall bring into the state all the Jews it is possible to bring . . . we shall establish a multi-faceted Jewish economy – agricultural, industrial and maritime. We shall organize a modern defense force, . . . and then I am certain that we will not be prevented from settling in other parts of the country, either by mutual agreement with our Arab neighbors or by some other means." Quoted in Michael Bar-Zohar, *Ben-Gurion: A Biography*, trans. Peretz Kidron (New York: Delacorte Press, 1978), p. 91. Also see Michael Bar-Zohar, *Ben-Gurion the Armed Prophet* (Englewood Cliffs, NJ: Prentice-Hall, 1968), pp. 57–58.

84. Samuel Kerstein, "The Congress Delegation Reports," *Jewish Outlook*, Sept. 1937, pp. 5–6; "Mizrachi On Partition," *Jewish Outlook*, Nov. 1937, p. 3.

85. General Zionists were neither socialists nor ultra-religious. The B faction generally opposed Chaim Weizmann, believing that he was too pro-British in attitude. *New York Times*, Aug. 6, 1937, p. 3: Laqueur, *History of Zionism*, p. 519; Hurewitz, *Struggle for Palestine*, p. 77; Neumann, *In the Arena*, pp. 136–37.

86. *New York Times*, Aug. 12, 1937, p. 1. Also see Neumann, *In the Arena*, pp. 136–37; Hurewitz, *Struggle for Palestine*, pp. 77–78. Szold to Mack, Aug. 16, 1937, Mack to Brandeis and Frankfurter, Aug. 6, 1937, and Aug. 11, 1937, Mack to Brandeis, Aug. 14, 1937, Wise to Brandeis, Aug. 17, 1937, all in Brandeis Records, Microfilm Roll #26, ZAL. Action of Hadassah's Summer Executive Committee, Aug. 11, 1937, Hadassah Papers, ZAL; Minutes of Hadassah National Board Meeting, Sept. 1, 1937, Hadassah Papers, ZAL.

87. *New York Times*, Aug. 12, 1937, p. 1; Weizmann, *Trial and Error*, p. 387; Laqueur, *History of Zionism*, p. 520; "Congress and Agency Act," *Jewish Frontier*, Sept. 1937, p. 27.

88. Minutes of Hadassah National Board Meeting, Sept. 8, 1937, Hadassah Papers, ZAL.

89. Minutes of Hadassah National Board Meeting, Nov. 3, 1937, Hadassah Papers, ZAL; Robert Szold to Brandeis, Nov. 2, 1937, Brandeis Records, Microfilm Roll #26, ZAL.

90. Minutes of Hadassah National Board Meetings, Dec. 15, 1937, and Jan. 19, 1938, Hadassah Papers, ZAL.

91. Wise to Szold, Nov. 11, 1937, Robert Szold Papers, Correspondence File X/15, ZAL.

92. Brandeis to Flexner, Nov. 11, 1937, *Letters of Louis D. Brandeis*, vol. V, p. 592; Szold to Brandeis, Dec. 8, 1937, Brandeis Records, Microfilm Roll #26, ZAL; Frankfurter to Harry Zinder, Dec. 23, 1937, Frankfurter Papers, Box 86, Microfilm Roll #2, Szold to Brandeis, Dec. 23, 1937, Brandeis Records, Microfilm Roll #26, ZAL.

93. Szold to Brandeis, Dec. 23, 1937, Brandeis to Wise, Sept. 23, 1937, Wise to Brandeis, Sept. 22, 1937, all in Brandeis Records, Microfilm Roll #26, ZAL. Also see "Summary of Dr. Adler's Views," July 12, 1937, Brandeis Records, Microfilm Roll #26, ZAL.

94. Szold to Brandeis, Dec. 31, 1937, Brandeis Records, Microfilm Roll #26, ZAL. Also see Louis Lipsky, "Toward a Jewish State," *New Palestine*, Sept. 3, 1937, p. 3.

95. Brandeis to Wise, Sept. 23, 1937, Brandeis Records, Microfilm Roll #26, ZAL; Brandeis to Wise, Nov. 1, 1936, Robert Szold Papers, Correspondence File X/14, ZAL.

96. Wise to Brandeis, Dec. 10, 1937, Brandeis Records, Microfilm Roll #26, ZAL.

97. Szold to Brandeis, Dec. 31, 1937, Brandeis Records, Microfilm Roll #26, ZAL; Brandeis to Szold, Sept. 2, 1938, *Letters of Louis D. Brandeis*, vol. V, p. 593; Brandeis to Szold, Jan. 16, 1938, *Letters of Louis D. Brandeis*, vol. V, pp. 593–94; Szold to Brandeis, Jan. 13, 1938, Brandeis Records, Microfilm Roll #27, ZAL.

98. Szold to Rose Jacobs, May 18, 1938, Brandeis Records, Microfilm Roll #27, ZAL.

99. "Mrs. Szold's Presentation of the Anti-Partition Position," attached to Minutes of Hadassah National Board Meeting, Mar. 2, 1938, Hadassah Papers, ZAL. Also see Robert Szold to Brandeis, Mar. 3, 1938, Brandeis Records, Microfilm Roll #27, ZAL.

100. Szold to Brandeis, Apr. 13, 1938, and Szold to Brandeis, July 1, 1938, both in Brandeis Records, Microfilm Roll #27, ZAL.

101. Wise's address can be found in the Stenographic Transcript of the forty-first ZOA Convention, July 1938, pp. 12–38, ZAL (hereafter: Transcript of 1938 ZOA Convention). Also see Brandeis to Szold, Apr. 14, 1938, *Letters of Louis D. Brandeis*, vol. V, p. 599.

102. Lipsky's address can be found in Transcript of 1938 ZOA Convention, pp. 44–60.

103. Silver's address can be found in *Ibid.*, pp. 126–50.

104. *Ibid.*, pp. 348–54.

105. *Ibid.*, pp. 264–80. Also see Mack to Solomon Goldman, July 8, 1938, Brandeis Records, Microfilm Roll #27, ZAL.

106. Hurewitz, *Struggle for Palestine*, pp. 81–90; Haim, *Abandonment of Illusions*, pp. 123–35.

107. *Palestine Partition Commission Report—Prepared by the Secretary of State for the Colonies to Parliament, October 1938* (London: 1938). Also see Rose, *Gentile Zionists*, pp. 149–65; M. Cohen, *Palestine: Retreat from the Mandate*, pp. 39–45.

108. Hurewitz, *Struggle for Palestine*, pp. 90–98; M. Cohen, *Palestine: Retreat from the Mandate*, pp. 66–74; Sachar, *History of Israel*, pp. 217–19.

109. Brandeis to Szold, Nov. 11, 1938, *Letters of Louis D. Brandeis*, vol. V, pp. 603–5. Also see Brandeis to Bernard Flexner, Oct. 12, 1938, *Ibid.*, vol. V, pp. 602–3.

110. Neumann to Wise, Oct. 23, 1938, Robert Szold Papers, Correspondence File X/16, ZAL.

111. Report on meeting of Louis Brandeis, Eliezer Kaplan, and Stephen Wise, Feb. 7, 1937, Brandeis Records, Microfilm Roll #26, ZAL; Report on Visit of Stephen Wise to Franklin Roosevelt, Oct. 5, 1936, Brandeis Records, Microfilm Roll #25, ZAL.

112. Minutes of Hadassah National Board Meetings, Dec. 16, 1936, and Feb. 17, 1937, Hadassah Papers, ZAL.

113. Wise to Brandeis, Sept. 2, 1936, Brandeis Records, Microfilm Roll #24, ZAL; Wise to Brandeis, Apr. 16, 1936, Brandeis Records, Microfilm Roll #25, ZAL.

114. Transcript of 1937 ZOA Convention, p. 418.

115. Robert Szold to Brandeis, July 6, 1937, and Wise to Brandeis, July 5, 1937, both in Brandeis Records, Microfilm Roll #26, ZAL.

116. M. Cohen, *Palestine: Retreat from the Mandate*, pp. 72–82; Porath, *The Palestinian Arab National Movement*, pp. 281–95.

117. *Palestine Statement of Policy Presented by the Secretary of State for the Colonies to Parliament by Command of His Majesty, May 1939* (London: 1939, reprint 1946); "British Statement of Policy, May 1939 (MacDonald White Paper), reprinted in *Book of Documents Submitted to the General Assembly of the United Nations Relating to the Establishment of the National Home for the Jewish People* (New York: Jewish Agency for Palestine, 1947), pp. 100–111, ZAL. Also see Hurewitz, *Struggle for Palestine*, chap. 7; Rose, *Gentile Zionists*, chaps. 8 and 9; M. Cohen, *Palestine: Retreat from the Man-*

date, pp. 72–87; Nicholas Bethell, *The Palestine Triangle: The Struggle for the Holy Land, 1935–48* (New York: Putnam, 1979), pp. 61–69; Peters, *From Time Immemorial*, pp. 335–40.

CHAPTER III

1. For example, see Israel Goldstein's address in the Stenographic Transcript of the forty-second ZOA Convention, June 1939, pp. 368–73, ZAL (hereafter: Transcript of 1939 ZOA Convention).

2. *Ibid.*, pp. 172, 224.

3. *Ibid.*, pp. 88–89.

4. *Ibid.*, pp. 23, 61–65, 201.

5. Brandeis to Szold, May 10, 1939, in *Letters of Louis D. Brandeis*, vol. V, ed. Melvin Urofsky and David Levy (Albany: State University of New York Press, 1971), p. 618.

6. See Solomon Goldman's comments in Transcript of 1939 ZOA Convention, pp. 41–45, 226–27. The British cabinet's decision to adopt an anti-Zionist policy was largely due to the government's desire to ensure Arab support in the event of a war with Hitler. However, there was some validity in Goldman's claim. By 1939, some English officials seemed to be grossly insensitive to the plight of the world's persecuted Jews. Chaim Weizmann reported that "Lord Halifax was strangely ignorant of what was happening to the Jews of Germany. During the St. James Conference he came up to me and said, 'I have just received a letter from a friend in Germany, who describes some terrrible things perpetrated by the Nazis in a concentration camp the name of which is not familiar to me,' and when he began to grope for the name I realized it was Dachau he was talking about. He said the stories were entirely unbelievable, and if the letter had not been written by a man in whom he had the fullest confidence he would not attach the slightest credence to it. For five or six years now the world had known of the infamous Dachau camp, in which thousands of people had been tortured and maimed . . . and the British Foreign Secretary had never heard of the place, . . ." Chaim Weizmann, *Trial and Error* (New York: Schocken Books, 1949, reprint 1966), pp. 404–5.

7. Minutes of Hadassah National Board Meeting, June 14, 1939, Hadassah Papers, ZAL.

8. Minutes of Hadassah National Board Meeting, May 23, 1939, Hadassah Papers, ZAL.

9. Minutes of Hadassah National Board Meeting, May 17, 1939, Hadassah Papers, ZAL.

10. "Mizrachi Convenes," *Jewish Outlook*, June 1939, p. 3. Also see "To the Convention: Symposium on New Orientations in Mizrachi," *Jewish Outlook*, May 1939, pp. 5–14.

11. Minutes of Hadassah National Board Meeting, June 14, 1939, Hadassah Papers, ZAL.

12. Minutes of Hadassah National Board Meetings, May 23, 1939 and May 17, 1939, Hadassah Papers, ZAL.

13. Brandeis to Robert Szold, Aug. 2, 1939, *Letters of Louis D. Brandeis*, vol. V, p. 623.

14. See the addresses of Abraham Goldberg and Solomon Goldman in Transcript of 1939 ZOA Convention, pp. 134–41, 14–57, 215–30; Brandeis to Flexner, July 12, 1939, *Letters of Louis D. Brandeis*, vol. V, p. 621; Brandeis to Szold, Aug. 2, 1939, *Ibid.*, vol. V, pp. 622–23.

15. *Parliamentary Debates* (Commons), 5th Series, vol. 347 (1939), cols. 2130, 2142. Also see Joseph Gorny, *The British Labour Movement and Zionism 1917–1948* (London: F. Cass: 1983), pp. 146–60; Norman A. Rose, *The Gentile Zionists: A Study in Anglo-Zionist Diplomacy 1929–1939* (London: F. Cass, 1973), pp. 201–20.

16. *Parliamentary Debates* (Commons), 5th Series, vol. 347 (1939), col. 2157.

17. *Ibid.*, cols. 2171–72, 2176, 2177.

18. *New York Times*, May 19, 1939, p. 5.

19. J. Bowyer Bell, *Terror Out of Zion: Irgun Zvai Leumi, LEHI and the Palestine Underground, 1929–1949* (New York: St. Martin's Press, 1977), p. 48.

20. Jacob C. Hurewitz, *The Struggle for Palestine* (New York: Schocken Books, 1950, reprint 1976), p. 92; *New York Times*, June 19, 1939, p. 4; *Ibid.*, July 4, 1939, p. 4.

21. *New York Times*, June 10, 1939, p. 9.

22. Yehuda Bauer, *From Diplomacy to Resistance* (Philadelphia: Jewish Publication Society of America, 1970), pp. 57–60.

23. *Ibid.*, pp. 60–63; Monty Noam Penkower, *The Jews Were Expendable: Free World Diplomacy and the Holocaust* (Urbana: University of Illinois Press, 1983), pp. 33–58; *New York Times*, June 2, 1939, p. 5. On July 3, British police seized a second boat with 697 "illegial immigrants" on board. *Ibid.*, July 4, 1939, p. 4.

24. Transcript of 1939 ZOA Convention, p. 381.

25. *New York Times*, Aug. 20, 1939, p. 15; *Ibid.*, Aug. 21, 1939, p. 2; Penkower, *Jews Were Expendable*, pp. 38–39; Bauer, *From Diplomacy to Resistance*, pp. 61–62.

26. Bell, *Terror Out of Zion*, pp. 48–49; Bauer, *From Diplomacy to Resistance*, pp. 16–24; Michael J. Cohen, *Palestine: Retreat from the Mandate* (New York: Holmes & Meier, 1978), pp. 1–9.

27. Wise to Brandeis, Aug. 30, 1939, Brandeis Records, Microfilm Roll #27, ZAL.

28. Action of Emergency Meeting of Hadassah National Board, Sept. 5, 1939, Hadassah Papers, ZAL.

29. Stenographic Transcript of the forty-third ZOA Convention, June 30–July 2, 1940, pp. 42–43, ZAL (hereafter: Transcript of 1940 ZOA Convention).

30. Penkower, *Jews Were Expendable*, pp. 3–4; Weizmann, *Trial and Error*, pp. 418, 422–24.

31. In May 1941, David Raziel, the Irgun's commander, was killed while on an espionage mission for the British in Iraq. Bell, *Terror Out of Zion*, pp. 51, 55–56.

32. *Ibid.*, pp. 62–73.

33. The best in-depth study of Jewish military developments in Palestine is Bauer, *From Diplomacy to Resistance*, chaps. 2–5. Penkower, *Jews Were Expendable*, chap. 2, is particularly informative about Zionist-British negotiations. Also see Weizmann, *Trial and Error*, pp. 424–25; Bernard Wasserstein, *Britain and the Jews of Europe 1939–1945* (New York: Oxford University Press, 1979), pp. 271–88; Hurewitz, *Struggle for Palestine*, pp. 124–31; and Cohen, *Palestine: Retreat from the Mandate*, pp. 98–124.

34. Weizmann, *Trial and Error*, pp. 419–20.

35. David Ben-Gurion's message can be found in Transcript of 1940 ZOA Convention, pp. 136–39. Also see Chaim Weizmann's message on p. 113.

36. Transcript of 1940 ZOA Convention, pp. 154–55.

37. *Ibid.*, pp. 65–66.

38. *Ibid.*, p. 304.

39. *Ibid.*, pp. 178, 332–34.

40. *Ibid.*, pp. 6–45. For similar views see the comments at the convention of Rabbi Barnett Brickner, p. 84; Henry Monsky, pp. 46–48; Rabbi James G. Heller, pp. 86–90; Israel Goldstein, pp. 155–62; and Louis Lipsky, pp. 55–66.

41. Emanuel Neumann, *In the Arena* (New York: Herzl Press, 1976), pp. 149–66; Melvin Urofsky, *American Zionism from Herzl to the Holocaust* (Garden City, NY: Anchor Press, 1975), p. 83.

42. Neumann, *In the Arena*, p. 167.

43. Szold to Solomon Goldman, Oct. 8, 1940, Robert Szold Papers, Correspondence File X/4, ZAL. Also see Brandeis to Szold, July 5, 1940, *Letters of Louis D. Brandeis*, vol. V, pp. 643–44; Szold to Goldman, Dec. 28, 1940, and Jan. 19, 1941, Robert Szold Papers, Correspondence File X/4, ZAL; Goldman to Szold, Jan. 19, 1941, in *Ibid.*, Correspondence File X/4.

44. *American Jewish Yearbook 5702, Sept. 22, 1941–Sept. 11, 1942*, vol. 43 (Philadelphia: Jewish Publication Society of America, 1941), pp. 569, 597, 602.

45. Thomas to James McDonald, June 6, 1941, MacDonald Papers, General Correspondence File #382, Herbert H. Lehman Papers, Columbia University, New York. On isolationism, see Manfred

Jonas, *Isolationism in America 1935–1941* (Ithaca, NY: Cornell University Press, 1966). On Thomas, see Stuart E. Knee, *The Concept of Zionist Dissent in the American Mind 1917–1941* (New York: R. Speller, 1970), pp. 165–68.

46. For Holmes in 1936, see chapter two of this book. On the Wise-Holmes relationship, see Carl Hermann Voss, *Rabbi and Minister: The Friendship of Stephen S. Wise and John Haynes Holmes* (Cleveland: World Publication Company, 1964).

47. Holmes, *The Christian Century*, Dec. 11, 1940, pp. 1546–49. Also see Holmes, *The Christian Century*, Nov. 8, 1939, pp. 1374–77; and Voss, *Rabbi and Minister*, pp. 291–98.

48. Melvin Urofsky, *A Voice That Spoke for Justice: The Life and Times of Stephen S. Wise* (Albany: State University of New York Press, 1982), pp. 134–42; Voss, *Rabbi and Minister*, pp. 138–53.

49. Voss, *Rabbi and Minister*, pp. 292–93.

50. *New York Times*, Feb. 12, 1940, p. 3.

51. Stephen S. Wise, *As I See It* (New York: Jewish Opinion Publishing Corp., 1940), p. 114. Also see pp. 222–27, 248–51.

52. Transcript of 1940 ZOA Convention, pp. 68, 329–31.

53. *New York Times*, Feb. 19, 1941, p. 14, and July 2, 1941, p. 5.

54. *Ibid.*, June 24, 1940, p. 34, and Nov. 24, 1940, p. 14.

55. *Ibid.*, May 20, 1940, p. 14.

56. Transcript of 1940 ZOA Convention, pp. 68, 329–31.

57. Lawrence H. Fuchs, *The Political Behavior of American Jews* (Glencoe, IL: Free Press, 1956), pp. 100–101, 72; also see chap. 11, "Sources of Jewish Internationalism and Liberalism."

58. Samuel Halperin and Irwin Oder, "The United States in Search of a Policy: Franklin D. Roosevelt and Palestine," *Review of Politics* 24 (July 1962): pp. 320–41; Selig Adler, "The Roosevelt Administration and Zionism: The Pre-War Years, 1933–1939," in *Essays in American Zionism 1917–1948, The Herzl Yearbook*, vol. 8, ed. Melvin Urofsky (New York: Herzl Press, 1978), pp. 132–48; Selig Adler, "United States and Palestine in the FDR Era," *American Jewish Historical Quarterly* 62 (Sept. 1972): pp. 11–79; Urofsky, *American Zionism from Herzl to the Holocaust*, pp. 414–15; Peter Grose, *Israel in the Mind of America* (New York: Alfred A. Knopf, 1983), pp. 134–40.

59. Weizman, *Trial and Error*, p. 417.

60. *New York Times*, Nov. 24, 1940, p. 14.

61. Silver to Neumann, Dec. 2, 1940, Stephen S. Wise Papers, Box 119, File 20, American Jewish Historical Society, Waltham, MA.

62. On Dec. 15, 1940, *New York Times* reported on page 7 that the Germans had completed constructing the walls of the Warsaw Ghetto.

63. *New York Times*, Dec. 14, 1940, p. 4, and Dec. 12, 1940, p. 4. Also see Penkower, *Jews Were Expendable*, p. 53; and Wasserstein, *Britain and the Jews of Europe*, pp. 76–78.

64. For the best account of the *Patria* incident, see Penkower, *Jews Were Expendable*, pp. 30–58. Also see Bauer, *From Diplomacy to Resistance*, pp. 108–9; Wasserstein, *Britain and the Jews of Europe*, pp. 60–68; *New York Times*, Dec. 19, 1940, p. 3.

65. On the *Struma*, see Penkower, *Jews Were Expendable*, pp. 56–57, 150–51; Hurewitz, *Struggle for Palestine*, pp. 140, 141; Bauer, *From Diplomacy to Resistance*, p. 244; Wasserstein, *Britain and the Jews of Europe*, pp. 143–57.

66. Penkower, *Jews Were Expendable*, pp. 50–53; Monty Noam Penkower, "Ben-Gurion, Silver, and the 1941 UPA National Conference on Palestine: A Turning Point in American Zionist History," *American Jewish History* LXIX (Sept. 1979): pp. 66–91; Bauer, *From Diplomacy to Resistance*, chap. 6; Michael Bar-Zohar, *Ben-Gurion: A Biography*, trans. Peretz Kidron (New York: Delacorte Press, 1978), pp. 101–5.

67. "Report of a meeting with Mr. Ben-Gurion held at the Winthrop Hotel," Dec. 5, 1940, Emanuel Neumann Papers, Ben-Gurion file, ZAL.

68. *Ibid.*; American Emergency Committee for Zionist Affairs (hereafter AECZA) Minutes, Nov. 28, 1941, Neumann Papers, AZEC File, ZAL. Also see Penkower, "Ben-Gurion, Silver, and the 1941 UPA Conference," pp. 72–73.

69. "Report of a meeting with Mr. Ben-Gurion held at the Winthrop Hotel," Dec. 5, 1940, Neumann Papers, Ben-Gurion file, ZAL.

70. *Ibid.*

71. *Ibid.*

72. Penkower, "Ben-Gurion, Silver and the 1941 UPA Conference," p. 75.

73. *Ibid.*, pp. 74–75; *New York Times*, Jan. 25, 1941, p. 1; Jan. 26, 1941, p. 25; Jan. 27, 1941, p. 5. The Zionists use of the term *Commonwealth* will be discussed later in this chapter.

74. "Statement of Principles" in the Stenographic Transcript of the forty-fourth ZOA Convention, Sept. 1941, pp. 91–95, ZAL (hereafter: Transcript of 1941 ZOA Convention).

75. Transcript of 1941 ZOA Convention, p. 20. Also see the comments of Mendel Fisher on p. 25 and Neumann on p. 48.

76. *Ibid.*, pp. 149–50.

77. St. Regis Hotel Conference, May 25, 1941, quoted in Isaac Neustadt-Noy, "The Unending Task: Effort to Unite American Jewry from the American Jewish Congress to the American Jewish Conference," Ph.D. diss., Brandeis University, 1976, pp. 149–53; Isaac Neustadt-Noy, "Toward Unity: Zionist and non-Zionist Cooperation, 1941–1942," in *Essays in American Zionism 1917–1941*, p. 152.

78. Chaim Weizman, "Palestine's Role in the Solution of the Jewish Problem," *Foreign Affairs* 20 (Jan. 1942): pp. 324–38.

79. *Ibid.*

80. Neumann's comments can be found in Transcript of 1941 ZOA Convention, pp. 167–69.

81. Weizmann to Meyer Weisgal, Oct. 13, 1941, letter #195 in *The Letters and Papers of Chaim Weizmann*, Series A, vol. XX, ed. Barnet Litvinoff (New Brunswick, NJ: Transaction Books, Rutgers University, 1979); Weizmann to Levinthal, Oct. 15, 1941, letter #197 in *Ibid.*; Neustadt-Noy, "Toward Unity: Zionist and non-Zionist Cooperation," pp. 149–65; David H. Shpiro, "The Political Background of the 1942 Biltmore Resolution," in *Essays in American Zionism 1917–1941*, pp. 166–77.

82. Salo Baron, "The Second World War and Jewish Community Life," in Baron, *Steeled in Adversity: Essays and Addresses on American Jewish Life* (Philadelphia: Jewish Publication Society of America, 1971), p. 455. Baron gave this address at the Conference on Jewish Relations on May 26, 1942, and at the National Conference of Jewish Social Welfare on June 6, 1942. For similar views, see Joseph Schlossberg, "The Jews After the War," *Congress Weekly*, Jan. 9, 1942, pp. 5–7; "Dr. Weizmann's Presentation," *Congress Weekly*, Jan. 2, 1941, p. 4.

83. "Extraordinary Zionist Conference, New York 1942, Stenographic Protocol," pp. 13–14, 278, ZAL (hereafter: Biltmore Protocol). The AECZA organized the conference and prepared the resolutions for the delegates to debate and vote on. AECZA Minutes, May 5, 1942, Neumann Papers, AZEC file, ZAL.

84. For the most comprehensive history of the Holocaust, see Raul Hilberg, *The Destruction of the European Jews*, 2d. ed., 3 vols. (New York: Holmes & Meier, 1985). On the mobile killing squads, see vol. 1, chap. 7.

85. Weizmann, Biltmore Protocol, pp. 20–40.

86. Ben-Gurion, Biltmore Protocol, pp. 51–52, 73–74.

87. Silver, Biltmore Protocol, pp. 460–63.

88. Ben-Gurion, Biltmore Protocol, pp. 81–82.

89. Biltmore Protocol: Szold, p. 145; Gellman, p. 153; Segal, p. 194; Goldmann, pp. 248–49.

90. Silver, Biltmore Protocol, pp. 456–78.

91. Grose, *Israel in the Mind of America*, pp. 168–69.

92. Weizmann's autobiography, *Trial and Error*, reveals the intensity of his devotion to Great Britain.

93. Weizmann, Biltmore Protocol, pp. 33–34, 499.

94. Ben-Gurion, Biltmore Protocol, pp. 71–72. For an enlightening discussion of Weizmann and Ben-Gurion's positions at Biltmore, see Yehuda Bauer, *From Diplomacy to Resistance*, pp. 234–42.

95. Sherman, Biltmore Protocol, pp. 179–82A.

96. *Ibid.*

97. Furmanksy, Biltmore Protocol, pp. 190–91.

98. On binationalism, see Walter Laqueur, *A History of Zionism* (New York: Holt, Rinehart & Winston, 1972), pp. 251–55; Arthur Goren, ed., *Dissenter in Zion: From the Writings of Judah L. Magnes* (Cambridge, MA: Harvard University Press, 1982); Susan Lee Hattis, *The Bi-National Idea in Palestine During Mandatory Times* (Haifa: Shikmona, 1970).

99. Greenberg, Biltmore Protocol, pp. 157–64.

100. Seigal, Biltmore Protocol, pp. 192–96.

101. Rose Jacobs, Biltmore Protocol, pp. 84–93.

102. Rosenblatt, Biltmore Protocol, pp. 93–107. Rosenblatt believed that the Arab component of a Federated Palestine should include Transjordan. He also held out the possibility that Palestine might eventually become part of the British Commonwealth or a larger federation of the Levant states.

103. Gellman, Biltmore Protocol, pp. 152–53.

104. Bublic, Biltmore Protocol, p. 192.

105. Gold, Biltmore Protocol, pp. 202–3. Also see Rabbi J. H. Lookstein, pp. 431–40.

106. Wise, Biltmore Protocol, pp. 4–5.

107. Szold, Biltmore Protocol, pp. 142–44.

108. Goldstein, Biltmore Protocol, p. 214.

109. Ben Halpern, *The Idea of the Jewish State*, 2d ed. (Cambridge, MA: Harvard University Press, 1961, reprint 1969) pp. 45–48.

110. Stenographic Transcript of the forty-fifth ZOA Convention, Oct. 1942, p. 432, ZAL (hereafter: Transcript of 1942 ZOA Convention). Also see Emanuel Neumann's address, pp. 131–33.

111. Transcript of 1942 ZOA Convention, p. 437.

112. Zionists also persuaded some of their Christian allies to adopt the postwar refugee formula. For example, see Senator Robert Wagner's greeting in Transcript of 1942 ZOA Convention, pp. 425–26.

113. *Ibid.*, pp. 459–60.

114. *Ibid.*, pp. 444–46.

115. *Ibid.*, pp. 135–44.

116. *Ibid.*, p. 415.

117. *Ibid.*, pp. 593–94.

118. *Ibid.*, p. 434.

119. *Ibid.*, p. 576.

CHAPTER IV

1. Weizmann, "Extraordinary Zionist Conference, New York, 1942, Stenographic Protocol," pp. 20–21, ZAL (hereafter: Biltmore Protocol).

2. Goldmann, Biltmore Protocol, pp. 231–57.

3. David S. Wyman, *The Abandonment of the Jews: America and the Holocaust* (New York: Pantheon, 1984), chaps. 2 & 3; Henry Feingold, *The Politics of Rescue* (New Brunswick, NJ: Rutgers University Press, 1970), pp. 161–71; Arthur Morse, *While Six Million Died* (New York: Random House, 1968), chaps. 1 & 2; Saul S. Friedman, *No Haven for the Oppressed* (Detroit: Wayne State University Press, 1973), chap. 6; Stephen S. Wise, *Challenging Years* (New York: Putnam's Sons, 1949), pp. 274–

76; Walter Laqueur, *The Terrible Secret: Suppression of the Truth about Hitler's "Final Solution"* (Boston: Little, Brown, 1980), pp. 158–64.

4. For example, see R. Lichteim to Arthur Lourie, Sept. 15, 1942, Emanuel Neumann Papers, AZEC File, ZAL.

5. Stenographic Transcript of the forty-fifth ZOA Convention, Oct. 1942, pp. 327–32, ZAL (hereafter: Transcript of 1942 ZOA Convention).

6. Transcript of 1942 ZOA Convention, p. 669.

7. *Ibid.*, pp. 484–85.

8. *Ibid.*, pp. 428–29.

9. In fact, Goldmann's and Rothenberg's comments account for only four of the more than eight hundred pages of the verbatim transcript of the conference.

10. Transcript of 1942 ZOA Convention, pp. 512–13.

11. *Ibid.*, pp. 665–66. Morris Rothenberg and Robert Szold called on Zionists to offer the world a "comprehensive" and "permanent" solution to the problems of Jewish misery and homelessness. *Ibid.*, pp. 432, 437. Also see Radiogram from British Zionist Federation, in *Ibid.*, pp. 513–14.

12. Transcript of 1942 ZOA Convention, pp. 485, 504.

13. Leon Feuer, *Why a Jewish State* (New York: R. R. Smith, 1942), pp. 69–72.

14. *Ibid.*, p. 15.

15. *Ibid.*, pp. 74–75.

16. *Ibid.*, pp. 80–81.

17. Wise, *Challenging Years*, pp. 275–76.

18. *New York Times*, Nov. 25, 1942, p. 10.

19. *Ibid.*, Nov. 26, 1942, p. 16.

20. Eliyho Matzozky, "The Response of American Jewry and Its Representative Organizations Between Nov. 24, 1942, and April 19, 1943, to Mass Killings of Jews In Europe" (Master's thesis, Yeshiva University, 1979), pp. 13–14.

21. Wyman, *Abandonment of the Jews*, pp. 71–73; Matzozky, "The Response of American Jewry," chap. 3.

22. Bergson to Levinthal, Dec. 8, 1942, Bergson Papers, 134 N3 (2), Yale University, New Haven, CT. For information on the Bergson groups, see Aaron Berman, "The Hebrew Committee of National Liberation and the Rescue of the European Jews," Division III project, Hampshire College, 1975; and chapter V of this book.

23. Wyman, *Abandonment of the Jews*, pp. 93–98, 102–3, 109–11, 120–21, 168–69; Edward Pinsky, "American Jewish Unity During the Holocaust—The Joint Emergency Committee, 1943," *American Jewish History* LXII (June 1983): pp. 477–94.

24. During this time the American government remained firmly committed to a restrictionist immigration policy. From Dec. 7, 1941, to V-E Day, only 10 percent of the available visas for refugees were used. The 1930s experience demonstrated that it was not possible to raise the quota limit. Instead the battle centered on convincing the State Department to issue all the visas that were available. Wyman, *Abandonment of the Jews*, pp. 5–6, 124–37.

25. *New York Times*, March 2, 1943, p. 2; Feingold, *Politics of Rescue*, pp. 176–77; Wyman, *Abandonment of the Jews*, pp. 88–89; "Program Action on the Rescue of Jews in Nazi Occupied Territories Adopted by the Joint Committee on the European Emergency Jewish Situation," n.d., Silver Papers, Manson File I–81, AHSMA

26. *New York Times*, Dec. 18, 1942, p. 26; March 3, 1943, p. 22.

27. *Ibid.*, March 3, 1943, p. 22.

28. In January 1944, under pressure from Congress and the Treasury Department, Roosevelt finally established the War Refugee Board, which has been credited with saving approximately 200,000

Jews. How many would have been saved if the agency had been established earlier, we shall sadly never know. Wyman, *Abandonment of the Jews*, p. 285.

29. A New York newspaper reported in March 1943 that Bulgaria had agreed to release over four thousand Jews. *New York Times*, March 3, 1943, p. 22; Feingold, *Politics of Rescue*, pp. 181–85; Wyman, *Abandonment of the Jews*, pp. 82–84.

30. Weizmann to Goldstein, Dec. 24, 1942, letter #360 in *The Letters and Papers of Chaim Weizmann*, Series A, vol. XX, ed. Barnet Litvinoff (New Brunswick, NJ: Transaction Books, Rutgers University, 1979).

31. "We Mourn and Protest," *Youth and Nation*, Dec. 1942, p. 3.

32. *New York Times*, Dec. 28, 1942, p. 15.

33. Minutes of Hadassah National Board Meeting, Dec. 9, 1942, Hadassah Papers, ZAL.

34. Hayim Greenberg, "Bankrupt!," reprinted in *Hayim Greenberg Anthology*, ed. Marie Syrkin (Detroit: Wayne State University Press, 1968), pp. 192–203.

35. "End the Conspiracy of Inaction," *Youth and Nation*, March 1943, pp. 3–4.

36. Wyman, *Abandonment of the Jews*, p. 108.

37. For example, see Weizmann to Halifax, Apr. 14, 1943, letter #23 in *Letters and Papers of Chaim Weizmann*, Series A, vol. XXI; Shulman to Silver, Apr. 5, 1943, Silver Papers, Manson File I–81, AHSMA.

38. Halifax to Wise, Feb. 4, 1943, Silver Papers, Manson File 1–96, AHSMA; Weizmann to Halifax, Feb. 16, 1943, letter #9 in *Letters and Papers of Chaim Weizmann*, Series A, vol. XXI.

39. For background on the Bermuda Conference, see Wyman, *Abandonment of the Jews*, chap. 6; Feingold, *Politics of Rescue*, chap. 7; Morse, *While Six Million Died*, chap. III; Friedman, *No Haven for the Oppressed*, chap. 7.

40. *New York Times*, May 4, 1943, p. 17.

41. Silver's May 2, 1943, address can be found in Abba Hillel Silver, *Vision and Victory: A Collection of Addresses, 1942–1948* (New York: Zionist Organization of America, 1949), pp. 1–12.

42. AECZA Minutes, May 3, 1943, #59, ZAL.

43. Weizmann to Dugdale, Jan. 8, 1943, letter #364 in *Letters and Papers of Chaim Weizmann*, Series A, vol. XX.

44. Minutes of AECZA Office Comm. Meeting, June 1, 1943, Silver Papers, AHSMA.

45. *Ibid.*

46. Weizmann to Wise, June 25, 1943, letter #42 in *Letters and Papers of Chaim Weizmann*, Series A, vol. XXI. Also see Weizmann to Weisgal, Aug. 23, 1943, letter #58 in *Ibid.*

47. Weizmann to Weisgal, Apr. 13, 1944, letter #151 in *Ibid.*

48. The idea of organizing a national conference was not a new one. Chaim Weizmann, among others, had suggested holding such a meeting. Minutes of Hadassah National Board Meeting, Jan. 6, 1943, Hadassah Papers, ZAL.

49. Monsky's letter is reprinted in *The American Jewish Conference: Its Organization and Proceedings of the First Session*, ed. Alexander S. Kohanski (New York: American Jewish Conference, 1944), p. 319.

50. Minutes of AECZA Office Committee Meeting, Jan. 7, 1943, Silver Papers, AHSMA: Samuel Halperin, *The Political World of American Zionism* (Detroit: Wayne State University Press, 1961), p. 223.

51. For a full list of those attending the Pittsburgh meetings see Kohanski, *American Jewish Conference*, pp. 320–21.

52. Naomi Cohen, *Not Free to Desist: The American Jewish Committee, 1906–1966* (Philadelphia: Jewish Publication Society of America, 1972), pp. 256–60.

53. Kohanski, *American Jewish Conference*, p. 325; Halperin, *Political World of American Zionism*, p. 225.

54. Halperin, *Political World of American Zionism*, p. 226.

55. AECZA Office Committee Minutes, Feb. 4, 1943, Silver Papers, AHSMA.

56. Minutes of AECZA Office Committee Meetings, Feb. 4, 1943, and June 1, 1943, Silver Papers, AHSMA.

57. Kohanski, *American Jewish Conference*, pp. 47–48; Halperin, *Political World of American Zionism*, pp. 231–33.

58. Kohanski, *American Jewish Conference*, p. 46; Joseph Halbert, "Minutes of the Palestine Committee, American Jewish Conference Sessions held Aug. 31 through Sept. 1, 1943," p. 210, ZAL (hereafter: Minutes of Palestine Committee).

59. Minutes of Hadassah National Board Meeting, May 12, 1943, Hadassah Papers, ZAL; Isaac Neustadt-Noy, "The Unending Task: Efforts to Unite American Jewry from the American Jewish Congress to the American Jewish Conference" (Ph.D. thesis, Brandeis Univ., 1976), p. 298; Emanuel Neumann, *In the Arena* (New York: Herzl Press, 1977), pp. 190–91; Emanuel Neumann, interview by Yehuda Bauer, July 21, 1967, p. 13, Neumann Papers, ZAL.

60. Kohanski, *American Jewish Conference*, pp. 56–57.

61. A detailed summary of Monsky's address can be found in *Ibid.*, pp. 67–70.

62. *Ibid.*, pp. 70–73.

63. *Ibid.*, p. 87–92. As part of an agreement to assure unity with the American Jewish Committee, Goldmann, Wise, and other Zionist spokesmen carefully avoided asking the Conference to endorse the Biltmore Resolution's demand for the immediate creation of a Jewish state. They believed that the American and British governments were jointly preparing to declare that they would not discuss the future political status of Palestine until the end of the war. Such a development, Zionist leaders believed, would be catastrophic because it would link the American government to Great Britain's anti-Zionist Middle East policy. American Zionists also understood that if this crisis situation developed, the financial and political resources of the American Jewish Committee would significantly strengthen the Zionist position in the United States. As a result, in return for solidarity on an anti–White Paper platform, Jewish nationalists toned down their rhetoric and program. Halperin, *Political World of American Zionism*, pp. 233–34; Neumann, *In the Arena*, pp. 190–91; Emanuel Neumann interview by Yehuda Bauer, July 21, 1967, p. 13, Neumann Papers, ZAL; Y. Ben-Ami to Bergson, Aug. 13, 1943, Committee for a Jewish Army Papers, 21/3/3H, Jabotinsky Institute, Tel Aviv.

64. Kohanski, *American Jewish Conference*, pp. 73–76.

65. Neumann, *In the Arena*, p. 191; Halperin, *Political World of American Zionism*, p. 234; Melvin Urofsky, *We Are One!: American Jewry and Israel* (Garden City, NY: Anchor Press, 1978), p. 27.

66. Silver's address can be found in Silver, *Vision and Victory*, pp. 13–21; and Arthur Hertzberg, ed., *The Zionist Idea: A Historical Analysis and Reader* (New York: Atheneum, 1959, reprint 1973), pp. 592–600.

67. Rose Halprin noted that "Dr. Silver's magnificent address won over to the cause of Palestine many unaffiliated and previously unenthusiastic persons." Minutes of Hadassah National Board Meeting, Sept. 8, 1943, Hadassah Papers, ZAL.

68. Minutes of Palestine Committee, pp. 108–15.

69. Kohanski, *American Jewish Conference*, pp. 133–34.

70. Minutes of Palestine Committee, pp. 73–77.

71. Rothenberg, Minutes of Palestine Committee, pp. 53–68, 239–50; Levinthal, Minutes of Palestine Committee, pp. 153–57.

72. Szold, Minutes of Palestine Committee, pp. 117–29; Greenberg, Minutes of Palestine Committee, pp. 190–98.

73. Neumann, Minutes of Palestine Committee, pp. 218–36. For other opponents of Robert Goldman, see Minutes of Palestine Committee: Rabbi David W. Pearlman, pp. 105–8; Herman Shulman, pp. 157–65; Rabbi David Shapiro, pp. 169–73; Harry Levin, pp. 184–90; Benjamin Shwadran, pp. 79–81.

74. Minutes of Palestine Committee, pp. 266–70; Kohanski, *American Jewish Conference*, pp. 178–81.

75. For a very fine discussion of the American Jewish Conference as well as the American Jewish Committee's relationship with the Conference, see Halperin, *Political World of American Zionism*, pp. 223–51, 129–44.

76. Stenographic Transcript of the forty-sixth ZOA Convention, Sept. 1943, pp. 39–55, ZAL (hereafter: Transcript of 1943 ZOA Convention).

77. *Ibid.*, pp. 189–202.

78. Neumann to Abraham Tulin, Sept. 15, 1943, Tulin Papers, File #32, ZAL.

79. Neumann, *In the Arena*, p. 187.

80. Weizmann to Lewis Namier, June 27, 1942, letter #301 in *Letters and Papers of Chaim Weizmann*, Series A, vol. XX; Weizmann to Wise, June 20, 1942, letter #298 in *Ibid.*; Neumann, *In the Arena*, p. 188.

81. Minutes of AECZA Meeting, Aug. 26, 1943, Silver Papers, AHSMA.

82. Jacobs to Silver, Sept. 27, 1943, Silver Papers, File #4–2–11, AHSMA.

83. American Zionist Emergency Council (AZEC) Minutes, Oct. 5, 1943, Silver Papers, AHSMA.

84. AZEC Executive Committee Minutes, Nov. 29, 1943, Silver Papers, AHSMA.

85. American Jewish Conference Digest of Minutes of Interim Committee, Jan. 25, 1944, Silver Papers, Manson File II–3, AHSMA; AZEC Executive Committee Minutes, Dec. 13, 1943, Silver Papers, AHSMA.

86. AZEC Minutes, Sept. 20, 1943, Silver Papers, AHSMA.

87. The American Zionist Emergency Council will be discussed in the next chapter.

88. Bergson to Chapter Offices of the Committee for a Jewish Army, Sept. 16, 1943, Bergson Papers, Hebrew Committee of National Liberation file #1 and Committee for a Jewish Army file #21, Jabotinsky Institute, Tel Aviv. The Bergsonites cooperated with Ben Hecht, journalist and Hollywood scriptwriter, in the preparation of a pageant dramatizing the crisis confronting European Jewry. "We Shall Never Die," produced by Billy Rose, staged by Moss Hart, with music by Kurt Weill, starred Paul Muni and Edward G. Robinson. It honored those Jews killed by the Nazis while the world kept silent and demanded that action be taken to prevent any more murders. Hecht's demand for rescue proved so successful at its March 9 premiere in Madison Square Garden that Hecht and the Bergsonites decided to have it performed in several other American cities.

89. Eri Jabotinsky to "Kitty and Ted," Jan. 11, 1944, Bergson Papers, Emergency Committee file #70, Jabotinsky Institute, Tel Aviv.

90. AZEC Minutes, Nov. 15, 1943, Silver Papers, AHSMA; "Memorandum Issued by the Interim Committee of the American Jewish Conference," Dec. 29, 1943, Wise Papers, Box 99, File 4, American Jewish Historical Society, Waltham, MA; *New York Times*, Dec. 31, 1943, p. 10; AZEC Executive Committee Minutes Jan. 3, 1944, Silver Papers, AHSMA; AZEC to various senators, Jan. 10, 1944, Bergson Papers, Hebrew Committee of National Liberation file #27, Jabotinsky Institute, Tel Aviv; Eri Jabotinsky to Taitel, Jan. 5, 1944, Bergson Papers, Emergency Committee file #70, Jabotinsky Institute, Tel Aviv; Minutes of interview with Senator Gillette, Jan. 17, 1944, Silver Papers, Manson File II–35, AHSMA; Gillette to Shapiro, Jan. 13, 1944, Silver Papers, Manson File II–35, AHSMA.

91. AZEC Executive Committee Minutes, Nov. 29, 1943, Silver Papers, AHSMA.

92. U.S. Congress, House Committee on International Relations, *Problems of World War II and Its Aftermath – Part 2 –The Palestine Questions, Problems of Postwar Europe, Selected Executive Session Hearings of the Committee, 1943–50*, Vol. II, (Washington, DC: GPO, 1976), pp. 217–43 (Wise testimony), pp. 235–38 (Rogers); Feingold, *Politics of Rescue*, pp. 238, 211–12; Wyman, *Abandonment of the Jews*, p. 199; Minutes of conversation with Congressman Sol. Bloom, Dec. 8, 1943, Silver Papers, Manson File II–21, AHSMA: *New York Times*, Dec. 2, 1943, p. 4. The Bergson resolution won the approval of the Senate but never reached the floor of the House. However, public pressure generated

by the resolution did contribute to Roosevelt's decision to create the War Refugee Board in January 1944.

93. Bergson to Halifax, June 10, 1944, reprinted in "A Statement of Policy Pertaining to the Entry of Hebrews into Palestine," published by the Hebrew Committee of National Liberation, Jan. 1945, Hebrew Committee of National Liberation file #50, Bergson Papers, Jabotinsky Institute, Tel Aviv; *Answer Magazine*, July 15, 1944, p. 22; *Answer Magazine*, Aug. 29, 1944, p. 28.

94. John Pehle to Edward Stettinius, March 20, 1944, Bergson Papers, microfilm roll #12, Yale University.

95. For more details on the plight of Hungarian Jewry, see Raul Hilberg, *The Destruction of the European Jews*, 2d ed., vol. 2 (New York: Holmes & Meier, 1985) pp. 796–860; Randolph L. Braham, *The Politics of Genocide: The Holocaust in Hungary*, 2 vols. (New York: Columbia University Press, 1981); Braham, *Eichman and the Destruction of Hungarian Jewry* (New York: World Federation of Hungarian Jews, distributed by Twayne Publishers, 1961); Feingold, *Politics of Rescue*, chap. 9; Morse, *While Six Million Died*, chap. XX; Friedman, *No Haven for the Oppressed*, chap. 9; and Wyman, *Abandonment of the Jews*, chap. 13.

96. AZEC Executive Committee Minutes, March 20, 1944, Silver Papers, AHSMA.

97. Sack to Abba Hillel Silver, Aug. 29, 1944, Silver Papers, AHSMA; AZEC Executive Committee Minutes, Aug. 31, 1944, Silver Papers, AHSMA; Arthur Lourie, "Draft Statement on Emergency Rescue Shelter Resolution," Sept. 6, 1944, Silver Papers, File #4–2–24, AHSMA; Silver and Wise to Hugh Scott, Sept. 6, 1944, Silver Papers, File #4–2–50, AHSMA; AZEC Executive Committee Minutes, Sept. 11, 1944, Silver Papers, AHSMA; John McCormack to Silver, Sept. 14, 1944, Silver Papers, correspondence files, AHSMA: AZEC Minutes, Sept. 14, 1944, Silver Papers, AHSMA.

98. Speech reprinted as "At the Congressional Hearings," in Silver, *Vision and Victory*, pp. 22–37; Draft Statement at the Foreign Affairs Committee, n.d., Silver Papers, File #4–2–3, AHSMA.

99. AZEC Executive Committee Minutes, Feb. 8, 1944, Silver Papers, AHSMA; "Draft Statement sent to FDR after meeting on March 9, 1944," Silver Papers, File #4–2–48, AHSMA.

CHAPTER V

1. American Emergency Committee for Zionist Affairs Minutes, Sept. 20, 1943, Silver Papers, AHSMA (hereafter: AECZA Minutes).

2. Samuel Halperin, *The Political World of American Zionism* (Detroit: Wayne State University Press, 1961), p. 247.

3. Discussed in chap. 3.

4. Halperin, *Political World of American Zionism*, pp. 279–80.

5. American Zionist Emergency Council Executive Committee Minutes, Oct. 5, 1943, Silver Papers, AHSMA (hereafter: AZEC Exec. Comm. Minutes).

6. *Ibid.*; Louis Segal, "Proposals to the American Emergency Committee for Zionist Affairs," Silver Papers File #4–2–11, AHSMA.

7. AZEC Exec. Comm. Minutes, Nov. 15, 1943, Silver Papers, AHSMA.

8. *New York Times*, May 11, 1959, p. 27.

9. Zaritsky to Abba Hillel Silver, Apr. 5, 1944, Silver Papers, File #4–2–19, AHSMA.

10. AZEC Exec. Comm. Minutes, Oct. 5, 1943, Silver Papers, AHSMA.

11. AZEC Exec. Comm. Minutes, Oct. 18, 1943, ZAL.

12. AZEC. Exec. Comm. Minutes, Nov. 29, 1943, and Jan. 13, 1944, Silver Papers, AHSMA.

13. Halperin, *Political World of American Zionism*, p. 179.

14. Carl Herman Voss, "The American Christian Palestine Committee," in *Essays in American Zionism: Herzl Year Book*, vol. VIII, ed. Melvin I. Urofsky (New York: Herzl Pres, 1976), pp. 242–43; Emanuel Neumann, *In the Arena* (New York: Herzl Press, 1976), pp. 110–14.

15. Minutes of an interview with Louis D. Brandeis, Aug. 20, 1941, Emanuel Neumann Papers, ZAL.

16. Yehuda Bauer interview with Emanuel Neumann, July 21, 1967, p. 4, Neumann Papers, correspondence file "Bauer," ZAL.

17. Voss, "American Christian Palestine Committee," p. 244; Halperin, *Political World of American Zionism*, p. 182.

18. Berlin, Confidential Memorandum, Feb. 24, 1943, Silver Papers, Manson File I–62, AHSMA.

19. Minutes of American Palestine Committee, Publicity Committee, June 19, 1941, Neumann Papers, ZAL.

20. AECZA Office Committee Minutes, June 1, 1943; AZEC Exec. Comm. Minutes, Jan. 13, 1944, Silver Papers, AHSMA.

21. Melvin Urofsky, *We Are One!: American Jewry and Israel* (Garden City, NY: Anchor Press, 1978), p. 38.

22. Halperin, *Political World of American Zionism*, p. 184; Neumann, *In the Arena*, p. 156.

23. AZEC Exec. Comm. Minutes, Nov. 29, 1943, Silver Papers, AHSMA; Halperin, *Political World of American Zionism*, p. 184.

24. On Catholic and Protestant views of Zionism and Jewish statehood, see Esther V. Feldblum, *The American Catholic Press and the Jewish State, 1917–1959* (New York: Ktav Publishing House, 1977); Hertzel Fishman, *American Protestantism and a Jewish State* (Detroit: Wayne State University Press, 1973).

25. AECZA Minutes, May 5, 1942, Neumann Papers, ZAL; Neumann, *In the Arena*, p. 156; Voss, "American Christian Palestine Committee," p. 245. On Bernstein's activities, see chaps. 2 and 4 of this book.

26. Voss, "American Christian Palestine Committee," pp. 245–46; Halperin, *Political World of American Zionism*, p. 374.

27. Niebuhr's views on Zionism will be dealt wth later in this chapter.

28. Voss, "American Christian Palestine Committee," p. 246; Wise to Neumann, July 29, 1941, Stephen Wise Papers, Box #128, File #8, American Jewish Historical Society, Waltham, MA. In 1946, the American Palestine Committee and the Christian Council merged to form the American Christian Palestine Committee.

29. AZEC Exec. Comm. Minutes, Jan. 15, 1945, Silver Papers, AHSMA.

30. For a very informative history of the AJC, see Naomi W. Cohen, *Not Free to Desist: The American Jewish Committee 1906–1966* (Philadelphia: Jewish Publication Society of America, 1972).

31. AZEC Exec. Comm. Minutes, Oct. 27, 1943, ZAL.

32. AZEC Exec. Comm. Minutes, Nov. 15, 1943, Silver Papers, AHSMA; Doreen Bierbrier, "The American Zionist Emergency Council: An Analysis of a Pressure Group," *American Jewish Historical Quarterly* LX (Sept. 1970): pp. 101–2; Halperin, *Political World of American Zionism*, pp. 134–35.

33. Herman Nederland, president of the Council of Jewish Organizations of Bensonhurst and Mapleton, to Proskauer, Jan. 16, 1944, Silver Papers, File # 4–2–15, AHSMA.

34. For the Zionist promise, see Abba Hillel Silver's speech to the American Jewish Conference. N. Cohen, *Not Free to Desist*, pp. 259–64, 293–303; Bierbrier, "American Zionist Emergency Council," p. 102; Halperin, *Political World of American Zionism*, pp. 134–42.

35. On the activities of the Bergson group, see Aaron Berman, "The Hebrew Committee of National Liberation and the Rescue of the European Jews," Division III thesis, Hampshire College, 1975; Monty Penkower, "In Dramatic Dissent: The Bergson Boys," *American Jewish History* 70 (March 1981): pp. 281–309; Sarah E. Peck, "The Campaign for an American Response to the Nazi Holocaust, 1943–1945," *Journal of Contemporary History* 15 (Apr. 1980): pp. 367–400; *Answer Magazine*, February 1946, p. 11; Yitshaq Ben-Ami, *Years of Wrath, Days of Glory: Memoirs from the Irgun* (New York: R. R. Speller, 1982).

36. Silver to Bergson, Feb. 12, 1941; Bergson to Silver, March 7, 1941; Bergson to Silver, May 25, 1941; Bergson to Wise, May 7, 1941; all in Bergson Papers, Series I, Box 1, File 5, Yale University, New Haven, CT (hereafter: Bergson Papers).

37. Wise to Bergson, June 4, 1941, Bergson Papers, Series I, Box 1, File 5.

38. "First Proposal made by the Committee for a Jewish Army to the Emergency Committee for Zionist Affairs, Dec. 3, 1941," Bergson Papers, Series I, Box 1, File 5; Van Paassen to Wise, Dec. 3, 1941, Bergson Papers, Series I, Box 1, File 5.

39. Yehuda Bauer, *From Diplomacy to Resistance: A History of Jewish Palestine 1939–1945* (Philadelphia: Jewish Publication Society of America, 1970), p. 236; Peter Bergson, interview with author, New York City, Aug. 30, 1974; Nachum Goldman to Bergson, Aug. 27, 1943, Bergson Papers, microfilm roll #1.

40. See preceding chapter.

41. *New York Times*, Dec. 31, 1943, p. 10.

42. David S. Wyman, *The Abandonment of the Jews* (New York: Pantheon, 1984), pp. 86–87.

43. *The Jewish Advocate*, Jan. 13, 1944, Bergson newspaper scrapbooks, Jabotinsky Institute, Tel Aviv; American Zionist Emergency Council to various senators, Jan. 10, 1944, Hebrew Committee of National Liberation Papers, file #27, Jabotinsky Institute, Tel Aviv.

44. Eri Jabotinsky to Irving Taitel, Jan. 5, 1944, Emergency Committee to Save the Jewish People of Europe Papers, file #70, Jabotinsky Institute, Tel Aviv.

45. Wyman, *Abandonment of the Jews*, p. 144.

46. AZEC Memo (Harry Shapiro) to Chairman Local Emergency Committees, May 11, 1944, Papers of the American League for a Free Palestine, file #49, Jabotinsky Institute, Tel Aviv.

47. *New York Times*, Aug. 9, 1944, p. 13; *Trend of Events*, June 9, 1944, "Palestine Assails Hebrew Committee," Hebrew Committee of National Liberation Papers, file #40, Jabotinsky Institute, Tel Aviv; *Trend of Events*, Aug. 11, 1944, "Resignations From . . . ," Hebrew Committee of National Liberation Papers, file #40, Jabotinsky Institute, Tel Aviv.

48. "A Petition from the Governors of Forty One States," n.d., Silver Papers, AHSMA. Thirty-nine state legislatures also endorsed the Zionist program. Bierbrier, "American Zionist Emergency Council," p. 91.

49. AZEC Exec. Comm. Minutes, July 24, 1944, Silver Papers, AHSMA; Reuben Fink, ed., *America and Palestine: The Attitude of Official America and of the American People Toward the Rebuilding of Palestine as a Free and Democratic Jewish Commonwealth* (New York: American Zionist Emergency Council, 1944).

50. U.S. Congress, House Committee on Foreign Affairs, *The Jewish National Home in Palestine—Hearings H. R. 418 and 419*, 78th Cong., 2d sess., 1944, p. 1 (hereafter: *Jewish National Home Hearings*).

51. Urofsky, *We Are One!*, p. 55.

52. Zvi Ganin, "Activism versus Moderation: The Conflict Between Abba Hillel Silver and Stephen Wise during the 1940s," *Studies in Zionism* 5 (Spring 1984): p. 76.

53. AZEC Exec. Comm. Minutes, Jan. 3, 1944, Silver Papers, AHSMA.

54. American Zionist Emergency Council Minutes, Jan. 13, 1944, Silver Papers, AHSMA; *Jewish National Home Hearings* includes scores of supporting statements.

55. *Jewish National Home Hearings*, pp. 24–31, 88–95.

56. *Ibid.*, pp. 110–20 (Goldstein), 232–33 (Wertheim).

57. *Ibid.*, pp. 150–56 (Epstein), 271–76 (Wise), 230–32 (Gold), 263–71 (Neumann).

58. *Ibid.*, p. 372.

59. *Ibid.*, pp. 192–93.

60. H. G. Nicholas, ed., *Washington Despatches 1941–1945: Weekly Political Reports from the British Embassy* (London: Weidenfeld & Nicholson, 1981), pp. 303–4, 314.

61. *Ibid.*, p. 325.

62. Ganin, "Activism vs. Moderation," p. 76; Nicholas, *Washington Despatches*, pp. 329–30.

63. Ganin, "Activism vs. Moderation," p. 77.

64. Wyman, *Abandonment of the Jews*, pp. 172–74; Ganin, "Activism vs. Moderation," pp. 79–81; Peter Grose, *Israel in the Mind of America* (New York: Alfred A. Knopf, 1983), pp. 147–48.

65. On the Wise-Silver conflict, see Ganin, "Activism vs. Moderation," pp. 78–95; Urofsky, *We Are One!*, pp. 84–93.

66. Arthur A. Ekrich, Jr., *Ideologies and Utopias: The Impact of the New Deal on American Thought* (Chicago: Quadrangle Books, 1969), pp. 246–52; Richard H. Pells, *Radical Visions and American Dreams* (New York: Harper & Row, 1973), chap. VIII; Margaret Mead, *And Keep Your Powder Dry* (New York: W. Morrow, 1942); Wendell Wilkie, *One World* (New York: Simon and Schuster, 1943), p. 203; Richard Pells, *The Liberal Mind in a Conservative Age: American Intellectuals in the 1940s and 1950s* (New York: Harper & Row, 1985), chap. 1.

67. Grose, *Israel in the Mind of America*, pp. 110–11; Marion K. Sanders, *Dorothy Thompson—A Legend in Her Time* (Boston: Houghton Mifflin, 1973), pp. 161–62, 184–85.

68. Discussed later in this chapter.

69. J. Joseph Huthmacher, *Senator Robert F. Wagner and the Rise of Urban Liberalism* (New York: Atheneum, 1968), pp. 306–7, 331–33; Halperin, *Political World of American Zionism*, pp. 182–84; Grose, *Israel in the Mind of America*, p. 192; Harold L. Ickes, *The Secret Diary of Harold L. Ickes*, vol. II, *The Inside Struggle 1936–1939* (New York: Macmillan Co., 1954), p. 304. Ickes spoke at the 1935 National Conference for Palestine: see chap. 1 of this book.

70. Niebuhr's address can be found in the Stenographic Transcript of the forty-fourth ZOA Convention, Sept. 1941, pp. 124–42, ZAL.

71. Reinhold Niebuhr, "Jews After the War," Parts I, II, *Nation*, Feb. 21 and 28, 1942, pp. 214–16, 351–52. Zionist leaders endorsed Niebuhr's articles and quickly sent letters to the *Nation's* editors. "Letters to the Editors," *Nation*, March 21, 1942, pp. 351–52. On Niebuhr and Zionism, see Richard W. Fox, *Reinhold Niebuhr: A Biography* (New York: Pantheon, 1985), pp. 209–11.

72. See chap. 2.

73. Ben Rosenblatt to Stephen Wise, Nov. 6, 1940, Stephen S. Wise Papers, Box 333, File 18, American Jewish Historical Society, Waltham, MA

74. Solomon Goldman to Robert Szold, Apr. 1, 1941, Robert Szold Papers, File: x/4, ZAL.

75. Walter C. Lowdermilk, *Palestine: Land of Promise* (New York: Harpers Brothers, 1944), p. 2; Neumann, *In the Arena*, p. 175.

76. Lowdermilk, *Palestine*, p. 3.

77. *Ibid.*, p. 5.

78. *Ibid.*, page preceding title page.

79. Neumann, *In the Arena*, p. 176.

80. Neumann to Lowdermilk, July 28, 1942; Lowdermilk to Neumann, July 31, 1942; A. Revusky to Lowdermilk, Sept. 3, 1942; all in Neumann Papers, Lowdermilk correspondence file, ZAL.

81. Neumann, *In the Arena*, p. 177; Neumann to Dr. and Mrs. Lowdermilk, Aug. 1942, Neumann Papers, Lowdermilk correspondence file, ZAL.

82. Neumann, "An Economic Development Plan for Palestine," Nov. 19, 1942, Neumann Papers, Lowdermilk File, ZAL.

83. Neumann, *In the Arena*, chap. 14; Neumann to David Lilienthal, Sept. 29, 1942, Neumann Papers, Lilienthal File, ZAL.

84. *Jewish National Home Hearings*, pp. 175–92.

85. Neumann, "An Economic Development Plan for Palestine," Nov. 19, 1942, Neumann Papers, Lowdermilk file, ZAL; Neumann, *In the Arena*, p. 178.

86. Neumann to Lowdermilk, Jan. 26, 1944, Neumann Papers, Lowdermilk correspondence file, ZAL.

87. AZEC Memo, Weisgal to Steinberg, March 31, 1944, Neumann Papers, Lowdermilk correspondence with others file, ZAL.

88. George Norris, "TVA on the Jordan," *Nation*, May 20, 1944, pp. 589–91.

89. AZEC Memo, Lourie to Steinberg, Feb. 9, 1945, Neumann Papers, Lowdermilk correspondence with others file, ZAL.

90. Typed Memo, n.d., n.a. (approx. late 1945), Neumann Papers, Lowdermilk correspondence with others file, ZAL.

91. AZEC Exec. Comm. Minutes, Dec. 13, 1943, Silver Papers, AHSMA.

92. List of names of people invited to be on committee of sponsors for testimonial dinner for Walter Lowdermilk, n.d.; Memo on Lowdermilk dinner, June 6, 1944; American Palestine Committee Press Release, n.d.; all in Neumann Papers, Lowdermilk Testimonial Dinner file, ZAL.

93. Alfred Kazin, "In Every Voice in Every Ban," *New Republic*, Jan. 10, 1944, pp. 44–46.

94. "The Massacre of the Jews," *New Republic*, Dec. 7, 1942, p. 728.

95. For information on Fry, see Timothy P. Maga, "The Quest for a Generous America: Varian Fry and the Refugee Cause, 1940–1942," *Holocaust Studies Annual* I (1983): pp. 69–87; Arthur Morse, *While Six Million Died* (New York: Random House, 1968), p. 307; David Wyman, *Paper Walls: America and the Refugee Crisis, 1938–1941*, (Amherst: University of Massachusetts Press, 1968), p. 142.

96. Varian Fry, "The Massacre of the Jews," *New Republic*, Dec. 21, 1942, pp. 816–19.

97. "Murder of a People," *Nation*, Dec. 19, 1942, pp. 688–89.

98. "Hitler's Subtlest Poison," *Nation*, Feb. 27, 1943, p. 293.

99. Freda Kirchwey, "While the Jews Die," *Nation*, Mar. 13, 1943, pp. 366–67.

100. Philip Bernstein, "The Jews in Europe: The Remnants of a People," *Nation*, Jan. 2, 1943, pp. 8–11.

101. Philip Bernstein, "The Jews in Europe: Seven Ways to Help Them," *Nation*, Jan. 9, 1943, pp. 48–51.

102. Philip Bernstein, "The Jews of Europe: Alternatives to Zion," *Nation*, Jan. 30, 1943, pp. 158–61.

103. Philip Bernstein, "The Jews of Europe: The Case for Zionism," *Nation*, Feb. 6, 1943, pp. 196–200.

104. Philip Bernstein, "What Hope for the Jews?," *New Republic*, April 26, 1943, pp. 555–56.

105. "The Jews of Europe: How to Help Them," *New Republic*, special supplement, Aug. 30, 1943.

106. "The First Front," *New Republic*, special supplement, Aug. 30, 1943, pp. 301.

107. "The Contribution of Palestine," *New Republic*, special supplement, Aug. 30, 1943, pp. 314–15.

108. "What Hope for the Jews," correspondence section, *New Republic*, May 31, 1943, p. 735.

109. Berman, "The Hebrew Committee of National Liberation," pp. 35, 62, 67; *New York Times*, Aug. 9, 1944, p. 13; *Trend of Events*, June 9, 1944, Aug. 11, 1944, Hebrew Committee of National Liberation, file #40, Jabotinsky Institute, Tel Aviv; "A Time for Harmony," editorial, *New York Post*, Jan. 3, 1944, Bergson clipping, Jabotinsky Institute, Tel Aviv; "Leader of the Crusade for a Free Palestine," *New York Post*, July 11, 1944, Bergson clipping, Jabotinsky Institute, Tel Aviv.

110. "The New Zionism," *New Republic*, Mar. 8, 1943, pp. 303–4.

111. *New Republic*, Aug. 30, 1943, p. 298, Dec. 6, 1943, Dec. 27, 1943, Jan. 24, 1944; *Nation*, Dec. 4, 1943, Dec. 25, 1943. For other ads, see *New Republic*, Nov. 8, 1943, Nov. 22, 1943 (inside cover), Dec. 20, 1943, Jan. 17, 1944, Jan. 31, 1944, Feb. 14, 1944, Feb. 21, 1944, Apr. 22, 1944; *Nation*, Nov. 27, 1943, p. 617, Dec. 18, 1943, Apr. 8, 1944, Apr. 29, 1944.

112. See chap. 4 of this book for more information. For American Jewish Conference statement, see *New York Times*, Dec. 31, 1943, p. 10.

113. "Crocodile Tears," *Nation*, Dec. 25, 1943, p. 748.

114. Berman, "The Hebrew Committee of National Liberation," p. 93; *New York Post*, Mar. 8, 1944, Bergson clipping, Jabotinsky Institute, Tel Aviv.

115. "Danger in the Near East," *New Republic*, Mar. 20, 1944, pp. 366–67.

116. Bergson to Halifax, June 10, 1944, and Telegram, Bergson to Churchill, July 15, 1944, reprinted in "A Statement of Policy Pertaining to the Entry of Hebrews into Palestine," published by the Hebrew Committee of National Liberation, Jan. 1945, Hebrew Committee of National Liberation file #50, Jabotinsky Institute, Tel Aviv; *Answer Magazine*, July 14, 1944, p. 22, Aug. 19, 1944, p. 28.

117. The response of American Zionists to the threatened extermination of Hungarian Jewry is discussed in chap. 4 of this book.

118. Freda Kirchwey, "Rescue Hungary's Jews," *Nation*, Aug. 26, 1944, p. 229.

119. Walter Laqueur, *A History of Zionism* (New York: Holt, Rinehart & Winston, 1972), pp. 251–55; Susan Lee Hattis, *The Bi-National Idea in Palestine During Mandatory Times* (Haifa: Shikmona, 1970); Arthur A. Goren, ed., *Dissenter in Zion: From the Writings of Judah L. Magnes* (Cambridge, MA: Harvard University Press, 1982).

120. For more on the binational state idea, see chap. 3 of this book. On the American Zionist response to Ihud, see American Emergency Committee for Zionist Affairs Minutes, Sept. 17, 1942, Neumann Papers, AZEC file, ZAL.

121. Judah Magnes, "Compromise for Palestine," letters to the editors, *Nation*, Dec. 23, 1944, pp. 783–84.

122. Following the publication of a similar letter in the *New York Times* in February 1945, the AZEC decided to send a letter to the newspaper and discussed asking prominent Jews, including Albert Einstein, publicly to oppose Magnes's plan. AZEC Exec. Comm. Minutes, Feb. 19, 1945, Silver Papers, AHSMA.

123. Bernard Joseph, "Dr. Magnes and Palestine," letters to the editors, *Nation*, Feb. 3, 1945, pp. 138–39.

124. Sumner Welles, *The Time for Decision* (New York: Harper Brothers, 1944), pp. 265–66.

125. *Ibid.*, p. 267.

126. "Compromise for Palestine," *New Republic*, Mar. 19, 1945, pp. 373–74. For follow-up, see James Read, "Which Way Zionism," *New Republic*, May 14, 1945, pp. 667–70; "Palestine and the UNO," *New Republic*, Oct. 1, 1945, pp. 420–21.

127. I. F. Stone, "Palestine Run-Around," *Nation*, Mar. 18, 1944, p. 326–28.

128. I. F. Stone, "Jewry in a Blind Alley," *Nation*, Nov. 24, 1945, pp. 543–44.

129. I. F. Stone, "Palestine Pilgrimage," *Nation*, Dec. 8, 1945, pp. 615–17. Stone's adoption of the binational state idea concerned American Zionist leaders who discussd how to respond to his article. AZEC Minutes, Dec. 7, 1945, Silver Papers, AHSMA.

130. Gerold Frank, "Europe's Children," *Nation*, Sept. 23, 1944, pp. 349–50.

131. Stephen Wise, "What the Jews Hope For," *Nation*, part II, Oct. 21, 1944, p. 487.

132. "Nowhere to Lay Their Heads," *New Republic*, Oct. 29, 1945, pp. 556–57.

133. "Blackmail In Palestine," *New Republic*, Nov. 12, 1945, p. 622.

CHAPTER VI

1. *The American Jewish Year Book 5706, 1945–46*, vol. 47 (Philadelphia: Jewish Publication Society of America, 1945), pp. 561–610.

2. AZEC Minutes, #23, Apr. 16, 1945, Silver Papers, AHSMA; Wise to James McDonald, April 9, 1945, James McDonald Papers, General Correspondence File #425 "Wise," Herbert H. Lehman Papers, Columbia University, New York. On the hostility of the State Department, see Peter Grose, *Israel in the Mind of America* (New York: 1983), chaps. 6 and 7; Ezekiel Rabinowitz, *The Jews: Their Dream of Zion and the State Department* (New York: Vantage Press, 1973), chaps. 6, 8, 9.

3. Nahum Goldmann, *The Autobiography of Nahum Goldmann* (New York: Holt, Rinehart & Winston, 1969), pp. 204–5; Emanuel Neumann, *In the Arena* (New York: Herzl Press, 1976), 198–99;

"Interview with Dr. Emanuel Neumann," by Yehuda Bauer, July 21, 1967, Emanuel Neumann Papers, correspondence file: Bauer, ZAL.

4. Melvin Urofsky, *We Are One!—American Jewry and Israel* (Garden City, NY: Anchor Press, 1978), p. 62. On Roosevelt's relationship with Jewish voters, see Grose, *Israel in the Mind of America*, pp. 112–16. On Truman and the Palestine dilemma, see Grose, chap. 8; Zvi Ganin, *Truman, American Jewry and Israel, 1945–1948* (New York: Holmes & Meier, 1979); Herbert Parzen, "President Truman and the Palestine Quandary: His Initial Experience, April–December 1945," *Jewish Social Studies* 35 (Jan. 1973): p. 42–72; Kenneth R. Bain, *The March to Zion* (College Station: Texas A&M Press, 1979); Evan M. Wilson, *Decision on Palestine* (Stanford, CA: Hoover Institution Press, Stanford University, 1979), chaps. 5–9.

5. Neumann, *In the Arena*, p. 201.

6. Chaim Weizmann, *Trial and Error* (New York: Schocken Books, 1949, reprint 1966), pp. 439–40; Urofsky, *We Are One!*, pp. 104–5; AZEC Exec. Comm. Minutes, Sept. 24, 1945, Silver Papers, AHSMA; Wise address, Stenographic Transcript of the forty-eighth annual ZOA Convention, November 16–20, 1945, pp. 131–32, ZAL (hereafter: Transcript of 1945 ZOA Convention); Abba Hillel Silver address, Transcript of 1945 ZOA Convention, pp. 137–59; Michael J. Cohen, *Palestine: Retreat From the Empire* (New York: Holmes & Meier, 1978), pp. 182–86. For an informative study of the Labour party's Palestine policy see Joseph Gorny, *The British Labour Movement and Zionism 1917–1948* (London: F. Cass, 1983), chaps. 10 and 11.

7. Urofsky, *We Are One!*, pp. 88–93; Ganin, *Truman, American Jewry and Israel*, pp. 35–37; Neumann, *In the Arena*, pp. 206–7. For more on the Wise-Silver dispute, see chap. 5 of this book.

8. Neumann, *In the Arena*, pp. 202–10; Melvin Urofsky, *A Voice that Spoke for Justice: A Biography of Stephen S. Wise* (Albany: State University of New York Press, 1982), pp. 341–46; Weizmann, *Trial and Error*, chap. 42; Walter Z. Laqueur, *A History of Zionism* (New York: Holt, Rinehart & Winston, 1972), pp. 574–77.

9. Raul Hilberg, *The Destruction of the European Jews*, 2d ed., vol. 3 (New York: Holmes & Meier, 1985), pp. 1048, 1201–20.

10. "Report of Ben Gurion Speech in Tel Aviv at JNF Exhibition in that City," n.d., Neumann Papers, correspondence file: AZEC sub-file: American Zionist Policy Committee, ZAL; Message from Senator Wagner, Transcript of 1945 ZOA Convention, pp. 5–6.

11. Epstein's address in Transcript of 1945 ZOA Convention, pp. 18–23; also see p. 8.

12. On the pogrom, see Leonard Dinnerstein, *America and the Survivors of the Holocaust* (New York: Columbia University Press, 1982), pp. 107–8. Interested readers might also see Yehuda Bauer, *Flight and Rescue: Brichah* (New York: Random House, 1970); Abram L. Sachar, *The Redemption of the Unwanted: From the Liberation of the Death Camps to the Founding of Israel* (New York: St. Martin's Press, 1983).

13. Hilberg, *Destruction of European Jews*, vol. 3, pp. 1141–53; Dinnerstein, *America and the Survivors of the Holocaust*, p. 278; Grose, *Israel in the Mind of America*, p. 208. Dinnerstein's is the best and most recent study of American immigration policy in the immediate postwar period.

14. Grose, *Israel in the Mind of America*, p. 105; Edward R. Murrow, *In Search of Light: The Broadcasts of Edward R. Murrow 1938–1961*, ed. Edward Bliss, Jr. (New York: Alfred A. Knopf, 1967), pp. 90–95; "Nazi Policy of Organized Murder Blackens Germany for All History," *Newsweek*, April 30, 1945, pp. 56–57; "They Look at Horror," *Newsweek*, May 28, 1945, pp. 34–35; "Letter From Germany," *New Yorker*, May 12, 1945, pp. 50–52; J. F. Krop, "The Jews Under the Nazi Regime," *Annals of the American Academy of Political and Social Science* 245 (May 1946): pp. 28–32; A. Timmenga, "Concentration Camps in the Netherlands," *Annals of the American Academy of Political ad Social Science* 245 (May 1946): 19–27; William D. Camp, "Religion and Horror: The American Religious Press Views Nazi Death Camps and Holocaust Survivors," Ph.D. diss., Carnegie Mellon Uni-

versity, 1981, p. 89; Charles H. Stember et al., *Jews in the Mind of America* (New York: Basic Books, 1966), chap. VI, pp. 144–54.

15. Robert F. Wagner, "Palestine: A World Responsibility," *Nation*, Sept. 15, 1945, pp. 247–49.

16. Transcript of 1945 ZOA Convention, pp. 137–38. Also see Louis Levinthal, "The Case for a Jewish Commonwealth in Palestine," *Annals of the American Academy of Political and Social Science* 240 (July 1945): pp. 89–98.

17. Howard M. Sachar, *A History of Israel* (New York: Alfred A. Knopf, 1976), p. 240.

18. Goldstein address, Transcript of 1945 ZOA Convention, p. 57; Weizmann address, *Ibid.*, p. 406.

19. Rothenberg address, *Ibid.*, p. 701; Weizmann address, *Ibid.*, p. 406.

20. Levinthal, "The Case for a Jewish Commonwealth in Palestine," p. 92. Also see Rabbi Joshua Lieban, Transcript of 1945 ZOA Convention, p. 371.

21. Frankfurter, Remarks phoned from Washington to dinner in honor of Dr. Chaim Weizmann, Nov. 27, 1945, Felix Frankfurter Papers, Box 86, Microfilm Reel #2, Library of Congress, Washington, DC.

22. Gerold Frank, "The Tragedy of the DPs," *New Republic*, April 1, 1946, pp. 436–38. Also see Joseph Dunner, "The Jews That Remain," *Nation*, July 6, 1946, pp. 15–16.

23. Henry Wallace, "The Problem of Palestine," *New Republic*, April 21, 1947, pp. 12–13; Henry Wallace, "In Rome, As In Palestine," *New Republic*, Nov. 17, 1947, pp. 12–13; Henry Wallace, "Palestine, Food and Chiang Kai-Shek," *New Republic*, Nov. 24, 1947, pp. 12–13.

24. Eleanor Roosevelt to James McDonald, April 28, 1946, McDonald Papers, general correspondence file #35 "E. Roosevelt," Herbert H. Lehman Papers, Columbia University, New York; Jason Berger, *A New Deal for the World: Eleanor Roosevelt and American Foreign Policy* (New York: Social Science Monographs, distributed by Columbia University Press, 1981), pp. 88–94; Joseph P. Lash, *Eleanor: The Years Alone* (New York: Norton, 1972), p. 118.

25. "Send Them to Palestine," *New Republic*, January 7, 1946, pp. 7–8. Also see Edward P. Morgan, "They Seek A Promised Land," *Colliers*, May 4, 1946, pp. 83–84.

26. Stone's articles were later published as *Underground to Palestine* (New York: Pantheon, 1946, reprint 1978).

27. Stone, *Underground to Palestine*, p. 47.

28. Freda Kirchwey, "The Palestine Problem and Proposals for Its Solution," special supplement, *Nation*, May 17, 1947, Part II. In particular, see these features of the supplement: "Are There Other Countries to Which Jews Can Migrate?" pp. 589–90; "The Need for Migration," pp. 587–89. On Kirchwey and Zionism, see Sara Alpern, *Freda Kirchwey: A Woman of the Nation* (Cambridge, MA: Harvard University Press, 1987), pp. 195–200.

29. Ganin, *Truman, American Jewry and Israel*, pp. 28–32.

30. Wise to McDonald, July 23, 1945, McDonald Papers, correspondence file #71 "Wise," Herbert H. Lehman Papers, Columbia University, New York. For information on the Harrison mission, see Grose, *Israel in the Mind of America*, pp. 196–201; and Dinnerstein, *America and the Survivors of the Holocaust*, chap. 2.

31. Neumann, *In the Arena*, p. 209.

32. I. F. Stone, "The Plight of the Jews," *Nation*, Oct. 6, 1945, pp. 330–31.

33. Ganin, *Truman, American Jewry and Israel*, p. 33; Herbert Parzen, "President Truman and the Palestine Quandary: His Initial Experience, April–December 1945," *Jewish Social Studies* 35 (Jan. 1973): pp. 42–72; Harry S. Truman, *Memoirs*, vol. 2, *Years of Trial and Hope* (New York: Doubleday, 1956), pp. 132–42. For an example of Zionist criticism of Truman, see Abba Hillel Silver's address, Transcript of 1945 ZOA Convention, p. 139.

34. Philip Bernstein's report, AZEC Exec. Comm. Minutes, #78, April 10, 1946, Silver Papers. While other Zionist spokesmen and leaders around the world enthusiastically seized on the DP issue, Abba Hillel Silver coolly, and perhaps wisely, warned that overemphasizing the refugee issue might sabotage the Zionist crusade. As he had done during the wartime rescue debates, Silver counselled

that the demand for mass Jewish immigration into Palestine should not be made on humanitarian grounds, but should be linked to the basic Jewish right to establish a state in Palestine. To do otherwise, Silver knew, was to invite the British and other opponents of Jewish nationalism to contend that Palestine lacked the natural and economic resources to accommodate the total Jewish refugee population. Silver reminded a ZOA audience that Zionism was not a "refugee movement." Even if the DP problem did not exist, he explained, Zionism would still be a "necessity" because "all the centuries of dispersion and the recurrent incidents of persecution . . . have persuaded the Jewish people that in order . . . to gain a measure of security, it needs a country of its own."

Silver and his principal assistant, Emanuel Neumann, knew that the very success of Zionism within the American Jewish community required a periodic reiteration of the basic tenets of Jewish nationalism. Neumann reminded American Jews that Zionism was a "revolutionary" movement in Jewish life, but that the tens of thousands of men and women who had joined the movement during the war years had been largely motivated by a desire to aid their persecuted brethren in Europe. Unlike the long-time veterans of American Zionism, the newcomers often lacked a coherent and deep sense of Zionist history and philosophy. A dangerous situation was developing, Neumann feared, because "in the past, the newcomer was a minority in our midst; today he is in the majority." Because Zionist organizations operated according to democratic principles, "old timers" had to "indoctrinate" and "convert" new members lest they divert the movement away from its great traditions. Transcript of 1945 ZOA Convention, pp. 146–53, 179–80. Also see Marie Syrkin, "Forum: Should Palestine Become the Jewish Homeland?–Yes: The Zionist Case," *Forum*, June 1946, pp. 912, 914–18.

35. Samir Shamma, "From An Arab Spokesman," *New Republic*, Jan. 28, 1946, p. 128; C. A. Hourani, letter to the editor, *New Republic*, Aug. 5, 1946, p. 143. Also see Kermit Roosevelt, "The Arabs Live There Too," *Harper's*, Oct. 1946, pp. 289–94; W. T. Stace, "The Zionist Illusion," *Atlantic Monthly*, Feb. 1947, pp. 82–86.

36. Samir Shamma, "From An Arab Spokesman," p. 128.

37. Transcript of 1945 ZOA Convention, p. 186. Estimate of Arab lobby budget from I. J. Cakplan, Transcript of 1945 ZOA Convention, p. 335. Arab lobbyists in the United States probably only wished that they were as powerful as Zionists believed. Kahil Totah, of the Institute for Arab-American Affairs, mournfully noted that in the United States, Jewish voters far outnumbered those of Arab descent. Kahil Totah, "Forum: Should Palestine Become the Jewish Homeland?–No: The Arab Case," *Forum*, June 1946, pp. 913, 918–22.

38. J. C. Hurewitz, *The Struggle For Palestine* (New York: Schocken Books, 1950, reprint 1976), chap. 11.

39. Eliahu Ben-Horin, "Have the Arabs A Case?," *Nation*, Oct. 20, 1945, pp. 399–401; AZEC Exec. Comm. Minutes #64, Oct. 29, 1945, Silver Papers, AHSMA; Goldstein address, Transcript of 1945 ZOA Convention, p. 31; Silver address, Transcript of 1945 ZOA Convention, p. 158. Also see *New York Times*, Sept. 25, 1945, p. 13.

40. AZEC Exec. Comm. Minutes, Jan. 30 and April 9, 1946, Silver Papers, AHSMA; Eliahu Epstein, "Middle Eastern Munich," *Nation*, March 9, 1946, pp. 287–88.

41. AZEC Exec. Comm. Minutes, June 11, 1946, Jan. 30, 1946, Apr. 9, 1946, Apr. 10, 1946, July 15, 1946, June 4, 1947, July 14, 1947, Sept. 17, 1947, Silver Papers, AHSMA. Also see the Minutes of Meeting, American Section of the Executive of the Jewish Agency for Palestine, Sept. 17, 1947, Silver Papers, AHSMA; American Christian Palestine Committee, *The Arab War Effort* (New York: American Christian Palestine Committee, 1947). Among the journalists to pick up Epstein's indictment of the Mufti were: I. F. Stone, "The Case of the Mufti," *Nation*, May 4, 1946, pp. 526–27; Del Vayo, "The People's Front," *Nation*, Dec. 7, 1946, p. 646; "The Mufti's Henchmen," *Nation*, May 17, 1947, pp. 561–62; "The Grand Mufti in World War II," *Nation*, supplement, May 17, 1947, pp. 597–99; E. A. Mowrer, "Call the Mufti! Author of Jewish Extermination Goes Free," *Forum*, March 1946, pp. 611–12. Stephen Wise in an October 1946 article for the *New York Times* accused the Mufti

of playing "a prominent role in the extermination of six million of my fellow Jews in Europe." *New York Times*, Oct. 6, 1946, p. 37. Also see *New York Times*, May 12, 1947, p. 3, and May 13, 1947, p. 12.

42. Kahil Totah, "Correspondence," *Nation*, Apr. 6, 1946, pp. 410–11. Also see *New York Times*, Oct. 6, 1946, p. 37, and May 13, 1947, p. 17.

43. Aside from polemical works, the strongest case against the Mufti is made by Joan Peters, *From Time Immemorial: The Origins of the Arab-Jewish Conflict over Palestine* (New York: Harper & Row, 1984), pp. 360, 363, 371–72, 435–42. Peters argues that "there was a symbiotic relationship between Muftism and Nazism" and cites a letter from the Mufti urging that Hungarian Jews not be allowed to enter Palestine, suggesting instead that they be transported to Poland. Raul Hilberg and Lucy S. Dawidowicz, the two historians who have systematically detailed and analyzed the Nazi genocide machine, give the Mufti no credit for inspiring or significantly abetting the German extermination of European Jewry. Both demonstrate that Hitler and Himmler were dedicated to the liquidation of world Jewry and needed little support or encouragement from the Mufti. See Hilberg, *Destruction of European Jews*, especially vol. 2, pp. 789–90, and vol. 3, p. 1071; Lucy Dawidowicz, *The War Against the Jews 1933–1945* (New York: Holt, Rinehart & Winston, 1975). Randolph L. Braham's definitive study of the extermination of Hungarian Jewry makes barely any mention of the Mufti, only noting that out of deference to him the Germans refused to sanction the evacuation of any Hungarian Jews to Palestine. Braham, *The Politics of Genocide*, 2 vols. (New York: Columbia University Press, 1981), pp. 945, 108.

44. AZEC Minutes, March 19, 1945, Silver Papers, AHSMA.

45. Eliahu Ben-Horin, "Have The Arabs A Case?" pp. 399–401. Also see Ben-Horin, "Palestine: Realities and Illusions," *Atlantic Monthly*, April 1947, pp. 72–77; and the comments of Dean Howard LeSourd, director of the American Christian Palestine Committee, Transcript of 1945 ZOA Convention, pp. 319–23.

46. Silver Address to Jewish National Fund Annual Dinner, Oct. 17, 1945, MSS. and Typescripts File #45–15 "JNF," Silver Papers, AHSMA.

47. "Statement by Dr. Silver, . . . at a Press Conference at the Mayflower Hotel," May 5, 1947, Silver Papers, MSS. and Typescripts File #47–4 "AZEC Press Statement," AHSMA. Also see Marie Syrkin, "Forum: Should Palestine Become the Jewish Homeland?"

48. "Statement by Dr. Silver, . . . at Mayflower Hotel," May 5, 1947, Silver Papers, MSS. and Typescripts File #47–4 "AZEC Press Statements," AHSMA.

49. Frank Gervasi, *To Whom Palestine?* (New York: D. Appleton-Century Company, 1946), pp. 2, 3; AZEC Exec. Comm. Minutes, #73, Jan. 30, 1946, Silver Papers, AHSMA.

50. Gervasi, *To Whom Palestine?*, pp. 161–62.

51. Bartley C. Crum, *Behind the Silken Curtain* (New York: Simon and Schuster, 1947), p. 155; McDonald to Joseph Hutcheson, June 26, 1946, McDonald Papers, Correspondence file #187, "Hutcheson," Herbert Lehman Library, Columbia University, New York. Reinhold Niebuhr, a long-time friend of the American Zionist movement, also condemned the alliance between British officials and "Arab feudalism." See Niebuhr, "Palestine: British-American Dilemma," *Nation*, Aug. 31, 1946, pp. 238–39.

52. George H. Gallup, *The Gallup Poll: Public Opinion 1935–1971* (New York: Random House, 1972), p. 554; Stember, *Jews in the Mind of America*, p. 175.

53. Freda Kirchwey, "British Policy Breaks Down," *Nation*, Nov. 24, 1945, pp. 540–41; Kirchwey, "Will the Arabs Revolt?." *Nation*, July 13, 1946, pp. 36–39; I. F. Stone, "Middle Eastern Forces," *Nation*, Dec. 29, 1945, pp. 726–28; Stone, "The Plight of the Jews," *Nation*, Oct. 6, 1945, pp. 330–31; Stone, "Jewry in a Blind Alley," *Nation*, Nov. 24, 1945, pp. 543–44; Also see Stone, "Palestine Pilgrimage," *Nation*, Dec. 8, 1945, pp. 615–17; Max Lerner and Martin Kingsley, "Sins of American Liberals," *Nation*, March 2, 1946, pp. 251–53; and "Introduction," *Nation*, special Palestine supplement, May 17, 1947, pp. 585–86.

54. Eliahu Ben-Horin, "Palestine and Grand Strategy," *Nation*, Oct. 27, 1945, pp. 424–25. The

editorial staff of the *Nation* also came to link Zionism with the American struggle against the Soviet Union. In May 1947, an editorial warned/that if Britain allowed the Arabs to create a state in Palestine that "a depressed economy would offer to the adherents of the Communist system . . . to stir up the miserable population against its rulers." "A Working Plan for Palestine," *Nation*, May 10, 1947, pp. 533–34. Also see Tulin to Silver, Jan. 17, 1946, Tulin Papers, file #35, "Corresp.: A. H. Silver," ZAL.

55. AZEC Exec. Comm. Minutes, #66, Nov. 14, 1945, and #70, Dec. 10, 1945, Silver Papers, AHSMA.

56. *Ibid.*, #66, Nov. 14, 1945, and #70, Dec. 10, 1945. For more on the Zionist reaction to the Anglo-American committee, see Neumann, *In the Arena*, chapter 18; Urofsky, *A Voice That Spoke for Justice*, pp. 350–51; David Horowitz, *State in the Making*, trans. Julian Metzger (New York: Alfred A. Knopf, 1953), pp. 28–35; Urofsky, *We Are One!*, p. 107.

57. Memo, Tulin to Silver, Jan. 17, 1946, Tulin Papers, file #35, "Corresp.: A. H. Silver," ZAL; Neumann, *In the Arena*, p. 216; Ganin, *Truman, American Jewry and Israel*, pp. 55–56. For an interesting account of the committee's activities, see Horowitz, *State in the Making*, chaps. 6, 7, 8.

58. On the Anglo-American Committee of Inquiry, see Ganin, *Truman, American Jewry and Israel*, chap. 4; Dinnerstein, *American Survivors of the Holocaust*, chap. 3; Grose, *Israel in the Mind of America*, pp. 202–5; Michael J. Cohen, *Palestine and the Great Powers* (Princeton: Princeton University Press, 1982), chap. 5; Bain, *March to Zion*, chap. 4; Amikam Nachmani, *Great Power Discord in Palestine: The Anglo-American Committee of Inquiry into the Problems of European Jewry and Palestine, 1945–1946* (London: F. Cass, 1987).

59. AZEC Minutes, #30, May 9, 1946, Silver Papers, AHSMA.

60. *Ibid.*, #30, May 9, 1946.

61. AZEC Exec. Comm. Minutes, #86, May 13, 1946, Silver Papers, AHSMA; "Statement Adopted by the Executive Committee of the American Jewish Conference," May 1, 1946, Robert Szold Papers, file VIII/3, ZAL.

62. Sachar, *History of Israel*, pp. 263–64; Hurewitz, *Struggle for Palestine*, pp. 247–50; Horowitz, *State in the Making*, p. 94; Gorny, *British Labour Movement and Zionism*, pp. 211–18; M. Cohen, *Palestine and the Great Powers*, pp. 109–15.

63. Sachar, *History of Israel*, pp. 267–70; Yehuda Slutsky and Yehuda Bauer, "Illegal Immigration and the Berichah," in *Immigration and Settlement* (Jerusalem: Keter Publishing House, Israel Pocket Library, 1973), pp. 35–49; Sachar, *Redemption of the Unwanted*, chap. 7. The most comprehensive study of illegal immigration is Bauer, *Flight and Rescue: Brichah*.

64. Sachar, *History of Israel*, pp. 264–65; Horowitz, *State in the Making*, p. 102; M. Cohen, *Palestine and the Great Powers*, p. 83.

65. Hurewitz, *Struggle for Palestine*, p. 254; Sachar, *History of Israel*, p. 265; Horowitz, *State in the Making*, pp. 103–7; M. Cohen, *Palestine and the Great Powers*, pp. 81–90. In response to the British arrest of Jewish Agency leaders, the AZEC initiated a national protest that included the picketing of British consulates and the staging of a large public demonstration in New York's Madison Square Park on July 2. AZEC Exec. Comm. Minutes, #91, June 29, 1946, and #92, July 1, 1946, Silver Papers, AHSMA.

66. Goldmann, *Autobiography*, pp. 225–41; AZEC Minutes, #30, May 9, 1946, Silver Papers, AHSMA.

67. Memo, Abraham Tulin to Silver, Jan. 17, 1946, Tulin Papers, file #35, "Corresp.: A. H. Silver," ZAL; AZEC Minutes, #30, May 9, 1946, Silver Papers, AHSMA; AZEC Exec. Comm. Minutes, #86, May 13, 1946, Silver Papers, AHSMA.

68. *New York Times*, July 11, 1946, p. 7; Ganin, *Truman, American Jewry and Israel*, p. 84.

69. AZEC Exec. Comm. Minutes, #95, July 25, 1946, Silver Papers, AHSMA; Ganin, *Truman, American Jewry and Israel*, chap. V; M. Cohen, *Palestine and the Great Powers*, chap. 6.

70. Goldmann, *Autobiography*, pp. 232–33; Ganin, *Truman, American Jewry and Israel*, pp. 88–

89; Horowitz, *State in the Making*, p. 117; Urofsky, *We Are One!*, p. 133; M. Cohen, *Palestine and the Great Powers*, pp. 141–47.

71. AZEC Exec. Comm. Minutes, #98, Aug. 1, 1946, and #99, Aug. 7, 1946, Silver Papers, AHSMA.

72. Ganin, *Truman, American Jewry and Israel*, pp. 90–94; M. Cohen, *Palestine and the Great Powers*, pp. 147–51.

73. AZEC Exec. Comm. Minutes, #101, Sept. 10, 1946, Silver Papers, AHSMA; Ganin, *Truman, American Jewry and Israel*, pp. 113–14.

74. Goldmann, *Autobiography*, p. 239; Weizmann, *Trial and Error*; Norman Rose, *Chaim Weizmann: A Biography* (New York: Elisabeth Sifton Books-Viking, 1986), pp. 418–21.

75. *New York Times*, Dec. 11, 1946, p. 25.

76. *Ibid.*, Dec. 10, 1946, p. 14; Neumann, *In the Arena*, pp. 231–32.

77. Urofsky, *A Voice That Spoke for Justice*, pp. 353–55. Silver went so far as to imply that Wise's loyalty to the Democratic party prevented him from criticizing Franklin Roosevelt for doing little to rescue the Jews of Europe, thereby contributing to their liquidation. See Silver's address to the World Zionist Congress, reprinted in Silver, *Vision and Victory* (New York: Zionist Organization of America, 1949), pp. 106–14. Also see Joseph Hutcheson to James McDonald, Dec. 18, 1946, McDonald Papers, General Correspondence file #352, "Hutcheson," Herbert H. Lehman Papers, Columbia University, New York.

78. Neumann, *In the Arena*, p. 228; *New York Times*, Dec. 12, 1946, p. 14.

79. *New York Times*, Dec. 11, 1946, p. 25.

80. The speech is reprinted as "The Vital Role of Tactics," in Silver, *Vision and Victory*, pp. 115–23.

81. *New York Times*, Dec. 25, 1946, p. 6, and Jan. 4, 1947, p. 17. On Basel Congress, see M. Cohen, *Palestine and the Great Powers*, pp. 177–83.

82. Hurewitz, *Struggle for Palestine*, chaps. 20, 21.

83. Arthur Koestler, "The Great Dilemma That is Palestine," *New York Times Magazine*, Sept. 1, 1946, pp. 5, 51–52; editorial, *Nation*, Sept. 14, 1946, pp. 281–82; "Peace for Palestine?," *Nation*, Jan. 11, 1947, p. 33; Joel Carmichael, "Crisis of Zionism," *Nation*, Jan. 25, 1947, pp. 90–92; "Some Proposed Solutions," *Nation*, May 17, 1947, special supplement, pp. 610–12; Henry Wallace, "Palestine, Food and Chiang Kai-Shek," *New Republic*, Nov. 24, 1947, pp. 12–13.

84. For an interesting insiders account of the U.N. drama, see Horowitz, *State in the Making*, pp. 151–248.

85. Grose, *Israel in the Mind of America*, pp. 233–36. The representative of Australia abstained.

86. Silver's address is reprinted as "We Shall Make This Sacrifice," in Silver, *Vision and Victory*, pp. 135–49; and in *Vital Speeches of the Day*, Oct. 15, 1947, pp. 10–15.

87. Grose, *Israel in the Mind of America*, pp. 243–45.

BIBLIOGRAPHY

MANUSCRIPT SOURCES

ZIONIST ORGANIZATION OF AMERICA PAPERS (including stenographic transcripts of annual ZOA conventions): Zionist Archives and Library, New York City.

HADASSAH NATIONAL BOARD MINUTES: Zionist Archives and Library, New York City.

HADASSAH CONVENTION MATERIAL: Hadassah National Office, New York City.

LOUIS BRANDEIS RECORDS (MICROFILM): Zionist Archives and Library, New York City.

FELIX FRANKFURTER PAPERS ON ZIONISM AND PALESTINE (MICROFILM): Library of Congress.

STEPHEN S. WISE PAPERS: American Jewish Historical Society, Waltham, MA.

ABBA HILLEL SILVER PAPERS: Abba Hillel Silver Memorial Archives, The Temple, Cleveland, OH.

EMANUEL NEUMANN PAPERS: At the time of my research these papers were located in Mr. Neumann's office. They are now at the Zionist Archives and Library, New York City.

ABRAHAM TULIN PAPERS: Zionist Archives and Library, New York City.

ROBERT SZOLD PAPERS: Zionist Archives and Library, New York City.

JAMES G. McDONALD PAPERS: The Herbert H. Lehman Papers, Columbia University, New York City.

AMERICAN EMERGENCY COMMITTEE FOR ZIONIST AFFAIRS (AECZA) MINUTES: Zionist Archives and Library, New York City; and Silver Papers, Abba Hillel Silver Memorial Archives, The Temple, Cleveland, OH.

AMERICAN ZIONIST EMERGENCY COUNCIL (AZEC) MINUTES: Zionist Archives and Library, New York City; and Silver Papers, Abba Hillel Silver Memorial Archives, The Temple, Cleveland, OH.

MINUTES OF THE AMERICAN SECTION OF THE ZIONIST EXECUTIVE: Silver Papers, Abba Hillel Silver Memorial Archives, The Temple, Cleveland, OH.

BERGSON GROUP PAPERS (including Papers of the Hebrew Committee of National Liberation, Emergency Committee to Save the Jewish People of Europe, American League for a Free Palestine, Committee for a Jewish Army): Jabotinsky Institute, Tel Aviv. Papers also available at Yale University, New Haven, CT, and on microfilm produced by Yale University.

NEWSPAPERS AND PERIODICALS

American Jewish Yearbook
Annals of the American Academy of Political and Social Science
Answer Magazine
The Atlantic Monthly
Christian Century

Bibliography

Christianity and Crisis
Congress Weekly
Foreign Affairs
Forum Magazine
Hadassah Newsletter
Harper's
Jewish Frontier
Jewish Outlook
The Nation
New Palestine
The New Republic
Newsweek
The New Yorker
The New York Times
The Palestine Year Book
Youth and Nation

PUBLISHED PRIMARY SOURCES

American Christian Palestine Committee. *The Arab War Effort: A Documented Account.* New York: American Christian Palestine Committee, 1947.

American Jewish Conference. *A Survey of Facts and Opinions on Problems of Post-War Jewry in Europe and Palestine. Committee on Preliminary Studies—Authorized by the Executive Committee for the Organization of the American Jewish Conference, N.Y., Aug. 1943.* New York: American Jewish Conference, 1943.

———. *Report of the Interim Committee and the Commission on Rescue, Commission on Palestine, Commission on Post-War to the Delegates of the American Jewish Conference.* New York: American Jewish Conference, 1944.

Ben-Ami, Yitshaq. *Years of Wrath, Days of Glory: Memoirs from the Irgun.* New York: R. R. Speller, 1982.

Crossman, Richard H. S. *Palestine Mission.* New York: Harper & Row, 1947.

Crum, Bartley C. *Behind the Silken Curtain.* New York: Simon and Schuster, 1947.

Feuer, Leon. *Why A Jewish State.* New York: R. R. Smith, 1942.

Fink, Reuben, ed. *America and Palestine: The Attitude of Official America and of the American People Toward the Rebuilding of Palestine as a Free and Democratic Jewish Commonwealth.* New York: American Zionist Emergency Council, 1944.

Gallup, George H. *The Gallup Poll: Public Opinion 1935–1971.* New York: Random House, 1972.

Gervasi, Frank. *To Whom Palestine?* New York: D. Appleton-Century Company, 1946.

Goldmann, Nahum. *The Autobiography of Nahum Goldmann.* New York: Holt, Rinehart & Winston, 1969.

Goren, Arthur A., ed. *Dissenter in Zion: From the Writings of Judah L. Magnes.* Cambridge, MA: Harvard University Press, 1982.

Haber, Julius. *The Odyssey of an American Zionist.* New York: Twayne Publishers, 1956.

Hecht, Ben. *A Child of the Century.* New York: Simon and Schuster, 1954.

Hertzberg, Arthur, ed. *The Zionist Idea.* New York: Atheneum, 1959, reprint 1973.

Hirschmann, Ira A. *Life Line to a Promised Land.* New York: Jewish Book Guild, 1946.

Horowitz, David. *State in the Making.* Translated by Julian Metzger. New York: Alfred Knopf, 1953.

Ickes, Harold L. *The Secret Diary of Harold L. Ickes.* Vol. II, *The Inside Struggle 1936–1939.* New York: Macmillan Co., 1954.

Israel, Fred L., ed. *The War Diary of Breckinridge Long: Selections from the Years 1939–1944.* Lincoln: University of Nebraska Press, 1966.

Jabotinsky, Vladimir. *The War and the Jew.* New York: Dial Press, 1942.

Karph, Maurice. *Jewish Community Organization in the United States.* New York: Bloch Publishing Co., 1938.

Kohanski, Alexander S., ed. *The American Jewish Conference: Its Organization and Proceedings of the First Session, August 29 to September 2, 1943.* New York: American Jewish Conference, 1944.

Lash, Joseph P., ed. *From the Diaries of Felix Frankfurter.* New York: Norton, 1975.

Lipsky, Louis. *A Gallery of Zionist Profiles.* New York: Farrar, Strauss and Cudahy, 1956.

————. *Memoirs in Profile.* Philadelphia: Jewish Publication Society of America, 1975.

Litvinoff, Barnett, Meyer Weisgal, Gedalia Yogev, and Leonard Stein, general editors. *The Letters and Papers of Chaim Weizmann.* Series A. 23 vols. London: Oxford University Press (vols. I–XI); New Brunswick, NJ: Transaction Books, Rutgers University (vols. XII–XXIII), 1968–80.

Lowdermilk, Walter C. *Palestine: Land of Promise.* New York: Harper & Brothers, 1944.

McDonald, James G. *My Mission In Israel 1948–1951.* New York: Simon and Schuster, 1951.

Mead, Margaret. *And Keep Your Powder Dry.* New York: W. Morrow, 1942.

Murrow, Edward R. *In Search of Light: The Broadcasts of Edward R. Murrow 1938–1961.* Edited by Edward Bliss, Jr. New York: Alfred A. Knopf, 1967.

Neumann, Emanuel. *In the Arena.* New York: Herzl Press, 1976.

Nicholas, H. G., ed. *Washington Despatches 1941–1945: Weekly Political Reports from the British Embassy.* London: Weidenfeld & Nicholson, 1981.

Palestine Royal Commission Report. London: 1937.

Proskauer, Joseph M. *A Segment of My Time.* New York: Farrar, Strauss, 1950.

Robinson, Jacob. *Palestine and the United Nations: Prelude to Solution.* Washington, DC: Public Affairs Press, 1947.

Rosenblatt, Bernard A. *Two Generations of Zionism: Historical Recollections of an American Zionist.* New York: Shengold Publishers, 1967.

Silver, Abba Hillel. *The World Crisis and Jewish Survival.* New York: R. R. Smith, 1941.

————. *Vision and Victory: A Collection of Addresses by Dr. Abba Hillel Silver 1942–1948.* New York: Zionist Organization of America, 1949.

Stone, I. F. *Underground to Palestine.* New York: Pantheon, 1946, reprint 1978.

Syrkin, Marie, ed. *Hayim Greenberg Anthology.* Detroit: Wayne State University Press, 1968.

Truman, Harry S. *Memoirs by Harry S. Truman.* Vol. 2, *Years of Trial and Hope.* New York: Doubleday, 1956.

U. S. Congress. House. Committee on Foreign Affairs. *The Jewish National Home In Palestine—Hearings on H. R. 418 and 419,* 78th Cong. 2d sess., 1944. Washington: GPO, 1944.

————. Committee on International Relations. *Problems of World War II and Its Aftermath.* Part 2. *The Palestine Question. Problems of Postwar Europe Selected Executive Session Hearings of the Committee, 1943–50.* Vol. II. Washington: GPO, 1976.

U. S. Department of Labor. *Annual Report of the Commissioner General of Immigration—1932.* Washington: GPO, 1932.

Urofsky, Melvin I., and David W. Levy, eds. *Letters of Louis D. Brandeis.* 5 vols. Albany: State University of New York Press, 1971.

Voss, Carl Herman, ed. *Stephen S. Wise: Servant of the People.* Philadelphia: Jewish Publication Society of America, 1964 (selected letters).

Weisgal, Meyer. *Meyer Weisgal . . . So Far: An Autobiography.* New York: Random House, 1971.

Weizmann, Chaim. *Trial and Error.* New York: Schocken Books, 1949, reprint 1966.

Welles, Sumner. *The Time for Decision.* New York: Harper & Brothers, 1944.

Wilkie, Wendell L. *One World.* New York: Simon and Schuster, 1943.

Bibliography

Wise, Stephen S. *As I See It*. New York: Jewish Opinion Publishing Corp., 1944.

————. *Challenging Years: The Autobiography of Stephen S. Wise*. New York: Putnam's Sons, 1949.

World Jewish Congress. *Memorandum on Post-War Relief and Rehabilitation of European Jewry: Submitted to the Councils of the UNRRA, Atlantic City, N. J*. New York: World Jewish Congress, 1943.

SECONDARY SOURCES: BOOKS

Abu-Lughod, Ibrahim, ed. *The Transformation of Palestine: Essays on the Origin and Development of the Arab-Israeli Conflict*. Evanston, IL: Northwestern University Press, 1971.

Agar, Herbert. *The Saving Remnant: An Account of Jewish Survival*. New York: Viking Press, 1960.

Alpern, Sara. *Freda Kirchwey: A Woman of the Nation*. Cambridge, MA: Harvard University Press, 1987.

Antonius, George. *The Arab Awakening*. Philadelphia: J. B. Lippincott, 1939.

Avineri, Shlomo. *The Making of Modern Zionism: The Intellectual Origins of the Jewish State*. New York: Basic Books, 1981.

Avneri, Aryeh L. *The Claim of Dispossession: Jewish Land Settlement and the Arabs, 1878–1948*. New Brunswick, NJ: Transaction Books, 1984.

Avnery, Uri. *Israel Without Zionism: A Plea for Peace in the Middle East*. New York: Macmillan, 1968.

Bailey, Thomas A. *The Man in the Street: The Impact of American Public Opinion on Foreign Policy*. New York: Macmillan Co., 1948.

Bain, Kenneth. *The March to Zion: United States Policy and the Founding of Israel*. College Station: Texas A & M Press, 1979.

Baron, Salo W. *Steeled in Adversity: Essays and Addresses on American Jewish Life*. Philadelphia: Jewish Publication Society of America, 1971.

Bar-Zohar, Michael. *Ben-Gurion the Armed Prophet*. Englewood Cliffs, NJ: Prentice-Hall, 1968.

————. *Ben-Gurion: A Biography*. Translated by Peretz Kidron. New York: Delacorte Press, 1978.

Bauer, Yehuda. *From Diplomacy to Resistance: A History of Jewish Palestine 1930–1945*. Philadelphia: Jewish Publication Society of America, 1970.

————. *Flight and Rescue: Brichah*. New York: Random House, 1970.

————. *My Brother's Keeper: A History of the Joint Distribution Committee*. Philadelphia: Jewish Publication Society of America, 1974.

————. *The Holocaust in Historical Perspective*. Seattle: University of Washington Press, 1978.

————. *The Jewish Emergence from Powerlessness*. Toronto: University of Toronto Press, 1979.

————. *American Jewry and the Holocaust: The American Jewish Joint Distribution Committee, 1939–1945*. Detroit: Wayne State University Press, 1981.

————. *A History of the Holocaust*. New York: F. Watts, 1982.

Bein, Alex. *Theodor Herzl*. New York: 1941, reprint 1970.

Bell, J. Boyer. *Terror out of Zion: Irgun Zvai Leumi, LEHI, and the Palestine Underground 1929–1949*. New York: St. Martin's Press, 1977.

Belth, Nathan C. *A Promise to Keep: A Narrative of the American Encounter with Anti-Semitism*. New York: Times Books, 1979.

Berger, Jason. *A New Deal for the World: Eleanor Roosevelt and American Foreign Policy*. New York: Social Science Monographs, distributed by Columbia University Press, 1981.

Bethell, Nicholas. *The Palestine Triangle: The Struggle for the Holy Land, 1935–48*. New York: Putnam, 1979.

Black, Edwin. *The Transfer Agreement: The Untold Story of the Secret Agreement Between the Third Reich and Jewish Palestine*. New York: Macmillan, 1984.

Braham, Randolph L. *Eichman and the Destruction of Hungarian Jewry*. New York: World Federation of Hungarian Jewry, distributed by Twayne Publishers, 1961.

―――. *The Politics of Genocide: The Holocaust in Hungary.* 2 vols. New York: Columbia University Press, 1981.

Brenner, Lenni. *Zionism in the Age of the Dictators.* London: Croom Helm, 1983.

―――. *Iron Wall: Zionist Revisionism from Jabotinsky to Shamir.* London: Zed Books 1984.

Brinkley, Alan. *Voices of Protest: Huey Long, Father Coughlin and the Great Depression.* New York: Alfred A. Knopf, 1982.

Caplan, Neil. *Futile Diplomacy: Early Arab-Zionist Negotiation Attempts 1913–1931.* London: F. Cass, 1983.

Cohen, Michael J. *Palestine: Retreat from the Mandate–The Making of British Policy 1936–1945.* New York: Holmes & Meier, 1978.

―――. *Palestine and the Great Powers 1945–1948.* Princeton, NJ: Princeton University Press, 1982.

Cohen, Naomi W. *Not Free to Desist: The American Jewish Committee 1906–1966.* Philadelphia: Jewish Publication Society of America, 1972.

―――. *American Jews and the Zionist Idea.* New York: Ktav Publishing House, 1975.

Dallek, Robert. *Franklin D. Roosevelt and American Foreign Policy, 1932–1945.* New York: Oxford University Press, 1979.

Dash, Joan. *Summoned to Jerusalem: The Life of Henrietta Szold.* New York: Harper and Row, 1979.

Dawidowicz, Lucy S. *On Equal Terms: Jews in America 1881–1981.* New York: Holt, Rinehart & Winston, 1982.

―――. *The War Against The Jews 1933–1945.* New York: Holt, Rinehart & Winston, 1975.

Dinnerstein, Leonard. *America and the Survivors of the Holocaust.* New York: Columbia University Press, 1982.

Ekrich, Arthur A. *Ideologies and Utopias.* Chicago: Quadrangle Books, 1969.

Elon, Amos. *The Israelis: Founders and Sons.* New York: Holt, Rinehart & Winston, 1971.

―――. *Herzl.* New York: Holt, Rinehart & Winston, 1975.

Feingold, Henry L. *The Politics of Rescue: The Roosevelt Administration and the Holocaust 1938–1945.* New Brunswick, NJ: Rutgers University Press, 1970.

―――. *Zion in America: The Jewish Experience from Colonial Times to the Present.* New York: Hippocrene Books, 1974.

―――. *A Midrash on American Jewish History.* Albany: State University of New York Press, 1982.

Feinstein, Marnin. *American Zionism 1887–1904.* New York: Herzl Press, 1965.

Feis, Herbert. *The Birth of Israeli: The Tousled Diplomatic Bed.* New York: Norton, 1969.

Feldblum, Esther Yolles. *The American Catholic Press and the Jewish State, 1917–1959.* New York: Ktav Publishing House, 1977.

Fineman, Irving. *Woman of Valor: The Life of Henrietta Szold 1860–1945.* New York: Simon and Schuster, 1961.

Finger, Seymour Maxwell. *American Jewry During the Holocaust: A Report by the Research Director, His Staff and Independent Research Scholars Retained by the Director for the American Jewish Commission on the Holocaust.* New York: Holmes & Meier, 1984.

Fishman, Hertzel. *American Protestantism and a Jewish State.* Detroit: Wayne State University Press, 1973.

Fox, Richard W. *Reinhold Niebuhr: A Biography.* New York: Pantheon Books, 1985.

Friedman, Saul S. *No Haven for the Oppressed: United States Policy Toward Jewish Refugees 1938–1945.* Detroit: Wayne State University Press, 1973.

Fuchs, Larence H. *The Political Behavior of American Jews.* Glencoe, IL: Free Press, 1956.

Gal, Allon. *Brandeis of Boston.* Cambridge, MA: Harvard University Press, 1980.

Ganin, Zvi. *Truman, American Jewry and Israel, 1945–1948.* New York: Holmes & Meier, 1979.

Gervasi, Frank. *The Case for Israel.* New York: Viking Press, 1967.

Gilbert, Martin. *Exile and Return: The Struggle for a Jewish Homeland.* Philadelphia: Lippincott, 1978.

Bibliography

Glick, Edward B. *The Triangular Connection: America, Israel and American Jews.* London: George Allen & Unwin, 1982.

Goldin, Milton. *Why They Give: American Jews and Their Philanthropies.* New York: Macmillan, 1976.

Gorny, Joseph. *The British Labour Movement and Zionism 1917–1948.* London: Frank Cass, 1983.

Gottlieb, Moshe R. *American Anti-Nazi Resistance 1933–1941: An Historical Analysis.* New York: Ktav Publishing House, 1982.

Greenstein, Howard R. *Turning Point: Zionism and Reform Judaism.* Chico, CA: Scholars Press, 1981.

Grose, Peter. *Israel in the Mind of America.* New York: Alfred A. Knopf, 1983.

Haim, Yehoyada. *Abandonment of Illusions—Zionist Political Attitudes Toward Palestinian Nationalism, 1936–1939.* Boulder, CO: Westview Press, 1983.

Halperin, Samuel. *The Political World of American Zionism.* Detroit: Wayne State University Press, 1961.

Halpern, Ben. *The American Jew: A Zionist Analysis.* New York: Theodor Herzl Foundation, 1956.

———. *The Idea of the Jewish State.* 2d ed. Cambridge, MA: Harvard University Press, 1969.

———. *A Clash of Heroes: Brandeis, Weizmann and American Zionism.* New York: Oxford University Press, 1987.

Hassan, Sana, and Amos Elon. *Between Enemies: An Arab Israeli Dialogue.* New York: Random House, 1974.

Hattis, Susan Lee. *The Bi-National Idea in Palestine During Mandatory Times.* Haifa: Shikmona, 1970.

Hecht, Ben. *Perfidy.* New York: Messner, 1961.

Heller, Joseph. *The Zionist Idea.* New York: Schocken Books, 1949.

Hilberg, Raul. *The Destruction of the European Jews.* 2d ed., 3 vols. New York: Holmes & Meier, 1985.

Hirsch, H. N. *The Enigma of Felix Frankfurter.* New York: Basic Books, 1981.

Hurewitz, Jacob C. *The Struggle for Palestine.* New York: Schocken Books, 1950, reprint 1976.

Huthmacher, J. Joseph. *Senator Robert F. Wagner and the Rise of Urban Liberalism.* New York: Atheneum, 1968.

Jonas, Manfred. *Isolationism in America 1935–1941.* Ithaca, NY: Cornell University Press, 1966.

Karp, Abraham J. *To Give Life: The UJA In the Shaping of the American Jewish Community.* New York: Schocken Books, 1981.

Katz, Shmuel (Samuel). *Days of Fire: The Secret History of the Irgun Zvai Leumi and the Making of Israel.* Garden City, NY: Doubleday, 1968.

Kedourie, Elie, and Sylvia G. Haim, eds. *Palestine and Israel in the 19th and 20th Centuries.* London & Totowa, NJ: F. Cass, 1982.

———. *Zionism and Arabism in Palestine and Israel.* London & Totowa, NJ: F. Cass, 1982.

Kimmerling, Baruch. *Zionism and Economy.* Cambridge, Eng.: Shenkman Publishing Co., 1983.

Knee, Stuart E. *The Concept of Zionist Dissent in the American Mind.* New York: R. Speller, 1979.

Laqueur, Walter Z. *A History of Zionism.* New York: Holt, Rinehart & Winston, 1972.

———. *The Terrible Secret.* Boston: Little, Brown, 1982.

Lash, Joseph P. *Eleanor: The Years Alone.* New York: Norton, 1972.

Learsi, Rufus. *The Jews in America: A History.* New York: Ktav Publishing House, 1954, reprint 1972.

Lesch, Ann Mosley. *Arab Politics in Palestine 1917–1939: The Frustration of a Nationalist Movement.* Ithaca, NY: Cornell University Press, 1979.

Levin, Marlin. *Balm in Gilead: The Story of Hadassah.* New York: Schocken Books, 1973.

Mason, Alpheus T. *Brandeis: A Free Man's Life.* New York: Viking Press, 1946.

Meyer, Michael A. *Response to Modernity: A History of the Reform Movement in Judaism.* New York: Oxford University Press, 1988.

Morse, Arthur. *While Six Million Died: A Chronicle of American Apathy.* New York: Random House, 1968.

Monroe, Elizabeth. *Britain's Moment in the Middle East 1914–1956.* Baltimore: Johns Hopkins University Press, 1963.

Murphy, Bruce A. *The Brandeis/Frankfurter Connection: The Secret Political Activities of Two Supreme Court Justices.* New York: Oxford University Press, 1982.

Nachmani, Amikam. *Great Power Discord in Palestine: The Anglo-American Committee of Inquiry into the Problems of European Jewry and Palestine, 1945–1946.* London: F. Cass, 1987.

Neuringer, Sheldon M. *American Jewry and United States Immigration Policy, 1881–1953.* New York: Arno Press, 1971, reprint 1980.

Neusner, Jacob. *Stranger at Home: "The Holocaust," Zionism and American Judaism.* Chicago: University of Chicago Press, 1981.

Parrish, Michael E. *Felix Frankfurter and His Times: The Reform Years.* New York: Free Press, 1982.

Patterson, James T. *Mr. Republican: A Biography of Robert A. Taft.* Boston: Houghton Mifflin, 1972.

Pells, Richard H. *The Liberal Mind in a Conservative Age: American Intellectuals in the 1940s & 1950s.* New York: Harper & Row, 1985.

————. *Radical Visions and American Dreams: Culture and Social Thought in the Depression Years.* New York: Harper & Row, 1973.

Penkower, Monty N. *The Jews Were Expendable: Free World Diplomacy and the Holocaust.* Urbana: University of Illinois Press, 1983.

Peters, Joan. *From Time Immemorial: The Origins of the Arab-Jewish Conflict over Palestine.* New York: Harper & Row, 1984.

Polish, David. *Renew Our Days: The Zionist Issue in Reform Judasim.* Jerusalem: World Zionist Organization, 1976.

Porath, Y. *The Emergence of the Palestinian-Arab National Movement 1918–1929.* London: Frank Cass, 1974.

————. *The Palestinian Arab National Movement 1929–1939: From Riots to Rebellion.* London: Frank Cass, 1977.

Rabinowitz, Ezekiel. *Justice Louis Brandeis: The Zionist Chapter of His Life.* New York: Philosophical Library, 1968.

————. *The Jews: Their Dream of Zion and the State Department.* New York: Vantage Press, 1973.

Raphael, Marc L. *A History of the United Jewish Appeal 1939–1982.* New York: 1982.

Rose, Norman A. *The Gentile Zionists: A Study in Anglo-Zionist Diplomacy, 1929–1939.* London: F. Cass, 1973.

————. *Chaim Weizmann: A Biography.* New York: Viking, 1986.

Rubinstein, Amnon. *The Zionist Dream Revisited: From Herzl to Gush Emunim and Back.* New York: Schocken Books, 1984.

Sachar, Abram L. *The Redemption of the Unwanted: From the Liberation of the Death Camps to the Founding of Israel.* New York: St. Martin's Press, 1983.

Sachar, Howard. *A History of Israel: From the Rise of Zionism to Our Time.* New York: Alfred A. Knopf, 1976.

Safran, Nadav. *The U.S. and Israel.* Cambridge, MA: Harvard University Press, 1963.

Said, Edward W. *The Question of Palestine.* New York: Vintage, 1979.

Sanders, Marion K. *Dorothy Thompson—A Legend in Her Time.* Boston: Houghton Mifflin, 1973.

Schechtman, Joseph B. *The Mufti and the Fuehrer: The Rise and Fall of Haj Amin el-Husseini.* New York: T. Yoseloff, 1965.

————. *The United States and the Jewish State Movement: The Crucial Decade 1939–1949.* New York: T. Yoseloff, 1966.

Schwarz, Leo W. *The Redeemers: A Saga of the Years 1945–1952.* New York: Farrar, Strauss and Young, 1953.

Shapira, Anita. *Berl, The Biography of a Socialist Zionist: Berl Katznelson, 1887–1944.* New York: Cambridge University Press, 1984.

223

Bibliography

Shapiro, Yonathan. *Leadership of the American Zionist Organization 1897–1930.* Urbana: University of Illinois Press, 1971.

Sherman, A. J. *Island Refuge: Britain and Refugees from the Third Reich 1933–1939.* London: Elek, 1973.

Sherman, C. Bezalel. *Labor Zionism in America.* New York: Labor Zionist Organization of America–Poale Zion, 1957.

Silver, Daniel J., ed. *In the Time of the Harvest: Essays in Honor of Abba Hillel Silver.* New York: Macmillan, 1963.

Silverberg, Robert. *If I Forget Thee O Jerusalem: American Jews and the State of Israel.* New York: Morrow, 1970.

Snetsinger, John. *Truman, the Jewish Vote and the Creation of Israel.* Stanford, CA: Hoover Institution Press, 1974.

Stember, Charles H., et al. *Jews in the Mind of America.* New York: Basic Books, 1966.

Stevens, Richard. *American Zionism and U.S. Foreign Policy 1942–1947.* Beirut and New York: Institute for Palestine Studies, 1962, reprint 1970.

Strong, Donald S. *Organized Anti-Semitism in America: The Rise of Group Prejudice During the Decade 1930–1940.* Washington, DC: American Council on Public Affairs, 1941.

Sykes, Christopher. *Crossroads to Israel.* Bloomington: Indiana University Press, 1965, reprint 1973.

Tartakower, Arieh, and Kurt R. Grossman. *The Jewish Refugee.* New York: Institute of Jewish Affairs of the American Jewish Congress and the World Jewish Congress, 1944.

Taylor, Alan R. *Prelude to Israel: An Analysis of Zionist Diplomacy 1897–1947.* New York: Philosophical Library, 1959.

Teller, Judd. *Strangers and Natives: The Evolution of the American Jews from 1921 to the Present.* New York: Delacorte Press, 1968.

Teveth, Shabtai. *Ben-Gurion and the Palestinian Arabs: From Peace to War.* New York: Oxford University Press, 1985.

Truman, Margaret. *Harry S. Truman.* New York: Morrow, 1973.

Tsur, Jacob. *Zionism: The Saga of a National Liberation Movement.* New Brunswick: Transaction Books, 1977.

Urofsky, Melvin. *A Mind of One Piece: Brandeis and American Reform.* New York: Scribner, 1971.

———. *American Zionism from Herzl to the Holocaust.* Garden City, NY: Anchor Press, 1975.

———. *We Are One!—American Jewry and Israel.* Garden City, NY: Anchor Press, 1978.

———. *A Voice That Spoke for Justice: The Life and Times of Stephen S. Wise.* Albany: State University of New York Press, 1982.

Volkman, Ernest. *A Legacy of Hate: Anti-Semitism in America.* New York: F. Watts, 1982.

Voss, Carl H. *Rabbi and Minister: The Friendship of Stephen S. Wise and John Haynes Holmes.* Cleveland: World Publishing Company, 1964.

Wasserstein, Bernard. *Britain and the Jews of Europe 1939–1945.* New York: Oxford University Press, 1979.

Wey, Nathaniel. *The Jew in American Politics.* New York: 1968.

Wilson, Evan M. *Decision on Palestine: How the U.S. Came to Recognize Israel.* Stanford, CA: Hoover Institution Press, 1979.

Wischnitzer, Mark. *To Dwell in Safety: The Story of Jewish Migration Since 1800.* Philadelphia: Jewish Publication Society of America, 1948.

———. *Visas to Freedom: The History of HIAS.* Cleveland: World Publishing Company, 1956.

Wyman, David S. *Paper Walls: America and the Refugee Crisis, 1938–1941.* Amherst: University of Massachusetts Press, 1968.

———. *The Abandonment of the Jews: America and the Holocaust, 1941–1945.* New York: Pantheon Books, 1984.

SECONDARY SOURCES: ARTICLES

Adelson, Howard L. "Ideology and Practice in American Zionism: An Overview." In *Essays in American Zionism: Herzl Year Book*, edited by Melvin I. Urofsky, vol. VIII, pp. 1–17. New York: Herzl Press, 1976.

Adler, Selig. "United States on Palestine in the FDR Era." *American Jewish Historical Quarterly* 62 (Sept. 1972): pp. 11–30.

————. "Franklin D. Roosevelt and Zionism: the War-Time Record." *Judaism* 21 (Summer 1972): pp. 265–277.

————. "The United States and the Holocaust." *American Jewish Historical Quarterly* 64 (Sept. 1974): pp. 14–23.

————. "American Jewry and That Explosive Statehood Question, 1933–1945." In *A Bicentennial Festschrift for Jacob Rader Marcus*, edited by Bertram W. Korn, pp. 5–21. New York: Ktav, 1976.

————. "The Roosevelt Administration and Zionism: The Pre-War Years, 1933–1939." In *Essays in American Zionism: Herzl Year Book*, edited by Melvin I. Urofsky, vol. VIII, pp. 132–48. New York: Herzl Press, 1976.

Baram, Phillip J. "A Tradition of Anti-Zionism: The Department of State's Middle Managers." In *Essays in American Zionism: Herzl Year Book*, edited by Melvin I. Urofsky, vol. VIII, pp. 178–94. New York: Herzl Press, 1976.

Baron, Lawrence. "Oswego's Reception of Holocaust Refugees, 1944–1946." *Holocaust Studies Annual* I (1983): pp. 119–33.

Bauer, Yehuda. "Genocide: Was It the Nazis' Original Plan?" *Annals of the American Academy of Political and Social Science* 450 (July 1980): pp. 35–45.

Berman, Aaron. "American Zionism and the Rescue of European Jewry: An Ideological Perspective." *American Jewish History* 70 (Mar. 1981): pp. 310–30.

————. "American Zionists, The Drive for a Jewish Commonwealth and the Holocaust." *Holocaust Studies Annual* I (1983): pp. 135–50.

Bierbrier, Doreen. "The American Zionist Emergency Council: An Analysis of a Pressure Group." *American Jewish Historical Quarterly* LX (Sept. 1970): pp. 82–105.

Burstin, Barbara. "Rescue in the Opening Rounds of the American Jewish Conference." *Holocaust Studies Annual* I (1983): pp. 151–65.

Capri, David. "The Mufti of Jerusalem Amin el-Husseini and His Diplomatic Activity During World War II (October 1941–July 1943)." *Studies in Zionism* 7 (Spring 1983): pp. 101–31.

Cohen, Henry. "Crisis and Reaction." *American Jewish Archives* V (June 1953): pp. 71–113.

Cohen, Naomi W. "The Specter of Zionism: American Opinions, 1917–1922." In *Essays in American Zionism: Herzl Year Book*, edited by Melvin I. Urofsky, vol. VIII, pp. 95–116. New York: Herzl Press, 1976.

Dawidowicz, Lucy S. "American Jews and the Holocaust." *New York Times Magazine*, Apr. 18, 1982, pp. 46–48.

————. "Indicting American Jews." *Commentary*, June 1983, pp. 36–44.

Dinnerstein, Leonard. "Jews and the New Deal." *American Jewish History* LXXII (June 1983): pp. 461–76.

Drinan, Robert T. "The Christian Response to the Holocaust." *Annals of the American Academy of Political and Social Science* 450 (July 1980): pp. 179–89.

Druks, Herbert. "Why the Death Camps Were Not Bombed." *The American Zionist* LXVII (Dec. 1976): pp. 18–21.

Eban, Abba. "Dewey David Stone: Prototype of an American Zionist." *American Jewish History* LXIX (Sept. 1979): pp. 5–14.

Bibliography

Feingold, Henry L. "Roosevelt and the Holocaust: Reflections on New Deal Humanism." *Judaism* XVIII (Summer 1969): pp. 259–76.

———. "Who Shall Bear the Guilt for the Holocaust: the Human Dilemma." *American Jewish Historical Quarterly* LXVIII (March 1979): pp. 261–82.

———. "Failure of Rescue European Jewry: Wartime Britain and America." *Annals of the American Academy of Political and Social Science* 450 (July 1980): pp. 113–21.

———. "'Courage First and Intelligence Second': The American Jewish Secular Elite, Roosevelt and the Failure to Rescue." *American Jewish History* LXXII (June 1983): pp. 461–76.

Feldman, Abraham J. "Abba Hillel Silver." *American Jewish Historical Quarterly* LIV (June 1965): pp. 474–80.

Feuer, Leon I. "Abba Hillel Silver: A Personal Memoir." *American Jewish Archives* XIX (Nov. 1967): pp. 107–26.

Friesel, Evyatar. "Brandeis' Role in American Zionism Historically Reconsidered." *American Jewish History* LXIX (Sept. 1979): pp. 34–59.

Ganin, Zvi. "The Limits of American Jewish Political Power: America's Retreat from Partition, Nov. 1947–March 1949." *Jewish Social Studies* XXXIV (Winter/Spring 1977): pp. 1–36.

———. "Activism versus Moderation: The Conflict between Abba Hillel Silver and Stephen Wise during the 1940s." *Studies in Zionism* 5 (Spring 1984): pp. 71–95.

Gelber, Yoav. "Zionist Policy and the Fate of European Jewry, 1943–1944." *Studies in Zionism* 7 (Spring 1983): pp. 133–67.

Goell, Yohai. "Aliyah in the Zionism of an American Oleh: Judah Magnes." *American Jewish Historical Quarterly* LXV (Dec. 1975): pp. 99–120.

Gottlieb, Moshe. "The Anti-Nazi Boycott Movement in the United States: An Ideological and Sociological Appreciation." *Jewish Social Studies* XXXV (July–Oct. 1973): pp. 198–277.

———. "Boycott, Rescue and Ransom: The Threefold Dilemma of American Jewry in 1938–1939." *Yivo Annual of Jewish Social Science* XV (1974): pp. 235–79.

Grobman, Alex. "What Did They Know? The American Jewish Press and the Holocaust, 1 September 1939–17 December 1972." *American Jewish History* LXVIII (Mar. 1979): pp. 327–52.

Halperin, Samuel, and Irwin Oder. "The United States in Search of a Policy: Franklin D. Roosevelt and Palestine." *Review of Politics* 24 (July 1962): pp. 320–41.

Halpern, Ben. "The Americanization of Zionism, 1880–1930." *American Jewish History* LXIX (Sept. 1979): pp. 15–33.

Huff, Earl D. "A Study of a Successful Interest Group: The American Zionist Movement." *Western Political Quarterly* XXV (Mar. 1972): pp. 109–24.

Kaufman, Menahem. "From Neutrality to Involvement: Zionists, non-Zionists and the Struggle for a Jewish State, 1945." In *Essays in American Zionism: Herzl Year Book*, edited by Melvin I. Urofsky, vol. VIII, pp. 263–83. New York: Herzl Press, 1976.

Knee, Stuart E. "Jewish Non-Zionism in America and Palestine Commitment, 1917–1941." *Journal of Jewish Social Studies* 39 (Summer 1977): pp. 209–26.

Kohler, Eric D. "Byways of Emigration: Panama, The Canal Zone, and Jewish Rescue Efforts, 1939–1941." *Holocaust Studies Annual* I (1983): pp. 89–118.

Kutscher, Carol B. "From Merger to Autonomy: Hadassah and the ZOA, 1918–1921." In *Essays in American Zionism: Herzl Year Book*, edited by Melvin I. Urofsky, vol. VIII, pp. 61–76. New York: Herzl Press, 1976.

Lipstadt, Deborah E. "Louis Lipsky and the Emergence of Opposition to Brandeis, 1917–1920." In *Essays in American Zionism: Herzl Year Book*, edited by Melvin I. Urofsky, vol. VIII, pp. 37–60. New York: Herzl Press, 1976.

Lowenstein, Sharon. "A New Deal for Refugees: The Promise and Reality of Oswego." *American Jewish History* LXXI (Mar. 1982): pp. 325–41.

Maga, Timothy P. "The Quest for a Generous America: Varian Fry and the Refugee Cause, 1940–1942." *Holocaust Studies Annual* I (1938): pp. 69–87.

Manson, Harold P. "Abba Hillel Silver—An Appreciation." In *In the Time of the Harvest*, edited by Daniel Jeremy Silver, pp. 1–27. New York: 1963.

Matzozky, Eliyho. "An Episode: Roosevelt and the Mass Killing." *Midstream* 26 (Aug.–Sept. 1980): pp. 17–19.

Meyer, Michael. "American Reform Judaism and Zionism: Early Efforts at Ideological Rapprochement." *Studies in Zionism* 7 (Spring 1983): pp. 49–64.

Neustadt-Noy, Isaac. "Toward Unity: Zionist and non-Zionist Cooperation, 1941–1942." In *Essays in American Zionism: Herzl Year Book*, edited by Melvin I. Urofsky, vol. VIII, pp. 149–65. New York: Herzl Press, 1976.

Panitz, Esther L. "'Washington Versus Pinsk': The Brandeis-Weizmann Dispute." *In Essays in American Zionism: Herzl Year Book*, edited by Melvin I. Urofsky, vol. VIII, pp. 77–94. New York: Herzl Press, 1976.

Parzen, Herbert. "President Truman and the Palestine Quandary: His Initial Experience, April–December 1945." *Jewish Social Studies* 35 (Jan. 1973): pp. 42–72.

———. "The Roosevelt Palestine Policy, 1943–1945: An Exercise in Dual Diplomacy." *American Jewish Archives* 26 (Apr. 1974): pp. 31–65.

Peck, Sarah E. "The Campaign for an American Response to the Nazi Holocaust, 1943–1945." *Journal of Contemporary History* 15 (Apr. 1980): pp. 367–400.

Penkower, Monty N. "The 1943 Anglo-American Statement on Palestine." In *Essays in American Zionism: Herzl Year Book*, edited by Melvin I. Urofsky, vol. VIII, pp. 212–41. New York: Herzl Press, 1976.

———. "Ben-Gurion, Silver and the 1941 UPA National Conference for Palestine: A Turning Point in American Zionist History." *American Jewish History* LXIX (Sept. 1979): pp. 66–78.

———. "Jewish Organizations and the Creation of the U.S. War Refugee Board." *Annals of the American Academy of Political and Social Science* 450 (July 1980): pp. 122–39.

———. "The Bermuda Conference and Its Aftermath: An Allied Quest for 'Refuge' During the Holocaust." *Prologue* 13 (Fall 1981): pp. 145–73.

———. "In Dramatic Dissent: The Bergson Boys." *American Jewish History* 70 (Mar. 1981): pp. 281–309.

Pinsky, Edward. "American Jewish Unity during the Holocaust: the Joint Emergency Committee, 1943." *American Jewish History* LXII (June 1983): pp. 477–94.

Porat, Dina. "Al-domi: Palestinian Intellectuals and the Holocaust, 1943–1945." *Studies in Zionism* 5 (Spring 1984): pp. 97–124.

Porath, Yehoshua. "Weizmann, Churchill and the 'Philby Plan,' 1937–1943." *Studies in Zionism* 5 (Autumn 1984): pp. 239–72.

Schmidt, Sarah. "The Parushim: A Secret Episode in American Zionist History." *American Jewish Historical Quarterly* LXV (Dec. 1975): pp. 121–39.

Shafir, Shlomo. "George Messersmith: An Anti-Nazi Diplomat's View of the German-Jewish Crisis." *Journal of Jewish Social Studies* 35 (Jan. 1973): pp. 32–41.

———. "American Jewish Leaders and the Emerging Nazi Threat (1928–January, 1933)." *American Jewish Archives* XXXI (Nov. 1979): pp. 150–183.

Shapiro, Yonathan. "The Zionist Faith." *American Jewish Archives* XVIII (Nov. 1966): pp. 107–27.

Sheffer, Gabriel. "Political Considerations in British Policy-Making on Immigration to Palestine." *Studies in Zionism* 4 (Autumn 1981): pp. 259–72.

Shpiro, David H. "The Political Background of the 1942 Biltmore Resolution." In *Essays in American Zionism: Herzl Year Book*, edited by Melvin I. Urofsky, vol. VIII, pp. 166–77. New York: Herzl Press, 1976.

Slutsky, Yehuda, and Yehuda Bauer. "Illegal Immigration and the Berichah." *Immigration and Settlement*. Jerusalem: Keter Publishing House, Israel Pocket Library, 1973, pp. 35–49.

Bibliography

Szajkowsky, Zosa. "The Attitude of American Jews to Refugees from Germany in the 1930s." *American Jewish Historical Quarterly* (Dec. 1971): pp. 101–43.

———. "Relief for German Jewry: Problems of American Involvement." *American Jewish Historical Quarterly* 63 (Dec. 1972): pp. 111–45.

Urofsky, Melvin I. "Zionism: An American Experience." *American Jewish Historical Quarterly* LXIII (Mar. 1974): pp. 215–30.

———. "Rifts in the Movement: Zionist Fissures, 1942–1945." In *Essays in American Zionism: Herzl Year Book*, edited by Melvin I. Urofsky, vol. VIII, pp. 195–211. New York: Herzl Press, 1976.

———. "HaMa'avek: American Zionists, Partition and Recognition, 1947–1948." In *Essays in American Zionism: Herzl Year Book*, edited by Melvin I. Urofsky, vol. VIII, pp. 284–309. New York: Herzl Press, 1976.

———. "A Cause in Search of Itself: American Zionism After the State." *American Jewish History* LXIX (Sept. 1979): pp. 79–91.

Voss, Carl H. "The American Christian Palestine Committee." In *Essays in American Zionism: Herzl Year Book*, edited by Melvin I. Urofsky, vol. VIII, pp. 242–62. New York: Herzl Press, 1976.

Wasserstein, Bernard. "The Myth of 'Jewish Silence.'" *Midstream* XXVI (Aug./Sept. 1980): pp. 10–16.

Westerbrook, Robert B. "The Responsibility of Peoples: Dwight Macdonald and the Holocaust." *Holocaust Studies Annual* I (1983): pp. 35–68.

UNPUBLISHED DISSERTATIONS AND MASTERS ESSAYS

Balboni, Alan R. "A Study of the Efforts of the American Zionists to Influence the Formulation and Conduct of United States Foreign Policy During the Roosevelt, Truman, and Eisenhower Administrations." Ph.D. diss., Brown University, 1973.

Ban, Joseph D. "The Holocaust—The Response of the Religious Press in the Pacific Northwest to the Anti-Semitics Policies of the Third Reich." Ph.D. diss., University of Oregon, 1974.

Camp, William D. "Religion and Horror: The American Religious Press Views Nazi Death Camps and Holocaust Survivors." Ph.D. diss., Carnegie Mellon University, 1981.

Dohse, Michael A. "American Periodicals and the Palestine Triangle, April 1936 to February 1947." Ph.D. diss., Mississippi State University, 1966.

Ferman, Yonah. "Analysis of an Interest Group: The Emergency Committee to Save the Jewish People of Europe (July 1943–August 1944)." Master's thesis, Hebrew University, 1965.

Fox, Maier B. "American Zionism in the 1920s." Ph.D. diss., George Washington University, 1979.

Grand, Samuel. "A History of Zionist Organizations in the United States from Their Inception to 1940." Ph.D. diss., Columbia University, 1958.

Hanauer, Edmund R. "An Analysis of Conflicting Jewish Positions Regarding the Nature and Political Role of American Jews, With Particular Emphasis on Political Zionism." Ph.D. diss., American University, 1972.

Huff, Earl D. "Zionist Influences Upon U.S. Foreign Policy: A Study of American Policy Toward the Middle East from the Time of the Struggle for Israel to the Sinai Conflict." Ph.D. diss., University of Idaho, 1971.

Hyatt, David M. "The United Nations and the Partition of Palestine." Ph.D. diss., Catholic University of America, 1973.

Lipstadt, Deborah E. "The Zionist Career of Louis Lipsky, 1900–1921." Ph.D. diss., Brandeis University, 1977.

Lookstein, Haskel. "American Jewry's Public Response to the Holocaust 1938–1944: An Examination Based upon Accounts in the Jewish Press and Periodical Literature." Ph.D. diss., Yeshiva University, 1979.

Lorimer, M. Madeline. "America's Response to Europe's Displaced Persons, 1945–1952: A Preliminary Report." Ph.D. diss., St. Louis University, 1964.

Marcus, R. W. "Stephen S. Wise: The Eclipse 1937–1946." Master's essay, Columbia University, 1974.

Miller, Donald H. "A History of Hadassah 1912–1935." Ph.D. diss., New York University, 1968.

Neustadt-Noy, Isaac. "The Unending Task: Efforts to Unite American Jewry from the American Jewish Congress to the American Jewish Conference." Ph.D. diss., Brandeis University, 1976.

Oder, Irwin. "The United States and the Palestine Mandate, 1920–1948: A Study of the Impact of Interest Groups on Foreign Policy." Ph.D. diss., Columbia University, 1956.

Pinsky, Edward D. "Cooperation among American Jewish Organizations in their Efforts to Rescue European Jewry During the Holocaust, 1939–1945." Ph.D. diss., New York University, 1980.

Schmidt, Sarah L. "Horace M. Kallen and the Americanization of Zionism." Ph.D. diss., University of Maryland, 1973.

Stewart, Barbara McDonald. "United States Government Policy on Refugees from Nazism, 1933–1940." Ph.D. diss., Columbia University, 1969.

OTHER SOURCES AND INTERVIEWS

Bergson, Peter. Interview with author. New York. Aug. 30, 1974.

Greenberg, Marian. Interview with author. Amherst, MA. April 21, 1979.

Merlin, Samuel. Interview with author. New York. Aug. 30, 1974.

Shpiro, David H. "The Stand of the American Zionist Leadership on the Question of Actions to Rescue European Jews—November–December 1942." Unpublished paper, n.d., available from the American Commission on the Holocaust.

INDEX

Abdullah, Emir, 43, 44
Alfange, Dean, 131, 143
Aliyah Bet campaign, 71–72, 73
Altneuland (Herzl), 41
Amalgamated Clothing Workers of America, 100
American Communist Party, 17
American Emergency Committee for Zionist Affairs (AECZA), 76, 82, 83, 85, 89, 107, 108, 110, 117–18, 124, 127
American Federation of Labor (AFL), 125
American Jewish Committee (AJC), 11; opposition to statehood, 60, 84, 89, 109; participation in American Jewish Conference, 109–10, 111, 112, 115, 116; position on Zionism, 32–33; secession from American Jewish Conference, 128–29
American Jewish Conference, 108–16, 120, 124, 128–29, 130, 132, 143, 154
American Jewish Congress, 32, 37, 38, 110
American Jewish Trade Union Committee for Palestine, 125–26
American Jews: and anti-Nazi boycott, 37–38; and Holocaust (*see* Holocaust, and American Jews); non-Zionist, 33, 88 (*see also* American Jewish Committee); position on Zionism, 31–33, 182; in Reform movement, 33; support for Roosevelt, 78, 152. *See also* Zionism, American
American Labor party, 125
American League for the Defense of Jewish Rights, 38

American Palestine Campaign, 35
American Palestine Committee, 126–28
American Zionist Emergency Council (AZEC), 148, 151, 172; anti-Arab propaganda of, 161–64; attack on AJC, 129; campaign against Bergson group, 120, 121, 122, 130–31, 133; and Christian support groups, 126–28; committees of, 125–26; and congressional resolutions, 132–35, 143–44; leadership of, 118, 119, 153; public relations function of, 131–32. *See also* American Emergency Committee for Zionist Affairs (AECZA); Zionism, American
And Keep Your Powder Dry (Mead), 136
Anglo-American Committee of Inquiry (AACI), 167–71, 172
Annals of the American Academy of Political and Social Science, 156
Anti-Semitism: in Europe, 29, 31, 37; Herzl's view of, 15; Nazi, 19, 22, 37, 40, 86; in Poland, 31, 45, 79, 155; in United States, 22–23; Zionism as solution to, 15, 29, 88–89, 113–14
Arabs, Palestinian, 12; and American public opinion, 47–51; and benefits of Jewish settlement, 41–43, 138, 141, 163; and binational state strategy, 91, 144–47; fear of Jewish domination, 45; and federated state strategy, 92; general strike of, 46; Jewish perception of, 13, 163–64, 184; opposition to partition, 63; opposition to postwar

231

Index

Aaron Berman is an associate professor of history
at Hampshire College. He holds the M.A. and Ph.D.
degrees from Columbia University.
The manuscript was edited by G. Aimée Ergas.
The book was designed by Selma Tenenbaum.
The typeface for the text is Bodoni Book and the
display face is Korinna.
Manufactured in the United States of America.